DATE			

Never Will We Forget

Never Will We Forget

Oral Histories of World War II

MARILYN MAYER CULPEPPER

PRAEGER SECURITY INTERNATIONAL
Westport, Connecticut • London

Library of Congress Cataloging-in-Publication Data

Culpepper, Marilyn Mayer.
   Never will we forget : oral histories of World War II / Marilyn Mayer Culpepper.
      p. cm.
   Includes bibliographical references and index.
   ISBN 978–0–313–34478–7 (alk. paper)
   1. World War, 1939–1945—United States.   2. World War, 1939–1945—
Personal narratives, American.   I. Title.
   D811.A2C85   2008
   940.53′73—dc22   2007037553

British Library Cataloguing in Publication Data is available.

Library of Congress Catalog Card Number: 2007037553
ISBN-13: 978–0–313–34478–7

First published in 2008

Praeger Security International, 88 Post Road West, Westport, CT 06881
An imprint of Greenwood Publishing Group, Inc.
www.praeger.com

Printed in the United States of America

The paper used in this book complies with the
Permanent Paper Standard issued by the National
Information Standards Organization (Z39.48–1984).

10 9 8 7 6 5 4 3 2 1

Extracts from Sam Dann, *Dachau 29 April 1945: The Rainbow Liberation Memoirs*
are used by Permission. © 1998 Texas Tech University Press.

For Tom and my parents

Contents

Introduction

For the most part, books dealing with the horrendous years of World War II focus on the battles, the generals, the amphibious invasions, the aerial warfare, or the savage ground warfare. These pages, however, are concerned with "the other side of war"—the personal side. Included here are excerpts from the reminiscences of some 400 men and women who evidence a variety of perspectives. Gleaned primarily from interviews and oral histories, the material reflects the World War II memories of male and female veterans; civilians on the home front, conscientious objectors; survivors of the *Indianapolis* and various typhoons; POWs of the Germans and Japanese; displaced Nisei; and participants in the Normandy Invasion, the Battle of the Bulge, Iwo Jima, and Okinawa.

These are brief personal interest accounts, vignettes not found in history books. Some are remembrances until now kept hidden in the dark recesses of the mind; others are experiences oft repeated to grandchildren. Not a few are anecdotes remembered and relived with old buddies at reunions; many are stories of rationing, discrimination, and sacrifices on the home front that generations later find difficult to believe. Some tug at the heart, some bring a smile, some foster the shock of surprise or awe; still others engender a surge of pride in America and Americans. These are glimpses of a world at war and the changes that radically transformed people and the world they lived in.

My gratitude and indebtedness go to the hundreds of people I have interviewed in person and via the telephone. In addition. I have appreciated being able to use excerpts from oral histories collected by the

University of Southern Mississippi; the Eisenhower Center for American
Studies at New Orleans; the Michigan Women's Historical Center; the
Women's Overseas Service League; the Historic Middletown Museum,
Middletown, Kentucky; the Nelson Poynter Memorial Library at the University of South Florida, St. Petersburg Special Collections Department;
and the Women's History Project of Northern Michigan. My dear late husband accompanied me on almost every personal interview and provided
wisdom and encouragement beyond all measure. He is sorely missed.

Scores of friends have shared tape recordings of families and friends.
Among the many people who helped supply tapes and DVDs, I would like
to thank Gladys Beckwith and Katie Cavanaugh at the Michigan Women's
Historical Center; Carolyn Boger; Pat D'Itri; Doris Key for special help
in securing important oral history tapes; Joanne Harvey; Karen Hummel;
Kaye Hummel; Debbie Jamieson; Doug Langham; Mary McCartney; Anne
Magoun; Judy Nash; Libby Otis; Sue Schulze; Polly Schwendener; Geneva
Wiskemann; Joan Witter; and Harry Zeliff. Allan Taylor was exceedingly
generous in sharing lengthy interviews he had completed in Minnesota and Wisconsin. Professor Jane Vieth graciously allowed me to plow
through hundreds of her MSU Honors Class semester reports on WWII.
John Shaw, assistant librarian at the G. Robert Vincent Voice Library at
Michigan State University; Jim Schnur, assistant librarian of Special Collections at the Nelson Poynter Memorial Library at the University of South
Florida at St. Petersburg; and Peggy Price, Head of Special Collections at
the Library of the University of Southern Mississippi; and Seth Paridon,
Director of Research at the National WWII Museum were particularly
resourceful and helpful.

There are hundreds of others who kindly devoted important time to
share their experiences and friends with me. Many of those I plan to use
later. Among the latter, I do wish to thank particularly Herman Bainder,
Ron Blanchard, Margaret Burke, Nina Clearman, Robert Carlson, Doro-
thy Chapman, Edward Coulson, Joan Coulson, John Cousins, Eleanor
Culpepper, Walter Davis, Elizabeth Denman, Dave Dietrich, Jean Draper,
Quentin Ewert, Maxine Eyestone, Mabel Flanders, Lindy Fries, Ethelyn
Gansoulin, Richard L. Garner, Maxine Giacoletto, Frances Gibson, Lia
Goll, Barbara Gray, Robert Guilivar, Ted Hacker, Don Hodgkiss, Joyce
Hoderman, John Hopkins, Julius Hoffman, June Judson, Judd Judson,
Sam Kamlet, Horace King, Dorothy Kelly, George R. Kelly, Gerald Kelly,
Laverne Klaver, Leland McLean, Don Larson, Pat McCarthy, Constance
McPherrin, Bill Magee, Gary Marshall, Carl Mescher, Warren Meyer, L. A.
Murray, Marilyn Overman, Stuart Parker, Josephine Paulone, Sam Pau-
lone, Truman Pound, Pat Ralston, William Reid, Marian Renaud, Elmer
Reynolds, Ruth Rice, Alma Rolenz, Ray Roots, Rae Ruff, Rex Sessions,
Reed Simpson, Robert Lee Sherwood, Russell C. Six, Shirley Sliker, Joan
Stevenson, Walter Sweeney, Frank Synk, Wally Travis, Joseph Vogt, Mark

Welborn, Robert Wiggin, Joseph Wilkerson, Doris West, Mary Jane Wilson, Bob Wright, and Bobbie Young. I especially appreciate the knowledge and encouragement supplied by my late Uncle Ross Mayer, who served in both World War I and World War II.

My veritable indebtedness, America's indebtedness, however, goes to the men and women who gave their lives for their country—for us.

CHAPTER 1

And the War Came

PEARL HARBOR BOMBED

Sundays were days of church activities, rest, football games, concerts, or movies—not for a Japanese attack on Pearl Harbor. Hundreds of history books recount the details of "The day that will live in infamy," December 7, 1941. The following paragraphs, however, present a kaleidoscope of the personal memories of civilians and servicemen of that fateful day. Some were eyewitnesses to the tragedy and chaos that attended the attack; others were apprehensive Americans caught up in the events that so traumatically changed the world forever after.

Concert halls, movie theaters, church gatherings, and football stadiums erupted with shock and disbelief that Sunday afternoon. Hosts of Americans were numbed into a stunned, stony silence; others fought vainly against tears; while still others experienced a violent surge of anger.

Football fans recalled the December 7th games being interrupted by ominous announcements for important military men to report to their headquarters. A Florida woman remembered attending a Redskins football game with her father on that day. "About half way through the game the loudspeaker announced that Admiral so and so should return to his office immediately. A little later a call over the speaker wanted General so and so to report to his office. After several more calls the voice came over the speaker again instructing all Marines to report to their barracks *now*. By this time interest in the game had ebbed and there was much buzzing in the stands about just what was happening. It wasn't until the game was over and we walked out of the stadium that we saw newsboys hawking EXTRAS and in big black letters—PEARL HARBOR BOMBED."[1]

At Pearl Harbor, at the time of the attack, Mary Sharp was living on Oahu with her husband, a First Lieutenant medical doctor with the Army. Her story, with its personal touches of the confusion and horror of the attack, unfolds in a letter written to her parents in Ann Arbor, Michigan. "Dear Mother and Dad. Wish there were some way I could reassure you that I'm okay & such." She apologized for sounding somewhat foolish "after having just written you that Oahu would never be bombed, but not quite as foolish as the Army & Navy who got caught with their pants down if anyone ever did."

December 6th had been a late night for the Sharps. "We had a lovely time at Bee and Harlan's dinner party and the fine cabaret show put on at the Officers' Club Saturday night," Mary told her parents. The Sharps were hoping to sleep in the next morning, when suddenly about 7:30 A.M., she and Mike, who were spending the night at their hosts' quarters on Gorgas Road, "awoke to the sound of gun fire—machine guns and bombs dropping." Thinking it an "alert" they went back to bed only to be startled moments later when one of Mike's fellow officers pounded on the door and insisted that they "Come on out and watch the Japanese planes. They are bombing Wheeler Field." Certain that their friend was kidding them and that they were simply watching a mock attack, they stood in the street and watched the planes "zooming and attacking Wheeler."

"Slowly it dawned on us," Mary wrote "that they were using real bullets and we could see the tracer bullets and the great cloud of black smoke rising from Wheeler." Mary continued: "Standing there like goops we suddenly realized a couple of planes were heading for us—very low, strafing the road. I can't say we properly dove flat for cover, but we got out of the way in the bushes very quickly."

A quick cup of coffee, "and Mike got into the car and headed for town," recalled Mary. In his memoirs, Mike wrote, "For some reason, I didn't feel hungry, unusual for me, and I also noticed that the cup I held clattered slightly on its fine China saucer." As the immediate tension subsided momentarily, Mary told her parents, "You probably think we acted very stupidly—we did. But it was and still is so incredible that Japan could pull such a complete surprise that no one believed their eyes."

Mike's assignment had been "in case of attack he was to establish 3 Aid stations around the harbor of Honolulu." "When I left Schofield," he explained, "I went out the gate nearest Wheeler Field. It was easy to see the wrecked concrete barracks and piles of planes burning magnificently including the fuel trucks." At the gate (no guard) a sickening sight awaited him: "a burning commander's car. Driver missing, Passenger half out of car. Head exploded, brains boiling."

As Mike Sharp rolled up his sleeves for emergency services, his first case was a soldier that he unfortunately was forced to give up on, a man Mike was later told was probably one of the first casualties of the war. Looking around him, Mike was dismayed to see the regular army officers "vomiting their heads off at the sight and stench of the war dead." As a medical doctor who was supposedly accustomed to dead bodies and cadavers, Mike was tapped by an officer to identify the dead. Actually, Mike said he didn't feel too well himself, his own stomach was doing flip-flops, but from fingerprints and dog tags he continued to help with the identification of the bodies. Meanwhile, a local lumberyard was making coffins as quickly as possible. Without a doubt, Mike said, many of the boxes contained more than *one* body. In a rapid assembly of bodies, arms and legs and hands were scrambled together to fill each coffin.

Back on Gorgas Road, Mary reported: "A soldier ran from door to door announcing 'WE ARE AT WAR—THE JAPANESE HAVE ATTACKED' and telling all officers to report for duty and all women and children (in our area) to report at the 19th Inf. headquarters barracks." At the barracks, "There was coffee and milk on the mess tables—soldiers in the various grounds dressing into full pack—motor trucks getting under way—guns being set upon roofs, etc.—and ambulances tearing out of the hospital drive to Wheeler." In response to a request for women to do bandage making, Mary volunteered to work in quarters a short distance away. "I don't think anyone was scared—at least I wasn't but there was a lot of nervous excitement."

Later that afternoon, "a soldier came by and said to report to 19th and be prepared to evacuate to Honolulu, which is just where I wanted to go." Upon arriving home in Honolulu, Mary provided two hungry young soldiers with a quick supper and remarked that "Both were cheerful and anxious to get back at the Japs—said 12 of their 'buddies' had been killed." As they ate, the soldiers laughed about one boy who, although he insisted he was not scared, had dived under the PX "bare nekked." The next morning, Mary must have cringed as she gazed into a hole from a shell in her neighbor's driveway that was "a beaut, can't see the bottom—about a foot across and on an angle."[2]

Years later Mike Sharp found himself breaking into uncontrollable tears for no known reason, but at the time, he realized he must remain calm and dared not break down before the other men. It turned out that necessity was the mother of invention, and at Pearl, the blood bank consisted of other soldiers. When blood was needed the doctors simply drew it from another soldier. Mike soon found that he could perform surgery that astounded even him. If he were in a tight place he convinced himself he could handle it, and his self-confidence grew by leaps and bounds.

Following his work at Pearl Harbor, Mike was sent to Australia and the Philippines. As a physician, Mike should have been somewhat accustomed to death and dying people, however, the tremendous loss of life at Pearl and in the Pacific continued to plague him. On one occasion, while standing at the rail of a ship, he recalled visiting with a young man and noticing his Beta Theta Pi ring. (This had been Mike's college fraternity also.) They talked amiably—each exhibiting a certain admiration for the other. Within hours, in a horrible turn of events, he saw that same young man had become a casualty of war, his abdomen completely blown away and one of the worst casualties Mike had ever seen. As Mike thought back to their conversation at the ship's rail, he was sickened by the potential of that young man that was lost to war.[3]

Ivan Wright was a Skipper on an Air Sea Rescue boat at Pearl Harbor on December 7th when "everything went to Hell." No one knew what was happening. Someone shouted "This ain't no drill, those are Japanese war planes."[4] For the next hours, Ivan and his men frantically hauled in men struggling to swim in the flaming oil and water. In one successful mission, Ivan, with the help of several of his crew, was able to save 14 men by cutting a hole and releasing the men from the *Oklahoma*.[5]

Charles Glasco had been in the Navy about a year and a half when Pearl Harbor was attacked. "Like many of my shipmates, I was loafing around after breakfast when General Quarters was sounded. Everyone knew we never had exercises on Sunday, so we ran to our battle stations. I stayed there until about five o'clock in the evening before I could get up to see what we were hearing about on the earphones. It was a mess." Fortunately, or unfortunately, Chuck's ship was in dry-dock. "Two destroyers ahead of us were destroyed. We took a 500 pound bomb and lost 34 men."[6]

At the time of the attack, Paul Gillesse was at Pearl Harbor aboard the destroyer the *U.S.S. Worden*. Because the ships were in too close proximity to each other, the *Warden* was at a loss to fire their guns. Afterward, however, the ship made her made way about battleship row, and the crew prided themselves in being able to pick up some 20 men from the fiery waters.[7]

An avid reader, Aviation Mechanic 3rd Ed Krenkel was not surprised by the attack. It was clear America would be attacked—but when? where? The preceding Friday the men had been ordered to get out all of the available munitions in readiness for a possible enemy attack. Yet, on Saturday, they were ordered to restore all munitions "to a place of rest." The threat of a possible attack was dismissed as unlikely. But surely something was in the air.

At the time of the bombing, Ed Krenkel was just leaving the mess hall after breakfast and "as I looked over my shoulder I saw the *California* come up one foot out of the water . . . torpedo hit . . . and gradually settle back down again. Now that's not normal," he reasoned. "After that everything went to hell." Subsequent bombs dropped from above detonated the *Arizona*'s ammunition and powder magazines, and the *Arizona* sank to the bottom in minutes. For three days pandemonium reigned. The fuel burning on top of the water created an inferno of flames and smoke. It seemed no one was prepared to give orders, and no one prepared to take orders.[8]

A SHOCKED AMERICA

On December 7th, the Hineses' home in Springfield, Illinois was brimming with company. With the intention of learning firsthand exactly what was taking place in the local schools, Mrs. Hines, a member of the Springfield School Board, was entertaining, as she did frequently, teachers from the local schools at a Sunday afternoon tea. The living room fairly exploded when one tardy guest arrived announcing that she had just learned that Pearl Harbor had been bombed by the Japanese. Immediately the radio was switched on (many families had only one radio), and tea, cookies, and dainty sandwiches took a back seat to the stunning news. Listeners clustered about the radio in dazed disbelief, many of them wondering where on earth Pearl Harbor was located. A courageous Mrs. Hines put up a brave front, knowing there would be serious ramifications for her seven sons and two daughters who would unquestionably be involved in the upcoming crisis. The repeated announcement for all military personnel to return to their bases sent son Harold (home on leave from his Marine Corps base at Jefferson Barracks in St. Louis) scurrying to gather up his bags and head out for his base.[9]

On their way from Tecumseh, Michigan to see *Hell's a' Poppin* at the Cass Theater in Detroit, Jon Young and his friends heard an ominous announcement on the car radio, something about some Japanese bombing Pearl Harbor. The news made little impression on the car's occupants who more or less laughed off the report as just another of Orson Welles's pranks. (Welles's radio play "War of the Worlds" on October 30, 1938, had spooked listeners into believing there was actually an invasion from Mars.) The theater was packed, the show was great, but at the end of the performance the manager came out on stage and solemnly announced "Pearl Harbor has been bombed. American lives have been lost." There was stunned silence, and not a word was spoken as the audience quietly left the theater and made their way to their cars. (At that time Jon Young was teaching at Tecumseh High School in Tecumseh, Michigan and was much involved in directing the school's production of Gilbert and Sullivan's *The Mikado*. Needless to say, the school board took a dim view of that activity and immediately canceled any further rehearsals.)[10]

The shock and anxieties experienced by their elders over the attack on Pearl Harbor quickly translated into fear and confusion in their young children. Having been bought up in Amity, a small town in Arkansas, 12-year-old Emily Hobbs (Wolf) had been well schooled in tales of the Civil War, and her fervent hope was that "I could out-smart 'Bushwhackers' if the country was again over-run by such people. My best thought of defense was to somehow hit each of them on the head, very hard, with a milk bottle." Emily's 9-year-old brother was extremely frightened when airplanes flew overhead and immediately made a beeline for the wash shed to hide under the wash tubs. Other children looked for safety in fruit cellars.[11]

When on her way to school on December 8th, Pat Rittenhour (Anderson) (about 12 years old) of Bucyrus, Ohio was shocked to hear her friends talking about the news of the bombing of Pearl Harbor. The savagery of the attack terrified Pat, and for days afterward she was afraid to look out the window for fear the Japanese would be bombing and invading Bucyrus. When the training Camp Millard was set up in town, Pat's older sister became friends with several of the soldiers stationed at the camp, and there seemed to be a constant stream of lonesome young soldiers brought home to Sunday dinners and backyard picnics—each soldier with a sad look about him, as though he were about to be sent into the lion's den or Beelzebub's fiery furnace. (One young soldier kept coming back repeatedly, ostensibly for the wonderful country style dinners—but more importantly for another look at Pat's beautiful sister—whom he eventually married.) It was sad, Pat recalled, as they watched the young men being marched down the street in front of their house to the trains waiting to carry them to far distant shores. Often many of the townspeople left their daily tasks and went down to the station to see the boys off.[12]

Having just turned 11, Rachel (Bunny) Bruner (McComb) was duly alarmed as shock waves rocked her household in Norfolk, Virginia with the announcement on the radio of the bombing of Pearl Harbor. It was especially traumatic for young Bunny as her father, Lieut. Commander Frank Bruner, was a career officer in the U.S. Navy and had been repeatedly transferred to various locations throughout the United States and abroad. "Oh, Momma!" Bunny cried, "Daddy isn't in Hawaii is he?" Fortunately the answer was in the negative. Her father was in Puerto Rico at the time.[13]

While thousands of people were mystified about where Pearl Harbor was located, Kathleen Allen knew immediately. Her junior high school student teacher was a native Hawaiian and had already instilled considerable interest in Hawaii in her young students.[14]

Irv Nichols, a teenager, was attending a ball game in Rocky Mount, North Carolina, when the news about Pearl Harbor broke. Surely there was a fortune to be made by racing downtown, buying up as many newspapers as he could carry, and reselling them for five cents apiece. As he wildly ran through the town hawking his papers, the cry "EXTRA! EXTRA!" drew eager residents to the street corners in droves. Of course, there was no television in those days and even radios were few and far between in small towns. Even a second batch of papers failed to satisfy the demand. Not only were the townspeople excited, even Irv got so excited, he later confessed, that he got sick and threw up.[15]

THE RUSH TO ENLIST

Word of the attack on Pearl Harbor was greeted by a rush of men all across the nation to enlist in the various armed services. Immediately after the news broke, David Anderson, of Lorain, Ohio, beleaguered his father to let him quit school and join the army. An indifferent scholar at best (later to complete a PhD and become one of the world's foremost authorities on Sherwood Anderson), Dave and his father reached a compromise. If Dave would finish high school, his father would sign the papers allowing him to volunteer for service with the U.S. Army. The morning following graduation, Dave was at the recruiting office with the necessary papers.[16]

One would be hard put to find a more eager volunteer than Robert Flores, who in 1943, at 13 years of age, lied about his age and enlisted in the U.S. Navy. He had lost his father when he was two years old, and his mother was hard put to support the family. As long hours and extra work kept her away from home for much of the day, Robert became more and more rebellious and difficult to manage. Forging his mother's signature on the enlistment papers, he was accepted and sent to boot camp. At first, things moved along rather well with the deception. He had already completed boot camp when a minor ailment sent him to the base hospital. There in very short order a doctor sized him up as underage, and following a severe reprimand, Robert quickly found himself on a train headed for home.

Undaunted by his dismissal and after another loathsome year of schooling, the persistent teenager became convinced that by now the Navy really needed him. Once again, he lied and with forged papers enlisted once more, and for a second time completed his boot camp training. (He still has two boot camp certificates in his possession.) This time he kept his distance from hospitals and was able to successfully pull off the deception. All went well until 10 years later (after several re-enlistments) the authorities finally caught up with Bob. Oh, boy! There could be big trouble ahead! Now he must face up to his deceit. A confession and a plaintive appeal to his superior officers for compassion sent the officers scurrying through voluminous pages of regulations. Finally, the problem was resolved when it was decided that the statue of limitations had run out. Robert was home free!

Did his fellow shipmates ever suspect his real age? It was not until their first post-war reunion in Memphis, Tennessee, some 25 years later, when his former buddies came up to him with "God damn, Flores, you haven't aged like the rest of us! What the hell are you doing to make you look so young?" It was then the truth came out.[17]

After Pearl Harbor, William M. Pace, of Iuka, Mississippi, "just couldn't wait to get into the war." Being underage, Bill was at the mercy of his parents' signing his papers, and they in turn were merciless in refusing to sign. "Since they wouldn't do it, I just signed it myself," he admitted, and ran away from home and joined up under the forged signature.[18] Kenneth Mac Donald also ran away from home in an attempt to enlist. He was caught, however, and his father finally signed his papers saying, "If you are going to join, I can't stop you."[19]

The Great Depression of the twenties and thirties influenced more than one young man to enlist in the military. Living pretty much on his own after the death of his parents when he was still a child, Don Kona was living in Florida working 10 hours a day, 6 days a week for about 10 cents an hour. A Marine poster promising $21 a month looked like an answer to his prayers. However, there was one catch: to enlist one had to be 18 years old. Dan was 16. Because he had no parents to sign for him, Dan succeeded in inveigling six adults to swear that he was 18. He was in! Suddenly, he had more food than he could possibly eat and more clothes than he had ever owned in his entire life. Life was good![20]

PROBLEMS OF EYESIGHT AND WEIGHT

Bern Engel had stayed up until 4 A.M. finishing a term paper, and about 11 A.M. that morning was awakened as the halls of his co-op at the University of Oregon came alive with news of the bombing of Pearl Harbor. Rumor ran rampant: one that the Japanese had shelled Santa Barbara; another that they had bombed a big oil refinery at Astoria, Oregon. Pranksters even marched down sorority row pretending to be Japanese invaders.

There would be no question about Bern's joining the armed forces. His father had been shot up by shrapnel and had lost one lung to gas in World War I. Bern knew he must carry on the family tradition of serving in the military. There was only one catch. Bern knew he was too nearsighted to ever pass the eye test. However, brains won out over myopia. As he stood in the long line of men waiting for their physical exams, he quickly memorized the eye chart and when his turn came he passed the test with flying colors.[21]

At the time of his enlistment, Charles Grosse was three pounds underweight, the minimum being 120, and eating bananas, drinking quarts of water, and even stuffing his billfold with silver dollars failed to produce the desired weight. While the examiners were otherwise occupied, Grosse cleverly traded places with a friend with problems of depth perception, and the friend weighed in for him. In short order, Grosse, thanks to his friend, had succeeded in passing the weight test and his friend, via Grosse, made the grade on the eye test.[22]

Three long-time friends in Lansing, Michigan, Don Langworthy, Bruce Kanouse, and Warren Meyer, talked it over and came to the decision that it was time to "'join up' and win the war as military pilots." Together they signed up to become pilots, although each in a different branch of the service: one in the Army Air Force, one for Navy Aviation, and one for Marine Aviation. Each passed his physical exam; however, Warren, on the first round, was three pounds under the minimum weight requirement for aviation cadets. Observing Warren's immense disappointment, a thoughtful sergeant called him back, gave him a dollar and told him to buy five pounds of bananas, eat every last one, drink gallons of water, and come back in an hour. Warren did as he was told, returned to the recruitment office and passed with no problem.[23]

On a hot summer's day in August of 1934, Frank Forsyth, who was living in Foxboro, Massachusetts, was swimming with some of his buddies when suddenly the brawniest of the gang announced that he would like to join the Marine Corps. The idea was contagious, and all six fellows took off for Boston to take their physicals. "Ironically enough," Frank laughed, "I was the only one that passed. They went home and I went into the Marine Corps."[24] It was a similar story for Conrad Taschner, who at the end of the high school basketball season joined the entire team in going to Detroit to enlist in the Marines. As it turned out, he was the only one of the team who passed, and he soon found himself headed for boot camp in San Diego.[25]

Because jobs were hard to get during the Depression years, David Ruff enlisted in the Marine Corps and served for four years from August 1937 to July 1941. The stunning news of Pearl Harbor was all it took for Dave, a member of the Marine Reserves, to head for the family home in Denton, Texas, and sign in. Money was still tight and Dave packed up his things and headed out to the highway to hitchhike to Denton. As luck would have it, the first car that stopped for him was a recruiting officer who immediately signed him up for recruiting duties.[26]

"There was no peace in the world," Hall Tennis remembered. Most people he knew had expected that the U.S. involvement in the war was imminent. "Even at that tender age (17), I knew that war was a bad idea—as an idea. I also suspected that it could be a bad experience for me personally. I did not like that thought. I also knew that I could not permit myself to hide behind my logical 'conscience' and sit out." In short order, the Marine Corps won out.[27]

Tom Dutch had been at the movies on Pearl Harbor Day and had come home to hear the news of the bombing. Pearl Harbor seemed far away in distance and in time, and he gave little thought to ever being in the military. His graduation from high school in 1942 and the draft made him realize that he would soon have to make some decisions. The Army? Or the Navy? A gentle push from his mother who had heard that the food was better in the Navy helped him decide. Two brothers already in the Navy clinched his decision.[28]

At Toledo, when Don MacKenzie and his buddy went to enlist, they found block-long lines of men waiting in front of the Army, Navy, and Marine offices. A short distance away there was a sign for Merchant Marines. Because there was no line, the men moseyed in and for several minutes listened to an enthusiastic Merchant Marine spiel. The talk, however, didn't go over at all well with Don's buddy who immediately turned away and left with a damning assessment: "That don't sound good to me." To Don it did sound good, and he immediately signed the papers and made ready to go home to await orders. There was no "going home" however. The Merchant Marines snapped him up at once, and that very afternoon he found himself on a train to Sheepshead Bay, New York. There was barely time for a quick call to his Mother who cried "You're what?" "Well, I guess I'm in the war," Don replied. "But I didn't get to say goodbye," his mother complained. "Well, goodbye!" and Don was off for New York.[29]

Levin Culpepper, of Why Not, Mississippi (there really is a town in Mississippi by that name) signed for the draft in 1942. At the Camp Shelby Induction Center, Levin tried to persuade the authorities that what he really wanted to do was to drive a truck in the Army. However, the government needed men in the Navy at that point, and Levin was sent to Hattiesburg, Mississippi to "volunteer" for the Navy. Once they discovered from the aptitude tests that Levin could easily distinguish between a claw hammer and a pair of pliers, the authorities decided that Levin would make a great mechanic.

Levin, himself, admitted that there "never had been a more shy or greener man than I was." (At his high school graduation Levin was too embarrassed to walk up in front of the audience to receive his diploma— there were eight in his class. Instead, he stood out in the parking lot and listened to the proceedings through an open door.) Small wonder that during his years in the Navy his greatest fear, he said, was the fear that some officer would ask him a question.[30]

Caught up in the draft in 1940, Jon Young was sent to Ft. Belvoir, Virginia, where after a few days of basic training, the Army decided he was too old (one month away from his 28th birthday!) and that they would have to discharge him. Just before his discharge, however, the army discovered he was keeping a journal, that not only could he write, but he could write well, and for the next six weeks the army kept him on to write training manuals for soldiers. His return to his teaching duties at Tecumseh, Michigan, lasted for 59 more days when he was again drafted and sent to Ft. Custer.[31]

Legrand K. Johnson was graduated from North Carolina State College in 1941 with "my diploma in one hand and my army orders in the other." At Michigan State University (Michigan State College then), Mel Buschman had enrolled in ROTC as a means of earning his way through college. Fortunately, the 4th year men in the Senior Class of ROTC were allowed to finish their senior year dressed in uniform and housed in fraternity houses. They marched to classes, drilled, ate their meals at the campus Union cafeteria, and studied to complete their requirements for graduation. The graduation ceremonies were held in the campus auditorium with each man wearing his cap and gown over his official military uniform. As the diplomas were handed out, each man walked off the platform, handed his cap and gown to a family member in attendance and proceeded 100 yards to a train waiting on a siding, and within an hour they were on their way to boot camp.[32]

Although he had enlisted in the Army reserves in August 1942, it was 1943 before Lloyd G. Wilson, a student at Michigan State College (later Michigan State University) was called up. Lloyd had just three months to go before graduation, and the prospects of finishing, so tantalizingly close, looked gloomy indeed. However, Michigan State as a co-operative measure for the war effort, sensed the plight of these young men (as did other universities) and offered a general exam to be taken prior to graduation. Those who passed were given their degrees despite lacking a term or a few credits and were sent on their way to fulfill their destiny. Lloyd Wilson was awarded his degree and proceeded to the Medical Replacement Training Center in Aboline, Texas.[33]

The attack on Pearl Harbor found Bob Hutchins working at a gas station and one semester away from graduation from high school. He immediately returned to school on Monday morning and informed the principal that he was enlisting in the Marines. The principal gave him a hard time, telling him that he should wait just a few more months until he had finished high school. Nothing would deter Bob, however, and on February 1, 1942, he was inducted into the Marines. Four years later that same benevolent principal, upon hearing that Bob had been discharged and had returned home, called him and made arrangements for him to take a few exams and be awarded his high school diploma. (Scores of high school principals made arrangements so that students inducted into the services who were only a few weeks or a couple of months away from graduation could receive their diplomas.)[34]

Although his father thought him too young for the Marine Corps, Rollie Dart was hell-bent on enlisting. Finally, realizing that there was no dissuading his son, Rollie's father signed the necessary papers, and Rollie was off to boot camp. It took just three days of grueling Marine Corps drilling before Rollie was beseeching his father on the telephone, "Dad, I know you and Senator Vandenberg are good friends. Please, please—get me out of this outfit. Bring me home. It is terrible! I never heard my dad laugh so loudly."[35]

DECISIONS, DECISIONS

Despite the onrush to enlist after Pearl Harbor, some months after the attack, there were some less than enthusiastic draftees who were anxiety-ridden about their situation. It was Fred Wickert's assignment, as a First Lieutenant with the Coast Guard Training and Replacement Center at Fort Heustis, Virginia, to arrange trainload after trainload of draftees to be sent to the Philippines. As a result of some of the tragic consequences aboard the trains, Fred had serious qualms about his job. A good many GIs accepted their "date with destiny" in good humor, took their assignments in stride, and looked forward to an exciting new adventure. Some deeply troubled young men sensed a deep foreboding, an irrepressible terror of what might lie ahead. Were they soon to be involved in savage fighting on some faraway battlefield? Could they ever bring themselves to kill another human being? What would life be like were they to lose an arm or a leg, or worse yet both arms and legs? How could one return to his family a disfigured, permanently hospitalized son or husband? For some harried draftees the stress became absolutely unbearable, and on almost every trainload that Fred sent off, the morning light brought the sickening news of at least one or two suicides. (It is interesting to speculate about what might have been the eventual fate of many of those GIs headed for the Philippines. They very well might have been captured at Corregidor or on Bataan and been the survivors—or nonsurvivors—of the Bataan Death March and the infamous Japanese prison camps. Could some of those men have been prescient as to their future?)[36]

To be a conscientious objector in WWII required immense courage and conviction. There were slurs, barbed comments, disparaging mutterings for a man not in uniform, despite the fact that the young man may already have enlisted and was waiting to be called up. The social pressure was unrelenting for men to enlist. Here and there, however, a sympathetic soul recognized the brave men who resisted the bandwagon enlistments. Ken Springer, partially as a result of his Quaker heritage, agonized over his choices of whether to plant trees in Montana, go to prison, or join up as a medic. Ken chose the latter. He was afraid people might think him a coward, a fear that no doubt prompted many an enlistment. His draft board gave him a rough time about his status, and even in the early days of his service Ken fended off snide remarks from some of his comrades. One day a stranger from another unit questioned him about his service, and when Ken responded that he was a medic, the man sneeringly remarked, "Oh, a pill roller." "Hey," Ken's buddy interrupted, "his name is 'Doc.'" With that, Ken knew he had been accepted and had secured his place with his comrades.[37]

Although from a Mennonite background, Mel Buschman opted for enlistment in the ROTC unit at Michigan State University, as noted earlier, as his only opportunity for a college education. All of his cousins declared themselves Conscientious Objectors, and although they refused to bear arms, they served as noncombatants. As a Conscientious Objector, Bill Worgul was assigned to the U.S. Medical Department at Percy Jones. When an opportunity arose for Bill to go to Officers Candidate School, he was denied admission unless he would refute his CO status. This Bill refused to do.[38]

Despite having two brothers in the army and one in the navy, Dan Suits, a Socialist from Kirkwood, Missouri, adhered to his convictions of being unwilling to participate in any war and became a Conscientious Objector. Men opposed to serving in the military had three choices: serving in the military as noncombatants, performing civilian service, or going to prison. Dan chose the Civilian Public Service option and for four years worked in Wellston, in northern Michigan, planting trees, fighting forest fires, and cutting timber. The camp was administered by the Church of the Brethren and was composed of two groups: the Brethren, boys who were conforming to the social mores of their upbringing in opposing war; and a second group, the liberated radicals referred to by the Brethren as "The Intellectuals." Dan had no regrets about his CPS work and noted that his service involved primarily out-of-doors healthful work, and in the long run probably added 10 years to his life. (Dan had completed his MA degree from the University of Michigan before his CO service. Afterward, he finished his PhD degree in economics and taught at the University of California at

Santa Cruz and at Michigan State University. Unfortunately, there were no GI bill advantages for Conscientious Objectors!)

There were many possible avenues of service for COs, including some "guinea pig projects" that involved volunteers for medical experiments involving the study of malnutrition, malaria, hepatitis, and typhus control. Dan told of one experiment that was "testing the effects of bed rest and you had to stay in bed for a month. Unfortunately, they didn't take me!" Dan laughed.[39]

The more compassionate civilians generally accepted the convictions of Conscientious Objectors who on religious or moral grounds refused to take up arms. Dorrie Souder told of a friend of hers who, as a Conscientious Objector, served in a TB hospital. In time the young man also contracted TB from one of his patients, but he eventually regained his health. The family did not question his stand, nor did he contest Dorrie's husband's decision to enlist in the U.S. Navy.[40]

THE NISEI

In the days before December 7, 1941, Iwao Ishino, a Japanese American, was completing his third year at San Diego State College. Following the Japanese bombing of Pearl Harbor and the mass hysteria that ensued, Japanese Americans on the West Coast immediately became suspect as possibly being accomplices in the attack. If not accomplices, then perhaps their ties to Japan might induce them to spy for the enemy or become saboteurs in the industrial plants. (Some critics claim anti-Japanese racism in Hawaii and on the West Coast had been brewing for some time, nearly 100 years earlier. Iwao Ishino indicated that it was not exclusively the possible threat of the Japanese as accomplices and spies that prompted the evacuation of the Nisei on the West Coast.)

In one of America's greatest miscarriages of justice, 120,000 Japanese Americans were ordered to be evacuated to camps in middle America where they would presumably present less danger to the national security. (Many people were convinced that their rich farmland and the lucrative businesses of the Japanese Americans were important factors in their removal.) Immediately following Pearl Harbor, the FBI began making random checks of homes and businesses, and rumor ran rampant. Friends and neighbors grew fearful of associating with the Nisei for fear they, too, would become suspect.

In March of 1942, rumor abated, and evacuation became a reality. Americans of Japanese descent were herded into assembly centers—Iwao and his family to temporary housing at the Santa Anita racetrack. Four months later, they boarded trains for an internment camp at Poston, Arizona, where the living conditions left much to be desired. Their quarters consisted of one room devoid of any furniture, save five army cots, for the five members of Iwao's family. Chairs and tables had to be constructed by the internees from scrap lumber. Frustration and boredom in the camps prevailed, and strikes and dissension were prevalent.

Although over 3,000 Japanese Americans were already serving in the military in December of 1941, following Pearl Harbor some were dismissed as "unsuitable for service." The whole problem was a "hot potato" for the Government. For a time, Japanese American men of draft age were reclassified from 1A to 4C and known as "enemy aliens." In 1943, however, the U.S. War Department reversed its stand and opened the door to Japanese American volunteers for combat service in Europe, and thousands of volunteers from the detention camps offered their service to their country. The famous 442nd Regimental Combat Team, a much-decorated unit, was made up of Japanese Americans.

As the war accelerated in the Pacific, a desperate need for translators became apparent. Where better to secure Japanese linguists than from the ranks of the Japanese American evacuees? Suddenly the lowly internees became valuable assets to the U.S. Government. Recruiters were sent out to make the rounds of the camps seeking volunteers of draft age to serve with the military. Iwao Ishino, with three years of college as background, was chosen as 1 of 15 men from the Poston camp to do survey work in the camp. His expertise and integrity were quickly recognized, and soon he was assigned work at the Pentagon in Washington, D.C, where he was sent to do research analyzing the interviews made with the Japanese prisoners of war following their capture. In addition, the Foreign Morale Analysis Division, in which Iwao served, sought to utilize Japanese diaries, letters, newspapers, and radio broadcasts to examine and evaluate Japan's strengths and weaknesses. Details gleaned from those Japanese POWs, such as strategies, death counts, knowledge of Japanese food, and materiel reserves, provided important information for the Allies.

When the Selective Service Board reversed its classification of Japanese Americans from 4-C to 1-A, Iwao was soon called into service. His draft call allowed him three weeks before he would need to report. (Way back in the Poston, Arizona camp, Iwao had met and been attracted to a pretty detainee, Mary Tomiko Kobayashi. Although time and distance separated them for some months, romance won out when they met once again at a United Service Organization (USO) dance in Washington. Mary had moved to Washington when two of her brothers were relocated to that area. Knowing he would have to report for service in three weeks and probably undergo another long separation Iwao proposed, Mary accepted, and they were married.) At Fort Meade, as the names were read off for assignment for basic training, Iwao, now 1-A, found his name was strangely missing. Upon questioning the officer in charge, he was told that he was special and had been assigned to his old job in Washington! "Oh, hell," Iwao joked, "I didn't have to get married after all!" (The Ishinos recently celebrated their 61st year of wedded bliss.) Following the war,

Iwao served with the Military Intelligence Service Language School, completed his PhD (thanks to the GI Bill) at Harvard, and accepted a position in connection with the occupation of Japan. This led to positions at Ohio State University and later to a job with Michigan State University. As he looked back at the bitterness the relocation engendered, Iwao spoke for thousands of Japanese evacuees: "We were forced to essentially prove our patriotism and our loyalties."[41] Hall Tennis recalled in a DVD account that as he was registering for classes at the University of Texas in 1942, "the guy next to me was a tall, ruggedly built oriental guy about my age. We talked some that day and several times later. He told me about his family being moved out to? Colorado, I think? And showed me photos of his family in front of their one story, barracks like, fenced in looking dwelling. I was appalled and confident that it was illegal and would have to be stopped, and perhaps this was just another of those many social events where the law, particularly the constitution, seemed to say one thing and people went ahead and did something else."[42]

It was ironic that Tom Oye, a Japanese American serving as a sergeant with the U.S. Army, married his wife, Martha, while she was a detainee in an internment camp. In her youth, Martha could not understand why people of Italian and German descent were not evacuated, as were the Japanese Americans.[43]

Yoshio "Bill" Abe, a Japanese American, from San Diego, California, had been serving in the U.S. Army for almost seven months at the time of the Japanese attack on Pearl Harbor. He was enjoying a three-day pass on December 7, 1941, when, upon his return to his base at Ft. Ord, California, general confusion prevailed about what to do with the Nisei serving in his unit. All Japanese Americans were immediately under suspicion, including those currently serving in the military. Could they be trusted? Would their true allegiance now be with the Japanese instead of with the United States? Might they attempt to pass on secret technical information to the enemy? Plans were soon formulated, as noted, to send thousands of civilian Nisei to retention centers. In fact, Bill's widowed mother and brother were soon dislodged and assigned to a Japanese American retention camp in Arizona.

The Nisei's presence in the military was becoming a serious problem. During the ensuing months and after being shifted around to several locations, Bill and some of his fellow Nisei were stationed at Camp Wolters, Texas, where they felt like prisoners of war and were consistently assigned humiliating tasks such as breaking rocks and hauling garbage. Finally, in May of 1942, the Army finally decided exactly what to do with Bill and 19 other lucky Nisei from Camp Wolters. What better use of their talents than to send them to the Military Intelligence Service Language School to learn to speak, read, and write Japanese? However, all during their intensive training, Bill and his comrades were considered security risks; their incoming and outgoing mail was "steamed opened and scanned." By December, apparently the Army decided they were truly loyal Americans and sent the men, now classified as language specialists, to the China-Burma-India Theater of Operations.[44]

Often the men did double duty not only as translators and interpreters but also as intrepid, death-defying infantrymen. Sometimes one or another of their team with a perfect accent would infiltrate the Japanese lines and shout out bogus orders that sent their men running pell-mell into a U.S. Army ambush. Sometimes a fellow Nisei would crawl up to little groups of Japanese soldiers to eavesdrop on their conversations. Often their talk paid off in vitally important information conveyed to Bill's officers.[45]

Years later, when asked if he could see anything worthwhile resulting from his more than four and half years of military service, Bill spoke with pride for many of his comrades, and those in the 442nd Infantry Regiment and the 100th Infantry Battalion, that were made up almost exclusively of Nisei: "We proved that we are loyal, patriotic Americans first and foremost."[46]

CHAPTER 2

Women Serving in the Armed Services and with the Red Cross

Just as men rushed to volunteer in the service of their country, women also quickly accepted the challenge of enlistment in the newly created women's branches of military service. In all, approximately 400,000 women served in the military in World War II. In 1942, the Women's Auxiliary Army Corps was formed, and in 1943 it became the Women's Army Corps—WAC. At the peak of enrollment almost 170,000 women had volunteered for the WAC. The WAVES (Women Accepted for Voluntary Emergency Service) numbered 76,000 enlisted women and 8,000 officers. The Coast Guard SPARS (from the motto *Semper Paratus*) attracted over 10,000 women. The Women Marines included 800 officers and 14,000 enlisted women. Not to be overlooked were the WASPS (Women Airforce Service Pilots) who numbered 1,074. In addition, some 60,000 women served in the Army Nurse Corps and 14,000 in the Navy Nurse Corps.[1]

CHOICES, CHOICES, CHOICES

There were almost as many different reasons for enlisting in a particular branch of the women's services in the War as there were women enlistees. An incredible number confessed that it was the sharp looking uniforms that convinced them to join the WAVES. The Marine Corps uniforms attracted another enlistee who vowed after seeing a Tyrone Power movie about Marines that if ever they let women in the Marine Corps she would sign up immediately. As for special training, Eleanor Robinson knew she wanted to be a link trainer the moment her mother's friend bragged that her daughter had qualified as a link trainer and added, "Your daughter can't be in that because it's a very special group."[2]

Posters, recruiters, pride, and the romance of military uniforms all served to attract young women into the services. Surprisingly, or perhaps not so surprisingly, thanks to its cast of handsome, daring young Marines, the movie *To the Shores of Tripoli* turned out to be the inspiration for dozens of enlistees. Marian Cyberski admitted, "That did it for me. And I signed up for the Army Nurse Corps and took one of my friends with me."[3]

After seeing the famous recruiting poster of Uncle Sam pointing and captioned, "I need you," Alice Haber just knew she had to enlist. Although she really didn't want to go, her conscience kept telling her that her country really needed her. Her motivation in enlisting in the Marine Corps was patriotism pure and simple, she insisted.

She scoffed at busybodies who sniffed: "'What's a matter? You can't find a husband?' Well, shoot, anybody could find a husband at that time. That was not the reason. I went because I thought Uncle Sam really needed me."

Although she had wanted to enlist earlier, Alice Haber had to wait until she was 21. Her father, who had served in World War I and was shell-shocked and mustard gassed, refused to sign her papers, believing "that the service was no place for a woman." All through the dinner hour each night Alice's father would keep repeating: "They only need girls in the service for one thing." "Well if you want to think that about your own daughter . . . " Alice replied. Actually, no one in Alice's family wanted her to enlist, "because it just wasn't the things girls did then."[4]

It must be remembered that service women were not universally applauded throughout the country. Some felt that women had no place in the military and looked down on women in uniform. Following Eleanor Smith's graduation in 1943 from nursing school, she and half of her class signed up with the Army or the Navy Nurse Corps. Everyone was doing it, she remembered. No one seemed to have any objections to her decision, other than one young sailor seated across from her on her trip home from having taken her physical at Hamilton, Ohio. Clearly, he was decidedly against women being in the military and caustically remarked, "You should have stayed home where you belong. Why are you doing this?"[5]

Harriet Wever, a SPAR, sensed that many of the men in the Coast Guard looked at them with amusement and failed to take the women seriously.[6] Adelaide Gould, who served with the WAVES, remembered, women were often disparaged for a seeming lack of morals.[7] It was surprising to Betty Drake to be turned away from several USO dances because she wore a Marine uniform, but at the same time young, single girls in the community were welcomed with open arms.[8]

As did many fathers, Dorothy Schieve's father had grave reservations about her joining the military. Dorothy's father was so upset with her enlistment that she was afraid her father would die of a heart attack.[9]

Chris VanderZalm's (Kittleson) father absolutely refused to allow her to join any of the branches of the women's services, although he, himself, served for three and a half years during the war as a physician in a station hospital in Australia. However, he did allow her to put her physical therapist degree to work as a civilian therapist at Percy Jones General Hospital, at that time the country's largest amputee hospital in the United States. (An added bonus was meeting and later marrying one of her patients!) At one time Robert Dole, Daniel Inouye, and Phillip Hart were patients at Percy Jones Hospital. It is also notable that a good many German POWs were assigned to the Hospital where they assisted with the heavy work in the hospital and did routine yard work. According to Chris Kittleson, they proved to be very responsible and extremely happy to be in America and not out risking their lives on the bloody battlefields of Europe.[10]

Betty Drake, an Alabamian, enlisted in the Marine Corps believing that women had a responsibility to their country as well as the men. Prior to her enlistment, her work buying war bonds, saving scrap metal, and even working in a plant in Grand Blanc, Michigan that manufactured Army tanks seemed inconsequential compared to the sacrifices GIs were making. Stipulations required that Marine enlistees be 21 years old, and because she was underage, Betty's father refused to sign her papers. Fortunately, her mother signed her in and following boot camp she was sent to Washington, D.C., where she worked on payrolls to enable Marines and their families to receive their rightful pay. "You can't believe how much paperwork it takes to run a war," she confessed.[11]

A "little" girlfriend of Alice Haber's, who knew she would be under the 95 pound weight requirement for the Marine Corps, tried desperately to enlist along with Alice. Determined to meet the weight requirement, the two girls immediately began a campaign to fatten up Alice's friend. "We fed her all day long. She ate—she still can eat like that—and she still doesn't put on a pound. And then at night, she lived across the street from me, and she'd eat dinner at her house, come over to my house and have dinner, then we'd take her to the ice cream parlor and feed her full of milkshakes."

Finally, a resolute Alice announced her plans to enlist with or without her still skinny friend. The friend pleaded so earnestly to go that Alice agreed, and the two of them headed off to Detroit to enlist. "And someone had told us if you eat bananas and milk it will weigh you up. So we went down the night before and we stayed in the Book Cadillac Hotel in Detroit. And then we went in the morning for our written test, and we passed our written test, and then we went for lunch, and so for lunch she had bananas and milk, and we went back to the hotel, and she got sick in the elevator and lost it all. So she still only weighed 93 pounds when we went back for our physical and she didn't pass, but I did." (Unfortunately Alice's friend, never did make it.)[12]

Essie Woods and her two sisters of Atlanta, Georgia, had been active in the USO that was associated with the airfield at Camp Gordon, and when several African American officers talked with them about enlisting, patriotism won out and all three girls signed up. At the physical exam at Camp Stewart both sisters passed, but Essie was turned away as being underweight. Naturally, her mother was delighted to be able to have one daughter at home, but Essie was humiliated. Immediately, the whole neighborhood, the grocer included, pitched in to help Essie take on weight, and 15 pounds later she went back and was sworn in.[13]

When she heard about plans to draft nurses, Hazel Percival opted to join the Army Nurse Corps. In April of 1945, Congress considered drafting nurses, but civilian hospital officials were not enthusiastic about losing many of their nurses and the matter was dropped. Some 15 percent of the 330,000 Registered Nurses in the United States at that time were already serving with the Army or Nurse Corps.[14] Kathryn Gutherie said she "never thought about *not*" joining the Army Nurse Corps, which she chose because she understood they did more "hands on" nursing. "I felt like I was as good as my brother and fiancé, and wasn't any better."[15]

During her senior year in high school, as the recruiters made their rounds, Gloria Smith (Bouterse) was attracted to representatives from the Cadet Nurses Corps who were offering four years of nurses' training at the government's expense. (The drastic shortage of nurses gave rise to the idea that if more young nurses were recruited, the older more experienced nurses might be freed up to volunteer to serve with the Armed Forces. Thus, the birth of the Cadet Nurses Corps.) The Corps suited Gloria perfectly—no loans, no expenses for the family, a free ride, so-to-speak, in a field that had interested her all of her life.

The war years constituted a particularly important time to be involved in the field of medicine—sulfa and penicillin were the new "miracle" drugs. Gloria distinctly remembered a vial of penicillin being passed around her freshman nursing class, the girls totally awed by its potential. A sad remembrance, however, was the untimely death of a classmate who had unknowingly been administered a toxic dose of sulfa. (Unfortunately sulfa's dimensions were not clearly understood at that time.)[16]

Marilyn Overman saw the world as much bigger than her small town in Iowa and decided enlisting in WAC was one way of seeing the real world. With two brothers in the service, Marilyn believed it important for her to do something for the war effort, also, and in 1943 enlisted in the WAC. Her parents were surprised that she would venture out of her small town life, but supported her decision completely. During her work as a library assistant with WAC in Arlington, Virginia, Marilyn was sure she would never get over the sadness of "listening to the dirges as another military person was buried and watching the horses carry the flag draped casket to its final resting place."[17] In joining the WAAC (later WAC), Edna Penny Rice claimed, "I had a lot of patriotism."[18]

As a very young girl, Ruth Riordan was so impressed by reading about the experiences of a World War I nurse that she vowed that if America ever did get in another war she would volunteer as an army nurse. Following Pearl Harbor in 1941 and her graduation in 1943, Ruth realized that ambition. Interestingly enough, almost half of her graduating class entered the service: three girls as Army nurses, two as Navy nurses, and two in the Air Force.[19]

While working for the telephone company in Jackson, Michigan, Eleanor Robinson and a half-dozen others decided to enlist. The general manager, however, hating to lose so many of his well-trained workforce, called the girls into his office and attempted to discourage them from enlisting. His efforts to convince them that they were doing as much for the war effort by remaining with the company fell on deaf ears, and the women strode right ahead with their plans.[20]

Curious to know whether she, a small town girl from Nebraska, could pass the Civil Service exam, Alma Mattison took the exam and sat back to await the results. Shortly thereafter, on December 8, 1941, at 2 A.M. her grades were mailed to her, and at 4 A.M. she received a telegram to report to Washington, D.C. for a job with the Department of the Army. Unfortunately, the timing was not right, and Alma turned down the offer. A few months later she did accept an assignment with the Office of Strategic Services (OSS; which was a predecessor to the CIA). With some hesitation, namely her aversion to the VI and V2 bombs, Alma accompanied her Washington bosses to London and served throughout the rest of the war in the OSS London offices. Had she accepted the first appointment, she noted, "I would probably have ended up in the Pentagon for the rest of the war typing up marching orders for the military. The fact that I reported directly to OSS changed my life forever." After the war, Alma's youthful desire to see more of the world than the view from the limited perspective of Nebraska was realized when she was sent to Guatemala, Rio de Janeiro, Paris, Calcutta, and New Delhi as well as other foreign offices during her 16 years of overseas service with the CIA.[21]

"Vanity, all is vanity." Although they hate to admit it today, a surprising number of women chose a particular branch of the service because of the uniform. More than one woman confessed to thinking she'd look better in blue than in khaki and enlisted in WAVES instead of WAC. Several women simply liked the lines of women's Navy uniform more than that of WAC's.

One enlistee chose the Marine Corps primarily because she liked the Marine Corps hats. "They had darling hats . . . Hattie Carnegie was a famous designer that designed the hat, and I still think they have the prettiest hats."[22]

Harriet Wever chose to join the SPARS rather than the WAVES because at that time, the middle of December, the WAVES were training in New York City and the SPARS were training in Palm Beach, Florida.[23] Lenore Woychik (Moe) laughingly admitted that in recent years she has no idea what prompted her to sign up with the WAVES.[24]

Actually, during the early days before the military had time to make and issue official uniforms, outfits were essentially catch-as-catch-can. Some women were given old World War I blue uniforms. Later, there were Hattie Carnegie designed uniforms (which, as noted, thrilled many of the wearers). There were pinks and greens and fatigues.

Although Frances Steen Suddeth Josephson, a senior majoring in biology at Goucher College, had planned to enter medical school following her graduation in 1942, her college president urged her to volunteer for secret work as a cryptographer in deciphering enemy codes. After graduation Fran was sent to Washington, and she and several other women who were recruited to take up this work were soon commissioned as U.S. Navy Ensigns and given special training for their future assignments. As Ensigns, naturally, they were expected to perform in formal military drill maneuvers. Now, one must remember, this was the first contingent of WAVES, and in those early days, as noted, there were no uniforms—they had yet to be manufactured and distributed. What a sight it must have been to watch the women as they drilled on a hockey field in dresses, hats with veils, and spike heels! The uniforms finally did arrive, but there were no uniforms in a size 6, and Fran practically disappeared in a size 14. Eventually alterations were made, and Fran took her place among the meticulously dressed WAVES.[25]

AND OH! THOSE DRILLMASTERS!

Stella Staley's father had been in World War I, had been wounded, and had received a Purple Heart. It was with great pride that he watched his only child carry on the tradition and enlist in the military. At first her dreams of enlistment were only wishful thinking—she was too young. However, the minute she learned that the minimum age had been lowered to 20 for WAVES, Stella immediately left her New Hampshire home and signed up in New York City. Stella considered herself hale and hearty, but her stamina was put to the test during her boot camp days at Hunter College. (The occupants of the apartments around the College had been forced to relocate, and the WAVES "luxuriated" in rooms with bunk beds and a couple of beaten-up old chairs.) The seasoned Marines who were in charge of Stella Staley's basic training course proved to be severe taskmasters. Often lacking enthusiasm for the Navy in the first place, in addition to being none too keen about the idea of women in the military, the Marines, who had recently returned from service on Guadalcanal, took little pity

on their female charges. Stella and her comrades were determined to finish their training, salute the Marines goodbye, and assume their first real
assignment.[26]

During the merciless drill by Marines, who really didn't want to waste
their time drilling women, Betty Drake admitted she grew up in a hurry.
"They had more ways to humiliate you than you can imagine. We were
expected to do the same marching and precision that the men did."[27]

Despite her patriotism and determination, Alice Haber was plenty
scared during her early days as a Marine recruit. By the time she got to
Hunter College in New York City she had developed alopecia, and to her
horror all of hair began to fall out. The drilling, parading, and physical
exertion all took their toll on Alice. It was a terrifying moment for a young,
naive Midwesterner to have an officer give her two dimes, point to the
subway, and tell her to find building H at the Brooklyn Naval Hospital. At
the hospital a sympathetic doctor took one look at Alice, sized up the situation, and asked: "The Marine Corps is scaring the hell out of you, isn't it?
You have alopecia and it's caused by worry." It took a while, but finally
the medicine worked, Alice's hair grew back, and in time, fortunately, her
anxiety subsided.

Perhaps all the early training had its positive side, for as her anxieties
diminished Alice saw her self-assertiveness grow. Early on at Camp Lejeune,
Alice was propositioned by a brash male Marine. Looking him straight
in the eye, an undaunted Alice retorted: "Hey, you know, I didn't do that
when I was a civilian, I'm certainly not going to do that since I put on
this uniform." Refusing to be denied, the propositioner shrugged, "'Well,
what do you think you're here for?' And I said, 'Apparently not what you
think I'm here for.'" With that curt put-down, the egotistical aggressor
immediately backed off.[28]

From the dirty tricks department Elizabeth Anesi, a WAC enlistee,
remembered that during boot camp their First Sergeant noticed that some
of the women were simply hustling on their overcoats over their pajamas
each morning, answering roll call, and then heading back to the barracks
for a few more minutes of sleep before breakfast. That habit came to an
abrupt end when the Sergeant forced everyone to turn around and jog the
length of the avenues and come back, and "in that time the pajama legs
would fall down."[29]

According to many of the recruits, the Marine drill officers really could
mete out punishment to men as well as women with little provocation.
Eleanor Smith, a Navy nurse, remembered one young recruit who had to
be sent to the hospital after his drill instructor caught him chewing gum.
The instructor, after observing the noisy gumming, had called a halt to the
marching, passed out sticks of gum for everyone in the platoon, ordered
the men to chew them to a nice, gooey consistency and then plaster the
sticky wads in the culprit's hair. That action, no doubt had a great deal to
do with curtailing gum chewing in that unit![30]

DIVERSIFIED SERVICE

Work within each of the services varied immensely: There were clerical workers; hospital workers at field, evacuation, station, and general hospitals; nurses on hospital trains and ships; women dietitians; as well as women pilots and air controllers to note a few possible areas of service.

Many Americans believe that women are not given half as much credit as they deserved for their immense contributions to the war effort. In 1943, Dorothy Schieve, who grew up in Mr. Pleasant, Texas, joined what was then the Women's Army Auxiliary Corps, later to be the WAC. Dorothy was eager for the opportunity to go overseas, and as a Technical Sergeant she performed clerical work for Eisenhower's Headquarters in London where she was involved in determining which correspondents from Washington would come to Europe and where they would be sent. Especially interesting, of course, were her meetings with the likes of Edward R. Murrow and H. G. Kaltenborn. In London and later in Paris she was assigned to write up and type out handouts for the correspondents at their frequent news conferences.

Naturally, problems arose from time to time such as the embarrassing moment when Marlene Dietrich announced a press conference at 11 A.M., the very hour a press conference had also been announced by General Charles De Gaulle. Eager to interview the glamorous Marlene Dietrich, the press lit out for her conference and left General De Gaulle with a paucity of attendees. There were just minutes to spare when orders went out to the clerical staff to put on their utility coats and attend the General's conference. Fortunately, there were a sufficient number of bodies so that the General was none the wiser.[31]

Working in London as a Corporal in the WAC, Elizabeth McIntee spent most of her time in the Office of Transportation doing paperwork preparatory to the D-Day invasion. The date, of course, was kept top secret, and no one could predict the exact time. Elizabeth said she would never forget the morning of June 6th, 1944, when an officer strode into her office and solemnly announced, "This is D-Day. Work will go on as usual." As a typist in the ammo division, Elizabeth and her fellow workers were kept frantically busy handling all the paper work (in triplicate) for transportation in and out of the United Kingdom.

In an attempt to escape the deadly devastation of the V1 and V2 rocket bombs, most Londoners holed up nightly, or in the event of a daylight air raid, in the comparative safety of the underground stations. (Of the 8,000 V1 bombs sent over by the Germans, some 2,000 took their toll in London.) WAC Corporal Elizabeth McIntee, afflicted by a bad case of claustrophobia, braved the congested quarters only when she was on duty checking names in the bomb shelter. When not on duty, she and several of her colleagues were granted official permission to remain in their homes.

Fortunately, they were billeted with Americans who owned homes in London but had turned them over to the army for housing of U.S. military personnel for the duration. At night, with every wail of an air raid siren, Elizabeth remembered one of her roommates jumping out of bed and getting on her knees and praying. Another roommate jumped out of bed and began singing hymns. Elizabeth said she stayed in bed and shook (and hoped she had said some prayers!).

As WAC Corporal Elizabeth McIntee made her way to work at the Office of Transportation through Hyde Park in London each day, she usually tossed out some crumbs for the birds to feast on. One day a tiny rabbit appeared to investigate the bounty. Here was a minuscule bundle of fur that had survived the bombing and devastation of the city. In awe, she waved over a young mother and her five-year-old daughter to see the furry miracle. When one recalls the ubiquitous food shortages that ravished London during the war, it was really not surprising that the little girl wishfully exclaimed, "Oh, Mummy, wouldn't he make a nice pie!"[32]

Barbara Brown's work in the WAVES consisted of serving as secretary to five officers in Washington, D.C. Life in the Capital during wartime pulsed with excitement. Barb's unit held their organized drill every Monday night next to the Washington Monument, and it was this group, representing WAVES from all over the United States, that Barb organized and drilled to march in President Franklin Delano Roosevelt's funeral parade in 1945.[33]

In Kansas City, as America geared up for war, Prudence Burrell, an African American Public Health Registered nurse, was sought out by the authorities in 1941 as a potential recruiter for the U.S. Army Nurse Corps. Informed that few African American women had volunteered for service, Prudence immediately rose to the occasion and in one fell swoop initiated and completed her recruiting role by enlisting in the Army Nurse Corps herself. "I recruited myself," she boasted.

In 1942, when she officially joined the Army Nurse Corps, there was no boot camp or extended preliminary training, and Prudence's group was soon sent out to New Guinea to Hospital Station 268, a medical facility where they were allowed to care only for African American soldiers. White servicemen were treated at a separate facility. One day Hospital Station 268 had a jolly time of it when a white soldier who was severely hemorrhaging from an accident was brought to the emergency room in their station for a desperately needed transfusion. Apparently the accident had taken place close to Prudence's hospital, and the soldier's condition was critical. Although the staff, of course, knew there was no difference between white blood and black blood, they, with tongue in cheek, toyed with the soldier for a few seconds explaining that they were very sorry but they could not give him the necessary transfusion for their blood was labeled "A" (for African blood). In anger, the soldier summoned what probably was his last remaining ounce of energy, rose up on his stretcher and shouted: "I don't give a damn, don't let me die!" The transfusion was completed, and the soldier survived! Years later Prudence laughed saying that if that man is still living, he should be aware of the fact that "he's walking around with African blood in him!"[34]

Ruth Marjorie Madole Riordan felt well compensated for her service on the 21st hospital train in France and Belgium from September 1944 until May 1945. The hospital trains, one recalls, were makeshift railroad "ambulances" that carried the wounded from the European battlefield and evacuation hospitals and transported them to rear or general hospitals or to ships that would carry the patients to England or to the United States. (At its height there were 55 hospital trains in Europe each staffed with nurses and physicians and boasting a dining car, surgical facilities, and a pharmacy.) The 21st Hospital Train could carry 240 stretcher patients and 64 ambulatory patients, and Ruth and her crew took pride in their three month's record in 1944–45 of traveling some 20,000 miles and evacuating more than 9,000 patients.

Each RN on a hospital train had 60 patients to care for. This meant busy days of changing bandages, administering medication, taking temperatures, feeding the enfeebled, fingering the vial of morphine always at the ready in their pockets, and often times just listening. Nurses had to be good listeners as they compassionately responded to oft repeated stories from their patients about the horrors of their experience on the battlefield, the details of their family life in the States, and their hopes and plans for the future. Providing answers to sobering questions about survival had to be one of the most difficult jobs. Ruth Riordan continued to wonder what more she could have said to the poor young soldier who had shared a foxhole with two buddies—one who had died instantly from artillery fire, another who had been dealt life threatening injuries by the same shell, and yet, he somehow had escaped unharmed. She prayed that her reply, "the good Lord has future plans for you," would provide the encouragement he so desperately needed.

For the most part, the hospital trains with their Red Cross identification were exempt from the bombings that decimated the countryside and took out thousands upon thousands of our soldiers. At the time of the Battle of the Bulge, however, there was a tremendous explosion as one of the bombs crashed near Ruth's hospital train, and a badly frightened crew hurriedly evacuated their patients for cover in an air raid shelter. Fortunately there were no casualties, and soon the train once again resumed its journey to the safety of a hospital in the rear.

Soldiers formed deep attachments to the nurses who hovered over them, fed them, and bandaged their wounds. Ruth Riordan smiled as she remembered allowing a group of patients in the day-room, when she was stationed at a hospital near Nottingham, England, to continue visiting and playing cards despite the 9 P.M. curfew stipulated by the hospital authorities. It was July and not even dark yet. When one of the Medical Colonels paid them a surprise visit, there was nothing for her to do but to accept responsibility for the infraction. As the day-room door closed behind the Colonel, her loyal patients were quick to fearfully inquire, "Lieutenant, did we get you in trouble?"[35]

As a member of the Army Nurse Corps, Ruth Johnson was assigned duties aboard a hospital ship plying the Atlantic. Often the work involved gathering up the wounded directly from the battlefields, work that took her close to the shelling on the front lines. On one occasion, her ship, the *Arcadia*, helped rescue survivors of a torpedoed American vessel during the North African campaigns and was cited by General Eisenhower for outstanding performance of duty.[36]

If patients were to get well they needed the proper food, and dietitians were an important part of the care-giving scene. Following her dietitian internship at Montefiore Hospital in the Bronx in New York, Irene Kenneck (Johnson) and many of her colleagues were eager to join the war effort as hospital dietitians with the U.S. Army. Following a year's service at Camp Carson in Colorado Springs, Colorado, Irene was headed to England as part of the 187th General Hospital Group. The 10-day trip across the Atlantic seemed interminable, but with a bit more maneuvering through England, Irene found herself stationed with two other dietitians at a general hospital located some 25 miles south of Salisbury, England, that housed about 1,000 patients. (En route from New York to Liverpool and then to Salisbury, England, Irene Johnson became friends with members of a group of 200 glider pilots en route to prepare for the D-Day Invasion. Although she knew that the longevity of glider pilots was not great, Irene was shocked upon her return to the States after the war to meet up on board ship with one of the pilots in the original group of 200 and hear him say that he knew of only six who had survived.)

At the time of Irene's arrival in England, D-Day was scarcely two months away, and secrecy was a top priority. Everything, of course, was hush-hush, and although rumor ran rampant, no one in the hospital had any idea when or where the invasion would take place. Taking advantage of the one day a week off from hospital work given to dietitians, on June 6th Irene Johnson was headed for an early morning shopping trip to nearby Devizes. Suddenly, her heart raced madly, and she caught her breath as from up above came the drone of a sky solid with planes. This was the big day: "D-Day had arrived." Soon the landing strips near their hospital would be throbbing with planes returning from the beaches bearing the wounded and dying. On the runways a fleet of ambulances would be readied to meet the planes from which nurses and orderlies gingerly transported the blood-soaked casualties to the hospital.[37]

Her job in a factory inspecting 40-millimeter shell cases for the Navy seemed a bit too tame for Wanda Kearns. She believed she could be doing more for her country by actively serving in the Navy, and in 1944 she enlisted, took her boot camp training at Hunter College in New York, and achieved her goal of being chosen 1 of 9 out of 2,000 WAVES to take training and serve as an air control operator. The stress at the Norfolk Naval Air Station was intense as controllers made sure that day after day all the planes—the fighters, sea planes, and transport planes—took off and landed safely. Furthermore, Wanda was convinced she was fighting three wars: the big one, WWII; the war with the male control operators who resented women replacing them; and die-hard southerners who took a dim view of all northern Yankees. The work was challenging, Wanda declared, especially when emergencies hyped up the adrenaline. It looked like a sure crash one day when a pilot on his way in radioed that he had a "dead stick" (his engines had stopped). There was a general alert, all aircraft were cleared from the area, and the shore patrol and emergency crews lined the runway as everyone held their breath. The savvy pilot came in nose down, slowed a bit, and then leveled off coming in for a beautiful landing that had everyone in a state of euphoria. There was an earsplitting cacophony of horns, whistles, and sirens as the fire engines, medical teams, and ambulance crews cheered the pilot as he emerged from the plane. In the control tower, Wanda uttered a silent thank you and breathed a huge sigh of relief. The remembrance of that moment still gives Wanda chills.[38]

While teaching physical education at McDonogh High School in New Orleans, Marion Schoor (Brown) jumped at the chance to learn to fly when the government offered opportunities for women to train as pilots for the Air Force under the Women's Pilot Training Program. After completing her training she was assigned to Romulus Air Force Base where she ferried small bombers and "trainers" from the various factories to Air Force Bases all over the United States and Canada. The work offered considerable more compensation than her $90 a month teaching job and included the added bonuses of travel and the excitement of sailing the wild blue yonder. Marion loved the work, but once the war was over the women were bumped for male pilots to take their places.[39]

Special Intelligence Staff Sergeant Shirley Martin (Schaible) served as a research analyst on Hollandia, New Guinea, Leyte, and in Manila working with enemy documents taken from dead Japanese bodies and POWs. Information gleaned from papers and letters about what ships they had served on, where they were headed, and whom they were serving under provided the authorities with top secret material for important briefing sessions and plans for future actions. Shirley remarked proudly that they were known as "enemy appreciationists."

Security was critical, and Shirley's special group consisted of two other women and a small group of Harvard and Yale lawyers. Their offices in

Leyte were tents that were unlocked to admit them, locked after they were inside, and unlocked when they closed down for the night. Each woman was given a helmet for protection were she to be caught in a Japanese assault and forced to dive for a foxhole. Each of the men carried a loaded gun that was put on his desk within easy reach. Associations with other army, navy, or marine personnel were strictly limited.

As the war wore on, Shirley remembered she had become so benumbed by death and dying that she found herself casually stepping over a dead Japanese who had been blistering in the sun for several days. Unthinkingly, she kept walking on to her tent.

After the news had circulated about the dropping of the atomic bomb, Shirley chided one of the officers for being so ecstatic about the ending of the war. "How can you be so happy when so many thousands of people have been killed by the atomic bomb on Hiroshima?" The officer coldly looked at her with disdain and said nothing.[40]

RED CROSS WORKERS AT PEARL AND NEW GUINEA

After several of her friends had volunteered to serve with the Red Cross, Sally Swiss in Saginaw, Michigan, felt conscience-bound to do what she could for the war effort. She returned the engagement ring she had accepted several months earlier, signed on with the Red Cross, and boarded a ship for an unknown destination. Because they left from the West Coast, there were rumors that they were headed for Hawaii—which in a few days' time proved to be true.

"Pulling duty" in Hawaii was not too painful, Sally admitted. In all three of her stations on Oahu, Sally and the Red Cross girls were expected to be available for conversation or cards with the servicemen—and to plan dances. Decorations for the dances were obtained by cutting down branches from the palm trees that lined the main street in Honolulu! (Nothing was too good for U.S. servicemen!) To assure dance partners for the men, trucks were sent into the city to a central place where there was always a lineup of women of every size, shape, and description ("all were welcome") waiting to be carried out to the base for an evening of jitterbugging, two stepping, or waltzing. Sally smiled as she recalled: "The marines really 'clean up good!' They could look scroungy during the day, but at a dance, their shoes sparkled and their trousers were creased and starched to the point where they could stand up alone."

The Red Cross women quickly learned the importance of being eager, patient listeners. Each GI had a story to tell—about himself, his hometown, his family. Often it was the same story, the same array of photos of a girlfriend, a fiancée, a wife, or children repeated every other week. An exception to the rule, however, was one amiable enlisted man, a bookie prior to his being drafted, who repeatedly offered to teach Sally how to make a bundle "betting on the ponies." Some of Sally's most creative work involved spending countless hours making charcoal drawings of the GIs—an activity that always garnered a noisy crowd around her as she worked. (Sally was and continues to be an extremely talented professional artist.)[41]

As for her service with the Red Cross as a Recreational Director in connection with the 13th General Hospital Red Cross unit in New Guinea, Mary Hoagland reported that, "Those two years were two of my most satisfying. I accomplished what I wanted to and they made me want to volunteer in hospitals the rest of my days." And that she did, working as a volunteer for Hospice.

December of 1944 looked to be a bleak Christmas for the weary, homesick patients at the hospital in New Guinea. Mary and her staff quickly decided to do something about that, although it took ingenuity and determination to galvanize the Christmas spirit among the aching bodies confined to wheel chairs, hobbling about on crutches, or swathed in bandages. They found local vegetation that could be fashioned into wreaths and garlands, and a little help from the Red Cross workers inspired the men to make personal gift cards for their distant families.

An SOS was sent out for help in making and filling 1,000 red stockings that were to be hung on each patient's bed at the hospital at precisely ten o'clock Christmas eve. Everyone joined in the project and turned it into a very Merry Christmas indeed. The antiseptic ward, thanks to wrapping paper and eager paint brush wielding patients, was transformed into a "snowy New England scene" complete with a white frame house with shutters and shrubbery. A walkway was covered with 50 pounds of Epsom salts to simulate snow, and a life-size snowman and snowlady presided over the house. The snowman and his wife were made of paper wadding on a wooden frame, tied with burlap, and covered with plaster of Paris bandages that were supplied by "the boys from surgery." To say the Christmas Open House and Christmas Pageant was a success was putting it mildly. For a few hours, Mary explained, peace instead of war prevailed.[42]

LIFE AMONG THE RUINS

The mass of rubble that constituted the once vibrant city of Le Havre staggered Margaret Oaks as she and the members of her Army Nurse Corps group arrived in France after crossing the Channel in 1945. As they marched in formation down through the town to the train station, "there was nothing but concrete foundations and columns and just rubble, every place. It occurred to me immediately that we in the United States don't even know what war is. We lose people from our families and our friends, but we never have had to suffer the destruction of everything else that we own. These people over there—everything was just utterly demolished, including their families."[43]

Following her enlistment and a brief period of recruiting service for the WAC in Newark, New Jersey, Dorothy Wilkie had hoped to be sent to England. Instead, in 1942 she was sent to Australia with the first group of WACs to be sent there. Her next stop was New Guinea and then on to the Philippines where she continued to serve as a secretary. Living conditions for the Filipinos following the bombings were horrible, Dorothy remembered. In Manila the "buildings were almost all bombed out, and the people who lived there, some of them would get a metal sheet, or wood, or whatever and make a lean-to and that's what they lived in. . . . You know, it's hard to describe what it was like, it was just unbelievable, unbelievable, because everything had been bombed, it was awful. We had the World Trade Center, that was nothing to what happened in the Philippines."[44]

As Marian Mosher and her group of Army nurses arrived in the Philippines in 1945, they watched as the recently released prisoners of war (with whom they were sharing tents) offered prayers of thanksgiving before eagerly devouring the breakfast of green-looking scrambled eggs that the nurses had turned up their noses at. Sharing toilet and shower facilities with the young, teenage male POWs caused some embarrassment for the nurses, but the boys thought the shared bathrooms a negligible problem indeed, in comparison with the appalling conditions of their prison life. Lavatory facilities for some nurses in the Pacific Theater consisted of "two holers" that the nurses shared with lizards and spiders. Water in many places was in such short supply that a bather took a chance on getting all lathered up and being unable to rinse herself when the water was turned off.[45]

Following the Japanese surrender, Catherine Cross's tour of duty was not yet over, and she and her unit were sent to Tokyo for two and a half months to care for the liberated American POWs. Catherine was aghast at the devastation of the city. Parts of Tokyo, she was told, had burned for 30 days after the Doolittle raid in 1942. "There were just shells of buildings left standing when we arrived in late August 1945. One exception to that was the pre-war mission hospital known as St. Luke's. American pilots purposely spared it and it was put to good use as soon as the war was over."[46]

COMMITMENT, PERSEVERANCE, AND STAMINA

The most difficult and depressing times, the military nurses and Red Cross workers all agreed, were caring for some of the tragic battle casualties. Even seasoned nurses cringed at their first experiences with the mangled bodies of young soldiers, merely boys, brought in off the battlefields, or incinerated sailors rescued from burning ships. It took time and cool-headed determination to cope with patients wracked with pain and clutching at life.

Putting in 12-hour work days, six days a week, fighting off the rats that invaded their tents, braving 148-mile per hour winds in typhoons, surviving on K rations (packages of emergency rations: spam, sugar, crackers, cheese, coffee, candy, etc.) three times a day, taking baths in steel helmets, and mushing through mud, mud, and more mud were simply part of the life of army nurses serving near the battlefronts in the South Pacific. The physical strain was minimal, however, compared to the emotional strain of witnessing the horrible suffering of the burned and wounded men, many of whom did not survive, and of hearing the plaintive cries of a 17-year-old Navy boy crying out "Mother, mother come and get me!"— memories that have been etched on Catherine Cross's mind and heart forever. Watching the kamikazes zero in on the ships near their field hospital and then seeing the casualties brought in, many too far gone to respond to treatment, took a devastating toll on Catherine and her fellow caregivers. "Most people would never imagine how much our men suffered with those terrible wounds. It was a pit of hell for many of them."[47]

Speaking later in life of her service as a Red Cross Hospital worker in Caserta, Italy, Helene Gram Forster recalled: "We were with those who had given everything. You got so that you didn't see anything, you didn't see any of the horror, and after all, we were seeing the horror of [war]. We were not on the front line, but we were awfully close to it. We lived in combat zones most of the time. . . So we really saw, and I think we realized that *this is* why we have given up a very comfortable position here in this country and volunteered to go into something in another country. It wasn't difficult as all at once you became indoctrinated to looking at the horror that you were seeing—with legs and arms and faces blown [away] and that kind of thing. It wasn't difficult anymore and you realized that your job was to help them, and to do what you could to make them as comfortable as possible and keep them in contact with their family. You were kind of the arm of the chaplain also."[48]

Following the fighting on Iwo Jima, Dorothy Drolett (Doyle) remembered some 700 hundred casualties a day being brought in to the hospital. "It was just horrible," she remembered with the young kids just begging "'Doc, please don't take my leg off, please don't take my arm off.' They had nothing they could do, they had to, it was very sad."[49]

Her stressful work on a plastic surgery ward brought on deep trauma for Kathryn Wetherby Guthrie, especially when young men were brought in with burned, mutilated faces "that even their mothers could not recognize." For some there was help. Others would be forced to go though life with faces so disfigured that they would forever be stared at and avoided. Almost immediately as the nurses arrived to assess their wounds, the poor, heartsick GIs would pull out a picture from their bill-folds to show the nurses how handsome they had once been before their injuries.[50]

There were horrific sights that made even seasoned nurses blanche. Marjorie Varner could scarcely hold back the tears when during one intake of casualties she reached under the covers to take a young, horribly wounded young man's blood pressure—but the young man had no arm. "So I reached for the other arm, under the covers,—but the young man had no extremity on that side either."[51]

Winifred Gansel had worked in a San Jose cannery to pay her way through the O'Connor Hospital of Nursing, and following Pearl Harbor she responded to the constant appeals on radio for nurses in the armed services. At Camp Roberts, Winnie claimed, "We all felt like pioneers because we were using sulfa drugs and penicillin drugs, which were quite new at that time." (Penicillin was so new and in such scarce supply that Carolyn Ryan, during her work with the Army Nurse Corps in Casablanca, Tunis, and Naples, found that to conserve the precious drug the hospital immediately separated the newly admitted men into groups of those who could live without it and those who were going to die without it.)

After volunteering for overseas service in 1945, her first duties at a field hospital just outside Manila involved long hours caring for boys sent directly from foxholes on the front lines. It was an eye-opening experience to some about the ravages of war as "most had been in the holes for 40–60 days. They came in with terrible diarrhea and vomiting and malnutrition."[52]

Dorothy Wilkie's sickening observations of Japanese brutality were to live with her for the rest of her life. In the mess hall in the Philippines she encountered a Filipino waiter whose tongue had been cut out by the Japanese because he would not divulge the information they wanted. A prisoner who had been held by the Japanese counted herself one of the luckiest persons in the world, for when she and her fellow prisoners were liberated by the Americans, they looked at the records and discovered that the Japanese had planned to shoot all of the prisoners at roll call the next morning, just hours after they were liberated. When Dorothy Wilkie, herself, was hospitalized with malaria, she, too, counted her lucky stars that she had not been there earlier when the Japanese had poisoned the water and killed a great many people in the hospital.[53]

Were all of the nurses able to tough it out for the completion of their tour of duty? No, indeed. They, as well as their patients, had to battle to survive malaria, dysentery, yellow fever, and jungle rot. Winifred Gansel saw at least three of her pals sent back to the states: one as a result of an injury from a jeep accident, one who suffered crippling bursitis from a yellow fever shot, and another who developed a serious lung disease.[54]

A SIMPLE SHAMPOO

Memories that keep surfacing in Army Nurse Martha Marshall Baker's mind involved a 19-year-old patient of hers during her service on Okinawa who had lost all of his limbs except his right arm. Despite his devastating losses, his most ardent desire was to have his hair washed. "I worked in supply," Martha recounted, "and I was able to ask the nurse's permission to take him down to our department and wash his hair; and I found it meant so much to him. This was at a time when all the wards were over-crowded with patients, so of course the nurses and the staff didn't have all the time to give these patients."[55]

On several occasions during the course of the next few weeks, Martha was able to wheel her young patient down to the nurses' department to honor his heart's desire for a shampoo. Soon, it was time for him to be evacuated to Hickam Field and from there to be returned to the States. One can scarcely imagine the anguish of the young patient as he read-ied for the trip home. "He was so nervous," Martha continued, but he begged once again, "Oh, if I could just have my hair washed!" It seemed such a little thing to do, she thought, but it was so very important to the young man's morale, and he was so appreciative of her efforts. As Martha wheeled him back to the ward he had one final plaintive request: "Will you make sure you come to the ward before I depart?"

The day became frantically busy and, "As it happened, when I returned he was already on the bus waiting to leave for Hickam. I hurriedly boarded the bus, and there he was on the lower level. As I came near him he beck-oned to me; and with his one arm, he just placed it around my neck and he kissed me. That was something I'll just never forget."[56]

A LOOK BACK

Catherine Cross, of south Minneapolis, assessed her time as an army nurse in World War II as "The most important time of my life." As for her war experiences, Catherine modestly shrugged off her demanding work car-ing for severely wounded and desperately ill men in field hospitals close to the front lines on Saipan and Okinawa as "just doing my job."[57]

"It was a growing up experience," Betty Drake believed. "One could never go back to being what you were before the war."[58] Shirley Schaible agreed. "I came back another person. I returned much older than my years, with a broader view of life's purposes and meaning. No regrets, but I can't watch war news on TV without feeling deeply for each and every person over there."[59] Elizabeth Anesi insisted that she got more serving in the WAC than she did "in all my years in college."[60]

Ruth Riordan encouraged "anybody, anybody, male or female, to do something for their country. Because if we don't do anything for our coun-try, we won't have it, we will not have it. . . I wouldn't take any amount of money for it. . . I have to feel that our form of government is the best form of government going."[61]

Asked if she would do it all over again and volunteer for the WAVES, Barbara Brown nodded, "In a heartbeat," but she was quick to point out that the WAVES "would probably not want a person my age."[62]

Would Essie Woods serve again? Yes, indeed. "It makes you a better person to understand human beings and it makes you dedicated to do something for someone else beside yourself. You're supposed to share and think about the people and not yourself and not be so self-centered."[63] Helen Minor felt her time in the WAC had been a great learning experience and that the discipline involved was vitally important to later life.[64] Elizabeth Brown's war experiences as a Red Cross hospital worker induced her to later join the Peace Corps.[65]

The stress involved in the exhausting day and night care of their patients took their toll on scores of nurses and caregivers for many years following the war. According to some of the nurses, their post-war adjustment was not an easy matter. Lillian Kivela pointed out, "It was a terrible adjustment. I think some of the awfullest times I spent in my life were after I came back from the service. We came back from all that activity—somebody around all the time—to nothing. Nothing!"[66]

Well aware of their devoted service in extremely dangerous situations and under appalling circumstances, nurses were unwilling to be accorded a second-class role in history. Having been a nurse in Sicily and other stations overseas, Virginia Rogers, at the end of the war, was invited to join the Auxiliary of the VFW. Her answer was a decided negative: "Absolutely not, I served just like the men did, I was in danger just like they were, and if I can't have full membership, then I'm not going to join." And join she did not until she was eventually given equal status with the men.[67]

THE BRIGHTER SIDE

Although it sounds as though it ought to have come from an *I Love Lucy* TV show, it was a true story that nurse Dorothy Doyle related about a friend of hers. As her friend was boarding a ship for a new assignment in New Zealand she was carrying her musette bag, containing the required "essentials" for three days, slung over her shoulder and at the same time juggling an armload of books. In the warm humid temperatures of the South Pacific it took about 15 minutes to wash and dry clothing, and each nurse carried several coat hangers hanging on her musette bag in readiness for a quick wash and dry. Dorothy's friend told her, "So I went aboard the ship and as you go aboard the ship the first thing you do is salute the Officer of the Deck. And my arms were full and I saluted the Officer of the Deck and I went to move and I couldn't move and as I turned around the coat hangers were caught in the Captain's fly. I had to back up until his

Navy boy got the coat hanger out of his fly." (Those were the days before zippers one should remember.) It took two days before Dorothy's friend could recover from her embarrassment and finally get up courage to go topside![68]

"Lights out" meant Lights *Out!* in WAC quarters in the States. Now and then the total blackout meant that a WAC emerging late from the shower room would be forced to find her way back to her bed in total darkness. Everyone had a good laugh when one of the women in Helen Minor's barracks, caught in the darkness after her nightly scrubdown, blindly struggled back to her bed, opened her footlocker, reached in, and slathered her underarms with deodorant. In the cruel light of day, what she thought was deodorant turned out to have been shoe polish![69]

Just for fun, because they all looked more or less like identical penguins in their WAC uniforms, the women in Helen Minor's barracks decided they could look even more alike if they all had the same hair color. Enough of this blonde and brunette business, they'd all be redheads! Out came the henna bottles, and the next morning at roll call the entire unit appeared identically uniformed and henna coifed. Unfortunately, the idea bombed with the officials, and everyone was immediately sent to the barbershop for short, short, short haircuts.[70]

The women in Eleanor Robinson's building (quarters that had formerly housed only men) found the urinals they encountered in the bathroom decidedly unfeminine and distasteful. They tolerated the eyesores for several days until one enterprising lady solved the problem by talking the cook out of a couple of sweet potatoes. These she planted in the urinals and whenever the women used the toilets, they took time to flush the urinals. The net result was a wonderful array of beautiful sweet potato plants. For months the women prided themselves on the fruits of their labors, that is until a "Captain's mast," when the Captain came in to inspect the facilities. In short order the little garden was relegated to the dumpster.[71]

Elizabeth Anesi had high praise for the Mess Sergeant of their headquarters in San Francisco who graciously volunteered accommodations at her parents' home in Mesa, Arizona for members of their company "who needed a place to go for a convalescent leave and either they lived on the east coast and the trip would be too much for them to go home or they just needed to get away." It took no prodding for the popular Sergeant to call up her mother and check to see whether the guesthouses on their ranch would be available on a particular weekend. The welcome mat was always out other than days when "Uncle Albie" was planning to come in with his retinue of friends and colleagues. Unfortunately, there would be no extra rooms at that time and a visit would have to be postponed until the next weekend. If "Uncle Albie" were not in town, the Sergeant's mother "would just take them in and baby them so." Out of curiosity Elizabeth once asked her friend: "Your Uncle Albie certainly travels around a lot, what does he do?" The answer turned out to be a real shocker: "Well right now he's the Vice President." "Uncle Albie" was Alben Barclay, the Vice President of the United States![72]

One of Helene Gram Forster's patients (she was serving as a Hospital Recreation Worker in Europe) had lost his right hand and was gradually losing his eyesight. "When he first looked at me he could very hazily make out the outline of my face." As she walked down the ward the other patients called to him, "'Here's the Red Cross girl, Dick.' And so I stopped and he said, 'Get my wallet out of the table,' which was on a bedside table next to each cot. I said, 'I don't need your wallet, Dick, I have nothing to sell you.' He said, 'No, no, I don't want my money.' He said, 'I want you to look at my wife's picture, I think you look like her.'" The entire ward and even Helene herself concurred on the likeness. From that time on the two became fast friends, Helene, as his amanuensis and in turn his reader of the loving letters from his wife. The friendship has spanned the decades with Helene visiting Dick and his wife as often as possible in their home in Lancaster, Pennsylvania.[73]

It was amusing for Gertrude Gay to see patients at Christmastime in 1944 in her hospital sitting on their beds making paper chains and cotton balls to use as decorations on their Christmas tree. Although there were no electric lights for the tree, patients painted light bulbs red and green and pretended they were Christmas lights. Santa Claus (the biggest toughest sergeant in the unit) passed out "presents" made up of cigarettes, candy, and chewing gum sent by the Red Cross to the patients who were being serenaded by a makeshift choir of nurses and technicians. In all it made for at least a few hours of diversion from their aches and pains and the overwhelming melancholy of homesickness.[74]

Anita Dean was a dietitian working in Women's Hospital in Detroit, Michigan and was barraged with telephone calls from the Army urging her to join the Women's Medical Specialists Corps. It was all new for Anita who took a very brief training course where they taught her how to salute, march in step, and maneuver a gas mask. Her assignment proved a decided contrast to less fortunate recruits. The Army had purchased the Greenbrier Hotel in White Sulphur Springs, Virginia and turned it into a general hospital. The golf courses, swimming pools, and deluxe housing made it seem more like a country club than a hospital.[75]

Anita was one of five dietitians who devised menus to tempt the most squeamish appetites. As can well be imagined, the war had produced not a few patients with stomach ulcers who were carefully monitored and restricted to special diets. Anita heartily approved of the dietitians' making the rounds with the physicians, learning and taking orders on the spot. (German prisoners of war were employed in some of the hospital kitchens where, according to the staff, they turned out to be responsible and most cooperative workers. Some worked on the golf courses at Greenbrier and naturally felt lucky that they were not engaged in the fighting that was taking the lives of so many of their former comrades.)

Dorothy Doyle, a nurse stationed in the New Hebrides, will never forget the evening she and several other nurses were invited to dinner aboard the *McCauley,* a troop ship that was temporarily docked near their quarters. The dinner was a meal to remember—including prime rib and *ice cold* celery, delicacies the nurses hadn't tasted for ages. As they were leaving, their hosts took them down to see their cabins and to the surprise of all of the nurses, each cabin had a mirror! The nurses gasped, for throughout their months of service they had had to make do with a tiny hand mirror.

There were even more surprises in store when they stepped down into the landing craft to return to their barracks. There, sparkling in the lights, were three full-length mirrors! Without tools the men were unable to detach the mirrors from the doors and therefore in their generosity they had removed the doors from their cabins and given the nurses the doors and all. The ship's captain might well have been upset over the munificent gifts; however, the nurses were ecstatic. "I'll never forget the mirrors, the full length mirrors. We hadn't seen our feet for a long time when standing," Dorothy exclaimed. A month later, Dorothy and her nurses heard that the *McCauley* had been sunk, perhaps near Bougainville. They were extremely thankful that none of their benefactors had been lost; furthermore, they were deliriously happy that the famous mirrors were not lounging on the bottom of the ocean. "We had 'em!" they rejoiced.[76]

CHAPTER 3

Normandy: "Operation Overlord"

By June 6, 1944, more than 10,000 war planes, over 5,000 ships and landing craft, and over 1 million troops readied for the invasion of Normandy, the greatest seaborne invasion force in history.

The immensity of the preparations for the Normandy invasion staggers the imagination. As GIs surveyed the immense accumulation of trucks, jeeps, troops, and supplies in England in preparation for D-Day, not a few jokesters predicted that if one more truck arrived surely Britain would sink beneath the weight. Upon arriving in Glasgow, Scotland, a wide-eyed Bruce Helmer was so awed by such a massing of ships that he thought he surely must be surveying the entire U.S. Navy.[1]

Everyone knew the invasion was coming soon—even the Germans. But thanks to ingenious deceptive maneuvers on the part of the Allied Forces, the Germans were convinced that the assault would be at Pas de Calais, the shortest distance to France across the English Channel. The Allies, of course, did everything possible to perpetuate that idea including dropping dummy parachutists and setting up dummy tanks and trucks made to look like a real invasion was in the offing.

Naturally, the exact date was a top secret. However, rumor ran rampant about the time and place of the invasion. When? Where? At what hour? While awaiting orders for the June 6th D-Day invasion, one Private First Class (PFC) in Al Alvarez's 16th Infantry Regiment, "had sneaked into the war room and saw the letters NOR . . . and bet his only five dollars we were going to *Norway!*"[2]

Shortly before the assault, William Burke was confused by the mess steward's reporting that the captain had informed them "We're going to the Riviera." It sounded great to William Burke, especially when all the ship's charts were specifically focused on the English Channel. Only when he looked carefully and found the village La Riviere on the Normandy coast near Bayeux was he able to understand what had been the Captain's feeble attempt at humor.[3]

It was crucial that the invasion be successful, and the training and preparatory exercises were endless. Several Normandy veterans explained that there were so many practice operations before the actual June 6th date that each time as the men prepared they never really knew which operation was going to be the real D-Day. John MacPhee, an infantry soldier, claimed that he "had spent so much time in the water" during the countless amphibious landings and maneuvers in preparation for the Normandy landings that "I thought I was in the Navy."[4]

Roland Johnston recalled that he and his buddies "were tired of training by the time the invasion came. We were glad to see it come, although I think I can speak for most of the fellows we were sacred to hell."[5]

REHEARSAL FOR D-DAY—SLAPTON SANDS

One of the most important, although little publicized, trial runs for the Normandy invasion was the "Slapton Sands" rehearsal conducted on April 28th. First Lieutenant Harold Cunningham was part of the units loaded on to LSTs (Landing Ships, Tanks) in the dark of night for a practice run to Slapton Sands near Plymouth, England. All went well, he explained, until German E-boats slipped into the convoy and sent some 800 men to their deaths.[6] Eugene E. Eckstam's dramatic description provides personal insights into the debacle—one so devastating that it was more or less hushed up for fear information would completely undermine the morale of the thousands of troops poised for the Normandy assault.

Eckstam's story starts in early January of 1944, when Eugene E. Eckstam, MD, of Madison, Wisconsin, had been part of a team assigned to examine some 1,600 recruits each day at the Great Lakes Naval Training Station. One day as he was engaged in his poking and prodding, his stethoscope thumping with heartbeats and deep breaths, the voice of a Lieutenant Commander thundered across the room: "Eckstam, we don't want you here any more. We're sending you overseas." "My knees started shaking." Gene recalled, "and so did those of all the birthday suited recruits."[7]

After a trip across the Atlantic, Gene arrived at Falmouth, England to ready for OPERATION TIGER, the all-important dress rehearsal in preparation for the Normandy invasion. The area near the village of Slapton Sands on the southern coast of England had been totally cleared of some 3,000 residents who had been evacuated and asked to keep secret the plans for the practice run. It was thought that in many respects the area resembled the geography of the Normandy beaches, and this would provide at least some of the invasion troops with a little practical experience for their upcoming contest. It was vital to see how the battle plan would work, whether troops could be moved efficiently and supplies could be dispensed quickly. Errors discovered on the trial run could be corrected quickly in time for the June 6th D-Day. The operation was massive. There were thousands of troops and hundreds of vehicles, ships, and "Defense" troops that would act as German soldiers trying to defend the beaches.

Unfortunately, the actual operation met with disaster when early in the morning on April 28, 1944, German E-Boats attacked several of the ships in the convoy carrying the men, supplies, and vehicles to be unloaded on the area's beaches. Some 749 soldiers and sailors lost their lives as a result of the torpedoing, a fact that was more or less glossed over for almost 40 years. Observers at the time called the operation a success, others deemed it a fiasco. Few people, however, would deny its importance to the success of the real D-Day some five weeks later.

Gene Eckstam, one of the survivors, was serving as a physician aboard LST 507, which was hit by the German E-Boats. His ship was carrying a capacity crowd. "There were 125 Navy as Ship's Company, plus our forty-two man medical groups and we took on about three hundred Army men with their trucks and jeeps. . . . The tank deck and the main deck were completely filled with vehicles and army personnel. They slept anywhere and received their 'C' rations on deck, parading around in a large circle about the main deck." For two days life aboard LST 507 was more or less routine while they waited for the other ships to load. Gene remembers, about 2 A.M. there was a terrific BOOM and the crunching of metal as the ship was struck by a torpedo from one of the E-Boats. The ship instantly exploded into an inferno. Slowly, Gene made his way through dark, unlighted passages that were not already in flames searching for men who might need medical attention.

"One of the most difficult decisions I have ever made," Gene confessed, "and one that gave me nightmares for years (and still does), was to close the hatches (doors) leading to the tank deck. I tried to call and go into the tank deck, but it was like looking and trying to walk into a huge roaring blast furnace. The trucks were burning, gasoline was burning, and small arms ammunition was exploding. Worst of all were the agonizing screams for help from the Army men trapped in there. I can still hear them. But knowing that there was absolutely no way anyone could help them and knowing that the smoke inhalation would end their misery soon, I dogged the hatches (closed them)."[8]

Soldiers near the fires started jumping over the sides, some headfirst, losing their inner tube life preservers on the surface of the water as they dove into the watery grave that awaited them. With the order to "Abandon Ship," men who sought safety in the lifeboats found the explosion had bent the lowering bars, and the bars were jammed. Most of the rafts were of little use as a result of rust. Life belts and a plunge into cold, 42 degree water offered about the only avenue to survival.

After swimming some distance away from the burning ship, Gene saw a life raft and joined the fifth or sixth ring of men clinging to the raft. With no means of tying the men together, Gene agonized as one after another of the men lost consciousness in the frigid waters and drifted off. Eventually, Gene "could reach between two guys and I twisted my hand around a rope that circled the raft, so I would not drift away. I was getting very sleepy and was no longer cold, and I knew I would be unconscious soon. The immediate concern of being strafed by the Germans after the sinking, now ceased to be a worry. The 507 was still burning brightly a couple of miles away."

Gene was very hazy about the rest of the night. "We were torpedoed at about 0205, and we were picked up by LST 515 at about 0600. Somewhere in between I was hauled out of the water" (and taken aboard a nearby LST). After a brief nap, Gene awoke and began making rounds of the wounded. Well aware of the regulations prohibiting the carrying of liquor on board ship, Gene issued a call for any booze that might be secreted away on board ship. "The number of whiskey bottles available was astounding. Good thing too, because we found out it worked as well, if not better than a lot of hypos, and it was easier to give in a mass casualty situation."[9]

Eventually, the survivors were checked over and reassigned in time for the official landings on Normandy. Three days after D-Day Harold Cunningham and other Slapton Sands survivors arrived on Utah beach.

During their shakedown missions in southern England in preparation for the Normandy invasion, William Burke considered himself fortunate indeed to have narrowly "missed participating in the Slapton Sands training exercise, which became one of the worst naval disasters of the war." Kenneth Almy's LCI (Landing Craft, Infantry) and its crew also luckily missed the Slapton Sands disaster as a result of a failed anchor that would have prevented the LCI from pushing off after dispensing their contingent of troops and their equipment.[10]

D-DAY ANXIETIES

The immense massing of ships for the Normandy invasion, according to Andrew Hertz (his impressions documented by almost every D-Day participant), "was an amazing sight. There were thousands upon thousands of ships on the water. And overhead hundreds or possibly thousands of planes flying toward the occupied land. It was a startling sight; it was unbelievable. It was overwhelming."[11] Po Weatherford remembered there were so many planes in the skies that one could scarcely see the sun.[12] Others observed that it would almost have been possible to walk from one landing craft to the next across the Channel.

One of Ed Boccafogli's most memorable experiences was General James Gavin's talk to the paratroopers as they prepared for the invasion. "'Men, what you're going to go through in the next few days, you won't want to change . . . but you won't want to go through it very often again. We're going to put our marbles into Normandy Campaign and if the Germans don't play the game our way, then we're going to get the hell out of there.' And even till today, I wonder how in the hell we would have ever gotten out of there," Ed wondered.[13]

On June 6th, tens of thousands of GIs crowded into landing craft that rolled and pitched in the giant, undulating waves as they made their way across the English Channel. Some put on a bravado designed to disguise the panic within. Some tried to mask their anxiety with a feeble wisecrack. Some sat eyes closed absorbed in silent prayer. Some nervously rechecked their weapons in readiness for the ordeal ahead. Some eagle-eyed the fast approaching shoreline looking for enemy machine gunfire on the beach. Some were so weary of the interminable pre-invasion training that they were eager to get the show on the road at last.

Germany's incredible espionage system astounded at the same time that it struck fear into the hearts of GIs. Paul Bouchereau told of headquartering near Nottingham, England, where he and his fellow paratroopers were going to attempt to make a practice jump preparatory to the invasion of Normandy. Tempestuous weather forced the jump to be called back, and in less than an hour they heard the radio propagandist "The Bitch of Berlin" (also called Axis Sally), who taunted allied forces via radio with threats and rumors, announce: "We extend our regrets to the men of the 508th who were to make a practice jump this evening but could not do so because of inclement weather. Come on over, paratroopers, Hitler's panzers are waiting. You will all be killed." Such threats did little to calm the nerves of paratroopers readying to make the real jumps over the coast of Normandy.[14]

There were anxious moments for both the novice and the experienced. On June 4th Ed Boccafogli and his fellow paratroopers had suited up, had taken off, and had flown around for about an hour when abruptly the invasion was called off because of bad weather. "It was really a let down. It just seems to take everything right out of our stomach." The next morning, Ed was disturbed by a young comrade, 16 or 17 years old, "standing there and he was staring into space. I went over to him and I said 'What's the matter, Johnny?' I get emotional just thinking about it. He said, 'I don't think I'll make it.' A very young kid. I said 'Nah, you'll be alright.' I sort of shook him because he was like in a daze. As it turned out, he was one of the first men killed in Normandy."[15]

Skipper of USS *LST 530* Anthony Drexel Duke told about one young seaman 2nd class who came up to his quarters shortly after the ship had been sealed, after leaving the Felixtown ramp and preparing for the trip across the English Channel for the Normandy landings.

He said to me, 'I'm only 15, Captain, and I don't want to go on this trip.' 'Well S,' I replied 'you are going anyway. You apparently fooled the Navy about your age if you are only 15.' 'Well, Captain I am scared, I want to get off, NOW.' 'Well, no way,' I said. 'We are sealed, and that's that.' I told him I felt sorry for him because I think he was scared. Well, so were all of us. But S was a young kid. I said, 'Why don't you report to me from now on at least once every watch. And that way, I'll be able to see how you're doing and you'll be able to see how I am doing.' Well, that's what he did for the next several days. By D-Day plus 2, he'd survived well, he called off that reporting, and for the next year or so, he grew up on the 530 and became a damn solid member of the crew.[16]

In the skies above the Channel, pilots' and paratroopers' hearts beat faster as they contemplated the challenges that lay ahead. As he and his fellow paratroopers waited for the jumpmaster's signal, Paul Bouchereau remembered, "We welcomed the darkness of the plane afraid the fear would show on our faces. Each of us wished to keep our emotions to ourselves."[17]

Another paratrooper, Edward Boccafogli, recalled that he took a more resigned attitude to the Normandy jump. "I was not actually scared. I was more nervous and tense. I figured, well, if it was going to be I wouldn't come back, that's the way it will be. I will just have to accept it." Still there was the haunting fear that Normandy might be another "Dieppe or another Dunkirk disaster."[18]

As a member of the 502nd Parachute Infantry of the 101st Airborne Division, Legrand K. Johnson was in fear of not even making it on takeoff from Greenum Common for the invasion of Normandy. "We were so grossly overloaded, that I didn't think we were going to make it, and I think the pilot didn't think we were going to make it either, 'cause I was standing up in the cockpit behind him, and boy, he was praying and cussing and pleading, and—it got up OK."[19]

As they were making their way to the Normandy beaches, Bill Lodge remembers that although the men were not necessarily happy "I think they were glad to be doing something because they'd been hanging on for so long." He continued, "We were thinking 'We're glad that we could go in on this journey.'"[20] Some veterans, such as George Loomis, thought that for the men on his ship, having already made dangerous invasions in North Africa, Sicily, and Anzio, the Normandy invasion would be almost routine.[21]

A member of the third wave on Omaha Beach on D-Day, Richard Crum, of Lodi, Ohio, figured he'd survived being on the first wave in the invasion of Sicily, so surely he'd make it on Normandy. The tendency was to believe that becoming a casualty was not going to happen to you. When told that two out of three would not make it, most men looked at the man to the right and the man to the left and thought: "I sure feel sorry for you two guys." Although there were not as many casualties as on the first assaults, the long lines of wounded at the water's edge were not exactly reassuring. Richard Crum noted that "Of the 219 members of Company C who landed on Omaha Beach it is believed that only between fourteen and eighteen are still living."[22]

En route to the D-Day landings, Victor Fast found himself on board ship with "some British Commanders who had landed at Dieppe, Dunkirk and Africa." Victor Fast noted: "They had seen some action we had not. We lay around on board cleaning our weapons and playing pinochle. The commanders joined in but were sweating blood, literally. None of us made any remarks about their sweating—inside, we knew (I think) what was going through their minds."[23]

A survivor of the first assault wave on Omaha Beach on D-Day, Louie Ryder, remembered jumping off his LST into 14 feet of water and swimming and sloshing to the beachhead with his 50-pound machine gun above his head and wondering if he'd ever make it. Seeing a score of men wiped out by a bomb as they started down the gangplank did little to calm his nerves. Once on the beach it was a gruesome scramble over dead bodies to the edge of the parapet. At one point he was talking with a friend, there was a thunderous noise and suddenly he found himself standing alone—there was no one else there. In the course of making his way through France and Belgium, he again lucked out by taking a bullet a couple of times—no serious harm done but "just enough to scare you that much more. . . . If you weren't scared," Louie admitted, "you just weren't there."[24]

Vast numbers of D-Day troops discovered another enemy almost as formidable as their German adversaries. For thousands of men the seasickness that plagued them from the time they left England to their arrival on Omaha Beach left them weak and enervated as they tumbled off the landingcraft and into the waist high (or higher) water. Struggling with their heavy equipment coupled with the tormenting cramps of seasickness made reaching the beaches a Herculean task. Infantryman John Kirkley had been one of those seasick for the entire two-hour LST trip to their Omaha Beach landing. Upon finally reaching solid ground "I fell on my back exhausted and still seasick. There was a lot of artillery fire. For a few moments I was hoping a shell would land in the middle of my stomach and end my misery."[25]

As they were crossing the English Channel, John Robert Lewis, Jr. remembered all the men gathering on the deck of the *Bayfield* to sing "The Battle Hymn of the Republic" and "Onward Christian Soldiers." "This was a very sobering time to sing the words 'as God died to make men holy, let us die to make men free.'"[26]

THE LANDINGS

During the Normandy landing, Harley Reynolds, from his unenviable position aboard one of the thousands of landing crafts that peppered the waters, recalled the confusion of the assault waves. "I was looking over the side often during these last minutes. We were moving slow because of other craft and obstacles the coxswain had to avoid. I saw direct hits on craft still far away from land. I doubt those on board not wounded made it to shore. I saw craft sideways, being upturned, dumping troops into the water. I saw craft heavily damaged by shell fire being tossed around by the waves—I saw craft empty of troops and partly filled with water as tho abandoned, awash in the surf. Men were among them struggling for the pitiful protection they gave."[27]

Ray E. Aeibischer did not deny having "a queasy feeling in the pit of my stomach" and being quite scared as he was about to parachute out of the plane on D-Day in Normandy. "And by the looks on the faces of my buddies, I'm sure they felt the same way." Fortunately, Ray landed safely in a churchyard in Ste.-Mere-Eglise. Machine gunfire down the street, a parachutist hanging lifeless in a treetop, and a dead comrade lying in the street provided a grim welcome to the town. Noiselessly, he crept up beside a soldier silhouetted in the moonlight, a figure he hoped would be a friendly American. His cricket, the kid's toy that was given to the men to use as identification, was somehow mashed, and Ray quickly whispered the password. To the relief of both parties, the figure responded with the reply, and as daylight appeared they joined other GIs, following the lead of the officer in charge. As Ray expressed it, "In reality, it was mass confusion. Not many of us had landed where we were supposed to." Happily the Germans also seemed to be confused and muddled, and there was very little gunfire. "So D Day for me ended on a rather quiet note," Ray Aeibischer recalled. The day seemed almost peaceful for "During the next six weeks in Normandy, there was plenty of action, with considerable loss of lives."[28]

Many years after that fateful day, Wallace Gibbs, Jr., of Fayetteville, North Carolina, noted that having gone through endless practices on the English beaches, as they landed on the Omaha beach "the feeling of myself and my men was pretty much the same, as we had experienced in our maneuvers, with no real apprehension, just a desire to get ashore and get off the boat." As enemy gunfire began plowing up the beach all around them, gut-wrenching fear quickly replaced calmness and more than one man divested himself of his breakfast. Luckily all of Wallace Gibbs' men made it through the day safely; however they counted their blessings the next morning as they surveyed the beach strewn with dead bodies that "were actually being piled up like cordwood. This continued for the rest of the day." Proud of having taken out an important enemy emplacement earlier in the day, Gibbs and his men dug out foxholes. "The day had ended with the coming of dawn and getting into the foxhole. I, like many others, spent a great deal of time before going to sleep praying both for salvation from the night and gratitude for having lived through the day."[29]

As things calmed down for a moment, there came a rush of emotion as men began to comprehend the reality of their experience and their near brush with death. Years later, Felix P. Branham recalled that several hours into the Normandy landing, during a brief respite, as he was furiously engaged in digging his foxhole, he would dig for a while and then "sit and watch with my rifle across my lap and I'd begin crying. I cried like a baby." When the solicitous buddy next to him stopped his digging to inquire about his distress, Felix confessed: "Look, I've been thinking about how close to death [I came], and the things that I've seen today. I don't know how we made it through all this." Putting down his shovel for the moment, his friend admitted "'Felix, I know exactly how you feel.' Then he would do the same thing."[30]

THE BLOODSOAKED BEACHES

Once on shore GIs discovered the bete noir of soldiers everywhere—mines that could send a soldier to eternity or merely blow off a foot or a leg. As Dick Conley of Scranton, Pennsylvania, and his buddies made their way up to high ground from the Normandy beaches, they observed one poor GI who had stepped on a shu mine and was "lying just off the trail with the front half of one foot gone. But he was smiling. He knew he'd be going home." As he reached the high ground above the beaches, Dick Conley found himself "shivering, shaking uncontrollably, and I was ashamed of it, until I noticed that all of the combat veterans of North Africa and Sicily were shaking just as much as I was. And I immediately felt better, to see the evidence that we all shared the same fear."[31]

The early days of the Normandy invasion brought many young servicemen face to face with death for the first time in their young lives. Andrew Hertz, of Boston and Bayonne, New Jersey, was shocked as he waded through the water to the beaches and saw dead bodies floating in the water around him. "This was a rather unpleasant experience. I had never seen a dead person before, and yet these were my fellow GIs who had been shot during the initial landing the day before." On the beach, Hertz recalled years later, "There was also the very, very unusual scary movement of the graves registration people collecting bodies on the beach. They moved right through the fire, walked right through any of the action that was taking place."[32]

Aboard his LST, during the Normandy landing, William Burke and his men saw their first corpse, a 20-year-old Iowan who had drowned in an attempt to reach the beaches. "Then," William Burke reported, "I looked at one of our crewmates standing nearby—also a 20-year-old Iowan—and realized how deadly serious war can be."[33]

Bill Pace was sickened by the sight of the beaches at Omaha with the vast numbers of half-sunk ships pulsating in the waves, landing craft disabled and blown apart, and dead bodies everywhere.[34] Some two weeks after D-Day Frank Keeley's Quartermaster's Corps made the rigorous Channel crossing from their base near Swinden, England and continued following the Allied troops into the interior of France. Fortunately, as they landed there was no enemy gunfire; however, there were still the chilling remains of the dead bodies that bulldozers had indiscriminately plowed under as they hurriedly attempted to clear the beaches for new arrivals.[35]

Not only were there appalling scenes of the deaths of one's buddies but also the dreadful slaughter of the enemy. During the fighting at St. Lo, Harold Cunningham was witness to the scene of the suicide of a German paratrooper who apparently was sleeping in a nearby field. As the paratrooper staggered awake and found himself surrounded, he instantly whipped out his gun, put it to his head, and pulled the trigger.[36]

Kenneth T. Delaney was so seasick from the three- to six-foot waves that rocked his troop ship and the LCI that carried him to Omaha beach on D-Day that he "just wanted to get onto that beach!!!!!" Just as he was getting off the LCI, Ken felt a sting in his foot, a wound that continued to be increasingly painful as the day progressed. As he and other wounded buddies took refuge in front of a wall, he watched as "WAVE AFTER WAVE" of men hit the beaches, "We watched them being shot and killed right in the water! They were floating all around us!! It was really a bad scene!" In the meantime Ken and his fellow GIs did what they could to bandage each other up, until fresh medics arrived to administer first aid. Most of the medics on the first boatloads to land, Ken remembered, were "shot; most were killed."[37]

Carrying two British doctors, Anthony Drexel Duke's ship was outfitted as a hospital ship for their return to England from the Normandy beaches. The night of June 6th, Duke remembered, "was a wild night." Suddenly a number of LCVPs (Landing Craft, Vehicle, Personnel) appeared alongside Duke's LST and began unloading wounded soldiers that the medics had picked up along the beach. In short order the wardroom was converted into an operating room where the two doctors and their assistants "worked all night saving some lives and losing others." Duke recalled, "Every once in a while I would come down from the bridge just to see what was going on and I remember splattering along the starboard boat deck which was filled now with men on stretchers waiting to go and be operated on, and I remember looking down and seeing myself standing in about a solid inch of blood that was running along that deck." The sickening sights of burns and wounds and amputations horrified Duke and his crew. During the next few months following the invasion, Duke and his crew made 42 trips across the Channel transporting troops and trucks to France and returning to England (sometimes carrying dying and wounded men) for another boatload and another crossing.[38]

Confusion often reigned on June 6th, and as a result there were giant snarls in communications—some with disastrous consequences. Carl Evans told of sighting a church steeple located part way up the high bluff above the Omaha beach. Germans clearly were operating out of the church steeple and wracking havoc on the LSTs unloading GIs beneath them.

Realizing the desperate need to take out that church, the Admiral of his ship requested permission to fire on that particular church, despite orders not to fire on churches and hospitals. The permission was 24 hours in coming; meantime the Germans in the steeple were taking a tremendous toll on the beaches. Finally, permission granted, two shots then finished off the church. Once the church and the steeple were destroyed, "The firing on our troops being landed at that spot stopped instantly."[39]

What John MacPhee's company commander had promised would be "like going into Coney Island," turned into a bloodbath. Years later, John MacPhee said that as he waded ashore that day, "I didn't care if Adolph Hitler was waiting for me. I was scared to death. I wanted to survive." Minutes later, three bullets found their mark, one in his lower back and two in his left leg. He figured it was all over for him. "I lost all my fear and knew I was about to die, made peace with my maker and was just waiting." Apparently some of the medics thought he was dead, and passed him by, but two of his buddies found him and risked life and limb to drag him out of harm's way. Later, long weeks of hospital care would eventually bring back John MacPhee to full speed, but nothing, absolutely nothing would ever erase the memories of that fateful day.[40]

Amid the slaughter on the D-Day invasion, Robert Hall, a Seabee with the 81st Construction Battalion serving on Utah beach, recalled a touching story that certainly brought a ray of sunshine into that gruesome day. Bob told of a frantic French farmer who approached them "seeking help for his very pregnant wife. As our casualties were very light, the battalion doctor went with him to his farmhouse, some 500 yards inland." Not long afterward the doctor returned proudly announcing that he had delivered the farmer's wife of a beautiful baby girl. A new life, a new hope amid the finality of life that carpeted the beaches. Hearts soared, prayers floated Heavenward amid the enemy gunfire that ravaged the beachhead. Deeply grateful for the doctor's help, the appreciative parents decided on the most appropriate name they could think of for their daughter—Sea Bee Marie.[41]

D-DAY PLUS

On D-Day plus 20, Paul L. Curry and his buddies waded ashore to the beaches of Normandy through water up to their armpits. After a miserable night in soaking wet clothes, Paul and his comrades woke up that morning and, in the eerie dawn, looked over a steep hill to the sobering sight of a sea of white crosses. For several weeks thereafter there were no complaints about army food or exhausting marches.[42]

As the fighting progressed beyond the beaches and into the French farmland, GIs discovered the hedgerows separating fields and farms to be incredibly frustrating obstacles. How had it come to pass that "in all the training we had undergone for over a year, we had never known about the *bocage,* the Normandy hedgerows," Ralph Eastridge wondered. The hedgerows that had existed since Julius Caesar's time consisted of trees and bushes that extended to a height of some six feet and were growing out of a mass of roots and underbrush. They provided a perfect fortress for the Germans to hide behind, and by shooting through the hedges the Germans held a tremendous advantage as the Allies advanced into the open field between the rows.[43]

Both sides made concerted attempts to gain the advantage through the use of propaganda and espionage. Ralph Eastridge told of the leaflets with which the Germans showered their regiment in the Bois De Bretel. "'ATTENTION! DANGER! WARNING! The Third Armored Division, ordered by stupid Allied High Command to break the iron ring enclosing your beachead, has been destroyed. Weary soldiers of the 115th Infantry! Your comrades lie dead in the foolish struggle against the might of the Werhmacht! The Imperial English dream of conquering Europe is doomed.' The leaflets went on about the German might and futility of fighting further."[44]

Instead of engendering fear in the Allied troops, the leaflets, Ralph pointed out, had the very opposite effect. "The result was an immense boost in morale. Seeing their regiment named had an exhilarating effect. If there is one thing that infantry men love, it is publicity. This was better than a story in Stars and Stripes!" Eastridge recalled. And a boost in morale was just what the 115th needed. Because of the tremendous losses, rifle companies ended up with more replacements than original members. "In fact the loss of so many officers and experienced non-coms resulted in the replacement soldiers having a lack of confidence in their leaders." New replacements at first "could not understand why we dug holes so deep. They soon learned," Ralph smiled.

As the trauma of the horrific first few days began to subside and the men had an opportunity to reflect on their experiences and to speculate on their questionable future, some men decided they had had enough of brutality and bloodshed. Some of the less committed GIs sought a way out: a nice hospital stay out of harm's way or an opportunity to sit out the rest of the war at home. While Cherbourg was being taken, Ralph Eastridge and his men experienced little action. "Soldiers are better moving than sitting around thinking," Ralph observed. "We began to have self-inflicted wounds, men shooting themselves, usually in the foot." During the temporary lull in fighting, Ralph remembered "We could hear the Germans singing at night across the field in front of us." With a touch of sarcasm, Ralph added: "But we knew the danger was small because we had majors and colonels coming around to inspect. When things were hot, we saw only lieutenants and a few captains."[45]

Despite the vast numbers of casualties incurred on the invasion, there were those who lived to tell about their great good fortune in making it through alive. "God must have been watching me," Ed Boccafogli, a New

York paratrooper, decided. The night before taking a bullet in the left shoulder from German gunfire, he had "taken the grenade off the left shoulder and put it onto the right, fortunately, because it would have blown—my head and body and everything would have been blown to pieces."[46]

Another D-Day paratrooper, Paul Bouchereau, surely had luck or a guardian angel at his side, for after landing, Paul was taken prisoner, shot in the leg, and marched for miles with blood squishing in his boot, until at last he fell to the ground unable to move. "A Kraut came over and rolled me over on my back. He cocked his rifle and put the business end to my head. I probably set a speed record for saying the rosary, but instead of pulling the trigger, the German laughed, then bent over me and offered me an American cigarette. I suppose I should have been grateful that my life had been spared, but instead I was furious at the physical and mental torture to which I had been subjected. My mind and head were filled with hate. I took the cigarette and enjoyed each inhalation while waiting to be transported to a German hospital. I dreamed of the day when I would repay them in full measure for my suffering."[47]

Personal confrontations with the enemy became uncomfortably frequent as the fighting continued. Dame fortune or divine intervention was known to smile on two cautious enemies one day when one GI peeking over the hedgerow realized he was looking directly into the eyes of a German soldier also bent on checking out the situation. Fortunately, both men quickly ducked in time to save themselves.[48]

Defying all the odds, Harold Cunningham was a lucky survivor of both enemy and friendly fire. Not only did he make it through the Slapton Sands disaster and the early days of the Normandy invasion, but he later survived being accidentally strafed by Allied troops. Fortunately, Harold's luck still held when an Allied plane dropped two bombs dead center of the unit's "ring of colors" (red and orange six-by-two-foot flags indicating an Allied position and designed to prevent erroneous shelling of the area).[49]

Making their way in light armored tanks through France several weeks after the Normandy invasion as part of the 2nd Army Cavalry Corps of the 3rd U.S. Army, the cavalry's primary assignment consisted of scouting the enemy entrenchments and reporting back to headquarters. This involved rain, mud, and in Alsace Loraine, heavy German resistance. "Don't tell me about sunny France," Ted Thomas warned. Furthermore, "Don't tell me about the charming vineyards of France," Ted insisted.[50]

Six months after D-Day, Reid Gilland of Charlotte, North Carolina (a member of a medical supply unit) found himself readying to board a 2,200 man ship to cross the English Channel on December 28, 1944, to help to provide medical services for the men fighting the Battle of the Bulge. As the men dumped their duffel bags alongside the dock, the collection of all-look-alike bags took on mountainous proportions. As the captain yelled to grab any bag and board the ship, Reid grabbed a bag too heavy for him to lift. Tumbling down the steep steps with his monstrous bag and prodded by the Captain's repeated orders to move it and stop holding up the line, Reid hurriedly shoved the bag onto a nearby bunk, made himself comfortable on top of it, and went to sleep. Later, when he discovered that the assigned quarters for the 16th Medical Depot Company in the lower decks were filled to capacity, Reid retreated to his original hideout and went back to sleep. Suddenly a crash sent the ceiling, walls, and bunks crumbling around him as torpedoes from German E-boats made a direct hit on the ship. How he emerged from the sinking ship, Reid never knew, but somehow he found himself on a lifeboat where he was being given morphine. It took hospital stays of two and a half years before Reid was well enough to return to normal life. As he looked back, Reid wondered that if he had not grabbed that heavy duffel bag, fallen down the stairs, and taken the first available bunk, he might well have been on the lower level and gone down with the ship. As Reid pondered, "Who knows?"[51]

There were those who admired their superior officers and those who hated their guts. After weeks of 24 hours a day work consisting of loading tanks on the shores of the Normandy beaches, picking up casualties, taking them to the hospital ships, picking up another load of tanks, and repeating the service, Captain Houston "Rip" Bounds of Stone County Mississippi was finally deployed to Liverpool and then to the United States where orders awaited him "to report to the commanding officer of the amphibious forces of the South Pacific." During their Normandy stint, Rip, in order to get the work done, had been a rigorous task master. Yet, despite his dictatorial mien, he had gained the respect and admiration of his men. As their crew split up following their Normandy service, Rip later proudly recalled, "Sweeney, my quartermaster, paid me one of the greatest compliments that I ever have been paid. Before we departed and separated, he walked up, and put his arm around my shoulder, and said, 'Skipper, you're the meanest son of a gun I've ever met in my life, but it was a privilege to serve under you and I love you,' He was a big Swede."[52]

Amazing as it might seem, at times the French citizens appeared oblivious to what was going on around them. Six days after the first waves of troops landed on the Normandy beaches, as B. Ralph Eastridge (platoon leader of an antitank company) and his men took over positions near St. Marguerite-sur Elle, he observed their forward observer directing fire from his strategic position in the church bell tower. Beneath him, the medics were manning an aid station. "And the strangest sight, one I remember, was the French farmers going in the church to mass, carefully stepping around the litters."[53]

"I have gone through lots of tragedies since D-Day," Felix Branham admitted, "but to me, D-Day will live with me till the day I die, and I'll take it to heaven with me. It was the longest, most miserable, horrible day that I or anyone else ever went through. But I am speaking strictly for myself. I would not take a million dollars for my experiences, but I surely wouldn't want to go through that again for a million dollars." (An oft repeated phrase!)[54]

For thousands of veterans there has been a constant mental revisiting of D-Day. "There is not a day that goes over my head that D-Day does not cross my mind," Felix Branham confessed. "I think of some of the things that I had done that day or some of the things that I did and shouldn't have done."[55] Years later, Dick Conley admitted, "reliving this day, the 6th of June, 1944, in such detail, even after nearly 46 years, the foul taste of fear returns very strongly."[56]

The Normandy beaches still bear grim testimony to the monstrous toll of war. Each year thousands of tourists, veterans, and relatives visit the sea of white crosses marking the ultimate sacrifices made on those memorable days in June in 1944. Tourists stand mute, awed by the magnitude of the scene; veterans mumble messages to their buddies of long ago; tears well up in eyes and spill down cheeks. And if you were lucky on your particular day, you might have looked down to see a fresh bouquet of flowers and a heartfelt note tenderly inscribed—"Daddy, we miss you."

CHAPTER 4

Europe

THE SICILIAN CAMPAIGN

Following the Allied victory in North Africa, the invasion of Sicily on July 9th and 10th, 1943, became the next step for the Allied forces. Once again the casualties escalated as waves of men assaulted the beaches and inched their way northward.

As Adolph Richard Elasky, of Minneapolis, Minnesota, and members of his platoon were waiting topside of an LST readying to disembark for an amphibious landing on Sicily, the pilot of a Stuka dive-bomber scored a direct hit on the ship. The bomb instantly killed all the men below deck, including the captain, and blew the rest of the men into the water—weapons, field gear, and helmets included. Luckily, Dick Elasky and several of his buddies were picked up by naval vessels; however, other men were not so fortunate. On that invasion attempt, over 50 percent of Dick's 693rd Airborne Machine Gun Battery were casualties.

Dick and other survivors were regrouped into the 451st Automatic Weapon Battalion and made their way to Messina, Sicily. (It was near Messina, one may recall, that the widely publicized "slapping incident" took place, when General Patton slapped a wounded soldier across the cheeks for what he deemed cowardice—using his injuries as an excuse for not returning to the scene of battle more promptly.) From Sicily it was on to Naples, Rome, then Marseille, and then to help rescue the American forces during the Battle of the Bulge. Finally, Dick explained, the Germans "knew their war was over and so began surrendering in droves. We couldn't feed them, so we disarmed them and just pointed them toward their POW camps in the rear and they marched off. I know they felt relieved because their war was over."[1]

A TRUE BONDING OF BROTHERS

Don Strand remembered threading his way with his buddies through the land mines that plagued Allied troop movements in Sicily. "Land mines were planted everywhere. We had to walk in the footsteps of the person in front of us. Every so often we would hear and see a big explosion up ahead and knew that the lead man got it. I hoped and prayed it would not be my turn next. We lost many men to land mines this way."

It should be remembered that not all battlefield surgeries were the result of wounds. It was during the Sicilian campaign that Don Strand began suffering excruciating abdominal pains that brought him to the point where he refused to dig a foxhole for himself, mumbling that he didn't care whether he lived or died. A doctor was called, the crew set up a cot under a tree, and out-of-doors, under greatly unsanitary conditions the physician removed an inflamed appendix that would soon have burst.

All the while he was recovering (he had been sent back to Tunisia), Don agonized over the fate of his buddies in his unit and his inability to be serving with them. Finally, although scarcely recovered, he took it into his own hands to do something about it. By hopping a train, catching a boat for Salerno, hitchhiking with an army truck driver, and taking a chance, he began walking to where he hoped his unit would be. His appearance as he entered the command post tent sent his old Captain into a state of shock. The Captain could scarcely believe his eyes and in very unmilitary fashion hugged Don in his enthusiasm at seeing him once again. The bonding with the members of one's unit was truly a bonding of brothers.[2]

During the fighting to take Rome in late May and early June of 1944, C. Andrew Ryan was captured and held prisoner in a POW camp in Poland until November when he succeeded in escaping amid the confusion of an attack on the camp. Through a fortunate series of events, Andy finally made it across the country and back to what was left of his company in Italy. Asked if he wanted to be sent home, he refused the opportunity preferring to stay with his comrades.[3]

As with Don Strand and thousands of other deeply devoted servicemen, esprit de corps proved a prime mover in war. Scores of other GIs testified that their great fear during the war was the constant threat of the possibility of letting down their buddies, of performing in a way that might diminish them in the eyes of their comrades.

Once reunited with his unit, Don Strand and his comrades found that the fighting from the landing in Anzio to Rome constituted some of the toughest combat in Italy. Mines, bombs, gunfire, and freezing temperatures plagued the troops. It was near the terrible fighting in Cisterna that Don Strand took a bullet to his chest that spun him around and left him dazed, wondering whether he was still alive or not. There seemed to be no blood and as he felt in his chest pocket, he pulled out his New Testament. To his amazement the New Testament had taken the brunt of the bullet. He was alive and well—and deliriously happy.[4]

The capture of Rome on June 4th received sparse media coverage in comparison with the news of the Normandy Invasion on June 6th. Don Strand and the members of his unit in Italy complained: "We heard about the 'Longest Day' that described D-Day. Well, we had many long days ourselves, moving up the Italian peninsula against fierce German resistance. We lost thousands of men along the way. We often felt there was no hope left, so all we had to go on was our faith in God and in the fighting qualities on the men of either side of us. We kept our helmets down, as the saying went."[5]

THE APENNINES

It was difficult to find experienced skiers in the ranks of the Army, and sometimes those most qualified somehow slipped between the cracks and were assigned to other branches of the service. Often the Army simply had to make do with what they had. Sometimes the military, Fred Wickert pointed out, had difficulties assigning people with very special qualifications into the niche most appropriate to their talents. For example, Fred, a lieutenant, working as Classification and Assignment officer at a replacement center at Fort Heustis, Virginia, was assigned to help put together a group of men with ski experience for ski troop training in Colorado. Despite contacts with high officials in Washington, he was never able to secure the assignment to the ski troops of one particular soldier experienced and skilled in fighting on skis as a result of his experiences in the Finnish and Russian fighting. Instead the soldier was relegated to routine army duties.[6]

Paul Niland, a PFC from Wisconsin, had been training at Camp Swift, Texas, with the 85th Mountain Regiment who were preparing to go overseas, but as a late arrival he had missed almost all of the ski training. His recreational skiing in his youth constituted almost exclusively his pre-army experience with skiing. As it turned out, instead of being sent to the northern European countries, the 85th Mountain Regiment was sent to Italy.

It was with the utmost secrecy that the 85th Mountain Regiment troops were transported from Texas to Italy. There was no visible light on the train as the men made their way to their embarkation point at Newport News, Virginia. All of the window shades throughout the cars were drawn. Their military insignia had been removed, and their trip across the Atlantic aboard the recently converted *U.S. United States* was shrouded in darkness. Again, there were no lights, and anyone wanting a cigarette at night had to light up below deck. Their debarkation in Naples and the jolting truck ride to their headquarters in the Apennines were also carefully calculated to obscure their arrival.

It was a shocker to Paul Niland and his regiment to find that the Germans were well aware of their whereabouts and, in fact, were waiting for them at their headquarters. Ominous notices nailed to trees threatened: "Welcome members of the 85th and 87th Mountain Regiments. This is no Cook's tour of Italy. You have seen Naples, now die!"

German intelligence had been hard at work successfully tracking their movements. Moreover, by citing only the 85th and 87th Regiments, the Germans were clearly aware that the 86th Regiment was not with them, but was serving elsewhere. So much for the meticulous secrecy and deception of that movement!

It was expected that as skiers the men of the 85th were good mountain climbers, and Paul's unit was summarily ordered to capture Mt. Belvedere, which was a big holdup in the Italian campaign. The mission was a success; however, the casualties were enormous, and unfortunately, there were no trained replacements to fill the losses. (Paul Niland smiled as he remembered that kids were brought in as replacements from Mississippi and Arkansas, kids who before the war had never even seen snow, much less skis.)

Following the capture of Belvedere, Paul's unit advanced and became the first American troops to cross the Po River after which they headed toward the Brenner Pass and arrived at Garda, where Mussolini was said to be ensconced. All was excitement as a patrol was sent over to try to capture Mussolini. Unfortunately, they were 12 hours too late. Mussolini had already been executed by partisans and, with his mistress, Clara Petacci, was hanging upside down by his toes in the marketplace of Milan.

On September 8, 1943, Italy surrendered to the Allies. Following the peace treaty, Paul and his unit were taken offline and sent back to Naples. Once again, on the return home to the States, there were cramped quarters and seasickness, but as the ship sailed into New York, wild cheering and jubilation broke out as the tugs came out to meet them shouting that the Germans had surrendered. The war was over in Europe. Jubilation was tampered, however, with the fear that everyone would then be sent to Japan.[7]

AN AWAKENING

Wounded by shrapnel from a mortar shell that hit less than four feet from his foxhole while he was fighting in Italy, Joe Spinosa was hospitalized for a couple of weeks, and despite his hope of picking up his mail and being sent home, he was returned, his arm still bandaged, to front line duty in the Apennines, near Bologne. There, a second wound sent him to a hospital in Florence and a couple of days later to a hospital in Naples. As a native southerner, Joe was somewhat taken aback as he looked around and found African Americans bedded in his ward. As he surveyed the scene, he realized that several of the African Americans were wounded more severely than he. Why should they not be given the same care, he reasoned, that he was being given? From then on racial prejudice was a thing of the past for Joe Spinosa.

It was a further learning experience for Joe Spinosa to see the herds of four- or five-year-old Italian children who came each day carrying a bucket in each hand, one for the scrapings left on their plates by the GIs, the other bucket to receive any leftover coffee from servicemen's coffee cups. These leftovers they eagerly carried home to their starving families. And yet, the servicemen in the chow line complained about their food![8]

BEYOND NORMANDY

There was little time for the Allies to gloat over the successful invasion of Normandy on June 6, 1944, and for the next 11 months the Allies were engaged in an unrelenting struggle to force Germany's unconditional surrender on May 7, 1945. There was horrendous fighting in an effort to take over tiny villages as well as to beat off the Germans in assaults at Caen, St. Lo, and Brussels, in the Netherlands; at the Battle of the Bulge; and on the Rhine River bridges. Each GI put his life on the line. Each GI had a story to tell. The following remembrances serve to sketch a brief picture of harrowing days of combat.

John R. Walker, of Crofton, Maryland, was reluctant to talk about his World War II army life until his son finally persuaded him to write up his experiences for the family. As a member of a front line infantry rifle company, John spent 18 months overseas in France, Germany, and Austria. Over 4 months of that time "were spent in vicious ground combat against a determined enemy, the Germans." John explained:

I served as the gunner and later sergeant squad leader of a 60-millimeter mortar squad. Our job was to support our three company rifle platoons with mortar fire in their efforts to defend our front line or to attack and overcome the German positions. We were in the front lines for a total of over 100 days. Our division, the 42nd Rainbow Division, suffered over 3000 men killed or wounded in that time. Some men I knew had the misfortune to become casualties within minutes or hours of coming under enemy fire. Others like myself had the good fortune (or misfortune, depending on how you look at it) of surviving the entire combat experience without a scratch.

If you survived without a scratch, it meant you experienced endless minutes, hours, days, and weeks of danger, fear, cold, snow, wet, hunger, misery, exhaustion, and innumerable close calls when your life was mysteriously and miraculously spared while a nearby buddy lost his. Many a time you wished and prayed for a "million dollar wound," one that wouldn't leave you dead, broken and limbless, but would release you from the numbing, endless hell of combat.

Nights were long and dismal (Winter 1944). My squad leader, Earl Owen and I shared a pup tent, two shelter halves buttoned together. We each had four blankets in our pack. We put four blankets on top of a raincoat under us and then the other four blankets over us. We also slept in all our clothes. We still froze. After a couple of chilly nights of this (at Comand Post 2 near Marseille) we brought another member of our squad, Earl Blundell, into our tent so we'd have an extra body and his four blankets too. It made the small pup tent awfully crowded but the extra body and extra blankets helped ward off the penetrating cold. In any case it made life a little more tolerable.[9]

A 24-hour pass from the harrowing life on the front lines in France was a taste of paradise for Walker and two of his buddies. In Nice, France, at the Red Cross Service Center, "It was heavenly for us three infantrymen to browse in the Red Cross library, lounge in the stuffed chairs and gorge ourselves on the coffee and doughnuts. A cup of coffee and 4 doughnuts cost 5 francs. I went through the line five times." The doughnut orgy no doubt had little effect on the hunger pangs that probably demanded attention about dinnertime. After a so-so meal in a restaurant the men headed back to their base. "We thoroughly enjoyed our brief vacation from the war, but the 45 caliber pistols we carried on our right hips reminded us of more serious business to come."[10]

It was a sobering experience for Wayne Lesher, B-17 Navigator, and his crew who had just landed at their Amendola, Italy, Twentieth Bomb Squadron, Second Bomb Group headquarters. Instead of a warm, hearty welcome, the men were mystified by their somewhat cool reception. They noticed a few of the ground crewmen talking to each other in muted voices, some were in tears. A haunting stillness pervaded the area. Minutes later they learned that word had just arrived that Mission 263, an entire squadron, had been wiped out by the Luftwaffe—7 planes had been downed, 70 airmen had lost their lives. Wayne and his crew were quickly caught up in the grief and fell silent as they were led to the recently abandoned tents and urged to go to the mess hall for dinner. Somehow, no one was very hungry that evening. It was particularly unnerving to realize that had not one of their crew members suffered a minor accident that held up their plane at Gander, they would have flown that mission and would have very likely been one of the 70 casualties. The next day, white sheets were spread out in front of each of the tents where the personal effects of the recent residents were bundled up to be sent to their respective families. What an introduction to the work that lay ahead for Wayne and his crew![11]

In Poupee Ville, France, Jon Young was assigned to accompany a *Life Magazine* correspondent on a tour of the town and its surroundings for a story for the magazine. The army had instructed all servicemen to avoid at all costs picking up any ammunition they saw on the ground, or touching a crooked picture in the interior of a house, or even tossing aside a piece of trash—all might be mined. As they jeeped through the countryside, ahead was a gruesome scene as a young army private innocently picked up a piece of wood that exploded in his face. With that, the *Life* correspondent fainted. As Jon sought to attend the dying man and at the same time revive the newsman, he cautioned the correspondent, "You better get used to this. You're going to see some pretty bad things."[12]

FIRST COMBAT

His first combat was indeed memorable for Lloyd Wilson as a PFC in northeastern France in October of 1944. His science major in college and his training at the Medical Replacement Training Center in Texas had led him to the front lines as a front line medic with a 45th Division rifle company as the army made their way across France and Germany.

There had been distant gunfire for several days as Lloyd and his unit were approaching a small village in northern France. Unexpectedly, a medic appeared with orders for Lloyd to be reassigned to the Second Platoon that was poised to attack the village. As the firing intensified, Lloyd and a newly met sergeant began struggling to make their way down a hill and through the unrelenting hedgerows. Suddenly, a groan pierced the noise of the firing, and Lloyd turned to find his friend tangled in the underbrush with a broken leg. Quickly, he fell to his knees to bandage his comrade as gunfire arched overhead.

Unfortunately, there was nothing more he could do but bandage his friend and tag him and leave him for the litter bearers. It probably took all of 15 minutes, but when Lloyd looked up from his patient, he found himself all alone with a frightening barrage of fire from above. Lloyd struggled to his feet, only to find himself really alone—completely alone. The Second Platoon had disappeared. Cautiously, Lloyd crept to the edge of the village, sure that as a lone soldier he was a perfect target for a German sniper. The streets were empty; there was no one anywhere to be seen. For a few minutes it appeared that Lloyd was going to be fighting the next hours of the war all by himself. Where had everyone gone? If he survived, was he to be a lone attacker of a German occupied town? Where was any protection? What way to turn?

Medics, Lloyd reasoned, were supposed to aid the wounded, not try to single-handedly and unarmed capture a town. Slowly he sidled into an open doorway. The lone occupant told him the Second Platoon was holed up in a house a short distance away. For a few hours there was the comfort of companionship and a bed to sleep on, albeit straw that a German had slept in the night before. Safety! In the morning it was discovered that the Germans had slipped away in the night. They were good at retreating in those days, he recalled.

In the midst of the slaughter that pervaded the battlefields, medics often experienced the "worst of times" and now and then the "best of times" in aiding in the survival of a comrade. During the Battle of Engwiller early in December of 1944, Lloyd Wilson found himself in the midst of crossfire emanating from the woods and either side of the road. Machine gun fire from the enemy drew return fire from the Allies. Suddenly, there was a piteous cry "medic," and Lloyd ran to the aid of a moaning, half-conscious soldier, a bullet having gone all the way through his chest. Instantly, Lloyd had his medic bag open, and fearing every moment would be the young man's last, he quickly administered aid and comfort to the desperate man. Knowing that the young soldier had but a slim chance of survival, Lloyd did his best for the young soldier, tagged him for the litter bearers, and hurried on to aid other wounded men. Later, Lloyd learned that his help had not been in vain, and that thanks to Lloyd's ministering the young GI fortunately had survived.[13]

BATTLE OF THE BULGE

After landing on Omaha Beach on August 25, 1944, Ray Young was part of the push of the Allied forces through northern France and Belgium to the Ardennes Forrest. For 113 days, he and men from the 602 Tank Destroyer Battalion had no rest and no time to maintain their equipment. Following a two-day rest period, Ray was back in the thick of it again, this time in the vicious fighting in the infamous Battle of the Bulge. The Germans poured everything they had into the Battle of the Bulge, a last ditch effort to bring about a German victory. The coldest winter Germany had had in years worked to the advantage of the Germans, and their savage barrage of bombings and gunfire gained them temporary advantages and sent the Allied forces into retreat. Soldiers who heretofore had been unwaveringly confident of their utter indestructibility, suddenly gave way to doubt and fear. Ray Young and thousands like him were now sure that they would never make it home alive. Every moment one stayed alive was a miracle in itself.[14]

In remembering the Battle of the Bulge, James Cecil Church, of Chicago and Minneapolis, recalled that the German attack was so surprising that some of the men could not even find a gun to fire. Patients from a field hospital in Liege, Belgium, where Jim Church was recovering from trench-foot, were hustled out of the town for fear of being overrun by the Germans. They constituted a motley group, and in the mass confusion of the moment, Jim admitted, "We assembled ourselves into makeshift squads and the leader was the guy with the most stripes."[15] German soldiers dressed in stolen U.S. army uniforms added even greater challenge to the fighting.

During the Battle of the Bulge, Lloyd Wilson, along with his comrades, experienced some of the most devastating fighting of the war. At temperatures of five degrees below zero, the Germans put forth their last mighty effort of the war. On the night of January 9, 1945, a satanic enemy barrage thundered through the skies, sending additional chills down the spine of Lloyd Wilson, shivering in a deep foxhole with two of his buddies. The shelling crept ever closer with one burst hitting just in front of their foxhole. Their relief was short-lived, for 30 minutes later a mortar shell hit a tree above them with a tremendous crash. "I'm hit," one of his companions, a sergeant, called out in pain. "I'm hit, too," Lloyd responded, and after hurriedly surveying the damage added, "but I think I'm ok." Fortunately, the lieutenant, the third man of the trio, survived unscathed.

It was two hours later before the medics arrived to pick up Lloyd, the sergeant, and six other wounded men. With the wounded clinging onto the top of the jeep and hanging on to the fenders, the driver set off on a high-speed dash through the snow. It was about 20 minutes later that the bewildered driver exclaimed: "I don't remember coming this way!" Suddenly, they realized they were heading straight into the German front lines. Weak and enervated as they were, the men struggled off the jeep and with almost their last ounce of energy, turned the jeep around and headed back to the battalion aid station in Wingen. Fortunately, a surgeon was able to remove the shrapnel, and things were indeed looking up for Lloyd Wilson; however, there was a long frigid boxcar ride, 20 men to a car and with doors wide open, for further hospitalization at the 23rd General Hospital. After several weeks of recuperation, Lloyd returned to the fighting, this time as a litter bearer.[16]

The Battle of the Bulge, Louie Ryder explained, involved taking over a town, having the Germans retake it, and then assaulting the town once again. Louie was afraid his luck had run out when during the Battle of the Bulge he got separated from his unit and was forced to spend three days and nights hiding from the enemy in the cellar of a building that been blown apart by gunfire and air strikes. It was the Christmas of 1944, and his single C ration and half of a canteen of water were long gone. Suddenly, outside in the street he could hear marching feet, and as he cautiously peered out between the bricks he saw the leggings of American troops. In seconds he was out of there and marching along with the Allies. His guardian angel was still watching over him.

During the Battle of the Bulge, Louie's commander was killed, and instinctively Louie quickly took over, urging the men, "Come on! Let's go! Let's go!" When a second officer suffered severe leg wounds and was unable to walk, Louie carried him by fits and starts to safety. As the gunfire rained down, he was forced to drop his wounded officer, step on up ahead, and shoot off a few rounds. Then he went back and picked up his officer, dropped him again as he dodged another barrage of gunfire, then went back and picked him up again until he had finally reached safety. Both men survived, and Louie says he will never ever forget when General Eisenhower himself pinned on a silver star for his heroism.[17]

During the freezing cold days that winter, the weather, as noted, proved as formidable an enemy as the Germans. Treacherous icy roads through steep mountain passes kept nerves constantly on edge. Sudden braking, a skid, or falling rocks all could spell disaster. A white-faced Ev Hohn nudged his buddy sitting next to him: "Hank, if we ever get out of this alive, remind me to write my mother and ask her how to pray." Staring straight ahead, similarly paralyzed with fear his friend responded, "Ev, just lean over close to me and listen. You'll learn real soon." And Ev did learn to pray during those frightening days in France. Now, he says, he avoids icy mountain roads—but he still prays.[18]

The casualties were enormous during the Battle of the Bulge—some 76,800 to 90,000 Americans killed, wounded, or missing in action. As he came in as a replacement during the fighting in the Battle of the Bulge, Walt Szpara was sickened as he saw truckload after truckload pass by loaded with stiff, frozen bodies of American soldiers stacked like cordwood. Unable to eat the good hot meal that was offered to him, he was likewise unable to make more than a few pitiful stabs at what was considered an "elaborate" Christmas dinner. It was a sight etched in his mind forever.[19]

As the troops made their way through the countryside, the desire to seek revenge ran high. As the Allies bombasted each little town, Ray Young's commander shouted, "Ok, this town is for . . ." and named one of their deceased comrades. "Let's do a good job!" Some days two or three little towns were bombed out—each time in the name of one of their former buddies.[20]

Suffering from a fever of 104, Joe Spinosa remembered the mutilated bodies brought in to his hospital during the Battle of the Bulge. The frozen feet and blood soaked lacerations of the wounded made his fever seem minimal. Finally, the assessment that "This soldier is unfit for further duty" was music to his ears.[21]

At the 191st General Hospital, at times only 30 miles from Battle of the Bulge front lines, Leroy Schroeder as a Master Sergeant Surgical Technician told of the 15 nurses, 19 surgical technicians, and 5 doctors who worked round the clock caring for the constant stream of patients suffering shrapnel wounds or frozen limbs. It was a relief to be able to patch up the mildly injured and a grisly job to help with the untold numbers of amputations of toes, feet, and legs as a result of the freezing temperatures. The hospital had been a mental institution in Villejuif that had been converted into a hospital following the evacuation of the mental patients. Leroy remembered being in charge of the 19 surgical technicians—2 former funeral directors, 2 chiropractors, and 1 veterinarian, the rest inexperienced young men not long out of high school. Time was of the essence as the cramped quarters left scores of servicemen freezing outside on stretchers as they waited their turn at the five operating tables inside. Surviving the zero temperatures was as chancy that winter as surviving the enemy gunfire. (Leroy was greatly impressed following his discharge and return home, when one day as he stopped at the post office he was handed a huge manila envelope. It was a thank you for helping liberate France signed by the President of France.)[22]

During the Battle of the Bulge, Gertrude Neff Gay's Field Hospital was being overrun with German prisoners. At one time, some 900 Germans were crowded into the stockade outside the hospital. What to do with them? Suddenly an idea hit. Why not put them to work as ward men, assign them KP duty, or put them on a work detail? Gertrude explained that they turned out to be good workers, that most of them had been forced into the German army, and that they were not SS troops. The German patients they were receiving were extremely malnourished, Gertrude observed, and had suffered three or four times the number of injuries of American patients.

Life was never dull for Gertrude. After the Battle of the Bulge, Gertrude's nursing duties changed considerably as the hospital more-or-less became a POW hospital for German prisoners and was soon moved to Carentan, France. One of Gertrude's saddest memories was the death of a young soldier that, considering the great strides being made in medicine during the war, should not have taken place. Instead of getting up and walking as soon as possible following surgery, patients were kept bedridden in those days, which resulted in the death of a patient who after days of bedrest, took his first step, had an aneurysm and a blood clot, and died. There were more changes in store when her hospital became an evacuation hospital where men with battle fatigue and psychiatric problems were given temporary treatment and then sent back to the United States.[23]

By the time of the Battle of the Bulge, Richard Crum had survived the invasion of Sicily and later Normandy, had dodged enemy gunfire through northern and central Europe, and emerged as "A Fugitive from the Law of Averages." The Bulge might have been his downfall had he not lucked out and been called back to assist the company clerk thus missing the Battle entirely.[24]

WOODROW WANTS "ACTION"

Fearing that his buddies would make fun of him, calling him 4F or worse, Woodrow Respects Nothing volunteered, despite the fact that he might well have been entitled to a deferment as an only son in a family. A Native American whose father had narrowly escaped the massacre at Wounded Knee, Woodrow wanted to see "action." And action he got as a member of the second wave of troops during the assault on Omaha Beach. "We were up against it right from the beginning. The German pillboxes had walls ten feet thick. We were very disorganized, but we got past them somehow."

"I was assigned to a 30 caliber machine gun, and for the most part, once we got past their coastal defenses, it was all hedgerow fighting squared off against the German positions at a couple of hundred yards. But against their armored vehicles, like a tank, firing a machine gun was like throwing peanuts against a wall." It looked like clear sailing once they reached western Holland in November, and they were convinced that they could ride out the winter there and then move on in the Spring. "But Hitler and the Germans thought otherwise. At 5:30 in the morning of December 16, we heard thunder up ahead of us. But it was winter and there was snow on the ground, so how could there be thunder?" It was shelling up ahead and not thunder; in fact it was the prelude to the Battle of the Bulge.

During the fighting around Bastogne, Woodrow remembered "a fierce mortar attack against us in a train yard. I crawled beneath a boxcar and lay flat between the two rails. A mortar landed close by, but the rail on that side was just high enough to shield me from some of the fragments. Another G.I. saw fit to relieve himself by a bowel movement and as he squatted to do so, he was killed."

That winter, Woodrow and his comrades battled not only the Germans but, as noted earlier, the snow and cold of one of the worst winters in that area for years. Shoe packs and cold weather gear helped to some extent to fend off the freezing temperatures, but, "We still had to sleep outside every night. We lived off what we could find in the countryside to add to our K rations. Eggs from chickens, and then the chickens went into the soup pot. Occasionally we shot a cow for fresh meat and our cooks served that up for us. We helped ourselves to the crackers, salami, and cheese from dead Germans we passed."

As they continued inching their way through enemy territory, Woodrow had a narrow escape with death when, during some hand to hand street fighting, as he cautiously rounded a building, his rifle at the ready, he found himself eyeballing a stout German soldier poised with his rifle also at the ready. One or both could be blown into oblivion. Traumatized by surprise, both soldiers stood paralyzed in a state of shock. A moment later in a most fortuitous turn of events, the German threw down his rifle, gestured "comrade," and Woodrow took him prisoner.

As the Germans began realizing the end was in sight, they surrendered by the thousands. There was no way for the Allied forces to effectively collect and corral them. "We just let them pass by us to the rear as we moved on to the front. We met the main body of Russian troops at the river Elbe and had a few parties with them. In that region, we set up a camp for displaced civilians while waiting for the signing of an unconditional surrender. We formed a tent city in a big pasture and housed them there," Woodrow explained.[25]

PFC Albert Fine, a medic from Brooklyn, New York, got his first baptism under fire when he spent 28 days in a foxhole in the Ruhr Valley, emerging only to race through the enemy gunfire from time to time to bandage a wounded comrade. Albert remembered that the foxhole occupants were conditioned once they heard the cough of the mortar to count 19 seconds and wait for the explosion. If you were still breathing you had luckily survived another shelling. At Christmastime in another move to a different spot there was the promise of a hot Christmas dinner, but unfortunately the food was served in tins that noisily alerted the Germans to their position. The steady firing of the enemy put a speedy end to the eagerly anticipated Christmas dinner.[26]

As Leonard Zimmerman and his men deftly set and took out minefields as they pushed the Germans back into their homeland, the enemy shu mines (hidden mines designed to explode and take off the foot of an unsuspecting GI) were the source of untold casualties. Leonard is still horrified as he travels back in time remembering the grisly operation performed on one victim of a shu mine. When three of his men failed to reappear at the agreed upon position in Klein Dorf, Germany, Leonard and a medic went back to search the battlefield for signs of life. Two of the men were wounded but could be taken to safe territory; however, the third man suffered a badly mangled foot. Apprehensively, the medic announced that he would have to remove the victim's foot before he could be moved. With a small shot of morphine as anesthesia the young soldier's foot was removed, and he was gently carried back to a field. Such were the scenes of the deadly shu mine casualties.[27]

Five months after the Battle of the Bulge, as Bill Worgul and his unit traveled through the battlefield area, they were astounded at the devastation: The trees and fields lay in ruins; empty foxholes punctured what had once been pasture land; and abandoned vehicles along with mangled parts of trucks and jeeps lay strewn about countryside. The area had become a wasteland. Along the Rhine some towns had been 97 percent destroyed.[28]

THE COUNTRY OF ONE'S GRANDFATHERS

Between 1942 to 1945, Everett William Hohn, of Dimock, South Dakota, chalked up 158 consecutive days of front-line duty in France and Germany. Following training at Fort Sill, Oklahoma and Fort Leonard Wood, Missouri, Ev arrived in Belgium in time to participate in the Battle of the Bulge as the radio operator for the company commander, where he rode in an armored group of 24 tanks. "The Germans liked to aim for the 200 gallon gas tank located at the side of our vehicle, somewhat close to where I sat. But it was always a near miss. We never got hit, even though we were in Bastogne and surrounded by Germans who wanted to serve up our heads on platters. Sometimes I had trouble with the fact that my grandfather, John Hohn, emigrated to the U.S. from Cologne, Germany when he was thirteen. And then here I was, in the land of distant relatives, blood relations and blood enemies, all in one time and place."[29]

In Germany, in particular, many soldiers had grave reservations, as did Everett Hohn, about the killing fields located in areas that were once the homes of their ancestors—and still might be the towns inhabited by distant cousins or great uncles. But this was war and orders were orders. "Seemed funny," William Wallace Henniger thought, "no, not funny really that my great grandfather immigrated from Baden, Germany, south of where I was just then, back in 1850 and moved to the States. So, I was back to the country of my cousins trying to kill them and they me. Almost like the Civil War. A crazy world."[30]

THE ALL IMPORTANT BRIDGES

Following the defeat of the German assault at the Battle of the Bulge, there was the mighty push to capture and secure the important bridges across Germany.

Kossie Akins, his company a part of Patton's Third Field Army, recalled his Army service during World War II as a time of building bridges. It was his company's job to build and rebuild bridges to facilitate the movement of supplies and troops across France and into Germany. Many times the work was an exercise in frustration. As the Germans retreated they, of course, attempted to demolish bridges in their wake so as to thwart the Allied advances. Case in point: As the Allies were making their way into Germany, a bridge over the River Saar had been destroyed by the Germans and had been hurriedly rebuilt by Kossie's company. It was a substantial bridge: 130 feet long, double wide, and double story. Proud of their work, the men had only a few hours before a German counterattack, and Kossie's men were ordered to tear down the bridge. When the counterattack failed, Kossie's unit immediately received orders to rebuild the bridge. All in all, within 36 grueling hours the bridge was built, dismantled, and rebuilt—a feat accomplished amid constant enemy gunfire. And yet not a man complained; they knew their work was crucial to winning the war.[31]

A RHINE CROSSING AND A CHAPLAIN

The early crossings of the Rhine River were nightmares for everyone engaged. Lloyd Wilson and his comrades found the view opposite Worms awesome. For miles, artillery lined the banks and soldiers, trucks, and jeeps inched forward. The first boats were sent over at midnight, but by the time Lloyd started across carrying medicine bags and plasma rolled up in liters, the Germans opened fire. Among the early casualties was Lloyd's sergeant, killed by enemy gunfire. Fortunately, the crossing was less hazardous than expected, for many of the Germans were still in their beds having anticipated the attack to be the next night instead.[32]

Although some men "got" their religion during their time in the military, Delbert August Kuehl brought his religion with him and shared it with his fellow paratroopers. Del earned a Silver Star, two Bronze Stars, and a Purple Heart as well as other commendations during his service as an airborne chaplain who chose to parachute with the men into enemy territory. It would have been simple for Del Kuehl to take the easy road and remain in the States as a minister in some nice quiet suburban church, safely removed from the chaos and hazards of war. He would have been exempt. Instead, he volunteered as a military chaplain. His studies in preparation for the ministry at Northwestern Bible School, Bethel College, and the University of Minnesota enabled him to enter chaplain school at Ft. Benjamin Harrison in Indiana, after which he volunteered for airborne training at Ft. Benning, Georgia.

As a new chaplain, eager to share the Christian message with his 1,800 fellow paratroopers, Del found it a bitterly disappointing experience when at this first service only two men showed up, one of them drunk. Undaunted, he continued to hold services, and as more and more men crowded in to hear his thoughtful homilies, his reputation as a courageous man of God spread through the ranks. His admiring fellow paratroopers kept repeating, "Chaplain, you don't know how much it means to us to have you go out the door of a plane with us."

For Del Kuehl, his most traumatic experience of the war involved crossing the Rhine River in 1944. Del was in the first assault wave floundering in capricious, folding canvas boats in the broad daylight with a storm of gunfire from German mortars, machine guns, and tanks peppering the water like hail. He was sure the commander must be insane to place men in flimsy, canvas boats in turbulent waters with paddles instead of motors for locomotion.

So, in short, on the afternoon of September 20, we were headed into a suicide mission. One officer showed what he thought of his personal chances for survival. He took one cigarette from a pack and threw the pack into the river. 'Guess I won't need the rest,' he said. Then he took out his Zippo lighter, lit his cigarette, and then threw the lighter in the drink as well. 'And I won't need that anymore either.' His premonitions were right. He was dead within the hour.

Just 12 of the 26 boats reached the far side of the river. The rest were shredded by gunfire and sank like sieves. The troops in them were either killed outright by the gunfire or drowned from the weight of their equipment. . . . Not many officers survived the crossing, but the men didn't need anyone to tell them what to do or lead the way. They did what had to be done and so were able to secure the area by the bridge [the Nijmegen Bridge in Holland]. Their action diverted some attention of the Germans from the G.I.s crossing the bridge on foot before the German could blow it up.

While the men who survived the crossing set about engaging the Germans in frenzied combat, Del was engrossed in looking after the wounded before sending them back to the other side. As he was attempting to administer first aid to one seriously wounded man, suddenly a shot rang out, and Del fell on top of the man he was caring for. Del himself had been hit by shrapnel. "Oh chaplain, did they get you too?" queried Del's solicitous patient. Even under the most dire circumstances, the men were vitally concerned about one another.[33]

The men's admiration for their chaplain continued to escalate as Del disregarded his own wound and for four hours continued to attend the injured and help in their evacuation. Thanks to his diligence and courage, 35 wounded soldiers were sent back to the safety of the south side of the river. Afterward, the men were in awe of his commitment to them and to his country. "We had to go, but you didn't. So why did you?" Del's response was immediate and heartfelt: "Because you had to I wanted to." (It should come as no surprise that after the war Del completed a Bachelor of Divinity degree at Bethel College and later served as a missionary to Japan and various other areas throughout the world. He continued to retain his rank as a chaplain in the reserves and now and then went on active duty for short periods of time.)[34]

After crossing the Rhine, Jim Church explained "As we entered towns vacated by German troops, our new concern was the civilian situation. After leaving France, Belgium, and Holland, we couldn't be sure of any more warm milk and cookies. Some of the locals could also shoot a pistol or rifle. So some of them got shot because we had reason to suspect them. We were jumpy. A curtain fluttering in an open window might be blasted. And we also had to be wary of 13 or 14-year-old kids. Some would pull out a handgun and shoot one of us. But by February, we could tell the resistance was fading. We met home guard units comprised of old men and young children."[35]

THE REMAGEN BRIDGE

The account of the crossing of the Rhine and the Remagen bridge is a familiar story dramatically recaptured in numerous books and movies. The miracle that the bridge was still standing, that the part of the explosives set by the Germans to blow it up somehow did not explode, enabled American troops and tanks to move across what the Germans had thought would prove to be one of their greatest defenses. The crossing was fraught with danger both from the possibility of untapped mining of the bridge and from the frantic Germans poised with artillery fire ready to meet the

GIs as they emerged from the bridge. Woodrow Respects Nothing and his buddies "crossed it by foot on the run, even though they were set up on the far side of the river, waiting for us." It was there that Woodrow succeeded in taking out a German machine gun nest that had his group pinned down. For his action, he was put in for a Bronze Star, papers that somehow got lost in the shuffle. "I didn't care," he said. "I came back from the war in good shape. That was good enough for me."[36]

CHAPTER 5

The Pacific Scene

The Allied island hopping through the Pacific, the Marshall Islands, Saipan, Guam, Iwo Jima, and the litany of other Pacific islands eventually spelled doomsday for Japan, but at horrendous costs in lives and property.

"UNDER WAY FOR WHERE ONLY GOD KNOWS"

It was an eerie feeling for tens of thousands of GIs as they said goodbye to their homeland, boarded ships on the west coast, and headed out to the great unknown. For Seaman Larry Deason, it was especially dramatic when he and his unit moved out of Pearl Harbor on May 29, 1944. Something awesome was clearly in the offing as one could see over a thousand ships in the harbor: every type of ship and class, including "transports loaded, aircraft carriers, battleships, cruisers, destroyers, old and new. It's not hard to see something big is cooking," Larry wrote his wife. "It's a queer feeling to know on those ships are thousands of men going to fight someone they don't know, or don't know where, or under what kind of conditions. It makes you feel small and insignificant." Several hours later he observed, "they are all out and we are now a task force consisting of thirty-two transports, fifteen destroyers and two carriers for plane protection and we are under way for where only God knows." Four days later, on June 2, 1944, Larry reminisced sadly, "Only one month ago today we were married. Little did we think then that I would be over 7,000 miles away in a month."

From his ship on the outskirts of what proved to be their objective, Saipan, Larry explained (the letters often blurred with perspiration from the heat), "We can expect to live at General Quarters and for days both eat and sleep on the guns. And we can expect almost anything. Honey, I am writing this with everything in because when you read it, it will either all be over or I will and if you don't think we are scared then you should be with us. But to a man, I don't think there is one that would turn back now for love or money. Even my love for you, which is the strongest in the world, couldn't keep me out of this now." On June 14th Larry continued, "There wasn't any G. Q. all day and the next one will be the real thing. No more practice. On this the eve of battle, everybody is in the best of moods, playing cards, and the usual confusion but as far as I am concerned, Honey, I can think of quite a few places I would rather be but still that feeling of—I wouldn't turn back now for anything. Everybody will sleep with their clothes on and close to their battle stations tonight."

In letters and a diary, Larry described the details of one of the most devastating battles (some 14,000 casualties) of World War II. (On Saipan the Japanese had conducted one of their suicide raids, in which every Japanese was instructed to take 10 Americans with him to their deaths. In the final analysis the raid proved futile, and some 2,000 Japanese lost their lives in the attack.) Finally, the U.S. forces took Saipan, which greatly helped in the eventual securing of Iwo Jima and Okinawa.[1]

ISLAND HOPPING

With word in July of 1942 that the Japanese were building an airstrip on Guadalcanal in the Solomon Islands, the Allies quickly landed 11,000 Marines to capture the landing strip and take possession of the island. (Capture of the airfield would help to prevent the anticipated Japanese invasion of Australia.) Although the airfield was secured in short order, the Japanese retaliated with air, sea, and land attacks and turned what was expected to be a brief battle into an operation involving six months of bloody warfare. The losses were extremely heavy for both the Japanese and the Allied Forces, but finally on February 7, 1943, the Allies drove out the last of the Japanese. Among the wounded during those savage battles was Robert Hutchins, a member of the 7th Marine Regiment, who less than four months following the first assault wave on Guadalcanal was caught by a piece of shrapnel that paralyzed his left arm. Surgery in Fiji, a trip home for recuperation, and guard duty at Great Lakes and then at the Naval Armament Department in Nebraska and Bob was sent back to Guadalcanal to join his unit for training in preparation for the invasion of Okinawa. A part of the first assault wave on Okinawa, Bob lasted 14 days when he next found himself the victim of shell shock on a hospital ship. As the ship hovered offshore, the kamikazes began their deadly suicide attacks in a final effort to save face in the war. Bob confessed that he had never felt so helpless in his life, as now there was no place to even dig a foxhole.[2]

The possession of the Marshall Islands was absolutely crucial to the success of the Allied Forces in the Pacific. The cluster of coral atolls, taken from Germany in World War I, had become an important base of operations for the Japanese attacks on American naval forces. The men of the 4th Marine Division were assigned to assault and take possession of the heavily fortified Roi-Namur in the vast Marshall Island chain. It was a hazardous assignment. The Marines knew the Japanese firepower would be intense. As Richard Sorenson and the members of his squad readied for the morrow's invasion (February 1944), the pulsing excitement of combat was tinged with the haunting anxieties of the unknown. That evening, in idle conversation, the men casually speculated on what they would do if a live grenade landed in their midst. Would they take the time to toss it back to the enemy hoping to make the pitch before it exploded or would they sacrifice themselves and fall on it with their own bodies in order to save the lives of their buddies? Sorenson remembered, "We mutually agreed that it would be better for one of us to take the hit than all of us die."

The next morning the carnage began as Sorenson and his buddies became prime targets in one of the first waves to confront the Japanese. "We began fighting our way across the island, eliminating enemy resistance as we went." About nightfall, as a result of their spirited assault, Sorenson and his comrades became aware that they had surged ahead of the other troops and an order to pull back had never reached them. Daylight found them cut off and surrounded in the basement of a half-destroyed building where they had taken refuge for the night.

As the Japanese opened up with a deadly barrage of gunfire, the Marines unleashed their own lethal arsenal of demolition. Suddenly, there was the terrifying thud of a grenade lobbed into their midst. "It fell in a near wall by me," Sorenson recalled. "I had no way of knowing whether I had time to throw it out and away. And there was no flashback to our talk about this the previous night. It just happened to land and then roll to a stop about a foot away. I remember being in a semi-crouched position, so the quickest way I could cover it was to sort of slide over to that side and sit on it. The right side of my body took the brunt of the blast when it exploded . . . buttock, thigh, leg and arm. Grenade fragments penetrated my bladder and messed up some other internal organs which I learned about later . . . I made a deliberate decision to do this, because if too many of us got wounded, the enemy would overrun our position and we'd all be dead."

Sorenson's survival was something of a miracle; had he covered the grenade face-forward he would have died. Sorenson credited expert medical care with releasing him "with just a slight limp, internal injuries, and shrapnel in my right arm, leg and abdomen." (Of the 433 men who received the Congressional Medal of Honor, 41 had purposely covered an explosive device to protect the lives of their comrades. Thirty-four men died as a result of their effort, and seven men lived to be awarded the

Medal in person. Richard Sorenson, at 19 years of age, received the Medal on July 19, 1944, at the Seattle Naval Hospital where he was still recovering from his wounds.)[3]

It was not Stanley Nelson's original intention to join the Marine Corps, but shortly after his induction into the army in 1942, "A Marine recruiter walked down a line of us inductees and picked out guys at random for the Marine Corps. I was one of them. There was no volunteering on my part. I had been working out some as an amateur boxer, so I probably looked in better shape than some of the rest." His training, he admitted, was merciless, including "seventy-five mile forced marches with just two canteens of water. The cadre didn't care if we collapsed from heat or exhaustion or both."

Engrossed in other assignments, Stan missed the swimming instruction that was given to guys who didn't know how to swim. "So one day we were towed two miles out to sea in rubber rafts with rifle and full pack. Then the cadre yelled, 'Everybody out,' so we had to jump in and then practice getting back in with all our gear on. I damned near drowned," Stan recalled. In the Pacific there were landings for Stan and his fellow Marines on Guadalcanal and Guam and finally on Okinawa. "When our LST got to the shoreline (of Okinawa), we had to go over the front of it because it didn't have the usual ramp. We didn't like that because we were momentarily good targets. . . The Japs were determined to defend it (the island) at all costs, so they came at us in two waves of banzai attacks. Screaming at the top of their lungs, they were drunk on rice wine. That made them lose any reserve or restraint or common sense they might have had. They also lost a lot of their troops."[4]

IWO JIMA

The battle for Iwo Jima, the five-mile long island with its two Japanese-held airfields that enabled the Japanese to wreck havoc with American bombers flying overhead en route to and from their missions to Japan, involved a bloody 36-day attack with appalling numbers of casualties. The number of U.S. casualties was estimated to have totaled 6,821 killed, missing, or died of wounds, in addition to 19,217 wounded.[5]

The famous picture of the raising of the flag at the top of Suribachi has been indelibly stamped on everyone's mind as a result of newspaper photos, magazine pages, best-selling books, and TV documentaries. To this day, however, there are many misconceptions about the picture. There was a first flag raising, before the picture so popularly recognized was taken. On that momentous occasion Charles "Chuck" Willard Lindberg played an important role atop Mount Suribachi and fortunately survived to tell about it.

Just as the members of his patrol were about to undertake the precarious ascent to Suribachi's rim, Chuck recalled that they were handed an

American flag and ordered that *IF* they made it to the top, they were to raise the flag as a monument to their successful climb. Crawling and zigzagging their way through rocks and loose ash, among caves alive with enemy forces poised and ready to put a quick end to their progress, the men struggled with stretchers to be made available for carrying the wounded down to Suribachi's base. "We each wondered to ourselves," Chuck remembered, "which of us would be coming back down the mountain on one of those stretchers."

Thanks to a devastatingly effective weapon, a flame thrower, Chuck and his fellow Marines could pour the liquid fire into the rocky crevices and Japanese hideouts along their way thus sealing the fate of the blood-thirsty enemy. The flame throwers were apparently doing their job well! Yet, with each step there was the potential of enemy sniper fire and disastrous land mines. Finally, what everyone thought would be a doomed mission, turned into a victorious ascension. The patrol had reached the top of Mount Suribachi!

The exuberance of their successful climb was now challenged with the necessity of finding a pole for the flag raising. An old piece of pipe discarded by the Japanese served the purpose, and Chuck Lindberg and five other Marines nestled the pole among the rocks and proudly hoisted the colors into the wind.

From the shoreline below thousands of Marines, navy personnel, and infantrymen cheered wildly while offshore ships whistled their thunderous applause. That day, Chuck Lindberg experienced "a happy chill" of pride and accomplishment that would be relived again and again for as long as life itself. For his bravery and his "cool-headed fighting," Chuck was awarded a Silver Star. A sentence from his presidential citation read: "As a member of the first combat patrol to scale Mount Suribachi, he courageously carried his flame thrower up the steep slopes and assisted in destroying the occupants of the many caves found in the rim of the volcano, some of which contained as many as seventy Japanese."[6]

Actually, it was Louis Lowery, a photographer for *Leatherneck Magazine,* who recorded the original flag raising on Iwo Jima and the Marines' treacherous climb up the volcano's side. However, it was not his photograph that received such tremendous publicity in the days and years to come. His climb up to the top with the original patrol and his photographic recording of the real hoisting of the flag had been withheld by *Leatherneck* in deference to the picture of the subsequent flag raising by the AP photographer, Joe Rosenthal. In a queer turn of fate, it was the picture of the second flag raising that became so widely publicized.

A short time after the Stars and Stripes first fluttered over Mount Suribachi, when it appeared that a serious contest was looming between the top brass and the battalion itself over possession of the original flag, Lt. Colonel Chandler W. Johnson took matters into his own hands.

Insisting that the flag belonged to the battalion and in order to preserve it as a treasured memorial, the Colonel immediately ordered that a larger, more impressive replacement flag be raised. The new flag was carried to the crater's rim, the original flag was brought down, and the second flag was raised with Joe Rosenthal, an Associated Press photographer (among others), catching the action. Although the second flag raising received only casual attention among the men atop Suribachi, because this was merely a replacement flag, in the end it was Rosenthal's picture of the replacement flag raising that made the front pages of newspapers all across the country. It was Rosenthal's picture that was awarded a Pulitzer Prize for photography.

Although the flag had been planted, the battle for even the top of Suribachi was far from over. Contrary to fact, some young inexperienced observers and millions of Americans back home assumed that the flag raising picture signified the capture of the entire island of Iwo Jima. The flag, a rallying point for the Marines, suddenly became a red flag for the Japanese who instantly emerged from their caves and tunnels as the Marines wheeled around with gunfire and flame throwers to defend their position. "All hell broke loose," Chuck Lindberg recalled. "Shooting our way back down was as tough as going up, and it was like kicking over a hornet's nest." Sometime later hundreds of Japanese were discovered who had resigned themselves to their fate and pressed grenades to their bodies or performed other acts of self-annihilation.

Unfortunately, it was not until over 36 days later, after some of the bloodiest fighting of the war, that Iwo Jima was really secured by the U.S. forces. In the months following, some 20,000 crew members returning from bombing raids on Japan owed their survival to the emergency landing strips that had been cleared thanks to the sacrifices of those brave men. It was Admiral Nimitz who sang their praises with the words: "Among the Americans who served on Iwo island, uncommon valor was a common virtue."[7]

The Japanese shelling of Iwo Jima rattled the nerves of even the most unflappable GIs. "The Japs had six inch naval guns pointed right down our throat every night for a week," Hall Tennis remembered. "The shells got there before you heard them coming; big bad concussion-They got to me a bit . . . It was quite shocking, beyond frightening," he continued. "You could feel the impact of the shock waves. You'd feel like your body turned to jelly."[8]

A member of the third assault wave to invade Iwo Jima, Marine Conrad Taschner remembered that at first there was only light opposition to the landings. In short order, however, with the third assault troops, "The Japs gave us hell." From their vantage point high on the hill, the enemy had a clear shot at everything on the beach. Gunfire swept the beaches, and even before he headed for the mountain Conrad Taschner had his first experience with death. Shortly after landing two of his buddies, one on either side of him, were mortally wounded. That he escaped unscathed he credited to the Lord's grace.

For months the island had been groomed as an impenetrable fortification for the Japanese homeland. An underground labyrinth of caves and tunnels had been carved out of the rock and lava, and any existing tree of any size had been cut down to shore up and camouflage the hideouts that Conrad Taschner likened to ubiquitous manholes. During the daylight hours the enemy remained secreted away in their caves, and only at night would they emerge as fiendish devils. As Conrad and four men from his unit took the point lead and struggled to make their way up the mountain, somehow the men got ahead of their lines, and within minutes Conrad was blinded by a grenade, and his friend Keith Rasmussen was shot in his hip. By now they were separated from the rest of the squad and the big problem was how on earth to get back to their base of operations. Necessity being the mother of invention, Keith climbed on Conrad's back and piloted the temporarily blinded Conrad as they crawled back to their own lines. After being treated briefly for head wounds, Conrad was then sent back to the States for further treatment. Fortunately, the health care providers were successful in restoring Conrad's vision, and he returned home in time to take his future wife to the senior prom—in borrowed dress blues![9]

As a member of the invasion forces on Iwo Jima, Rollie Dart had a scary time as he went ashore on a DUCK (an amphibious military truck). "Sitting on top of a pile of White-Phosphorus 105 shells, we were [scheduled] to land on East Shore at the narrow neck of the Isle. The DUCK lost power, the surf was running high and we were drifting into the East Face of Suribachi. They were lobbing shells closer and closer to us, along with direct fire but unbelievably not one direct hit. Finally we got engine power again and worked our way back through the smoke to a beach that was indiscernible. This island was a place without any growing things; I can remember seeing things that *used* to grow. The isle was bombed steadily for days before we went ashore. There was sadness in remembering the caves," Rollie recalled. "I remember guiding the 5th Corps Flame flowers unto cave after cave. We needed to be sure we would not have snipers at our backs." (Repeatedly cautioned *not* to eat any Japanese food, Rollie's company ignored the warnings and found the cans of Japanese fish found in the burned-out caves a gourmet delight, a far cry from the unappetizing K-rations that had sustained them for so long.)[10]

During his trip up to the mountain's summit, Chuck Lindberg's helmet was dented by a piece of shrapnel, but fortunately he escaped injury. Five days later, however, he was not so lucky—although in the long run perhaps he was exceedingly lucky. As the fighting advanced to the north end of Iwo Jima, Chuck was again involved in entombing the enemy with his flame thrower. This time, however, he suffered a gunshot wound in his arm and was sent to hospitals in Saipan and later to Great Lakes. Over the years, Chuck came to realize that he probably owed his life to that wound. During the rest of the fighting on Iwo Jima, 90 percent of the men in his platoon were either killed or wounded.[11]

Following a barrage of dynamite blasting on Iwo by the combat engineers to seal off the ubiquitous enemy caves and tunnels, the commandant ordered the unit to set up a bivouac and fall back for a rest. Dead tired, George Dike and a fellow Marine decided to take turns napping and maintaining the radio watch. Suddenly, George was awakened by another Marine frantically signaling him to move immediately. As George looked back to exactly where he had been sleeping, a hand was sticking up out of the rubble and in the hand was a Japanese grenade. Joined by other Marines the body was unearthed. He was alive, and apparently he had been covered by the previous day's dynamite blast. He was quickly dispatched to regimental headquarters as George and his comrade returned to "other business." So much for sleeping with a live Japanese with a live grenade in his hand![12]

Among Hall Tennis' assignments were orders to go to the front lines to report the exact positions of troops, run phone wire back to the artillery and hook up their phones, and direct air support planes where to strafe and bomb. The trick in making one's way back to the Allies was to remember the password. In all the chaos and confusion, it was easy in the panic of the moment to forget the password. Hall had the answer. He'd start swearing. "I could do that for a minute and a half without repeating myself. That way the guards were sure I wasn't Japanese."

Once Iwo was secured, Hall's anxieties were still not over. It was his unit that was assigned the perilous job of cleaning up all the unexploded munitions on the airfield and on Surabachi. Only extremely deft handling determined the difference between life and death.

During his stay on Iwo Jima, Hall Tennis reported, "For 'intelligence' I probably grubbed about more mangled bodies than most big-city morgue workers; I know the touch, smell, feel and taste of dead and dying enemies in large numbers. 'Banzai' counterattacks do that."[13]

BRUTAL WARFARE

During his 17 months' service with the Seabees in the Aleutians, Ray William "Buck" Wells, from Hattiesburg, Mississippi, realized he had been lucky not to have been in the front lines in the European theater. Upon being sent to Samar in the Philippines to build hospitals to receive the wounded who would be coming in from the anticipated invasion of Japan, Buck knew "this was coming down to the real gritty nitty of it, and there was a lot of people were going to lose their lives." Buck and his buddies realized, "the United States thought that they were going to have to fight the Japanese to the last man, and it was going to be a bloody, bloody mess." Service in the Aleutians had consisted of long hours and hard physical labor, but now it would be the real thing.[14]

As Donald R. Rudolph, Sr. maneuvered his way along with the American forces invading Luzon in January of 1945, the path was alive with Japanese machine gunners entrenched in caves, pillboxes, and bunkers camouflaged with bamboo, sod, and dirt. By courageously and persistently lobbing grenades into Japanese hideouts, seemingly without regard for his own safety, Don earned a battlefield commission as a second lieutenant as well as a Congressional Medal of Honor for his heroism and leadership in the invasion of Luzon. In a daring escapade, Don climbed up on a disabled Japanese tank, opened the turret, and tossed in a white phosphorus grenade. "The only way to get them out was to get some explosives inside it. The whole inside of the tank started to burn; that's how white phosphorus works. The shells in the chamber of the tank gun also exploded. None of the Japs got out." Why would he single handedly take on such a dangerous job? "I was available to do it," Don shrugged. "Someone had to. We had to knock it out. Otherwise, they could wait for night, then crawl away to safety."[15]

Clarence "Clink" Joseph Stubbs believed he "was lucky to have lasted twelve days on Leyte. It was brutal." Actually there were some who didn't think he had survived. The life expectancy of lieutenants was traditionally short, and as he was returning to battalion headquarters following the bloody fighting on the beach, he met two GIs who inquired about the location of his platoon. "We're from Quartermaster Graves Registration," they explained, "and we're going to identify and mark Lieutenant Stubbs' grave."

A few days later Clink thought the grave registers might have been clairvoyant when a cluster of Japanese entrenched in a bunker opened fire on his platoon. "First a sniper's bullet got me in the hand but it wasn't very serious. But the medic who dressed it had to fill out a report, and because of that, I got a Purple Heart. Later in the withdrawal, I was blown over by a mortar round. When I started walking again, my left arm felt numb. I looked down at my sleeve and noticed it was getting soggy with blood. Then, I noticed the arm was flopping sideways instead of a natural backward and forward arm-swing while I was moving along fast. My elbow was shattered; partly blown off is another way of putting it." Clink brought home painful, physical reminders of that day, and for years afterward, despite hospitalization and considerable rehabilitation, pieces of shrapnel continued to surface on various parts of Clink's body.[16]

Death surely stalked Richard Newton Scott, but it took almost 50 years to catch up to him. Although his work in the Minneapolis-St. Paul Northern Pump Arsenal, a manufacturer of ammunition for the government, was classified as essential to the war effort and would have exempted him from military service, Richard Newton Scott saw all of his buddies leaving for the service and decided he should sign up too. "I didn't see why I shouldn't be among them. Holding a job which made me exempt wasn't a good enough reason."[17]

According to the testimony of almost every veteran interviewed, each was tenaciously convinced that he would make it through the war and return safe and sound to his family. An incredible succession of brushes with death, however, prompted Dick, aka "Scotty," (Scott) to give serious thought to his own mortality. (On the other hand perhaps, at the time, his survival assured that he was, indeed, invincible.)

As a member of the 503rd Parachute Infantry Regiment, Scotty was temporarily knocked out in a hard landing over Corregidor. His slight concussion was a far better fate, however, than the slow, excruciating death that befell several of his fellow paratroopers who landed on bombed out buildings and became skewered on steel girders and were unable to extricate themselves. Some of the paratroopers never reached the island at all and sank into the briny depths dragged under by their equipment. Here and there a friend was rescued by a hovering Navy ship.

The carnage on Corregidor was appalling, Scotty remembered. "The Japs didn't come out of their caves at first. It took us about three weeks to clean them out. After one heavy day of fighting, my sleeves were littered with bullet holes, but I wasn't scratched. When it was over, we could walk across bodies without stepping on the ground in areas where the fighting was the heaviest."

Intuition or a subconscious impulse to duck, dive for cover, or change positions saved countless lives—Dick Scott's life, for example. Scotty's brushes with death during his service in the South Pacific are almost unbelievable. A few days after his arrival on Corregidor, Scotty flopped down atop an old map room bunker and grabbed a few precious hours of sleep. Sometime later, he awoke with a nagging feeling that he should move immediately—somewhere—anywhere—even to what might be a far less comfortable spot. Dazedly, he repositioned himself flat on the ground some 15 feet from the bunker. An hour later the spine chilling screams of the enemy in a suicidal Banzai attack rent the air. In the morning light, some 15 Japanese and American bodies were strewn atop the very bunker where Scotty had been positioned just a few hours earlier.

Scotty had escaped the Banzai charge, but later a Japanese soldier had crept up to within 10 feet of Scotty. As Scotty raised his rifle in defense, horror of all horrors the gun jammed. It was a sure shot for the Jap, and Scotty figured his time was surely up. There was a second's lapse, and suddenly, the Japanese soldier toppled over dead. A buddy had spotted the gunman about to take out Scotty and had downed him with a single bullet.

Later that day, a replacement for Scotty arrived at the bunker, got off one shot, and in seconds lay dead—slain by a Japanese gunman waiting just outside the bunker for the perfect opportunity to pick off one of the enemy.

Days later, Scotty's captain sought him out for information about the enemy's position in the field, and as they were talking the captain dropped to the ground with a bullet in the head. Sometime afterward, his buddy was shot in the head and collapsed into his arms. As Scotty was attending his friend, a shot rang out, and a Japanese gunman primed to kill Scotty fell dead thanks to the keen eye and expert marksmanship of a fellow GI.

As death became ever more threatening, Scotty began asking himself, "What's going to happen to me if I get killed like some of my buddies?" In his quest for answers he appealed to the unit chaplain and found solace in a deep and abiding religious experience. In fact, he became so spiritual as a result of his religious experience that he attracted the attention of his commanding officers who suspicioned that Scotty had gone off his rocker or was using his religion as a pretense to be sent home. Scotty was immediately dispatched to the company psychiatrist, and then to the guardhouse. Even his friends marveled at his transformation—he cleaned up his speech, changed his lifestyle, and even his attitude took on new dimensions. His conversion mystified the officers at the base, and he was sent back to New Guinea for further evaluation. There, five more psychiatrists proceeded to interrogate Scotty, and in desperation concluded that he must have "combat fatigue." "Were going to send you back to the States. You've had enough over here."

Finally, Scotty convinced them that he was truly a "born again" Christian and should be reunited with his unit now stationed in the Philippines on the island of Mindora. The next stop was Negros as the unit readied plans for the invasion of Japan, but in August the bombs dropped on Hiroshima and Nagasaki revolutionized life for Scotty—and the rest of the world. "We went berserk with joy. It was over, No more of this mess. I could drink water again anytime I was thirsty without boiling it. I could sleep nights and any other time I was tired without fear of someone sneaking up on me." Christmas that year at home in Minneapolis was a fabulous celebration, Scotty exulted. "My brother, brother-in-law, and I came back from the War alive and reasonably well."

For the records, Scotty's conversion was no temporary "foxhole pledge." Following the war he enrolled in Northwestern Bible School in Minneapolis where evangelist Billy Graham was serving as president. He soon became a member of the staff of the Navigators, the para church ministry associated with the School, and later served with other independent missionary groups including a stint in Japan. Instead of killing Japanese people, Scotty had now turned to ministering unto them.[18]

OKINAWA

As the Allies moved ever closer to Japan. the Japanese became ever more vicious in attempting to defend their homeland. It was eventually a victory for the United States, but at a cost of 12,500 killed and 36,000 wounded. The Japanese lost over 109,600 fighting men and some 109,000 Okinawan residents.[19] Earlier, the fire-bombing raids on Japan had caused 260,000 civilian deaths. And one can only speculate what the costs to both the American and the Japanese would have been had the Allies invaded Japan!

In *Tennozan: The Battle of Okinawa and the Atomic Bomb,* George Feifer details the bloodbath that consumed Okinawa. Feifer notes that "more innocent civilians died on Okinawa, and in greater agony, than in Hiroshima and Nagasaki and that the cultural damage was incalculably greater than that of the two atomic bombs."[20]

Although he was working in the Tacoma shipyard helping to build Liberty Ships, Chuck Larrowe chose to volunteer in the American Field Service. Following a tour of duty that took him through Libya, Egypt, and Syria, Chuck returned to the United States and signed up for the army, preferring "to be a participant rather than a bystander in the war." Once in the army he found himself anything but a casual observer. Even his sendoff from San Francisco was a bit unnerving when, as he and his unit were leaving for the Philippines, a group of Japanese War Prisoners on Angel Island waved them off with an ominous "So long, suckers."

Upon his arrival on Leyte (the same time and place as General MacArthur!), Chuck's first assignment to head up the hospital's ambulance unit might have been a relatively safe placement; however, he soon felt compelled to criticize and make suggestions on what he considered mismanagement. Chuck deemed the hospital's organization "a mess." Finally, an officer annoyed with Chuck's constant harassment announced: "Larrowe, I know you're a Communist." "Why?" came Chuck's query. "Because you're always criticizing the captain and me." With that Chuck sought a transfer to the 7th Division as a replacement and was sent to help with the invasion of Okinawa.

Although for the first few days the landings on Okinawa were relatively unopposed by the Japanese, "After four days, however, the Japanese opened up with full power," Chuck Larrowe explained. "Their objective was to kill as many Americans as possible so we wouldn't invade the main islands." As at Iwo Jima, the flame thrower (Larrowe had had special training) constituted a powerful instrument for dispatching diehard Japanese soldiers holed up in small crevices and underground tunnels.

"The flame thrower would aim at a Japanese in a small cave which would suck the air out of the cave and asphyxiate the enemy." Chuck and his unit made excellent use of their lethal weapons.

Bit by bit the Japanese were driven back, and the fighting began to wind down on Okinawa. One seemingly uneventful day, a driver arrived to summon Chuck from the foxhole he shared with two buddies and take him back to the Army headquarters (10th Army) to be checked out for a possible field promotion. The interview went well, but upon his return as he stepped out of the jeep, he was traumatized to find two corpses in his foxhole—a mortar shell had hit just minutes before, and his two buddies, a radio man and a runner, had been its victims.

There was precious little time for recovering from the shock or for grieving for his buddies as the Japanese held Chuck's unit at bay with renewed firing. A few days later, on the last day before the fighting on Okinawa ended, a Japanese sniper's bullet caught Chuck on the shoulder. His good fortune prevailed, however, and following a stretcher ride on a jeep to an airfield, another stretcher attached to a helicopter and a flight to a hospital ship, a ship to Guam for a month's hospital stay, a hospital ship to Washington, and a train ride to Walla Walla, Washington for another month—at last the war was over for Chuck Larrowe.[21]

In 1945, by then well trained, after two bootcamps, Robert Flores was assigned to the *U.S. Butler* and was sent to the South China Sea where, for nine days before the D-Day invasion of Okinawa, his ship cruised up and down the island where it was soon joined by the big fleet to form a picket line around the island in readiness for the April 1, 1945 invasion. Up until that point, Robert, like most young GIs, was sure he would make it through the war alive.[22] The fighting was incredible at Okinawa, and Robert's eye witness to the shocking death and destruction aboard his ship and others in the fleet gave him gut-wrenching fears that he indeed might not make it home after all. Any kamikaze direct hit on a ship could cause extensive damage, but by the time the *U.S. Butler* had taken 17 hits by kamikaze planes the ship had become a floating hell. The sickening sight of ships that had been engaged in the invasion now barely afloat with their hulls caved in and their decks strewn with dead and wounded bodies marked Robert for life. Dead and dying sailors were slipping off the decks into the ocean where they were quickly devoured by fish. Even most of the wounded that were rescued by nearby ships, according to Robert, soon succumbed to their burns and injuries and died. Fortunately, in Robert's own words, "God was with me and I did make it through alive."[23]

Dave Ruff, typical of the young, confident youth of his day, said it never entered his mind that he might possibly be killed. He was eager to get into the middle of the fighting. And that he did, serving with the Marines on the landings at Guadalcanal, Guam, and Okinawa. Amid the hail of enemy gunfire during the April 1st landings on Okinawa, however, his convictions gave way to wondering whether he really would make it home. There were lots of close calls, Dave recalled. Once, he was awakened from a deep sleep in his foxhole and informed that he was needed on the firing line. Within seconds of his departure the dugout was obliterated by enemy machine gunfire. Eighteen bullet holes in the dugout were reminders of what might have been.[24]

GRAVES REGISTRATION

Identifying dead bodies on the field after a battle makes for gruesome, depressing work, but somebody's got to do it. Straight-away following graduation, Walter Maner (Bud) was off for training at Columbus, Ohio and San Antonio, Texas, and then put on a Liberty Ship for the 30-day trip across the ocean to New Guinea. There, surprise of all surprises, he found his tentmate was a buddy with whom he had gone all the way through school from kindergarten through college.

Bud described himself as an "undertaker," for it was his grisly assignment as a member of a Graves Registration Company to traverse the battlefields attempting to find dogtags or some other personal belongings that would serve to identify the lifeless bodies abandoned on the battlefields. During his next assignment he was sent to Luzon in the Philippines, where the fierce fighting had left hundreds of hapless victims and no place to bury their remains. It was left to Bud and his men to "confiscate" a plot of land, create a "cemetery," and make sure the bodies were as properly interred as the facilities at hand allowed. Once Bud and his company reached Manila, there was a brief respite before General MacArthur asked them to go on an expedition to the Bataan Peninsula to trace the path of the Bataan Death March victims and to identify the bodies of those who had died along the way.

The job was not any easy one. The Death March, one recalls, took its toll on hundreds of American soldiers who were too weak and too ill to make the enforced 60-mile walk to San Fernando. Scores were carried or dragged by their comrades along the march, others were too far gone and simply fell by the wayside and had to be abandoned. Compassionate Filipinos in the tiny villages along the way had tried to bury some of the bodies that were strewn along the road. By the time Bud and his men arrived, it was extremely difficult to locate the simple unmarked graves that now were covered over and almost obscured. By calling a meeting in the center of each little village, Bud and his company were able to enlist the help of the Filipino natives in recovering and attempting to find information identifying the bodies that the kindly villagers had laid to rest in hastily dug graves. Appalling though the job was, the Graves Registration crew took heart in their good fortune—the fact that they had not been among the ill-fated walkers on that notorious death march.[25]

CHAPTER 6

Tragedy at Sea

One of the most tragic episodes of the war surely had to be the sinking of the USS *Indianapolis* shortly after midnight on July 30, 1945, in the Philippine Sea some 600 miles from Leyte. The story of the disaster is a long involved account, the record of men reportedly "killed in action" who in truth were "killed by inaction." Space here allows for only the briefest retelling by some of the survivors of those traumatic hours.

After dropping off her top secret cargo (which the crew later learned contained important components of the atomic bomb) at Tinian, and after a short stop at Guam, the cruiser *Indianapolis* was proceeding unescorted through what were assumed to be safe, enemy free waters to Leyte. It was thought to be a routine trip. However, shortly before midnight, the ill-fated *Indianapolis* was sighted by a prowling Japanese I-58 submarine. Within minutes Japanese Captain Hashimoto fired six torpedoes, two of which unerringly found their mark on the starboard bow and underneath the bridge of the *Indianapolis*. Within 12 minutes the *Indianapolis* had disappeared from view into the dark waters of the Philippine Sea. Of the 1,197 men on board, some 880 men deftly jumped, stepped, or walked off the decks of the rapidly vanishing ship. As a result of a gigantic snafu in responsibilities, the failure of the *Indianapolis* to berth in Leyte on July 31st was given only casual attention, and for five interminable days the seamen were abandoned to the frigid, shark-infested waters. As the hours dragged on, one man after another succumbed to shark attacks; salt water nausea; ulcers, open wounds, and burns; a blistering sun; or withering, water-logged life jackets, until finally, on the fifth day, only 317 men survived to be rescued.

Jerry Mitchell, Seaman First Class, recalled that the watches had just changed that night, and he had climbed up to his station on the main deck where he was assigned the manning of a five-inch gun. Suddenly, a thunderous explosion rocked the ship. A volcano of timber and metal erupted skyward, instantaneously showering the decks with fire and debris. Walls of flames sealed the fate of men in the crew's quarters below deck, while topside men ran for their very lives to escape the fires that were ravenously devouring everyone and everything in their paths. Clearly the *Indianapolis* had taken a direct hit, and within minutes the ship began listing. With the communication systems knocked out by the crash it was hopeless to try to call for an "Abandon Ship!"

Chaos reigned supreme. It was every man for himself. For Jerry Mitchell, with fires everywhere, his only avenue of escape appeared to be to crawl along the side of the ship and then into the water. The plan was a good one until suddenly Jerry became entangled in a loosened rope that tripped him up and snake-like wrapped around his leg. The next few moments were a blur for Jerry. In retrospect, Jerry reasons he actually must have gone down with the ship but thanks to the miracle of being caught in an air bubble, he surfaced and survived. Now in command of his faculties, Jerry found himself a block or two away from the ship, where looking back he could still see the propellers turning as the ship descended into the murky depths.

Alone in the pitch-black night, Jerry frantically floundered among crates of potatoes and pieces of debris, all the while vomiting up the saltwater he had unavoidably ingested. In a great stroke of luck, out of the eerie darkness came the sound of men yelling to him from a life raft a few feet ahead. A few speedy strokes, and he was quickly hauled aboard. Moments later he and the two half-drowned occupants of the raft located two more men. Soon a few other small life rafts were spotted floating nearby. By tying the overcrowded, nearly submerged rafts together, despite being half submerged themselves, the little group managed to stay afloat. A large net that had floated free from the ship had been a godsend for some 140 to 150 men who had found their way to the life net and were clinging to its ropes with death grips.[1]

Also onboard the *Indy* that fateful night, Richard Thelen, Seaman Second Class, continues to be haunted by the explosion. As he was sleeping topside on the *Indy*, a relief from the stifling heat of his sleeping quarters two levels below, he was awakened by a blast that sent him Heavenward. Only partially recovered, Dick was knocked down by the second explosion. As the ship pitched to the starboard side and the water inched up to his knees, Dick made a desperate effort to swim away from the ship to avoid being sucked under as the ship went down. Years later he laughingly commented: "I didn't jump off; the ship left me."[2]

Convinced that they would be rescued as soon as the authorities realized that the *Indianapolis* had failed to appear in Leyte, the men weathered the first hours and even the first two days with, if not confidence, then at least with bravado. As the hours wore on, however, the salt water began its blistering deviltry, chaffing open wounds and abrading tender skin around mouths, ears, and eyes. Drinking the salt water or inadvertently ingesting too much of it was the death knell for hundreds of men who succumbed within two or three hours of their folly. In the sky above an unrelenting sun blackened the scalps, faces, and arms that the ubiquitous spreads of fuel oil had not already discolored. Jerry Mitchell was not alone in experiencing a frightening, temporary blindness as a result of the fuel oil gouging his eyes.

And yet, the merciless sun, saltwater, and fuel oil were the least of it. The real enemy proved to be the appearance of voracious sharks that dispersed blinding terror throughout the group as they nosed about delighting in bruising legs and snatching a limb or two, or even the whole torso of their hapless victims. All around were dead bodies floating among the waves, many to abruptly disappear beneath the waters as a shark ravenously clasped his jaws around dinner.

THE HOURS AND DAYS GO BY

Hour after hour passed, and still there was no sign of a rescue ship. Each day without food or water left the men more and more weakened and distraught. Frantic yelling and wild waving to planes overhead went unheard and unnoticed by otherwise preoccupied pilots. Each day, as their life jackets leaked air and took in water, the men sank farther and farther into the sea. Water that was waist high the first day had soon inched up to their shoulders by the third day, and by day five, the men were finding it difficult to keep their chins above the waterline. Richard Thelen survived thanks to parts of three lifejackets: the one he grabbed as the ship was sinking, another salvaged from a dead seaman, and one that miraculously floated by within reach.

Hallucinating was rife, and it became impossible to restrain traumatized men from happily swimming off to an island that they were convinced was only a short distance away. Others, never to reappear, dived down to start the ship's engines, to get a drink of fresh water, or a glass of orange juice. A group of 25 elected to swim to Leyte and were never heard from again. In their hallucinations, the men often pummeled their fellow crewmen, one insisting that his shipmate had swiped the keys to his car. One seaman swam away to aid a woman he was convinced was having a difficult time in childbirth and needed help desperately. Another was sure his little group was surrounded by Arabs on camels. One man spotted a rootbeer stand open and just waiting for customers. Survivors remembered having witnessed unspeakable acts of vampirism and even cannibalism as men became deranged by thirst and excruciating hunger. The screams of the men snuffed out by shark attacks, the despairing moans of men speculating on, "What is my wife going to do without me?" "What will become of my kids?" sent chills down the spines of even unmarried, heretofore swaggering, self-sufficient 17-year-olds.

Floaters and men clinging to the life rafts sent promises Heavenward to stop smoking, attend church more regularly, stop swearing. At least two men promised to give their lives to the church—and kept their promises after the war and became ministers. Bob Gause called his time in the water his "109th-hour conversation with the Lord."[3] Some even prayed to die. Death seemed a welcome relief to their agony.

An officer, Gause remembered, began a prayer, "and told the Lord where we were and why he didn't want to die. He had things he wanted to do at home. Everybody that prayed, prayed virtually the same thing. "When it came my turn," Gause wrote, "I corrected our location to the Lord, since I'd been keeping the log, and prayed about the same thing as the others."[4]

Hope and patience were both wearing despairingly thin when miraculously on the fifth day a pilot, Lieutenant Wilbur Charles Gwinn, swooped down out of the sky to investigate what looked like an oil spill that he observed on the ocean below him. Only then were the woeful, rapidly disappearing islands of seamen discovered. Within hours his report sent planes and ships converging on the pitiful scattering of men spread over a distance of some 120 miles.

On assignment patrolling the Philippine Sea searching for Japanese submarines, Ensign Peter Wren, hometown Buffalo, New York, heard the announcement over the speaker system, "Proceed with all possible haste for unknown subjects in the water." At that moment his ship the USS *Bassett* was 10 hours away from the "unknown objects" and no one had any idea as for what or for whom they were looking.

As Peter and his men finally approached the human floes, the bedraggled, half-deranged men appeared to be a cloud or perhaps an oil slick on the water. Suddenly, oil- and sun-blackened faces and parts of shark-eaten bodies became discernible amid the six- to eight-foot waves. In the dark of midnight, however, it was almost impossible to determine which men were alive and which men had died. Most were comatose, Peter Wren, explained.[5]

These tiny clusters of men milling about in the dusky waters were a complete mystery to their deliverers. Who were they? Where did they come from? What were they doing thrashing about in the six- to ten-foot swells? Early on the rescuers were warned that these men might well be Japanese navymen engaged in a ruse to kill off a few more Americans. The faces of the men were so besmirched from the fuel oil that at first there was a real question about their nationality. Officers suggested that rescuers ask at least two questions to determine whether the men really were Americans.

Ensign Jack Broser, of Brooklyn, New York, a member of the LCVP USS *Bassett* rescue ship, as a precautionary measure, leveled his 45 pistol at the bewildering collection of humanity clinging to the floater net. His first question brusquely demanded the name of their ship. However, the quick response "The *Indianapolis*," was only partially convincing. The answer to the second question was critical. "Ok, men, now, what city do the Dodgers play baseball in?" A hearty "Brooklyn!" resounded from the men. There was no further delay. "It's ok," Broser shouted to the rescuers, "they're Americans all right. Pick 'em up guys—and hurry!"[6]

Some of the most heartrending tragedies were the deaths of men who within minutes of their rescue sank beneath the waves from exhaustion and dehydration. Spotting a life raft about 100 yards away that had been dropped from Gwinn's plane, Dick Thelen and three of his buddies struck out to reach the raft. Dick was the only one who made it. The other three died of exhaustion in the attempt. At that point, Dick was too weak to be able to climb up on the raft and secured himself by tying himself to the raft.[7]

Too weak to handle the ropes that were lowered to rescue them, not a few men had to be basket-lifted to a ship's deck. Burned skin broke lose in the hands of rescuers as they groped for a secure hold on the arms and legs of the survivors they were carrying to safety. "It was a nightmarish scene," the men recalled. Even hardened sailors aboard the rescue ships openly wept as the oily, emaciated half-dead bodies were brought onboard. Those who cringed at the sight were admonished, "Come on, get with it. It's not going to get any better."[8] Jerry Mitchell remembered weighing 165 pounds before his ordeal. He was down to 118 pounds when he was finally rescued.[9]

Ensign Peter Wren, an officer aboard the USS *Bassett*, one of the early rescue ships on the scene and a member of one of the LCVPs that was lowered to assist the survivors, wrote of attempting to lift a water-soaked survivor over the gunwale of the rolling and pitching craft. "This man lets out a scream of agony that would pierce a mother's heart. I feel like I am pulling his flesh and muscle away from the bone. I let go quickly and grab on to the life jacket and continue to lift him while waiting for the next wave to assist me."

"My next survivor," Wren continued, "which I have a good hold on his life jacket, decides I am a Jap trying to capture him and he commences to flail his arms at my head as the gunwale is protecting my body. He clobbers me pretty good but I managed to get him in the LCVP."[10] Obviously, at first the survivors were as wary of their saviors as the rescuers were of them. Wren recalled the heroism of Jack Broser who dove over the side of his LCVP to swim after and retrieve a man who resisted rescue thinking that he was being captured by the Japanese. (One should remember that the water was alive with sharks. Jerry Mitchell reported that the sharks went wild, churning up the waters, as the rescuers completed their mission of mercy. Could they possibly have sensed that their meal tickets were fast disappearing?)[11]

That there were as many survivors as there were was probably due to the fact that many of the *Indy's* crew were heretofore hale and hardy young 17- and 18-year-olds. For many of them, their total time at sea had consisted of 17 days, 5 of which they spent in the Philippine Sea clinging to life from ropes tied to a life net. To what, other than strong bodies, did the men attribute their survival? There were dozens of answers: prayer; divine intervention; sheer determination; luck; predisaster swimming ability; their youth; Chuck Gwinn, "their angel"; Adrian Marks having disobeyed orders and landing his PBY in the open sea; aid from a buddy; aid from an unidentified fellow seaman; the crews of the rescue ships; and the doctors and nurses at the hospitals.

Heroes? You better believe it! *Indianapolis* survivors continue to be unending in their praise for the pilots and crewmen from the rescue ships and planes who so courageously jumped into the shark-filled waters and swam about to rescue men too weak to swim or move. Without question, survivors achieved instantaneous hero status in giving up their semisafe place on a raft, as did Jerry Mitchell and other crewmen, and regularly trading places for hours on end with a fellow sailor who was gripping a rope on the side and immersed in a game of life and death with sharks.

Lyle "Duke" Pasket was overcome with the realization that they had been saved and promptly "passed out once I got on board." "A PBY," he noted, "spotted other survivors in the area and landed in their midst. The plane's crew eventually fished out 56 men who perched on the plane's wings, its hull, and crammed inside until the USS *Doyle* could move into that area and take those men aboard. That PBY crew were heroes to us that day."[12] Jerry Mitchell corroborated "Duke's" praise for the PBY crew who kept diving into the water again and again to recover the men who were so weakened that they kept slipping off the wings of the plane and into the sharked waters. As he was pulled aboard the PBY and transferred to the USS *Doyle*, Stan Wisniewski overheard two doctors and a nurse deciding that he probably was not going to make it, and he was administered last rites. Thanks to antibiotics and tender nursing care, a most grateful Stan did make it![13]

Although untrained for such a disaster, the seamen aboard the rescue ships were incredible in providing TLC for the survivors. On board the *Bassett*, for example, one-third of the crew of 206 maintained the mandatory ship's watch, while the rest of the men took over an almost a one-on-one bedside vigil with their more than 150 survivors.[14]

In all, the USS *Bassett* gathered up 152 survivors, the USS *Doyle*, 93, the USS *Talbot* 24 (there is a slight discrepancy in the exact number of men each ship picked up), for a total of 317. From the rescue ships, many of the men were taken to the Medical Facility on Samar, others to Peleliu and then to a hospital in Guam before finally being returned to the States.

Robert Rubert, a radio operator on one of the planes that transported sur-vivors to Guam, remembered the disorientation of the *Indy* men who knew not who they were, where they were, or where they had been.[15] During their recuperation, the *Indy* survivors learned, as noted, that their stop on Tinian three days before the sinking of their ship had been to drop off vital components of the atomic bombs that would be dropped on Hiroshima and Nagasaki and lead to the formal surrender of the Japanese on Sep-tember 2, 1945, less than a month after their harrowing ordeal. (Survivors were incensed to note that newspapers carried headlines of the Japanese surrender and only a brief news story at the bottom of the page informed the public for the first time that the *Indianapolis* had been sunk.)

BLAME FOR THE TRAGEDY?

Who would take the blame for the sinking and the appalling loss of life? A lengthy trial beginning in December of 1945 resulted in a court-martial for Captain Charles B. McVay III, the chief charges being that he did not order a zigzag course for the *Indianapolis* and did not call for an abandon ship in time. (Actually, many authorities think a zigzag course attracts more attention and often does more harm than good. Even Captain Mochitsura who had been in command of the villainous Japanese submarine and was brought to the United States for the trial, testified that zigzagging would have in no way saved the *Indianapolis* from the torpedo hits. Furthermore, McVay was never informed of any submarine action in the area. With the communication systems out it would have been almost impossible to order an abandon ship that could be heard throughout the *Indy*.) Much essential information that would have cleared McVay was omitted from the trial. Jerry Mitchell, Richard Thelen, and many of the *Indianapolis* survivors—perhaps all—felt that McVay was given a hatchet job and that he was used as a scapegoat and should never have been court-martialed in the first place. "We would've rode to hell with Captain McVay," one survivor insisted.

At the first reunion of the survivors in 1960, McVay was greatly appre-hensive about meeting with his former crew. Would his reception be a chilly one? Did his men hold him responsible for the sinking? How did they really feel about him, now, 15 years after their harrowing experience? As he emerged from the plane, it was impossible for McVay to choke back the tears. There lining the runway were the *Indy*'s survivors, each man saluting, each man's cheeks wet with his own tears.[16] The men worked tirelessly to clear McVay's name. On October 12, 2000, an amendment was passed by Congress that exonerated McVay, but it was too late. In the ensuing years after his court-martial, McVay was plagued by the stigma of the trial and the hate mail that continued unending from parents of sons lost at sea. Throughout the years and especially at Christmastime, McVay received hundreds upon hundreds of cards and letters from parents, brothers, and sisters accusing McVay of being responsible for the deaths of their loved ones. Finally, McVay could stand it no longer. On November 6, 1968, Charles McVay put a gun to his head and pulled the trigger. On that day, yet another casualty was added to the long list of victims of the *Indianapolis* disaster.

THE MENTAL SCARS

Peter Wren recalled, "Although more than fifty years have passed I can still see our crew of young faces laboring with the task before them. I can still see those oily blackened faces in the sea and I can hear their cries of agony. When we sing the Navy Hymn I still well up when we come to the last line 'For those in peril on the sea.' It will never leave me."[17]

For years afterward, Jerry Mitchell had nightmares about his experiences and to this day steadfastly refuses to watch movies or TV shows that portray violence. One summer in July 2002, when watching a film that suddenly began depicting shipwrecks on the Great Lakes, Jerry became traumatized, exited the theater, and waited for his friends outside. His ordeal, he believes, actually had a positive side in that in the long run it has made him more compassionate, more loving in later life. Even today, although Jerry loves to fish, he refuses to go out of sight of land.[18]

One of the *Indy*'s survivors, Tom Goff, explained that after his horrendous experience, he "takes only showers these days." He had "all the time he will ever need soaking some fifty plus years ago."[19] For similar reasons, another survivor confessed that he had been swimming only once since the disaster. A chaplain who recited the "Lord's Prayer" over the bodies of the deceased as they were pushed out to sea admitted that even now he can never bear to hear that prayer without weeping.

It took seven years before Richard Thelen was able to talk about his ordeal, even to his wife. In time, comrades at the *Indy* survivors' reunions finally encouraged Dick to open up about his experiences. In recent years, Dick has given hundreds of talks to students informing them of the realities of war and the supreme sacrifices made by men and women in World War II to ensure their freedom. He credits his swimming ability, honed as a member of his junior high school swim team, with having greatly contributed to his survival and encourages young people to take advantage at an early age of swimming instruction at schools and pools. How was he able to hold up under such horrendous odds when so many others failed? His father had had to sign for Dick because he was only 17 when he enlisted. Prayers and the image of his father's face as he bid him goodbye at the railroad station kept him going. "I want you to come back," his father had insisted. "Every time I was ready to give up, I saw my dad's face there."

Not a day passes that Richard Thelen does not think about his ordeal. Nightmares murdered his sleep for years. Today, even a glass of water or the smell of tar from a roofing job can trigger chills and palpitations. Unwilled, remembrances keep cropping up of that fateful day in the spring of 1945 while stationed in Shoemaker, California, when several hundred seamen were lined up and ordered to count off—one-two-one-two—down the line. All the "ones" were sent to the USS *New Jersey* at Bremerton, Washington, and the "twos" went to the USS *Indianapolis* at Mare Island.[20]

Most of the survivors admitted that sleepless nights and daily thoughts of the tragedy continue to plague their survival. At least one seaman wondered if those who died at sea had actually been the most fortunate in not having to battle bouts of deep depression and survivor's guilt. "I know that only death will bring peace to me by blocking my mind of these horrors," Cozell Smith wrote. "I sometimes think that my shipmates who were killed or eaten by sharks were the lucky ones. We who were left have had almost fifty years of mental pain. After 50 years, dates and faces lose their distinction, but the horror never goes away. I suffer long periods of depression and I cannot shake the feeling. The older I get the more it bothers me."[21] Louis D. Campbell's daughter wrote: "Part of my dad went down with her [the *Indianapolis*]. He was never the same, physically or mentally."[22]

On the brighter side, Herb Miner wrote: "It gave me a greater degree of self-confidence. It also made me more tolerant of life's many *un*important problems and more appreciative of life's simple pleasures."[23] "I learned a hell of a lot about life and death from that experience," Dick Thelen admitted. "After that I looked at life completely differently." The "me first" attitude died long ago, and since the war his life has been devoted to helping other people and meting out respect and compassion to all of his fellow men. Some measure of satisfaction has derived from his extensive volunteer activities. When he gave some vague thought to re-enlisting, Dick's mother became so unglued that Dick immediately abandoned the idea.[24]

Historians and veterans, of course, are prone to ponder the "ifs" of life: "What would have happened if . . ." In *The Pacific Campaign,* author Dan van der Vat reflected: "The unforgivable carelessness on the U.S. Navy's part is bad enough; one can only speculate how differently history might look had I58 caught the unlucky ship on her way *into* Tinian. The US nuclear stockpile at that time consisted of two bombs, with scant prospect of a third for some months."[25]

A sidelight, but one that surely should be included with the memoirs of the *Indy's* survivors, was another much happier drama unfolding thousands of miles away. Buried in Gus Kay's personal account of his survival of the tragedy was a heart-warming story that surely warrants recounting.

Eager to sign up with the Navy, Gus had forged his mother's signature on his enlistment papers in order to enable him to volunteer at 16 years of age. As a teenager a long, long way from home, Gus sorely missed his family back in the States. Years later, Gus wrote that while he was struggling for survival during the *Indianapolis* disaster, back at home, "my Greek born-mother went to get her citizenship papers. The judge asked her many questions about the United States. She could not answer. All she could reply was, 'I don't know.' The judge said. 'If you cannot answer these questions then you cannot get your citizenship papers.' Then (in desperation) the judge asked her, 'How many stars are on the American Flag?' She replied, 'There are three stars.' The judge said, 'If there are 48 states why are there only three stars?' My mother said that the President of the United States had sent her a flag with three stars for her three sons fighting overseas." There were no more questions as the judge immediately gave the order to "Give this lady her citizenship papers—and take her out to dinner."[26]

A DEADLY FOE

On occasion, nature proved to be a more deadly foe than gunfire, bombs, or murderous kamikaze planes. Typhoons, of course were the bete noire of seamen, and violent storms took no holiday during the war years. Men, such as Harry George, who aboard the Attack Transport the USS *Eastland*, weathered the monstrous typhoons in the Pacific and watched in horror as their ship heaved with the swells, lurched, almost turned over, and gave the men serious concerns about their survival. Whether they should jump, believing that the ship was about to go down, or wait around and hope for survival became a life and death choice.[27] Asked about war's most terrifying moments, Hall Tennis summed them up succinctly in saying one's days in a Pacific typhoon "were probably as impressive as anything a war can provide."[28]

It was terrifying enough to be aboard a ship rolling and pitching in 30-foot waves; consider for a moment being on board an airplane being buffeted by unrelenting rain and winds that threatened to demolish the plane and its hapless crew. Forget about parachuting out or finding a safe landing on an aircraft carrier. Being caught in a typhoon in the Pacific was by far the worst experience of his life, Radio Operator Robert Rubert claimed. Once their pilot realized he was unable to circle the typhoon, the crew were in for a wild ride in blinding rain and winds up to 130 miles per hour. The storm, Bob feared, would surely shear off the wings and turn the plane upside down. The aerial had to be disconnected for fear of a lightning strike; the radar was useless; it was impossible to see any stars and consequently the navigator was at a loss to even guess at their position. Bob said he and the crew never prayed so hard in their lives. Here they were totally lost in the middle of the Pacific. (Bob still has nightmares thinking about their near disaster.)

Once they emerged from the storm, the next big problem was to find a landing field before they ran out of gas. Finally, they spotted a tiny island,

and fortunately there was an airfield—but was the airstrip held by friend or foe? After several circles around the island, they discovered it was Eni-wetock, an atoll recently captured by the Allies. Terra firma, no doubt, never looked so good.[29]

In one of the most savage typhoons in the Pacific on December 18, 1944, the storm claimed 790 officers. Three destroyers, the USS *Hull*, the USS *Spence,* and the USS *Monaghan,* capsized and disappeared beneath the waves. In addition, over 100 aircraft were lost as a result of fires, collisions, or ocean swells. According to Captain C. Raymond Calhoun, 3 light carriers, 2 escort carriers, and 1 cruiser suffered major damage, and 19 other ships escaped with lesser damages.[30]

During the course of the typhoon, waves up to 60-feet high buffeted ships, turned over others, and indiscriminately swept men overboard. In the distance, the ominous shout of "man overboard" resounded from ship after ship. Mountainous waves and high winds added up to almost zero visibility and the very real possibility of a collision with another ship. Some ships rolled 70 degrees or more and yet miraculously survived. The electrical power on ships went out along with radio contact. Planes broke loose from their moorings and skidded across the deck, into each other, and into the ocean. The loss of 32 planes that had been swept overboard from the flight deck of the *Cape Esperance* no doubt lightened her load and saved her from certain disaster.[31] Smoke stacks fell and crashed onto the decks as well as onto unsuspecting seamen. Even the optimists turned pessimistic as steering became impossible and ships were "in irons" unable to maneuver. The *Hull,* the *Spence,* and the *Monaghan* jettisoned seamen into the ocean where a few lucky ones feebly held on to a raft or a life net as they bobbed against the waves.

Joseph C. McCrane, Water tender Second Class, a survivor of the sinking of the USS *Monaghan,* wrote of being washed off the ship and wildly thrashing about in the murky waters as the ship gradually disappeared from sight. Thanks to a buddy's voice signaling him to grab onto a raft, McCrane and 13 other men struggled to keep afloat amid the gigantic billows. Lifejackets offered only temporary protection, and the chance of being rescued seemed slim indeed. Sharks circling the survivors looking for dinner added to the terror of the night.[32]

A. S. Krauchunas, a survivor of the USS *Spence,* described a similar experience as his ship capsized and went down.

Upon sliding into the water, I swam towards a floater net, which was adrift at least twenty yards away. I picked up a life jacket in the water and put it on. I reached the floater net, which contained approximately twenty to twenty-five men, and the net floated back to the ship, which by this time was completely capsized. The men struggled to push the net away from the hull. Soon the *Spence* was shut off from our view by the gusts of wind and rain. The net was turned over completely and men were shaken off, including myself. I was pulled beneath the surface for a great length of time. . . I finally broke the surface and saw the floater net twenty yards away. I reached it and found that several men had not returned. The storm was so severe that one could not face directly into the wind. After what seemed several hours . . . an inflated yellow rubber raft came floating by. Two or three of the men inflated it and jumped in. . . . The yellow raft was immediately blown out of sight and we were left alone again.[33]

As the USS *Hull* heeled over and capsized, some 100 unfortunate members of her crew of 263 met a watery death trapped below decks. Of those who managed to make it into the inky waters, some found temporary asylum by grasping onto three life rafts that had floated free of the ship. Others, with only lifejackets for support, somehow braved—or succumbed to—the ravenous waves that sought to devour them.[34]

At first rescuers discovered survivors almost by accident when a small light or a sharp whistle from the watery depths below alerted a ship to a fellow seaman in peril for his life. Immediately after the first survivors were rescued and word of the sinkings came to light, rescue ships in the vicinity banned together to make an intensive search to locate more survivors. Ships' crews lined up against the rails anxiously scanning the water for signs of life; however, the darkness and the violence of the storm made rescue work a hazardous, almost impossible task.

Unquestionably the heroes of the days—and nights—were the courageous, stalwart swimmers from the rescue ship the USS *Tabberer* (Louis A. Purvis and Howard J. Korth) who selflessly dove into the water to bodily lift seamen too weak to maneuver themselves to the safety of the ship. Despite the possibility of being detected by Japanese subs, Lieutenant Commander Henry Plage of the *Tabberer* threw caution to the wind and every 10 minutes turned on the ship's giant searchlights in an attempt to discover more survivors. (Plague was awarded the navy's Legion of Merit for his heroic service. Other rescue ships included the USS *Robert F. Keller,* the USS *Cogswell,* and the USS *Brown.*) By the conclusion of the search on the 22nd of December, 98 officers and men had been pulled from the waters. The devastating loss of life and the costly ship and airplane damage of the December 18, 1944, typhoon in the Pacific were attributed to problems of weather forecasting, command errors. and ship stability.[35]

Bill Emerson, Seaman First Class, pointed to the precarious situation of the USS *Buchanan* in the December typhoon as recorded in the ship's log. "The mountainous seas lifted screws and rudder out of the water and sent *Buchanan* rolling 50 degrees to port. Vent ducts on the port side and the forced draft blower intakes at the base of the stacks became submerged. Water poured into engine rooms and fire rooms; 20mm and 40mm gun shields clogged with water; provisions accumulated on the port side.

All hands jettisoned stores and punctured gun shields with axes while *Buchanan* hung with maximum power on engines."

Suddenly a voice on the speaker system ordered "all hands to starboard." This added weight, probably saved the ship from capsizing, Bill remembered. It was a scary time and, according to Bill, the sheer terror of the ship's possible rollover, "turned a lot of seamen to religion, at least for a short time."[36]

Lt. Ralph Moulton, meteorologist aboard the USS *San Jacinto,* was intricately involved in the December 18th typhoon where his ship "was tossed about like a match stick." "Spare engines, aircraft, and other rubble broke loose in the hangar deck, and crashed again and again into the bulkheads, severing ventilation ducts, wiring, and water pipes." It was a frightening experience as "the mountainous waves rolled the ship more than 30 degrees each way, repeatedly submerging the damaged ductwork and permitting a vast amount of seawater to pour down to the lower decks and engine room." Flooding problems were merely part of the problem, however. "Additional threats to survival erupted when broken wiring set fire to the oil and gasoline soaked debris. Heroic efforts of the ship's officers and crew eventually quenched the fire." Many hours later, the *San Jacinto* emerged from the killer typhoon with 30 members of the crew injured, but fortunately none seriously.

"It was a harrowing time," Ralph commented. "This long drawn out experience almost made a kamikaze attack seem like a walk in the park." Ralph's ship was involved in yet another typhoon that caused serious damage but "without quite the excitement of the previous storm." To be sure, weather studies and radar advances in the years following the war have greatly reduced the destructive forces of typhoons. Nevertheless, Mother Nature still continues to vent her anger with malicious intent on land and on sea.[37]

The typhoon of December 18th was just one of many typhoons that took their toll of men and ships during the war. Not always was it the man behind the gun but instead Nature itself that was the determining factor between life and death. Cool hands saved the day when a sister ship to Bill Noonan's patrol frigate was dead in the water in the northern Philippines, the high waves of a typhoon having drowned out the boilers.[38] Without power, the ship was at the mercy of a wrathful King Neptune. Tossed about and dragged through the typhoon at least twice, the ship appeared doomed. In desperation, the crew gathered up every available scrap of wood and paper on board ship, stuffed them in the boilers, lit a blowtorch and fortunately built up enough power to at least get them out of the eye of the storm. When the ship finally tied up next to Bill's ship, Bill's crew were aghast at the destruction. The water and winds had bent back one-eighth inch steel like an orange peel. In a fortunate turn of events, although there were some broken bones and bloody lacerations, there miraculously was no loss of life. However, it was a reality lesson that sometimes typhoons can be mightier than either the pen or the sword.[39]

As if the frigid temperatures of the Aleutians were not torment enough, nature heaped insult upon insult with her violent storms. Having unloaded their troops on January 12, 1943, the crew of the USS *Worden* were making their way out of the harbor into the Bering Sea when a violent storm blew up, buffeting their ship between the rocky sides of the channel until "it cut open the ship like a can opener." In answer to the immediate call to "abandon ship," Yeoman Paul Gillesse, quickly grabbed the ship's service records, stepped over the side into the icy waters, and swam to the nearest rescue ship, the USS *Dewey*. Chances for survival in the freezing waters were abysmal at best and once aboard, Paul joined the *Dewey* crew scanning the waters for more survivors. At least one very fortunate seaman owed his life to Paul as Paul yelled out, "Hey, there's the old man," and the unconscious captain was pulled from what would have been certain death. Despite the closeness of several rescue ships, 14 members of the crew died from overexposure. Mother Nature was having her way again.[40]

One tends to forget that in addition to nature's vengeance, German submarine warfare was wreaking havoc with merchant ships in the Atlantic, particularly during the early months of the war. "In the month of January alone (1942) 43 ships were sent to the bottom of the sea, with the loss of more than a thousand lives."[41] Bill Noonan, essentially involved in the patrolling operations, told of hundreds of ships being lost in the south Atlantic during the four months after Pearl Harbor.[42] The Germans were sinking merchant ships faster than the United States could build them. The U.S. ships had no protection, and citizens on the coast failed to dim their lights and thus made it possible for the enemy to move in close to shore without being spotted. The demand for more ships and the vigilant patrolling of the waters along the eastern seaboard were critical. Finally, the initiation of a system of convoy ships and air coverage helped reduce the German threat.

CHAPTER 7

German POW Camps

CAPTURE AND IMPRISONMENT

For those airmen whose planes were shot down by enemy gunfire, the order (or need) to "bail out" was merely the first step in possible survival. The parachute had to open, the enemy gunfire had to miss both parachute and parachutist, the landing had to be successful, and one had to be fortunate enough not to be shot summarily upon landing. Paul Van Oordt's grueling ordeal of bailout, capture, and imprisonment was re-enacted ad infinitum as enemy gunfire and flack brought down airmen by the thousands in Europe.

In mid-1943, Paul Van Oordt had to complete only three more missions before he would be sent home. Actually, he was scheduled to go on R and R and not even be on the flight (an escort mission to a site near Naples) when his plane took a direct hit that knocked out the right engine on August 20, 1943. As the plane became engulfed in flames, Van bailed out, waited until he could no longer hear the plane's single motor, and for the first time in his life pulled the ripcord on a parachute. His parachute opened, and 12,000 to 15,000 feet later, he was deposited on a mountaintop near Mount Vesuvius. Torturous burns incurred during his bailout and pulled tendons rendered him unable to walk.

As he struggled to disengage himself from his parachute, he suddenly found himself eyeballing two gun barrels aimed squarely at his head and wielded by two burly, zealous Italians (probably civilians as they were not in uniform). Any confrontation on Paul's part was, of course, useless, and his captors immediately dragged him off to the Italian authorities, then to a small village jail, from which he was dispatched to Rome and thrown into solitary confinement. Days later he was put in a room with several other prisoners. There, his captors hoped that the men would talk among themselves so they could glean intelligence that their ceaseless interrogation sessions had failed to yield.

Just how effectively the German–Italian intelligence system had been working came as a surprise to Van and other prisoners. In some instances the Germans seemed to know more about the Allies' activities than even the Americans themselves knew. Van remained mute, but he was indeed shocked when, during one of the interrogations, Van was shown a picture of a captured P-38. In it Van recognized one of his classmates!

Frustrated when the men failed to divulge any further information than the required "name, rank, and serial number," their interrogators gave up, and Van and several other men were sent to a regular prison in Pesaro. There the prisoners were "treated" to straw mattresses spread out on the floor and fed a so-called balanced diet that included figs for breakfast and cheese for lunch. Once the Italians capitulated in early September 1943, Van and his comrades became German prisoners.

As the men were being transferred from Pesaro to Stalag VII-A, near Moosburg, a small town in Austria, the prisoners were moved by train, in boxcars where for six days each man was sardined into five feet of space, and where there were no toilet facilities save a hole at the end of the car. At Bolzano in the Brenner Pass, American pilots, unaware that the train was carrying American prisoners, accidentally dropped bombload after bombload aimed at the train in an attempt to thwart the Germans by destroying a river bridge. Van and the other prisoners, knowing that if they remained it meant certain death, made a valiant, life-or-death effort to escape and finally succeeded in breaking out of the boxcars. In short order they were rounded up and sent to Stalag VII-A. By now Van had decided that seeing the war from the air had been a blessing rather than meeting the enemy face to face. From Stalag VII-A, the men were sent to yet another prison camp, Stalag Luft III near Sagan, Poland, 60 miles from Berlin, a camp where primarily Air Force officers were imprisoned.[1]

EACH MAN HAS A STORY TO TELL

When James Edward Clark was shot down near Braunschweig, Germany on May 8, 1944, upon hitting the ground he was immediately surrounded by a posse of what he later decided were home guards. "Some of them had bugle-shaped old antique weapons. Some of them had pitch forks. They had everything. That posse had me, anyway."[2]

In 1944, while on a bombing mission over Vienna, Austria, James Moye, pilot of a B-24, and his crew, were forced to bail out when their plane was hit by enemy fire. On the ground, as Jim attempted to evade a posse of German soldiers that were scouring the countryside for him, he found a ditch and was crawling along when he suddenly "looked up the side and there was a pair of feet going along by the side with a gun shoved down at me. You know, your heart can be willing to run, but your feet freeze at a time like that, so I surrendered."[3]

During a bombing run over Budapest, Hungary, Patrick E. Carr, a native Mississippian and a gunner on a B-24 bomber during the war, was momentarily knocked unconscious when on his fortieth run, flack hit his plane and the explosion tore the plane in half. As the plane was spinning around, Pat regained consciousness, jumped out of the open end of the plane, and parachuted down amid the gunfire aimed at him and his parachute. "I really hadn't been afraid when I was shot down, not because I was brave, but [I] just didn't have time; I was rendered unconscious when the shell hit, and when I came to I had no difficulty in getting out, I bailed out. I really hadn't had time to assess things and really be conscious of the danger that was involved at the time. But when they started shooting, and I realized they were shooting at me, of course, I really got scared."

Bomber crews had been warned during their training that if you get shot down, "If you get in the hands of soldiers you are apparently, relatively safe, if it's civilians there's no telling what will happen to you." That warning proved true for Pat Carr when within seconds of being shot down a civilian accosted him with his rifle aimed and ready to shoot. Fortunately, a German soldier suddenly appeared and ordered the civilian to drop his rifle, an order that unquestionably saved Pat Carr's life.

As with other POWs, Pat was amazed at what his captors knew about him. During his interrogation, Pat refused to divulge more than the required name, rank, and serial number; however, the Germans already had a tremendous amount of information about him—even his age, schooling, and hometown. For his refusal to supply further information or to assent to or to deny any of their questions, he was sentenced to 19 days of solitary confinement.[4]

Robert E. Lee Eaton, a native Mississippian and Commander of the 451st Bomb Group, recalled his luck in not being killed on a run over Ploesti when an 88-millimeter shell "made a clean hole right smack through the cockpit." Missing his feet on the rudder pedal by inches, the shell "went right smack through the top. If the fuse had worked on that thing, we would have had a quick trip to heaven or wherever aviators go."[5]

On his seventeenth bombing mission (the target was a jet-aircraft factory) over Munich, Germany on July 11, 1944, radio operator Carl Moss' plane (a part of the 389th Bomb group) suffered immense flack damage, and the crew was ordered to bail out near Lille, France. In short order, Carl was captured by the Germans and sent through Brussels, to Frankfort, Germany, then to Dulag Luft Wetzler through Berlin, and finally to Grosstychow near the Baltic Sea. As Carl and his fellow prisoners departed the train, they were greeted by a menacing line of German guards well equipped with rifles and threatening police dogs. "Well, at least they're not going to kill us on the spot," Carl and his men thought. A few minutes later they were not so sure about their fate as just before they embarked the captain of the guards began yelling that they were gangsters and responsible for the bombing of the German cities and the killing of the women and children. Mass confusion broke out and the prisoners were chased by dogs and angry guards for a seven kilometer run up to their new camp Stalag Luft IV. Any of the men who fell behind were attacked by the vicious dogs; others were repeatedly jabbed by the guards with piercing strokes of their always-at-the-ready bayonets. "Suddenly shots were going off, the guards yelling, the dogs barking, and some POWs were screaming as they were getting jabbed with the bayonets and bitten by the dogs. I thought they were going to kill us." Carl believed he was fortunate to be hit only a few times when he fell back from the man in front of him. The next day more new prisoners were mercilessly chased up to the camp. Fortunately, a day later the National Red Cross paid a visit to the camp, and the savage chases appeared to be abandoned. This brutal treatment was simply a foretaste of what was to come in Stalag Luft IV.[6]

On May 24, 1944, Morris Williams' plane sustained a hit by enemy gunfire and burst into flames near Munster, Germany, on his forty-fifth combat mission. Morris bailed out and landed safely, but he was immediately captured. For the next few days Morris was kept on tenterhooks while his interrogators used every possible means, fair or foul, to extract information from him. A menacing German colonel insisted: "You are going to be shot as a spy because you have no identification unless you tell us what we want to know." Insisting on his right to reveal only his name, rank, and serial number, Morris grew more and more nervous as the colonel became more and more threatening. In time the exasperated colonel gave up, and Morris was returned to a cell and kept in solitary confinement. There his tension mounted by the hour until finally three days later, when the cell door opened, he could scarcely believe his good fortune when told that he was being sent to Stalag Luft III. "And that was the first I knew that they had not planned to kill me. I was really sweating that out because they really could have been perfectly within their rights to have shot me."[7]

As a bombardier flying bombing missions in a B-17 from Polebrook, England, over targets in Germany, Charles Boyd Woehrle, of Pine City, Minnesota, found his days in the air numbered. "At the stage of the air war over Europe we were in, we had to fly without fighter escort, a very risky business, as I soon learned." On May 29, 1943, following Chuck's fifth mission, a raid on St. Nazaire, France to wipe out the submarine pens there, his plane was hit by an anti-aircraft shell that exploded *inside* the plane—the bomb bay doors were still open. "It was a crippling hit," Chuck explained, and realizing their hopeless situation, the crew soberly watched the rest of their squadron fly away. "There was obviously nothing any other plane could do for us."

"As our plane began to lose altitude," Chuck continued, "German fighters rose to encircle us with flaming guns, killing four of our crew. The pilot gave the order to bail out, so I buckled on my parachute and went out the forward hatch." The exploding shell and the hail of enemy gunfire were the least of Chuck's worries when his parachute failed to open despite his frantic tugging at the ripcord. Finally able to pull out the small chute that triggered the main chute, Chuck felt the silk shoot open with a jolt that dislocated his shoulder and fractured his jaw—minor injuries, he concluded, compared to his fate in a free fall.

Things began looking up with a safe landing in the Bay of Biscay where he paddled around in his inflatable life vest until two French fishermen rescued him and took him to their nearby home. French hospitality was cut short, however, with the arrival within the hour of two German officers who had watched his descent, sighted his position, and arrived to escort him to the nearest Wehrmacht office in Vannes where he was imprisoned in a filthy medieval castle dungeon. Several days and several moves later, Chuck found himself in Lower Silesia, at Stalag Luft III. There he counted his blessings at being quartered among English RAF men. "They had been prisoners of war since 1939 and knew the ropes of survival. They were fine men," Chuck declared enthusiastically.[8]

Willis Emmanuel Eckholm, a paratrooper from Willmar, Minnesota, made his first combat jump on July 9, 1943 behind German lines in Sicily. Luckily, he escaped the disastrous friendly fire from Navy ships of the Seventh Fleet who thought that they were Germans and accidentally shot down hundreds of U.S. planes loaded with paratroopers. Minutes later, however, he and the members of his group were accidentally dropped in the middle of a German military post, two miles away from their proposed target. At that point, as he and his group attempted to open their chutes, German artillery fire opened up in earnest, the assault resulting in most of the men being either killed or wounded. Once again, the German intelligence was working overtime. "The first thing I heard was an English-speaking German officer. . . . 'You surprised us. We expected you two miles up the road.'" That was to have been their exact drop zone target.[9]

Jim Tyler told of his harrowing experiences on December 20, 1942, as a radio gunner with the 91st Bomb Group of Flying Fortresses headquartered in Basingstoke, England. There had been four consecutive briefings earlier that day regarding the target, Romilly-sur-Seine, a "refueling airdrome in France where enemy planes were refueled on their North Africa missions."

As they neared the target the crew grew increasingly nervous as they encountered heavy casualties as the enemy planes "started picking off, one by one, the bombers from the rear of the formation. The plane flying next in formation to our craft was singled out and the 20 millimeter shells from the guns of the FW-190s were so heavy that the tail section was soon sheared off and ten friends plunged headfirst to the ground to their deaths."

"Next in formation to receive the brutality of war" was Jim Tyler's plane. As the enemy fighters made repeated passes at the planes they "came so close that one could actually see the color of the Jerry pilot's eyes." In minutes, three of the four engines took hits and were set aflame. An explosion sent pieces of shrapnel into Jim's lung and body. Other hits took out the pilot, the engineer-top turret gunner, the tail gunner, and both waist gunners. The ball turret gunner also caught bullets.

With the order to "bail out," Jim strapped on his parachute, struggled out of the burning plane, jumped, and landed safely amidst a herd of cows. "Since I was unable to walk and was bleeding profusely, my only alternative was to await being picked up by the Gestapo to be carried to the American hospital in Paris for treatment. Soon the German guards arrived in a closed van, and the fear of my unknown destiny enveloped me—a genuine case of being in the wrong place at the wrong time." Following nine weeks of hospitalization in Paris, Jim was escorted to Dulag Luft at Frankfort, Germany.[10]

LIFE IN GERMAN POW CAMPS

Most POWs in both the German and Japanese prisoner of war camps had little good to say about their treatment by their captors. As a prisoner of war in Stalag XVII-B, Lamar Rodgers spoke for thousands of POWs when he portrayed his imprisonment as involving "the harshest, most cruel treatment, I guess, that anyone could imagine."[11] (The Japanese gave their POWS much harsher treatment considering the fact that almost seven times the number of prisoners in the Japanese prison camps died as in the German and Italian POW camps. The death rate was 4% in German and Italian camps and 27% in Japanese POW camps.)

Fear pervaded life in most of the camps—fear of being disciplined, beaten senseless, or shot dead for the least infringement of rules. In addition there was the very real fear of dying of starvation as a result of the inhumane food rations provided for their sustenance. The threat of death was a constant companion. As prisoners watched the death detail go by each day, there were grim thoughts about how many days it would be before they themselves would be carried out.

Jim Clark learned in a hurry that when their German captors said do something, "do it." Straight off, when Jim and his fellow prisoners were introduced to their POW barracks, the Germans instructed the men not to go in and out of the windows of the barracks and not to lean on them but to use the front door. When one man leaned his arm on the window in response to a call from a friend outside, the Germans shot him. "From then on we knew what they said they meant."[12]

Jim Tyler's account of his experiences in various German POW camps parallels those of thousands of other prisoners held by the Germans. Scores of books have been written about the prison camps and the men incarcerated in them; however, Jim's brief story of his imprisonment provides a window on some of the aspects of life in a German prison camp.[13]

Immediately following his capture, the interrogators at Dulag Luft, near Wetzlar, turned their attention to Jim who was questioned "repeatedly and repeatedly, and repeatedly." In turn Jim responded "repeatedly and repeatedly" with his name, rank, and serial number. In time, the interrogator finally gave up and "in sarcasm and disgust, blurted out more information about my outfit than I knew myself." Carl's Moss's interrogator was similarly upset with Carl's refusal to provide more than the required name, rank, and serial number. After about 10 minutes of questioning, "he looked at me and started yelling in German, his face got red, and I could see the veins in his neck swell. He pulled out his lugar and pointed it right at my face, but didn't shoot. If his intentions were to scare me, he certainly did. I thought I was a goner."[14]

There was more trouble ahead for Jim Tyler. Within weeks he was moved from Dulag Luft at Frankfort to Stalag VIII-B, near the Czechoslovakian border, where once again fluid ominously began collecting in his lungs. Thanks to a British "masseur" who provided massages and instructions in deep breathing exercises, Jim's lungs were restored to normal. Once his lungs were healed, Jim learned that he was being sent to Stalag VII-A, near Moosburg, Germany. "The fear of the unknown constantly remained with me, and this segment of my prison journey was no different."[15] In a POW camp, Gilbert Blackwell explained, "You either lived or died according to what your health, your age, and . . . whatever your infirmity was."[16]

As in the other camps, Jim Tyler reported, "the standard rations of soup, potatoes and black bread continued to repulse one's appetite . . . For lunch or dinner we had a couple of potatoes, or maybe a watery soup, which we called 'bed board soup.' It got that name because we could sometimes find pieces of wood in it. At supper time, we had the same conglomeration, with maybe a few pieces of rotten horsemeat thrown in for flavor. I even found a cat's claw once, not to mention other pieces of strange meat with hair on it."[17]

In most of the camps, the food allotment, as Jim pointed out, was minimal at best. Lamar Rodgers remembered that when times were good they might get a quarter of a loaf of bread as their week's ration. Their steady diet consisted of reconstituted cabbage soup that almost invariably was infested with worms that floated around on the top of the soup. For a few days the men would scrape off the worms, but when hungry enough, the men downed the soup worms and all. Cats who haplessly wandered into the camp suffered an extremely short life span as they were quickly incorporated into the heretofore meatless menu. Malnutrition and cold, damp living conditions in time wrought havoc with men's teeth, bones, and lungs.[18]

"The German rations were not enough to live on very long and we were certainly grateful to the Red Cross for the parcels that did get through to us, as this is what kept us alive," Jim Tyler explained. Unfortunately, the eagerly anticipated Red Cross food parcels were few and far between as a result of bombed railroads and terminals. In time, however, as the Allies gained ground in North Africa and Italy, Red Cross food parcels found their way to Stalag VII-A more frequently, and "trading reached a fever pitch." Candy bars, cheese, and cigarettes were popular items in the bartering business. The seemingly ubiquitous trading provided the barterer with a couple of bucks to sock away and procured for the bartee an extra liquor or cigarette ration.

Although the contents of the Red Cross parcels varied, Jim enumerated the contents of a typical package.

One Red Cross parcel contained the following articles and was supposed to be a week's supply (but never once did I ever receive two packages in succeeding weeks during my entire confinement of 21 months.): five packages of cigarettes; two small bars of face soap; one pound box of cubed or diced sugar; a one pound tin of what we called butter, but was animal or vegetable fat; one box of twelve crackers, and were called C-rations; two D-bars; one twelve ounce cake of American cheese; one can of sardines or salmon; a small can of jam or jelly; and a one pound can of the G.I.'s favorite meat . . . SPAM! Two of the most valuable articles were a one pound can of powdered milk, and a twelve-ounce can of powdered coffee. Another food was a six-ounce can of orange paste, which when mixed with water and sugar, was a pretty good tasting beverage. A six-ounce can of liver paste at times took the place of the orange. (All tins were punctured at the time of issue by the Germans to keep one from storing up food for an escape attempt. With all the tins being punctured, one would have to eat the food quickly before spoilage.) It is a shame that we didn't get a parcel every week as we were supposed to. I often wonder what the Germans did with the parcels we did not get that were sent.[19]

"Lights Out" often brought on a time of nostalgia and reflection. Jim Tyler mused:

Many nights, after all was quiet. I lay thinking of my life and would wonder what I could have done differently during the first twenty-one years of my life. I would dream of the things that I would like to accomplish when I got home. I would dream of my folks and feel their concern for me not yet knowing whether I was dead or alive. I'd think how heart broken they would be if I were killed while a prisoner. Then, I'd get to feeling sorry for them and, more, so sorry for myself and a lump would swell in my throat and I would nearly cry. Other times, sound from the darkness would penetrate my thoughts as muffled weeping, trying to keep others form hearing, drifted across the barracks from the bunk of the most recent prisoner. This weird sound of a grown man crying filled me with compassion. Later, I would seek that person out and try to explain the sterling quality of 'living one day at a time'—that's the only way I made it.[20]

As new prisoners arrived, "We had forty-eight notebooks nailed to a wall, one for each state, and each prisoner would sign in his respective state's book. Then I [JimTyler] would spend some time looking up the ones from my home state, asking the latest news, and trying to impart my knowledge of the importance of 'living one day at a time,' since there's nothing more heartbreaking than seeing a comrade go 'stir-crazy,' or 'wire happy'—just walking continuously around the inside of the barbed wire fence, all day long, around and around, not uttering a word to any one. There were other types of degeneration equally as heartbreaking."[21]

Word of a transfer to a new Luftwaffe camp was greeted with wild enthusiasm by Jim Tyler and his buddies. Hopes were soon dashed, however, when their new camp proved equally as appalling as their old accommodations. Travel to their "new" camp, Stalag XVII-B near Krems, Austria, involved a grueling train trip with box cars so overcrowded that it was impossible for all the men "to sit down or sleep at the same time. Turns were taken by some sitting, some standing, and some sleeping." The train trip was seriously debilitating, and what the men had hoped would be greatly improved conditions turned out to be grievously disappointing.

At least in the "new" camp the Red Cross parcels came in a little more frequently, and the men formed combines and attempted to cook what meager supplies were sent in. An "intelligence man" was elected to represent them to the Germans, and the Red Cross supplied some sporting goods that helped relieve some of the boredom of their confinement. "One barracks was designated for a gymnasium; but after a few months in an escape attempt, a tunnel was dug beneath it and the Germans tore the barracks down. Likewise, a barracks was set aside and was used for a Chapel but when a tunnel was found, this barracks was also destroyed."[22]

"MEANER THAN HELL"

Pat Carr's guards were brutal and malicious at his POW camp, Stalag Luft IV, near Stettin. "They had two or three guys there that were just meaner than hell as individuals; 'Rat Face' and 'Big Stoop' were the two in our compound. Big Stoop [was] always moseying through the compound and he was just meaner than hell. He would slap the hell out of you, you know. Then just walk past you. [He] walked around with his hands behind him and he'd come into the room nosing around, we're sitting along the bed, and one guy would get it one time and another guy another time." Big Stoop, apparently a sadist, ordered the men to strip down in order to examine them for contraband and any possible escape materials. Then, "He'd just double that big German belt and almost pick me off of the floor."[23] The sadistic streak in Big Stoop was corroborated by Carl Moss who was maliciously thrown up against a wall by Big Stoop for simply sitting down on a bench during the strip search. Other men were sent to the doctor for ear problems resulting from being cuffed up by the "Stoop."[24]

One day, while Colbert Graham was nursing a leg wound and standing with a group of fellow POWs in Stalag Luft IV, a German working on the wiring on one of the poles in the camp made a wrong connection and was summarily electrocuted. Pent-up anger over their prison camp incarceration erupted in loud cheering by the prisoners who quickly drew fire from the German guards.[25]

"Wheeling and dealing" with the guards was a common practice in most camps. As a German prisoner of war for 22 months in Stalag VII-A and XVII-B, Lamar Rodgers discovered that almost anything could be procured from their German captors in trade for a chocolate bar. There was little demand for cigarettes, but oh, a chocolate bar from a Red Cross parcel was as good as gold. Although the packages were a Godsend to the prisoners, sadistic Germans often cut their rations after the receipt of a Red Cross parcel. Some camp commandants considered the POWs lucky to have "anything at all to eat."[26]

The fact that many of the German guards could be bribed for favors turned out to be a lucky break. Most camps had a radio that had been put together from parts secured by bartering with the guards. After listening to the nightly news from the BBC, the prisoners took their radio apart and each man was responsible for hiding a certain item. The parts were so cleverly concealed that despite frantic searches the Germans could never locate where their prisoners had cached the components. In Stalag VII-A, according to Paul Van Oordt, the men had a radio, and delighted in scheming to keep the Germans at bay. Even before their liberation, the men, relying on radio reports that the war was not going well for the Germans, grew increasingly more confident of being rescued. (Sounds of the Allies' bombing of Berlin just 60 miles away provided additional reassurance.)[27]

In Stalag XVII-B, Lamar Rodgers also told of their radio, the parts similarly obtained through bribery with the Germans, that was cleverly hidden in the wall of the barracks. The Germans looked everywhere for the radio.

They knew it was there, but they never could find it. We had more news actually than the Germans did with this thing, but we traded our food for this. We traded rations of food for the pieces of this radio. What we'd need we'd tell the German guards and they'd bring it in. When they'd bring that, then we'd give them so much of this food that we'd kind of take from each barracks. This was the only saving part of any part of it for us because they would have given anything for chocolate. They were eighty kilometers from Vienna, I hear. They could go into Vienna and trade that chocolate on the black market, and they could come out with a wealth of anything they wanted, because chocolate was a premium. They couldn't get it. It was the first thing traded, always, was the chocolate bar.[28]

Inside the barracks the prisoners worked in committees that governed everything in the camp—health problems, psychological problems, or escape attempts. The prisoners were indeed their "brothers' keepers." It was the unity and camaraderie of the men that became such an important element in survival. In one case in Stalag VII-A, the men succeeded in helping a fellow prisoner, who spoke German fluently, to escape by setting up false identity and providing him with German clothing. He made his escape but was soon apprehended, returned to camp, and executed.

According to Willis Eckholm, there was a considerable difference in their guards. Once, when a fellow prisoner who served as a volunteer chaplain led the group in a chorus of "Onward Christian Soldiers," it "unglued one hardnosed guard. He rushed forward shouting at them to quit it. He felt the military overture was more of a threat than its intended symbolism. He called it 'American propaganda!'"[29]

On another occasion, in a surprising turn of events, a lay chaplain followed his church service with an invitation to anyone who would like to make a commitment to Christ to come forward. The POWs were in a state of shock when one of the guards moved to the improvised podium, placed his rifle beside him, and knelt in prayer. After a few moments, without a spoken word, he gathered up his rifle and returned to his guard post.

It should be remembered that each POW camp was different. In contrast to the brutal treatment and starvation in most of the camps, it was a different story in some of the German POW camps. In Stalag III-B, for example, the discipline was much more relaxed. In some camps it was possible to take classes taught by fellow prisoners who were well-versed in a particular field. Often camps supported theater groups that presented plays and vaudeville shows. Others maintained fairly well-stocked libraries. Ice skates and sports equipment were provided by the Red Cross in some of the camps. It was surprising, Lamar Rodgers recalled, that the Germans allowed the POWs to play softball. In his camp the men had the softballs but had to manufacture their own bats by cutting down a sapling in the woods and whittling it down to bat size.[30]

In other camps, the prisoners made bootleg whiskey from a little stolen sugar and potato peelings. Now and then a guard would surreptitiously whisper to a prisoner, "We don't want this war either." Apparently in camps housing Air Force men the prisoners were accorded far better treatment than the men in camps devoted primarily to enlisted men.[31]

Although millions of Americans regaled themselves over the popular TV series "Hogan's Heroes" and the movie made of American German POWs, veterans of the appalling hardships in the camps were incensed that their trials as prisoners had been made into a parody, a farce for audiences to laugh over. For many of the former POWs, there was nothing funny about their imprisonment.

GERMAN POW ESCAPES

Despite the odds, some men thrill to the adventure and danger of a possible escape and refuse to be confined for very long periods of time before they begin devising some method of escape. Unfortunately, attempts to escape usually resulted in prisoners being caught and lined up before a firing squad. Lamar Rodgers told of several men being held in Stalag XVII-B who attempted an escape using a blinding snowstorm as cover. Just as they were making it under the restraining wire, the snow stopped. "They stood up, held up their hands, tried to surrender and were shot, just killed right there." After that, the guards "turned their rifles loose on the barracks."[32]

An attempt to escape through a sewer proved foolhardy for Lamar Rodgers and some of his buddies. They got out and succeeded in reaching the woods, but without detailed maps they were quickly caught and spent 60 days in solitary confinement—after 30 days, they were released for 1 day and then returned for 30 more days.

One man attempted to escape seven or more times. The last time the man was captured he was sent to Stalag XVII-B where he dug a hole and buried himself underneath the floorboards. The other men kept him hidden, and Lamar Rodgers bragged: "In fact he walked out of there with us." Unfortunately, according to Lamar, the escape artist "became a total alcoholic at the end of World War II. I mean he was just nothing. He became such an alcoholic, trying to forget all of this."[33]

Asked if they tried to escape from prison camp, Fred Williams explained that "there wasn't anywhere to go." They didn't know where they were. Twice they tried, but with limited success. When a guard yelled at them with his gun drawn, they threw their "hands up and went running back."[34]

Three times during his seven and a half months' incarceration as a POW by the Germans, Jim Moye attempted to escape his captors. Twice he was recaptured, but the last time he made it back to the American lines. On their last attempt, Jim and his buddy saw a group of Hitler Youth marching their way. They immediately jumped in a little gully to hide convinced that "This group of little monsters was the greatest enemy that flyers had because these kids would kill you in a hurry. They were a vicious bunch of little things twelve [or] fourteen years old." Jim had seen them "training those kids one time over there and [with] the training they gave those little fellows [and] the hate they instilled in them, it's amazing to me that the people have made as good an adjustment as they have made over there after that experience."

The British POWs, in Jim Moye's mind, displayed remarkable ingenuity in assisting in escape plans. The British kept two "ghosts" in camp. These were two men who did not appear for roll call one day, although the Germans searched everywhere for them. The next day's roll call and thereafter the roll call number was two short; meanwhile, the two men, were carefully hidden by their fellow prisoners. Then when someone had a feasible escape plan, the two men, who had been hidden, took the real escapees' place at roll call, and the Germans, of course, came up with the right count of prisoners. This gave the men trying to escape a five-day head start before the Germans discovered they were missing. Jim was also impressed with the British tunneling and the escape of some 80 men that has received considerable publicity over the years.[35]

THE GREAT ESCAPE PLAN

After months of imprisonment, the RAF men in the North Camp of Stalag Luft III decided that with careful planning and a little bit of luck they surely could outwit their German captors. If all came to naught, then even punishment and possible death might be preferable to their wretched life in Stalag Luft III. With the utmost secrecy, a select group of men embarked on a masterfully executed plan for a tunnel escape—"The Great Escape" that has been memorialized in books and movies. (As the numbers of captured American airmen began arriving in droves, a South Camp had been added and thus some Americans were included in the devious scheming.)[36]

Originally there were three tunnels under construction called Tom, Dick, and Harry. Progress was painfully slow. Forged passes, maps, civilian clothing, and compasses all had to be "manufactured" in secret workshops. Just as an escape was beginning to look like a real possibility, a German spy discovered "Tom," and it was immediately destroyed. The work on "Dick" had to be abandoned, leaving only "Harry" with 120 feet completed and 220 feet to go. On March 24, 1944, in the dark of night, all was in readiness as 80 men squirmed through the narrow tunnel. "Just three made it to freedom," Chuck Woehrle groaned. "Of the rest who were recaptured, 50 were executed by a Gestapo firing squad on orders of Hitler himself . . . I lost two roommates who were in on that escape effort and who were among those executed."[37]

CHAPTER 8

Liberation

THE GREAT MARCH

As 1944 was drawing to a close, the Germans were beginning to see the handwriting on the wall as they felt pressure from the Russians on the east and from the Allies on the west. Caught up in mass confusion, the Germans quickly attempted to move their POWs to other camps. Because many of the POW camps had access to radios, as described earlier, concocted from parts acquired by bribing the guards, many of the prisoners suspected their liberation would come in the not too distant future. Stalag Luft III inmates, however, were stunned when on January 27, 1945, the order was given for all prisoners to gather up their meager possessions and be ready in 30 minutes to move out. In deep snow and zero degree temperatures, well over 10,000 prisoners from four camps formed a line 20 miles long and began the "Great March," yet another test determining the survival of the fittest. (Prisoners from other camps were similarly moved to avoid their being taken over by the Russians. It is estimated that there were three broad migration routes composed of thousands of prisoners.)[1]

Only the hardy could survive the bone chilling winds, the temperatures that hovered between 10 degrees below zero and 20 degrees above zero, the prolonged marching, and the lack of food. "Our chaplain," Chuck Woehrle pointed out, "began to attend to the emotional needs of men who showed hypothermia and exhaustion. He ministered to those who would soon die from starvation and exposure to the cold."[2]

"We marched continuously from morning until midnight for five days with occasional rest stops in barns and churches," Chuck Woehrle continued. (Using margarine to attempt to weatherproof their boots helped a little, but scores of prisoners succumbed to the frigid temperatures, frozen feet, and over-exhaustion.)

"Finally we were completely exhausted when we reached Spremberg where we were herded 50 or 60 to boxcars, and packed in so that we could only sit herring-bone fashion. We had no latrine facilities so the train stopped alongside snow-covered fields so we could relieve ourselves. We rode that way for three nights and four days. The only good news was that we were getting away from the oncoming Russians, even if they were supposedly our allies in this war. They sent thousands of prisoners they found in the German POW camps to Siberia as laborers. One could guess their eventual fate."

Once off the trains the men were imprisoned in a grossly unsanitary camp near Moosburg, Bavaria, that came to be known as "The Snake Pit." There, 300 hundred men were herded into a shelter with one latrine and one spigot of water to be shared by all. The food was minimal and often nonexistent, partly as a result of the Kommandant's having pilfered any Red Cross parcels that arrived and sold them on the Black Market for money to line his own pockets. For six weeks the men slept in their clothes on flea-infested straw mats.[3]

The forced march, the inhumanely scanty food allotments, and the horrendous conditions at Stalag VII-A steadily decreased the ranks of prisoners. Paul Van Oordt, a 15-month veteran of Stalag Luft III, was among the survivors of the long 5-day march through the frigid winter snow drifts as the Germans drove the Stalag Luft III prisoners to Stalag VII-A. He, too, was imprisoned in the filthy box cars en route to Stalag VII-A. Rather than submit to the foul odors and unsanitary conditions of the appallingly overcrowded Stalag VII-A barracks, Van and many of his comrades dug slit trenches and slept in the bitter cold. Helplessly, the prisoners watched their numbers erode as comrade after comrade succumbed to starvation and disease.[4]

Knowing that they would eventually be liberated, the men were beside themselves with anxiety. What was taking so long? Would their rescuers ever appear? Would they live long enough to be rescued? "But relief came on April 29 when General Patton and his tank units of the Third Army liberated us," Chuck Woehrle recalled. "We were hanging onto the main fence, watching our liberation. We saw the German swastika come down from the Moosburg Platz flagpole and in seconds the Stars and Stripes fluttered in its place. We were free at least! Hanging on the fence and with tears streaming down his face, a Scotsman beside me said in his brogue, 'Laddie, I dun wanna sound unpatriotic, but that's the bloodiest foinest flag I've ivver seen!' It was an overwhelmingly ecstatic moment, and is still indelibly etched in my memory."[5]

"A Sherman tank, covered with sandbags, charged into the camp and we immediately mobbed it. We were elated at the sight of our liberators.

Then came General Patton himself in his command car. Obviously we were deliriously happy and excited." Deeply moved by the miserable conditions of the camp, Patton promised the men better things to come. He advised the men to stay together until they could be evacuated and "warned us against taking off on our own. Some did. At that time Stalag VII-A camp held some 100,000 POWs so it was going to take several days for food and evacuation arrangements."[6]

As Patton's forces rolled in on April 29, 1945, to liberate Stalag VII-A, the prison camp near Moosburg, Morris C. Williams, a Mississippian, was pleased to have had the distinction of giving Patton directions to the camp commander. (Most of the Germans, knowing the camp was to be liberated, had panicked and left.) "I was right by the gate and here comes his jeep," Williams recalled. "And in the jeep on the right-hand side there was a most highly polished helmet I have ever seen. And out of it stepped the big boy. He was an exclamation point of a man. Just neat as a pin. And he had two guns on—he had his service gun on his right side and his pearl-handled pistol on his left-hand side. And he returned my salute and he said, 'Where can I find the commander?' And I gave him directions. He went down and he came back up. By that time many prisoners had grouped around the gate, around his tank that knocked the gate. And when he came back, he stood up and he said, 'Men, what I have seen today amazes me at the way the American prisoner of war has conducted himself and kept yourself so clean and so organized.' And he blasted out with an invective against the Germans which I won't repeat. And he said 'I've got a war to fight and let's get out of here.'"[7]

On the day following their liberation, Chuck Woehrle volunteered to go into town to try to hunt up some bread to supplement their grossly inadequate rations. Spying an American GI with a good-looking camera, Chuck begged to buy the camera. (He had been a publicity photographer during summer vacations at Glacier Park, Montana and knew his way with cameras.) There was only one problem—he, of course, had no money. After settling on a price of $20 for the camera and five rolls of film, the deal was consummated by the GI's tearing out a clean page from a spiral notebook and asking Chuck to write a draft on his hometown bank.

Armed with his new camera, Chuck photographed every aspect of the camp, their quarters, their food, and the squalid conditions. It so happened that the photographs turned out to be a speedy ticket home for Chuck. As he was being processed for departure to the United States, his films came to the attention of government officials who were looking for evidence for the upcoming trials of German officers. He, his camera, and his photographs were quickly sent directly to Washington. With a sigh of relief he concluded, "My war was about over, and I was alive."

As a postscript to the notebook-page "check," Chuck recalled, "After I got home my father told me one day that a funny little hand-written check cleared my account that was still in the bank. He asked what that was all about. I enjoyed telling him."

Upon his return home in May, Chuck was reunited with his longtime sweetheart, and on June 14, 1945, they were married. It was a banner day in more ways than one. It seemed that everyone in St. Paul, Minnesota was flying a flag in honor of his service to his country and in celebration of their wedding. It was all very flattering until someone reminded them that it was Flag Day. "Oh, well," Allan Taylor noted, "it was a way of never forgetting future anniversaries."[8]

As Patton's troops rapidly pushed forward, it was clear that his supplies were inadequate for his own troops and that it would be quite some time before the Allied supply lines could begin to provide enough food for the thousands of prisoners at Stalag VII-A. Although most of the GIs waited out the miserable rations in camp, Paul Van Oordt and three of his friends, impatient with the lack of food and the squalid conditions of Stalag VII-A, took matters into their own hands and headed out on their own. As they entered Munich they met up with two Frenchmen near a gas depot where the Americans were refueling Allied vehicles. The Frenchmen were absolutely irate when the Americans refused to give them any gas and begged for help from Paul and his comrades, who agreed to try to procure fuel for the Frenchmen's car. The success of their venture took a happy turn when the American attendant, after gassing up the car, realized that Paul and his buddies were POWs. Knowing they had suffered immeasurably in the German camps, he slyly suggested they sneak out the back way. Voila! They quickly appropriated the Frenchmen's car (they knew it had to have been a stolen car), revved up the motor, and left the two Frenchies in the dust.

As they made their way across country, they made it a practice to check in at Army bases where sympathetic GI's repainted the car and put fake license plates on their bumpers indicating it was an "official" car. All went well until finally the car broke down, and the men abandoned it. Hitching a ride on a U.S. Army truck, they arrived at Nancy, went to the airport and luckily caught the last plane that was hauling POWs from Stalag VII-A. A stop at Le Havre and then it was Camp Lucky Strike—the staging area for deployment back to the United States—and home sweet home.[9]

AT STALAG XVII-B

When the Russians were closing in on Stalag XVII-B near Krems, Austria, Lamar Rodgers and his fellow POWs simply walked out of their prison camp on April 9, 1945, and headed for Salzburg, Austria, a walk that took them 18 days. The night before they started, the Germans had announced, "We're leaving tomorrow morning at roll call time. You can either walk with us or you can stay here and wait on the Russians." Having heard stories of Russian atrocities, all that were ambulatory walked out. "Some two hundred that couldn't walk, were about six months behind us getting home."[10]

In a surprising gesture of compassion, after lights out on the eve of their dismissal, one of the guards came in and addressed the men. "I hope all you guys make it, because I'm leaving." Quizzed about where he was going, he replied that he was going home. His family lived in an area that had recently been taken over by the Russians, and he was eager to determine their well-being. Armed with civilian clothing he was deserting, never to be seen again by Lamar and his men.

Along the way food was somewhat more accessible as the prisoners raided the countryside and now and then were aided by handouts from sympathetic farmers. One malicious guard, however, with hatred still in his eyes, walked ahead of the men and spread the word in each town that the prisoners were actually American gangsters and warned the citizens to be careful and not give them anything to eat. As they crossed the Danube at Linz, citizens lined up to spit on them and barrage them with insults.

The camaraderie engendered in the prison camps was the salvation of many of the internees. Shoes were always a problem, and the 18-day walk out of Stalag XVII-B to Ranshofen really put shoes to the test. Lamar Rodgers' buddy had been issued Serbian civilian shoes that not only didn't fit but were ill-suited for prolonged walking over rough dirt roads. In a heroic act of generosity, Lamar Rodgers swapped shoes with his friend. They both wore the same shoe size and every third day Lamar traded shoes so that his friend could walk comfortably. "We walked that 18 days by me letting him wear my shoes part time [and] I'd wear his part-time."[11]

WHEN THE GOING GOT TOUGH

Despite the fact that they were freed from the confines of their POW camps, there were still dangers ahead as the men walked through the countryside. There was the real possibility of being bombed or strafed by Allied planes whose pilots did not recognize them as American prisoners. In one "foul up," British or American planes strafed a column of POWs, killing some 30 men. Pat Carr attributed the tragedy to "some young pilot, inexperienced," who thought he was firing on German troops. Shortly before their liberation, Pat Carr and his fellow POWs had a near miss when they looked up one day and saw a P-51, whose pilot, not realizing they were Americans, was readying for a strafing run on them. "We were just waving like anything and apparently he recognized what it was and didn't fire." Later, Pat gave the pilot the benefit of the doubt and conceded, "Maybe he didn't intend to fire anyway, maybe he intended to buzz us only." Nevertheless, the men were taking no chances.[12]

As their liberation appeared imminent, a fellow prisoner of Leland McLendon's who could understand a little German overheard a guard in their camp Stalag IV-B saying the war would be over tomorrow. The next day the Germans opened the prison gate and "here we went to walking then—all of us. And they told us which way to go." "Mac" and his fellow prisoners were told "That's it, go ahead!" Unaware of where they were and hoping to make contact with American GIs, the men marched along a highway and suddenly lo and behold there was an abandoned German truck. "What's wrong with this thing? Nobody's in it," they wondered. It took just an instant before one of the men ordered: "'Let's everybody pile in here. Get in the back!' He cranked up and he said, 'Maybe I know how to run it and get this thing [to] shift,' so he got in there and here we went to riding then." Their luck continued to hold when they, too, narrowly escaped bring strafed by Allied planes.[13]

On February 6, 1945, Carl Moss and the men from Camp Stalag Luft IV near Grosstychow, Germany were ordered out of the camp and marched some 600 miles through rain, snow, and sleet for 86 days until they were liberated by the British on May 2, 1945. Just before leaving camp the men were sent through the commissary and invited to pick up one or more Red Cross parcels for the trip, which the Germans announced would be only "a few kilometers." (These were the Red Cross parcels that had been sent to the camp for the prisoners, but had been hoarded by the guards for their own consumption. Those who opted for two parcels were soon to regret it, for it was one more burden for what turned out to be not "a few kilometers" but a march of 600 miles. Urged to "buddy up," Carl and his friend Edmund Boice grabbed a parcel each and headed out for the first day's march of 27 miles. That night they eagerly devoured the Red Cross parcel's can of liver pate, which turned out to be a huge mistake. Within hours Carl and his buddy were ravaged by food poisoning from the liver pate. Carl believed "the liver pate was spoiled." The guards or whoever received the Red Cross parcels, opened all the parcels and punctured the cans, to make sure there were no knives or guns in them (that was the German excuse). The parcel with spoiled liver pate had not been passed out before and sat in the warehouse for several weeks or months and therefore became spoiled. For the next five days, Carl had little knowledge of what was happening to him. With help from Dr. Leslie Caplan and several of his friends, Carl apparently was dragged or carried until he could struggle along on his own. Without their help, Carl knows he never would have made it.

The first 30 days were the worst Carl remembered, for there was almost no food other than a few potatoes or kohlrabi that could be scavenged from some farmer's meager stockpile of food for his hogs. A "sick wagon," a farmer's produce wagon, was used to pick up the dead and dying. Many of the scores of men who fell by the wayside simply had to be abandoned.

His own survival Carl credited partially to the fact that he was in relatively good shape for a prisoner, for each day during his confinement he had circled the camp repeatedly for exercise and conditioning. David Dennis corroborated the grim details of the 600-mile forced march from their prison camp Stalag II-B westward whereby the Germans hoped to keep the prisoners from being "liberated" by the Russians.[14]

Mushing through deep snow and seeking a few hours sleep at night in company with horses, pigs, and cows in some farmer's barn or just bedding down in the snow with spruce branches for cover, the prisoners put all of their energy into just staying alive. Dozens of prisoners, already weakened by hunger and malnutrition, were unable to keep up on the 25-kilometers a day marches and simply fell by the wayside where freezing temperatures and wild animals took their toll. At one stop a kindly old lady supplied hot water, cooked some food for the men, and allowed them to wash up in her kitchen. For her hospitality, she gained the gratitude and preferential treatment by the POWs.

Other less hospitable farmers drew the wrath of some of the marchers. Prisoners who had been badly treated by their prison guards sometimes took out their anger on the civilian German farmers and upon occasion destroyed homes, out-buildings, or household furnishings in retaliation. Chicken coops all along the way were considered fair game, and an observant David Dennis commented in his diary: "When I arrived at the chicken pen all you could see was chicken feathers flying and chickens being beheaded. The chicken was very good," he added slyly.[15]

The Russians clearly evidenced little sympathy for the German guards, David Dennis wrote in his diary. Once the Russians caught up with the marchers and their guards, "There were no questions asked—the German guards were lined up and shot. . . . They rolled to the bottom of the ravine and the Russians told us if we bothered them we would be shot."

May 1, 1945, turned out to be a day David Dennis and hundreds of their comrades would remember always. Following the several hundred-mile trek through snow and ice from their prison camp II-B near Danzig, they were finally liberated by the Russians. It was the day they had hoped and prayed about for months and years. "We were thankful to be alive and liberated. Some of us have been POWs for over two years and now we are free. No gun in our backs," David Dennis rejoiced. "We were thankful to be alive and liberated. The church group held a Thanksgiving Prayer service and quite a few of us got on our knees and thanked God."[16]

LIBERATION AT STRASBOURG

Earlier in the war, in November of 1944, the French Resistance secured the liberation of Willis Lott and his comrades who were being held as POWs by the Germans near Strasbourg, France. There, Willis and his unit had been assigned the work of digging foxholes around the city for the Germans to use if attacked by the Americans. In a surprise visit one morning, the Germans came into their compound and announced that they would not be going out that day. That was most unusual. As they peered out the windows of their barracks, Willis and his men were amazed to see a few bicyclists, soon to be joined by greater and greater numbers of cyclists riding through the area.

Somehow there was an eerie suspense about the day. Something was about to happen, but what? Suddenly, about three o'clock that afternoon, a flag, the Free French flag, was gallantly raised on the steeple of a nearby church and immediately all hell broke loose. "And that was a signal for all of those who had been coming in on bicycles. They had guns run down their pant legs" and were ready for action. The bicyclists, the French resistance, had tentatively secured the town for the Allied capture of the town. "About that time we could hear artillery, and it was our artillery. We didn't know it. But when that flag went up there on that church, there was ten thousand guns went off at the same time, little rifles and things. They took that town over in an hour." Within minutes DeGaulle's tanks had covered the town.

Although liberated, the war was certainly not over for Willis and his men. They were sent back to their companies and continued on with the war. Willis had survived the Normandy invasion (having gone in on the fourth day), had helped liberate Cherbourg, had been captured by the Germans, but on his return to his company his luck ran out; he was wounded and at long last he was headed home.[17]

LIBERATION, RESISTANCE GROUPS, NAZI COLLABORATORS

"The war is over for you!" should have been joyous news for Russ Hilding, B-17 pilot with the 447th Bomb Squad stationed in Rattlesden, England. The ominous tone and the gun leveled at his head by a wrathful Nazi, however, gave rise to Russ' feeling that this might well be the end of the road instead of the end of the war.

Russ had participated in the D-Day invasion—"the biggest day in our lives," he wrote his parents. Next there were some 12 missions over Germany, and then on the 13th of July, 1944, an attack by German fighter planes "shot the daylights out of us." The bailout and the successful parachute jump landed Russ in a wheat field just as two men (working for the French underground) drove up in a Citroen to pick him up and hide him in homes of members of the French Resistance. What a break! In a few days Russ was joined by his bombardier, co-pilot, and one waist gunner, whereupon the four decided they were lucky to be alive.

Suddenly their world was turned upside down when one morning a seemingly responsible woman beckoned them away from their hideaway over to a waiting car. At her insistence they got in naively expecting to be transferred to another safe shelter. At that point the door banged closed and a strange man in the front seat turned around, pointed his pistol at them and announced: "The war is over for You." In a state of stark disbelief they quickly realized this was *not* a move to another hideout. They had been betrayed by Nazi sympathizers!

In very short order they, along with many other allied airmen, were crammed into boxcars and transferred to the infamous Buchenwald concentration camp. There, for two months, they suffered freezing temperatures and near starvation food rations, and at least two of their comrades succumbed to pneumonia. Just as the days of fear and anxiety were beginning to appear unending, things started looking brighter when a zealous officer finally arranged for them to be sent to POW camp Stalag Luft III near Sagan. "Leaving Buchenwald was the happiest day of my life," a relieved Russ confessed.

New and clean clothes and more and better food rendered life at Stalag Luft III considerably more bearable. By January 27th, the Russians could be heard approaching, and Russ and the other POWs were told to pack up. Following a five-day march through the ice and snow (noted in other POW accounts in this chapter), they were loaded into boxcars and sent to Nurenberg and from there transferred to Stalag VII-A at Moosburg. Time moved slowly until April the 28th when the sound of an L-4-piper cub plane was heard in the skies. The prisoners in Camp Stalag VII-A went wild knowing this was a spotting plane for Patton's Army and they would soon be liberated.

Once liberated, the next move was to Camp Lucky Strike at Le Harve, where there was food aplenty, however, prisoners were put on a stringent diet as a result of their malnutrition. A troop carrier took them to Southhampton to pick up medical patients and then it was a long, happy trip to the Statue of Liberty and New York harbor! At last the war was finally over for Russ and his comrades.[18]

All had been going well for Henry Wolcott, a B-24 pilot flying missions from England over Belgium in 1944 with the Army Air Force. Their missions, directed by the OSS, involved dropping supplies—cargo and bombs—for the Belgian resistance agents. Eighteen missions had been successful, but on the nineteenth mission, Henry's plane was hit by enemy anti-aircraft gunfire near Brussels, and the crew was forced to bail out. Fortunately, Henry made a safe landing in a wheat field, and after disentangling himself from his parachute, he cautiously cased the area for sanctuary with someone from the Belgian resistance. Picking a house at random and in a great stoke of luck, Henry was greeted by a family fully committed to the resistance movement. There he and several of his comrades were accorded regal treatment, but for fear of their being discovered, their benefactors moved them five different times to homes of other underground sympathizers. Their safety seemed assured—that is until they were betrayed by German collaborators.

One day one of their "safe homes" turned out to be extremely unsafe. As they were comfortably seated around a table at one of their "hideaways" chatting about the war, a seemly personable couple entered and joined the group. Amiable conversation continued until suddenly the talk changed to the need for a "surefire" escape route out of Belgium to safer territory. "If anyone wants to go to Switzerland, we can get you there," the couple promised. Naturally Henry and the others jumped at the offer only to find out a few hours later that the "friendly couple" were in reality Nazis (unknown, of course, to the Resistance) who herded them onto a train headed for Buchenwald! Fortunately, the train engineer was a Belgian, and he and his crew resorted to every avenue of sabotage to keep the train from running. Finally the Germans were convinced that the train was so disabled that it would not move, and Henry and his comrades were marched into an old Belgian prison, St. Giles, in Brussels. There the accommodations were almost unbearable: 8 by 10 foot cells and one meal a day of watery soup.

A few weeks later as the British overran Brussels, they were liberated from their despicable quarters, and Henry and 50 Allies and 1,500 Belgian civilians who had been working for the Resistance were sent on "The Ghost Train" to other camps and then finally released.

Many years later, in 2001 Henry, his wife and their four children made a special trip to Belgium and there were reunited with Emil Boucher and his family who had kept Henry and several members of his crew hidden for more than a month some 60 years ago. In an effort to thank the Resistance, the Wolcotts helped to dedicate a memorial in honor of the Resistance and to lay flowers at the graves of comrades who did not make it home. In turn they were royally feted by the Belgians who were eternally grateful for the help of the Allied Forces.[19]

LIBERATION OF CONCENTRATION CAMPS

If there were any possible doubt in a GI's mind about why he was fighting, all uncertainty was quickly dispelled as the troops moved into Germany and witnessed firsthand the appalling concentration camps and furnaces that had sent some six million Jews to their deaths.

The war in Europe was winding down during the early days of April 1945, but some of the most horrifying sights were yet to be experienced—the Nazi concentration camps, and the shocking scenes of mass graves, and the deteriorating bodies of victims only recently incinerated. Although Auschwitz had been liberated by the Russians in January of 1945, the first Nazi death camp to be liberated by American troops during WWII was Ohrdruf on April 4, 1945. Ray Young was one of the first American servicemen to witness the gut-wrenching sights of the German atrocities at

Ohrdruf. One of Raymond Young's prize possessions is a document reading, "The United States Holocaust Memorial Council hereby expresses appreciation to Raymond Young for valiant service during the 1944–45 liberation by Allied Forces of Nazi Concentration Camps."[20]

On April 3rd, as a member of the 602nd Tank Destroyer Battalion, Ray was assigned to check out the terrain ahead to see if the ground was solid enough to enable the heavy tanks to move through the area near Ohrdruf, Germany. Suddenly shots rang out over their heads, and Ray and the sergeant accompanying him immediately returned fire. Within minutes five SS men raised white flags and surrendered. Early the next morning, a lone German bomber dropped two bombs in an attempt to obliterate the hideous scene that awaited Ray Young and members of Company A. About daybreak, the town came under attack by the Allied Forces. As the tanks opened fire, Ray and several of his men charged ahead with 30-caliber machine guns.

As they made their way through a fence, they were aghast at what they saw. "The bodies were all there in a pile. As the sun rose, I grabbed a camera I had picked up earlier off someone's table and took pictures of the pile of lime-covered bodies in a shed, as well as the pile of freshly killed people, including one with American air corps boots on." (Ray's picture of the sickening scene was later to appear in *Time Magazine*.)

For many people there had been confusion about the Nazi death camps and the millions of Jews and Nazi dissidents who were put to death in those ghastly concentration camps. Although Ray and his comrades, after months of combat, had seen hundreds of dead bodies, the Germans' unconscionable, methodical slaughtering of their fellow human beings shocked them to the core. One of the camp's survivors directed them to the mass graves, "each of which was seventy-five to one hundred yards long. Along the sides were burning pyres with partially burned pieces of bodies they had not yet scraped into the ditches." Boxcars loaded with layers of wood and layers of bodies had been set afire, their remains still smoldering. The demoniacal scene of outrage and the stench of wholesale death were gruesome memories that Ray and his comrades would never be able to forget. In the next few days Generals Eisenhower, Bradley, and Patton came to witness first hand the atrocities at Ohrdruf. During their tour of bodies and skeletons, Patton became so sickened by the stench that he turned away to vomit. Eisenhower immediately dispatched Washington to send photographers and journalists to Ohrdruf to validate for the public the scenes of horror and inhumanity. Unfortunately, the liberation came too late for 3,000 Jews who were murdered the day before what would have been their liberation.[21]

Daniel P. Mc Carthy was also one of the first Americans to experience the grisly sights at Camp Ohrdruf. Dan remembered all too well the mass graves where here and there a gaunt hand or a leg emerged from the grotesque pits.

Rather than face worldwide vilification, the mayor and his wife committed suicide, and the townspeople of Ohrdruf were ordered to walk single file through the camp to view and smell the carnage of the mass murders that had been so ruthlessly committed almost in their very backyards. Later, Ray and his men learned that Ohrdruf was a satellite of Buchenwald. (As the enemy was slowly closing in, all of the able-bodied men in the camp had earlier been lined up and made to march to Buchenwald.) A few days later, both Dachau and Buchenwald would be discovered and liberated.[22]

Ted Thomas concurred that one of his most emotionally disturbing experiences of the war was helping to free the prison camp at Ohrdruf. The half-dead, emaciated skeletons of men who survived the holocaust and the sickening piles of remains of those who did not were horrors that to this day continue to shadow the hearts of the liberators. "Don't tell me there were no German Concentration Camps," Ted Thomas threatened.[23]

After the heinous sights at Ohrdruf, Ray Young and the Allies gave no mercy to the Germans in the confrontations that followed. Ray Young, Walter Adams, and hundreds of others reported that they took no prisoners after witnessing the inhumanity of the death camps. The spectacle was so revolting that Henry Kane and his comrades turned over their guns to the prisoners of one of the camps they had helped liberate, and told the prisoners to use them as they wished on their guards. One enfeebled inmate was given a gun by a GI who suggested he use it on his captors. Instead, the prisoner returned it to its owner. Refusing to emulate the merciless murders committed by the guards, he declared "No, I don't want to be like them."[24]

DACHAU

John Walker, gunner and later sergeant squad leader of a 60-millimeter mortar squad, was a member of the 42nd Rainbow Division that on April 29th and 30th, 1945, helped liberate some 33,000 prisoners in the infamous Dachau concentration camp. The horrified liberators would never forget the hideous scene at Dachau. Time, sheer numbers, and a war still to be fought made it possible for only a few of the men in John's battalion to inspect the interior regions of Dachau. Those who did were in for the shock of their lives. Their experience marked them forever. First was the grisly sight of 50 or so freight cars on a railroad siding loaded with the bodies of some 1,500 dead men. The prisoners, who clearly had been dead but a short time, were stacked like cordwood, some even lying outside the cars, their remains no doubt scheduled by the Germans to be incinerated in nearby crematoriums or callously dumped into mass graves. Although the entrance to the camp presented a most inviting appearance with its attractive flowerbeds, sparkling fountains, and well-manicured green lawns, inside, however, was a nightmare. Inspectors concurred, "This must be what Hell looks like."

Thousands of prisoners, barefoot and in rags, pushed and shoved each other as they frantically cheered their liberators in a Babel of languages. There was a mad crush to hug and embrace or merely touch one of their rescuers. Yet, amidst the wild scene of ecstasy, there was tragedy in store for at least one hapless inmate who was swept up in the crowd, pressed against the charged barbed wire fence, and electrocuted. It took only seconds for terrified officers to shut off the power supply.

Other prisoners sat in a dazed stupor leaning against a wall, their minds long since effaced by savage beatings or the maniacal experiments of their captors. Bodies of the dead, the half-dead, and the dying littered the walkways and lay waist deep in "The Waiting Room." Typhus was almost universal.

John Walker remembers, "Many of the SS camp guards were killed and others surrendered. Most of the prisoners were in terrible shape: emaciated, starving, diseased, and victims of a wide variety of tortures and cruelty. . . The next morning, we then rumbled slowly in a column of tanks and other vehicles past the high wire fences of the concentration camp. The fences were crowded with hundreds of emaciated prisoners in their blue and white striped prison garb. They cheered and waved and shouted to us in many languages as we slowly rode atop our tanks by the fence. We waved and shouted back to them and tossed a few items of K-rations over the fence."[25]

"THE BEST PICTURE IS THE ONE I DIDN'T TAKE"

Onlookers had already been hardened by the carnage of the battlefield, but the scenes at Dachau drove the stark reality of man's inhumanity to man to new dimensions. Officials, journalists, and photographers flooded the camp. Among the historical documents of the Rainbow Division is an excerpt from the haunting account of journalist T-3 James Creasman, HQ Company, 42nd Infantry Division. "An officer pressed through the mobs of forgotten men of all nations, wept unashamedly as limp ghosts under filthy blankets, lying in human excreta, tried to salute him with broomstick arms, falling back in deathly stupor from which most would never rouse."[26]

One photographer, T-5 Robert Steubenrauch, of the 163rd Signal Photo Company, later confessed in Dann's book *Dachau*: "The best picture was the one I didn't take." He thought he had seen it all. "I'd had thirty months overseas by this time. I had experienced many grim sights in combat. I took more pictures than I can remember. But the best picture was the one I didn't take. I was about to photograph a group of inmates who obviously didn't have more than thirty minutes to live. I just couldn't bear to see the look in their eyes. So, I lowered my camera and simply walked away."

In the women's barracks, over 400 gaunt women bore testimony to their repeated rapings by the German guards. For many observers, Dachau became a turning point in their lives. Dachau made it painfully clear for every soldier "why we were fighting this war."

On April 30th, Lloyd Wilson and the men of the 45th Division reached Munich and set about continuing the liberation of Dachau. The scene was hideous. A buddy summoned Lloyd to the interior of the camp. "You just got to see this." It was a sickening sight to see boxcars packed with dead bodies and fences lined with more dead bodies. Outside the camp long columns of emaciated German slave laborers in striped clothes begged for help from the Americans. Already those that could be helped had been separated and sent to the rear where medics quickly administered intravenous feeding and bound up festering sores. In a stroke of luck, that day Lloyd and his comrades were assigned occupation duty and taken out of combat. "The European war was over for the 45th Division!"[27]

Andrew Candler Leech told of liberating "several prisoners of war of all types, but what did us the most good was to free some of our own men and watch them kiss the tanks and shake our hands. The most pathetic thing of it all was the refugees at the forced labor camps we liberated, and there were many. Those prisoners were living in terrible conditions with very little food and clothing. They were crowded together in shacks where they were dying by the hundreds from malnutrition and other diseases. We liberated a large concentration camp near Munich [Dachau] and it was unbelievable to see the conditions these people were in. They were walking skeletons that had run away—some of them that were able to, to the mountains in the snow. They had no food and very little clothing that was tattering about them. They escaped because the Germans were lining them up and mowing them down with machine guns before the Americans came in. We were in one town where they had mowed down 500 of them the day before we entered. When they saw that we were Americans, many of these walking skeletons wobbled down to greet us and beg food. They said they hadn't had anything to eat in about eight days. We sat down in groups as we were in position firing on the next town. And when we got time we took down our own rations, built fires, and cooked them for these people. They ate it and told some awful weird stories in the meantime. When they had finished, they thanked us and wobbled off toward the road which was about a hundred yards away. Two of them fell dead by the time they reached the road."[28]

Within days after the liberation of Dachau, Kossie Atkins' platoon checked out the camp and were staggered by the gruesome piles of dead bodies stacked and ready to be thrown in to the ovens. To people who refuse to believe the existence and atrocities of the German concentration camps, Kossie declared: "I would like for them to have seen that!"[29]

At least one GI was so traumatized by grisly scenes at Dachau that the experience changed his entire life. Donald R. Brown, Emeritus Professor of

Psychology at the University of Michigan, all too often remembers being the first man into Dachau when it was liberated. The experience proved so devastating that it served to change the direction of his life. Prior to the war, Don had been majoring in biochemistry at Harvard. The sickening sights at Dachau gave him cause to wonder about the merits of biochemistry in preventing atrocities such as the Germans were perpetrating on their fellow human beings. Perhaps the answer lay in social psychology; perhaps a study of men's minds and social behavior could forestall such execrable acts in the future. After the war Don returned to college on the GI Bill for his undergraduate and graduate work with a major in social psychology and a deep commitment to perpetuating concepts of tolerance and nonviolence in his young students.[30]

Few men could find words to describe the grisly sights at the concentration camps they helped to liberate. At the Nordhausen concentration camp, Bern Engel was stunned by the sight of seeing 3,000 bodies lined up in three neat rows waiting to be taken to the crematoriums. The cavernous ovens, the skeletons, and the lethal "shower" rooms all bore mute testimony to the ghastly reality of the camps and the atrocities perpetrated there.[31]

June Bohn still shudders remembering her husband's account of the grueling experience of trying to aid the sick and dying who remained in the Nazi concentration camp at Mauthausen (near Linz, Austria) after its liberation earlier by American troops. Prisoners who had been well enough to walk had been liberated. It was the incapacitated, near-death prisoners who, of necessity, had been left behind for the medical teams to attempt to resuscitate. From May 12 to June 22, 1945, Armin Bohn, a T5 Dental Technician with the 64th Medical Regiment, and his team worked to evacuate to Allied hospitals the men for whom there remained even some faint hope of recovery, and to tag and send to the morgue those who had drawn their last breath. Armin had told June of being appalled by the human skeletons, the living-dead, who had been victims of TB, overwork, starvation, and disease. It was heartrending work as not a few of the barely alive men succumbed, even as the medics were making every effort to revive them. One day the rescuers got the shock of their lives as one of the men who had been thought to be dead came tottering back from the morgue to the crew of workers. It was almost a Lazarus story. As the medics regained their senses, suddenly it became very quiet as the poor man slowly staggered back to his bed and fell atop it. The two men who had carried him to the morgue quickly disappeared, and the work continued.[32]

Certainly Charles Grosse's most unforgettable experiences were stopping at former German concentration camps. The sight of decapitated bodies, lampshades made of human skins, blood still visible on the walls of the rooms where Jews and other victims had been gassed, and scratches on the doors where people had sought to escape left imprints that lived with him for life. In a visit to Dachau, Betty Leiby was shocked by the blood stains 12-feet high on the wall where the Germans had piled the bodies of their victims. The nauseating sights while helping to liberate Buchenwald camp are images that continue to murder Po Wetherford's and hundreds of other GIs' sleep at night.[33]

CHAPTER 9

Japanese POW Camps

Imprisonment for most of the thousands of POWs held in Japanese camps involved not only confinement and unconditional subservience to authorities, but also savage beatings, beheadings, and near or real starvation. Disease, lack of medical supplies, and overwork compounded the death toll in the camps.

THE BATAAN DEATH MARCH

Thousands of prisoners got their first taste of Japanese brutality when following their capture they were herded into groups for the long merciless Bataan Death March. Two of the marchers, Philip Brain and John Hinkle, dramatically remember scenes from the march and their imprisonment thereafter.

Philip Sidney Brain, Jr., grew up in Minnesota, was inducted into the army in April 1941, was sent to the Philippines, and on April 10, 1942, joined 12,000 American and 64,000 Filipino soldiers in the notorious Bataan Death March up the Bataan Peninsula in the Philippines. Statistics vary, but estimates indicate that some 700 American soldiers and about 5,00 Filipinos, faint from hunger, weakened by dysentery, and debilitated by malaria, died on the march. Any men unable to keep up were shot or bayoneted on the spot. Compassionate Filipino civilians along the way who tried to surreptitiously pass out a little food or water to the marchers were similarly dispatched. A pregnant Japanese woman who bravely attempted to offer a piece of bread to one of the marchers was callously gunned down and tossed aside. Surprisingly, the Japanese were equally merciless with any of their own guards who could not keep up with the marchers.

Thousands more men succumbed to the brutal treatment and unsanitary conditions of the POW camps to which they were sent. For Phil Brain and his group, surviving the march was just the first test of survival. Next was a smothering railroad trip in boxcars with no latrines and no food that finally ended at Camp O'Donnel, a former Philippine training camp, where there were almost no beds or blankets or chairs. There, Phil Brain was put to work digging latrines and graves—the latter a devastating assignment considering the fact that an estimated 1,000 men died in the first month at the camp. The work was backbreaking, especially because Phil's dysentery, a pervasive illness among the POWs, had reduced him from 168 pounds to less than 100 pounds. After a move to Camp Cabanatuan for 10 months, a thousand men, including Phil, were transferred to Mindanao, where Phil was relieved of his shovel and assigned a 12-hour day in the rice fields.[1]

After being captured when the Bataan peninsula fell in 1942, John Lewis Hinkle, Jr., also became a member of that infamous Bataan Death March. The lack of food was inhumane, he explained, but the worst misery was the lack of water. Although there were a number of artesian wells along the way, "when you would get near one, they would put a man over it with a rifle and a bayonet. And even though you might want water, you knew it was immediate death if you broke the line. Now some of the people got to where they just couldn't stand it and they would break the line, and they would either bayonet them or shoot them."

For six days there was no food. It took courage and resolute determination to continue. Often it was thanks to the prodding or physical assistance of a fellow marcher that made the difference between life and death. On about the fourth day of the march, the Japanese in a surprising gesture of compassion allowed the marchers a brief rest stop and a quick gulp of water at one of the artesian wells beside the road. But by then John Hinkle was ready to give up. He had valiantly struggled to keep going as he passed scores of his comrades who had fallen by the wayside, too exhausted, too dehydrated, or too brutalized by the guards to continue. The future looked hopeless. Before most could get a thirst-quenching swallow of water, the guards began shouting at them to fall back in line.

A few feet away, John heard his friend call to him: "Let's go Hinkle." It was a moment, John emotionally recalled, that he would remember for the rest of his life. "I said, 'I'm not going.' He said 'What do you mean?' I said, 'Well, it's just a matter of whether you are going to get it today or tomorrow. All of us are going to die.' He said, 'Come on and fall in.' I did, and he got to talking to me. He said, 'What would your mother think, or what would the Lord think? You are just being a quitter.' I'll tell you that kind of woke me up, and I prayed to the Lord that day like I never have since. It may seem strange, but actually, He answered me and told me that I was going to make it back. I never had any doubts that I wasn't coming back. . . That was in that same afternoon in the march. It wasn't an audible voice, but it was something that just told me that it was going to be tough, but I could make it. I often think about that, and every time I talk to Sam now, I thank him for that. And I feel like if it had not been for him and the Lord, I wouldn't be here today."[2]

LIFE IN JAPANESE POW CAMPS

After serving in Shanghai where the Fourth Marine Regiment had been protecting the area as an international settlement, Frank S. Forsyth, a Marine from Massachussetts, was sent to Corregidor and there became a prisoner of the Japanese when Corregidor fell in May of 1942. Excerpts from his experiences in various camps in the Philippines and in Japan, along with the testimony of other survivors, paint a vivid picture of the quality of life in a Japanese POW camp.

Survivors of the Japanese POW camps, among them Frank Forsyth, repeatedly testified to the ruthless brutality of the guards who frequently beat the prisoners to within an inch of their lives for not working fast enough, for wheeling and dealing with the guards, for any minor infraction of the rules, or for no reason whatsoever. Beatings were a way of life the prisoners declared. One could expect to be beaten at least once a day. Although not directly concerned with the physical work of the prisoners but responsible for overseeing the projects, American officers got their share of beatings—as did Japanese workers themselves. Even the guards were taken to task by their superiors. "They got the beating too," Cecil Chambliss remembered. "They'd line each other up and beat them just like they'd beat us."[3]

In part, the Japanese brutality to their prisoners could be attributed to the Japanese tradition of considering surrender or capture not only cowardly but also disgraceful. Better death by suicide than dishonor by surrendering. The shame of submission would reflect gravely on the soldier and eternally shroud his family's name as well. To the Japanese, their POW captives deserved no quarter whatsoever. They were beyond redemption and deserved the inhumane treatment they were often accorded.[4]

Respect for the Japanese authorities was mandatory. Severe beatings and vicious attacks kept the prisoners in line. In some camps, following roll call and instructions for the day, the internees were ordered to bow their heads to the camp's commandant. Failure to do so could result in brutal punishment—or even beheadings in front of their fellow POWs.

Apparently one of the most difficult—if not the most difficult—problem of imprisonment was restraint, that is, not retaliating when, as prisoners, they were insulted or beaten. Sam Abbott knew very well that the results would be disastrous were he or any of the POWs to attempt to strike back when being beaten by a Japanese prison guard. Once when Sam Abbott was taking too long on a cigarette break, the guard "started hitting me with his rifle butt and kicking me with his hobnailed shoes. And, as I would go down, I'd get back up, and he'd knock me down again. I had it in my mind 'I know I can hit that guy a couple or three times and knock him right on his back,' because he was just a little fellow. But that's what they wanted you to do. They wanted you to fight back, and then they could take their bayonet and use you as bayonet practice. So, you had to take the indignities. It's pretty hard to do when you're [mad]—and [have to] bow to them like you were some subservient slave or something."[5]

It was especially difficult, John Hinkle agreed, for large muscular men to be slapped around or belittled by the small-framed Japanese guards and not strike back. Their captors seemed to take great pleasure in taunting and knocking them around knowing full well that if their victim dared to retaliate he would face "an almost certain death."[6]

"Most people weren't interested in it but the Japanese would want to wrestle us. Some of them would want to wrestle sumo, the sumo type of wrestling—where you take, I don't know, I guess where you take, go around and see who could throw each other to the ground. . . Not too many Americans would take them on, because even though the Japanese were little, they were strong. We were all too weak. But in good shape, we could have taken them and heaved them 30 feet."[7]

The Japanese were pitiless in their treatment of many of the POWs. Frank Forsyth told of being able to sneak a little rice to one of the men he felt sorry for and telling him to hide it. Minutes later the recipient of the rice was crying, saying "'Pavlokas took it away from me and beat me up." It turned out Pavlokas, instead of eating the rice himself, had traded it for cigarettes. When the Japanese heard about the incident they decided they could do without Pavlokas; he'd been a disturbing influence throughout the camp. Taking justice into their own hands, "they starved him and he died."[8]

In at least one Japanese POW camp, internees caught gazing at the skies watching for U.S. planes of liberation were forced to keep their eyes steadily focused on the tropical sun for five hours.

During part of his three-year internment in Santo Tomas (Manila), Hal Rather was assigned to assist the camp's dentist in filling and extracting teeth. Hal found it a rather cushy job compared to his other assignments on janitorial and garbage disposal details, and the opportunity for revenge was irresistible. When their Japanese/Korean guards came in for emergency treatment, extraction, whether needed or not, was standard procedure. "For these cases we had prepared novocain capsules filled with tap water. Once pressure was put on the dental forceps, our patient would let out a scream—a natural reaction when the injection was not painkilling novocain but rather tap water." At that point the dentist would take special pains to convince the patient that the "novocain" was a Japanese product, and, of course, would be superior to any other painkiller. "With this 'fact' established, and his loyalty to the Rising Sun, he would clutch on to the arms of the dental chair for dear life while the 'sore tooth' was pulled." Ah, sweet revenge!

Several of the veterans of the Japanese prison camps felt that the Japanese were as cruel to their own people as they were to their prisoners. One veteran recounted his observations of a Japanese's cruelty to a desperately hungry man in the neighborhood, who heard it rumored that the prisoners were getting good food, while those at home were going hungry. One night he sneaked into the camp, scrounged around for delicacies, and finding little else stole a cup of rice. He was quickly apprehended and strung up on a pole as an example for everyone to see. Every hour the guards came out with long sticks and beat him until he was dead.

Prisoners who were not beaten to death or starved to death often met their fate from overwork. In Frank Forsyth's POW camp in Japan, many of the able-bodied (and also a vast contingent of not-so-able) were sent to work in a nearby under-the-sea mine. The mine had been closed down and condemned earlier; however, now the Japanese were so desperate for fuel that they reopened the mine and put the prisoners to work. Many a prisoner succumbed to the devastating exhaustion of strenuous manual labor from sunup to sundown, 7 to 10 days at a stretch. In addition, the imminent dangers of cave-ins and flooding and the meager sustenance of a cup of rice for breakfast served to compound the hellish mine work. Not infrequently the work became so horrendous that as many as a man a day sought to maim himself or pay a fellow prisoner to break his arm or leg to keep him from being sent to the mine. As the Japanese suspiciously counted up more and more unaccountable injuries, they ruled that they had to *see* the man break his arm. The solution was to break an arm or a leg then go to the mine and pretend to fall in front of a foreman. Only then might the injured man be exempt from the grueling mine work.[9]

In Omuta, 65 miles across the bay from Nagasaki, Sam Abbott recalled that everyday was a workday for the prisoners, Sundays included, from morning to night. Sam remembered that even their Yasume day, a "rest day" awarded every tenth day, was a misnomer. That was the day they were chased out of their barracks so the Japanese could search for any contraband or any evidences of escape plans or diggings. That was the day the POWs washed and scalded their clothes to get rid of body lice. Unfortunately, it was usually an exercise in futility, for once one returned to the barracks there would be a new onslaught of lice. "We kept our heads shaved," Sam Abbott, remembered. "We had no razors per se but we did have access, or, I got ahold of GI case knives and would sharpen them to a razor sharpness, and would shave each others' heads. We had very little soap to keep the body lice out of our heads."[10]

Frank Forsyth credited much of his kind treatment to his dog, Lucky, a Chow dog that he had picked up in China. For some strange reason one of the officers of the prison camp at Nichols Field, a much feared and "utterly vicious man," took a liking to the dog, despite the fact that the dog hated him, always snarling and tugging at his chain. The "White Angel" (an immaculately white-uniformed Japanese naval officer) seemed to relish the fact that "He doesn't surrender; you surrender." Surprisingly, he ordered a Japanese sentry to care for the dog and make sure he was fed and brushed and kept free of fleas. The dog somehow created a bond between the bully and Frank.[11]

FOOD! PLEASE, FOOD!

Their inability to survive on their daily ration of two cups of tasteless rice gruel sent many prisoners to an early grave and rendered others prone to disease and digestive ailments. Food was a top priority. In the "wheeling and dealing" system in both the German and Japanese POW camps, food was power among prisoners. It could be traded for favors, for money, for almost any item. Unfortunately, the "weed" was most important to some inveterate cigarette smokers who would trade their ratio of soup for cigarettes, a trade that could eventually lead to their demise by starvation.

As the men grew increasingly debilitated, the thought of food became an absolute obsession. Countless POWs recalled constantly hallucinating about food. At night they dreamed about food; during their waking hours they fantasized about luscious cakes, potatoes au gratin, brownies a la mode. Survivors remembered that they spent hour upon hour talking about food. The men shared "recipes" conjured up by the imagination of the moment, dreamed of triple cheeseburgers "with all the fixins," and spent whole evenings concocting imaginary mile-high sandwiches. Talk about sex was of secondary importance when their stomachs were empty.

Prisoners in some of the Japanese camps were forced to go to any lengths to keep from starving. Case in point: A few days after the Japanese surrender, navyman Joe Kish and his unit were the first units in Tokyo Bay sent to northern Japan to pick up POWs who had been sentenced to the exhausting work in one of the Japanese coal mines. Internees, several of them veterans of the Bataan Death March, told Joe of being daily marched to the mines through the streets and being pelted with rocks by the civilians lined up along the streets. To look back or to shout back at them would have meant instant death. The long hours and insufficient food rations rendered the POWs human skeletons. When asked about the food during their incarceration, the men told of supplementing their starvation menu by eating cockroaches, worms, and rats. Asked how without stoves or kitchen facilities they were able to cook the rats, the men answered directly and succinctly, "We didn't."[12]

George B. Thornton, of Raleigh, Mississippi, had enlisted in the service of the U.S. Marine Corps in 1938 and had been taken prisoner by the Japanese in May 1942. In a POW camp in the Philippines, George told of the prisoners being allowed to raise a few garden vegetables, supposedly for their own use. The idea was great, but when the cabbage, onions, eggplant, and lettuce were harvested, "the Japanese got the bigger part of it. We would take litters out and would gather ten litters, and the Japanese would get nine, and we would get one. So, we got very little of what we raised."

One day, while working with his fellow prisoners in the fields adjoining his POW camp, George nearly missed being sent to eternity for a momentary lapse of attention.

Food was the top of the list on every subject. So, this particular day, we were working. The signal for one of us to shut our mouth, the other would hush and start to working fast. That was our signal. But something happened to my signal that day. I got so engrossed on talking about food that I had to eat back home and if I ever got back what I was going to do, and I missed my cue. Boy, I missed it a sight. The jolt that brought me back to reality was a shadow and I said, 'Oh, my Lord, help me!' I saw a shadow come up raising a bamboo pole. The guards carried bamboo poles or 2 x 2s, anything. But, they usually carried the bamboo because it was light, hard and would kill a fellow if you hit him right with it. Anyway, this shadow coming up and out the corner of my eye, I saw Glyn [a fellow prisoner from Mississippi] way on down the row. So, I knew I had had it. So, I just said, 'Oh, Lord, I've had it.' The shadow come on up, and through no power of my own, I was transferred about two rows over. I don't remember even flexing a muscle. I was picked up and sat down a couple of rows over there. Instead of getting clobbered aside the head, which was normal, I felt a tap on the shoulder and the Japanese was grinning. That was something that they didn't usually do. They didn't usually smile about nothing. Especially when there was a work violation or something. But this Japanese had lowered his cane, tapped me on the shoulder, and told me to get back over there and get to work. Of course, he spoke in Japanese.[13]

Not only lack of diligence but also eating any produce in the fields was a capital offense. "If the Japanese caught you eating something, they would break an arm, or hit you over the head, anything. It didn't matter. Even when you were working, in what we thought was ours, when we were working in the vegetables, if they caught us eating anything, they [would] just as soon kill you right there as not, So, you didn't take too many chances even then."

MORALE

Keeping up one's morale amidst the deplorable camp conditions was a daily challenge. Some survivors attributed their survival to their faith in God, or to lucky breaks, or possibly to some lucky charm, or to their belief in good eventually triumphing over evil, or to their conviction that eventually the war would end and they would be rescued, or to an innate conviction that somehow they would make it home safely come what may.

In the Santo Thomas internment camp, during the latter part of December of 1944, the Christmas spirit came alive (and with it the fervent hope of deliverance) when American planes flew over dropping thousands of cheery Christmas cards. Perhaps it was a way of saying, "Hang on. We know where you are and we're coming to free you." The gesture was electrifying, Hal Rather pointed out, and morale instantly skyrocketed. "The cards were in trees and bushes and literally covered parts of the Santo Thomas campus like gigantic snowflakes."

At most of the Japanese POW camps there were few church services. Sometimes a chaplain would gather a handful of men together and conduct a brief service. Frank Forsyth indicated, "There is a great deal of religion in a foxhole, but right after the war when you're a prisoner, there's really not that much religion."[14]

Fortunately, Sam Abbott recalled, he was able to retain and read his New Testament. "Well, the Japanese, I can say this, they did not try to brainwash us. They did not try to keep you from practicing your religion, if you were religious. They had no such, like the communist brainwashing, there was none of that. They had no doctrine or philosophy except their domination of the Greater East-Asia Co-Prosperity Sphere. That was what they wanted." Sam confessed, "I don't know whether we had any chaplains per se or not, but I don't remember that. But they didn't try to discourage or encourage."[15]

As for burial services, "When they died, he [the chaplain or a fellow prisoner] just dug a big trench, a long trench, and carried them out. Every morning they had a body detail, and you'd carry them out and throw them out into the trench, and that's all there was to it." In Cabanatuan there were some 100 or 200 deaths per day, usually from the ravages of malaria, dysentery, beriberi, pellagra, dengue, or tropical ulcers as well as other tropical diseases.[16]

The distribution of a few Red Cross packages and the receipt of some vital medical supplies proved tremendous boosts to morale. "Then along in 1943, the death rate started curtailing. I can remember well what a joyous day it was," John Hinkle reminisced, "when the day passed where there weren't any deaths, going from forty or fifty a day to none. Then your hope and spirit really began to perk up there."[17]

JAPANESE CAMP POW ESCAPES

With such horrendous treatment one would think that plans to escape would be a top priority for every prisoner. Not so. Unfortunately, the penalty for attempting to escape usually involved death before a firing squad. In many camps, in order to prevent escapes, the Japanese guards divided their prisoners up into squads of 10 men, and the prisoners were warned that if 1 man escaped, the other 9 men in the squad would be killed—a threat that was summarily carried out sans trial or investigation on many occasions.

On one of those occasions, Frank Forsyth, himself, narrowly escaped death. "As a matter of fact, when I was in Nichols Field (near Manila) one man in my squad escaped. They later captured him, but they lined the other nine up. That's when the "White Angel" [the irascible Japanese naval officer always dressed in an immaculate white naval uniform] was there and he debated whether or not to kill the nine. But then, just about the time they were making up their minds to go ahead and kill us, he captured the fellow. They took him out front and tied him to a pole and practically beat him to death, and then they shot him. But it was a very good way to keep people from escaping."[18]

Another time when the Japanese captured six disorientated, sick men who sought to escape from Cabanatuan Number 3, Frank Forsyth was an eyewitness to their execution. The men were ordered to dig their own graves and as one of the men took a last drag on his cigarette, he angrily stubbed it out on the Japanese officer's forehead. In an instant the firing squad had mowed him down. As he struggled in the final throes of death to get up, there were even tears in the eyes of some of the Japanese who were greatly impressed with his courage and fortitude.

Samuel W. Abbott, who had grown up in Texas, enlisted in the U.S. Navy in August 1936. On May 6, 1942, he was captured on Corregidor and for 42 months remained a prisoner of the Japanese. Sam corroborated Frank Forsyth's gruesome tales about Japanese guards' treatment of their POWs. Sam and his fellow prisoners were admonished, as were Frank Forsyth and his men, that "if one of the men in your squad escapes, the entire squad would be executed."[19]

Although they had not been long in the Cabanatuan area, Sam Abbott was sickened when he saw "four Americans that were hobbled, tied-up—you know, the Japanese, the Orientals can put you in an awful bind as far as binding you up—and hobbled them to where they were just in severe pain and torture, lying out there in front of the Japanese, what they had said was the headquarters of the Japanese. [It was] not very far from where we were in the camp, and in that hot sun all day long and by the end of the day, they were begging to be shot. They were just in such misery. Well, they marched those four guys, unhobbled them, and they marched those four guys right by our barracks. They had four little shallow graves not very far out there. They lined them up and then blindfolded them and gave them a cigarette and shot them right there." The men had been caught trying to escape. Luckily, the rest of their squads escaped a similar fate; however, the sight of those four men's torture and execution was enough to discourage any serious attempts to escape.[20]

As time passed, there were fewer and fewer escapes. The men quickly came to the conclusion that the escapee as a Caucasian could be quickly identified, and without food and water, his only hope was to get connected to some of the guerrillas, and that was not an easy task. In addition, there was the gnawing fear for the safety of the other nine men in one's squad.

OTHER AVENUES OF ESCAPE

At least one man, without even leaving the camp, found another avenue of escape from the beatings and beheadings. "But there was some that worked their way out of it," according to Frank R. Forsyth, who spent almost three years as a captive of the Japanese.

There was one man, we called him Red Dog, who grabbed a broom and used to walk all over the camp, supposedly crazy. And he remained stooped over sweeping. After a while—the Japanese are kind of leery of people who are crazy—and he'd just sweep all over the place. That's all he did: [he] took the broom to bed with him, would get up and sweep anywhere at all. [He'd] walk in the commander's office and sweep in there. They'd look at him [and] call him *bakka*, which means crazy. Well, he continually did that. [He] worked his way out of the mine and they had him hanging around camp. The day that they announced the surrender, he took the broom, threw it off to one side and said 'I don't need that son-of-a-bitch anymore.' He had remained in that position. The doctors had looked at him and they said that the muscles had formed by being continually stooped over [and] that he'd never be able to straighten up. That day he stood straight up. The doctors sat there and they couldn't understand it.[21]

There were, of course, hundreds of distraught prisoners who escaped into a world of their own. The backbreaking work in many of the Japanese camps, the severe beatings, debilitating disease, the lack of food, and the relinquishing of hope that they would ever be rescued often gave way to depression and the abandonment of the will to live. Some men became completely unhinged, walking around with glazed-over eyes, in a stupor that no amount of prodding or attempted reassurance could penetrate. J. Cecil Chambliss still grieved for the men who simply gave up and died. "They would just have absolutely no desire to live. They just couldn't face it. That's all there was to it. Of course, once they developed that attitude, unless we could snap them out of it, which we would try to do, it was just a matter of time before they would go."[22]

"Of course, there were a lot of prisoners in that camp that died because they wanted to die," Frank Forsyth recalled. "The Dutch are probably the worst of that. A Dutchman will turn over, face the wall, and he's going to die." The doctors would be "madder than hell and say, 'There's not organically a thing wrong with that man. He's just as healthy as you and I are, and yet he'll be dead tomorrow morning.' And they would die [for] that reason."[23]

It seemed surprising that often it was the young people who gave up hope first. "They seemed to say it's no use," John Hinkle observed. "However, until you have really looked death in the eye, I don't think you realize how grateful we are for life."[24]

A MOVE TO JAPAN

In the fall and winter of 1944 when the Japanese camp commanders decided to move as many of the able-bodied prisoners as possible to Japan to use as slave labor, there was another horrendous trip for many POWs, this time by boats with men jam-packed into minuscule, unventilated quarters. Conditions were so unbearable that, "We seriously prayed that a sub would sink us and put an end to this. We were that desperate. And I was on the last prison boat to Japan that wasn't sunk. One that came after us had our prayers answered for them. That ship, with 1,600 POWs was sunk. The survivors were put aboard another vessel and that one was also sunk. Only 175 prisoners survived of the 1,600 that started out."[25] The Japanese had not marked the ships, and Allies, unaware that the ships were carrying American prisoners, ruthlessly bombed and torpedoed the ships, known as "The Hell Ships." Estimates run as high as 5,000 men who died as a result of the bombings of the Hell Ships. On one ship alone more men died than on the Bataan Death March.[26]

Not only the bombing and torpedoing of the Hell Ships but the oppressive heat, suffocation, and even murder and cannibalism took the lives of many of the prisoners on the Hell Ships. At least one survivor of the Hell Ships, Henry Stanley, claimed: "That ship [the *Taga Maru*] was the worst part of the whole deal; that ship made the Death March look like a picnic. They died like flies." Manny Lawton agreed, "by far the worst of all was the . . . journey from Manila to Japan on the Hell Ships."[27]

The POWs who survived the Hell Ships and other relocation attempts were sent to various areas to work in shipyards, on railroad tracks, in mines—wherever needed to build up the Japanese labor supply. It would seem that conditions could not get any worse than the camps in the Philippines, but on Honshu Island, Phil Brain was assigned work in a copper mine. "We had to get up at 4 A.M., eat millet or barley mush, walk three miles to the site, then down 478 steps to the mine itself. Late in the evenings, we retraced those same steps back to the surface. The guards rode the elevators. One worker was badly crushed between two ore cars but the guards would not allow us to send him up on the lift. We had to carry him up those 478 steps."[28]

Day after day the debilitating work continued until, "One day in mid-August, 1945, a guard told us that America had surrendered. We knew differently, but wondered why he would try out such a rumor on us. The following day we were told that America had dropped a big bomb which caused the Japanese to surrender. We were free."[29]

FROM JAVA TO NAGASAKI

In November of 1941, Roger H. White, Jr. of Texas, a sergeant with the U.S. Army, was sent to San Francisco, from there via Pearl Harbor (as a part of a convoy that had left Pearl three days before the Japanese attack) to the Fiji Islands and Australia to help set up an Army base on Java. The Japanese were determined to take over Java, the key to the Indies, as an important part of their expansion plans. Unfortunately, the Allies came up too late with too little to stave off the savage Japanese assaults, and on March 9–10, 1942, the Dutch East Indies were surrendered to the Japanese despite heavy fighting by the men in the Allied field artillery. Thus, Roger became a prisoner of the Japanese, a member of the "Lost Battalion" in the Pacific, and he was sent to Singapore and then to Nagasaki to work in the shipyards. Other POWs (there were some nine other camps nearby) were sent into the mines to dig for coal.[30]

Only the strong could survive the overwork, the starvation, and the cruel beatings by the Japanese guards. Prisoners were housed in barracks, 60 men to a room some 20 by 30 feet, and were given half cups of rice or rice gruel twice a day as their daily food allotment. In addition, insects—bedbugs, body lice, maggots, rice worms, mosquitoes, and other insects—almost ate them alive. It was a precarious existence, and one never knew when he would be beaten senseless or killed on the spot. Once, when Roger accidentally dropped a drill, a Japanese guard rushed over and beat him savagely until he was almost dead. Roger got even, however, through sabotage on his job—by driving the rivets into the steel a little off the mark so that they would sheer off and cause leaks when the ship was launched and put in heavy sea. (POWs everywhere would attempt sabotage whenever possible.)

In August, the first news of the atom bomb came when an old Japanese official came running into Roger's POW camp awed by word that the biggest bomb ever heard of had been dropped on Hiroshima. Although the prisoners took little notice of the report, they, too, were awed when they heard the thunder of 500 B-29s in the skies, a sortie that lasted six hours. Soon the Japanese commander announced that hostilities had ceased, and the war had ended. The prisoners were euphoric, however, the news angered throngs of Japanese who seized the opportunity to pelt the prisoners with rocks. It was therefore suggested that the prisoners remain in camp.

Food was still scarce, and a plea for more food ended with an emissary's appeal and the report that the Japanese themselves were little better off by way of food than the POWs. Soon, however, Allied planes began dropping huge parcels of food and clothing. Unfortunately, the planes' low altitude and the size of the drums of food actually killed some of the soldiers who ran out with arms outstretched to get first choice of the manna from Heaven.

Aware of the desperation of the prisoners, the Allied forces were extravagant in their attempts to supply food, medicine, and clothing to the POWs awaiting evacuation from their prison camps. One soldier told of 2,000 pairs of shoes being dropped on his camp; an inordinate amount because their numbers had dwindled as a result of starvation and disease to only 280 survivors.

The pilot of one of the planes dropping provisions to the prisoners at a camp on the island of Kyushu, James Romero, described the scene from the perspective of the crew of the supply plane after they had dropped their cargo. "I came around for one more run at the camp and began a descent to buzz them. As we approached, I dropped to about 150 feet and we saw a prisoner hobbling at a near run toward the south fence. He climbed the barbed wire fence rapidly, hooked a leg around a fence post and, as I passed over his head, he blew kisses at us. I made a steep climbing turn over the camp and wiggled my wings in salute to the prisoner and we headed for home. The return trip was quiet, but we were satisfied with a job well done."[31]

It took about four weeks later for liberation to became a reality, and Roger White and his fellow POWs (they had been moved from the shipyards to Nagasaki to Orio some 120 miles northwest to dig for coal) began being shipped out to be sent home. At the first stop en route home, a group of Red Cross ladies were passing out coffee and donuts. It was a welcome sight, and Roger's British friend exclaimed with big tears rolling down his cheeks: "You know, Rog, those are the first white women we have seen in four years!"[32]

THE BURMA SCENE

J. Cecil Chambliss, of Purvis, Mississippi, had enlisted in the U.S. Navy in 1934 and was serving aboard the USS *Houston* when it was sunk by the Japanese on March 1, 1942. Fortunately, he survived the disaster, but was taken captive by the Japanese, and for the next 42 months he lived out the war as a POW, first in Java and then in Singapore, Burma, and Saigon. In Burma he spent 20 months as forced labor working on the 365-mile Thailand–Burma railroad, where he estimated one-third of the 90,000 to 100,000 men died building that railroad.[33]

The Railroad, called "The Death Railway," was designed to connect Kanchanaburi, Thailand and Thanbyuzayat in Burma. The Japanese believed the route south of Singapore was too vulnerable to Allied bombing and also was too time consuming. Therefore, the Japanese high command ordered the importation of tens of thousands of POWs to take on the backbreaking job of building the railroad. It is estimated that there was almost one death for every sleeper laid on the Burma–Thailand railway. Overwork, Japanese brutality, starvation, disease, and lack of medical facilities accounted for the deaths of 12,000 POWs. (Among this number were Australian, British, and Dutch POWs, as well as Americans. This number was greatly surpassed by the deaths of untold numbers of Southeast Asians.) The little plots on the sides of hills that were used as cemeteries filled up fast, and the lonely, mournful sound of the bugler blowing taps at a new gravesite was a sound that ever after sent shivers down J. Cecil Chambliss' back. (Men were moved around in the numerous camps, usually numbered according to their distance from the headquarter's base, that lined the railroad track.) The same brutalization of prisoners and starvation diets appeared to prevail in Burma as in the other Japanese POW camps. J. Cecil Chambliss told of the fate of three men who tried to escape the forced labor POW camp in Burma. Following their capture, other prisoners were forced to dig their graves for them, and the escapees were unceremoniously executed. Two more men tried the same thing and suffered similar consequences. The jungle usually succeeded in entrapping any would-be escapees.

Once in Burma, when someone had been caught buying something from the natives, J. Cecil Chambliss recalled, "They lined us all up in front of the guard house and made us kneel down there. Then they started beating the fool out of us. They'd come by and one of them [would] hit you on one side and then come back on the other side. He'd slap the fool out of you. Then they kept us kneeling there, I don't know how long, for hours on end, just for some little minute [infraction of the rules]. So we were beginning to get a taste of what was to come later, you see."

The death tolls in the various camps were considerably augmented by the lack of doctors and medical supplies. Proper medicine and even a novice surgeon could have saved so many lives. Cecil Chambliss remembered a man who had appendicitis. As there was no way to operate, the appendix ruptured. "He just actually laid there and died. That's all, with a ruptured appendix. It could have been corrected in five-minute's time, he could have been saved."

In the prisoners' starving conditions almost anything was fair game for food. As they were building the Burma Death Railroad, American POWs survived their starvation rations by eating the eggs from bird nests that they stumbled upon in the trees. A dinner of king cobra proved not too displeasing. "There was nothing wrong with that meat. Just the only thing wrong was we didn't have enough of it," Cecil Chambliss recalled. Bugs, worms, and horsemeat all served to provide the mandatory protein. Squeamish eaters ended up in the cemeteries.

In the Burma camps apparently there was little news of the outside world. During their POW incarceration in Saigon however, the acquisition of parts for a radio and its final assembly brought renewed hope for J. Cecil Chambliss and his fellow prisoners. Over a period of time some of the men were able to pick up the different parts needed, and with the help "of one guy that was the brains of the thing" they put together a radio. The radio was secreted under one of the huts, and at the precise time of the BBC broadcast, guards would be stationed about the hut and one man would be positioned under the hut to listen to the news. That prisoner told his buddies and they grapevined the news to the rest of the men by word of mouth. Although the Japanese made feverish attempts to find the radio, practically tearing the huts apart, they were to no avail. The Japanese were clued that there must be a radio somewhere when they sensed that the prisoners were "in too good a mood."[34]

True to American ingenuity, there were always some would-be entrepreneurs in the camps who made a bit of money by concocting devious methods of outwitting their Japanese captors. "Wheeling and dealing" was ubiquitous in many prison camps, and Frank Forsyth found it particularly prevalent during his imprisonment in the Cabanatuan camps. Knowing that there were very severe penalties for Japanese guards who contracted a venereal disease, Frank Forsyth made the most of his talents and ingenuity by concocting "sulfa" pills that he made and sold to the guards. Sulfa drugs were in their infancy and difficult to procure, and Frank developed a thriving business by molding a little plaster of Paris, baking it in his homemade oven, putting a little glycerin on top—and voila "sulfa" pills. These he insisted must be swallowed whole in order to be effective and would cure most types of venereal disease. The business proved a real moneymaker—that is until one of the guards, who apparently was finding no real cure, took the pills to a chemist to have them analyzed. From then on, Frank's days were spent hiding out, under, above, and behind buildings, anywhere in an effort to evade his irate ex-customers who were on the warpath ready to kill him. Finally the guards were transferred leaving Frank congratulating himself on his clever deception.[35]

As in other POW camps, a positive attitude appeared to be an all-important key to survival. J. Cecil Chambliss recalled, "The thing I think that helped some of us, probably a lot more so than others was we were able to keep a little bit more positive attitude and not become so mentally depressed. Not that we didn't. I'm sure we all did at one time or another. I know there were times that it would have been so simple just to lie down there and not get up, but, then, the desire to live and come back was sufficient . . . I know that there were times that each and every one of us, and I know myself, that it just didn't seem possible that I could pick one foot up and put it ahead of the other in carrying this dirt, hauling it, building that railroad, and especially, get back to camp."[36]

FREEDOM

From the safe distance of his POW camp about 80 miles away, Frank Forsyth actually heard and saw the explosion resulting from the atomic bomb dropped on Nagasaki. Thinking the Americans had bombed some huge Japanese munitions dump, Frank and his comrades knew nothing of what had happened at Hiroshima and shrugged off the noise as a monstrously successful bomb drop. It was later that they learned of the magnitude and devastation—and controversy—caused by the dropping of the world's newest instrument of mass destruction. A few days later, the prisoners were called out for a speech from the Japanese commandant who announced that the Emperor had graciously consented to end the hostilities. He instructed the men to conduct themselves honorably as free men and "share their Red Cross packages with the poor people of Japan." What insanity! It took a wild stretch of the imagination to think that the prisoners would generously divvy up any forthcoming Red Cross parcels with captors who had beaten them almost to death, had kept them teetering on the brink of starvation, and had withheld the distribution of Red Cross packages and eaten the contents themselves.[37]

As a radioman on LCI (L), Sam Greene helped land the Army's 6th Rangers at Lingayan Gulf as they prepared for the raid on the Japanese POW camp at Cabanatuan. The raid, detailed in books, movies, and TV programs, was an attempt to attack the camp and bring the prisoners out alive, an assault that proved to be one of the most dangerous and adventuresome of the war. It was a 30-mile trek to the camp, much of it made by the Rangers crawling through the undergrowth at night for a surprise attack. Sam's ship lay off shore, and Sam and his fellow radiomen kept open radio communications with the Rangers and the 6th Amphibious Command. The raid was heralded a great success in that it succeeded in liberating 512 POWs at the cost of one Ranger (Dr. Capt. Jimmy Fisher, the son of the famous author Dorothy Canfield Fisher) and 200 of the enemy.

Sam had high praise for the Rangers and their perilous mission to rescue the POWs. "I saw quite a bit of action in the Pacific and met a lot of Marines and soldiers whom we landed on various islands and beaches, but the 6th Rangers were a group set apart. To a man they were the bravest, friendliest and most relaxed group that we transported on our ship."[38]

Three years as a Japanese prisoner of war, stamped J. Cecil Chambliss and others like him for life. Troubled with depression, dysentery, malaria, stomach troubles, and lung problems, it took Cecil another three and a half years of hospital confinement in the United States after the war to even begin to regain his health and strength following his imprisonment and forced labor on the Burma railroad.[39]

CHAPTER 10

Luck, Fate, Providence, and Guardian Angels

In war there is survival—or death. There were men who took a fatal bullet their first day of battle. There were others who dodged the bullet for four years of combat. There were men (almost without exception) who were resolutely convinced they were going to make it home alive. There were also those who were equally convinced that they would survive, whose bodies filled the cemeteries and the ocean depths. There were men who credited their personal survival to the grace of God, others called it great good luck, others deemed it fate. Over the passage of time, however, even at the moment of crisis, a conclusion that steadily gained credence was the realization that survival was an extremely chancy affair.

Incessant machine gunfire, strafing from German planes that "buzzed off like a giant annoying mosquito," and bombs that exploded scarcely two feet away took a fearful toll on John Walker's army buddies serving in the front lines during the bloody warfare that persisted through France and Germany. "We were in the front lines for a total of over 100 days. Our division, the 42nd Rainbow Division, suffered over 3,000 men killed or wounded," John recalled. "Such happenings made us all realize how little control we had over our fate in the war. No matter how well trained you were, how alert, how cautious, how competent a soldier, you could easily become a casualty at the whim of a shot or shell addressed 'to whom it may concern.' This fact has become more and more apparent to me as I've reflected these many years on those frightful days in combat so many years ago."[1]

Sixty years later, Ted Thomas looks back with almost disbelief that he could have been so fortunate as to have survived a gunshot wound to his ankle and a mine explosion that left him the sole survivor of his tank crew. For 11 months Ted faced the enemy close up every day and every night—and somehow lived to tell about it. Even on the trip overseas, Ted was feeling pretty lucky when an enemy bombing and a barrage of four torpedoes missed their mark and left his ship unscathed.

Brushes with death seemed to follow in ever increasing ascendancy. In one hairsbreadth escape in Germany, Ted was confronted by a German officer who quickly drew his gun; fortunately, Ted succeeded in outdrawing him. Some of Ted's most terrifying experiences were the various river crossings before the bridges were constructed. There was no place to hide, and everyone was at the mercy of heavy machine gun fire from the enemy. Over time, Ted made it across the Rhine, the Mosel, and the Saar in rubber rafts and watched in stark terror as gunfire took out two of his friends as they attempted to cross the Merderet, southwest of Ste.-Mere-Eglise. Luckily, Ted escaped unscathed from the devastating hedgerow fighting and terrible Battle of the Bulge that proved so costly to the Allies.[2]

Strangers did a double take during the war at seeing the Hinses' front door replete with a service flag with nine blue stars. (A blue star in the window or on a door indicated a member of the family serving in the armed forces; a gold star was a reminder that a member had died in the service of one's country.) Springfield, Illinois neighbors and townspeople, however, knew that Herb, Wally, and Marshall were serving with the Army; Bedell with the Navy; Paul with the Marines; Harold and Burton with the Army Air Force; daughter Marion with the Waves; and daughter Mildred with the Navy Nurse Corp. Their youngest son, Don, was too young (11–14 years old) to serve in any of the services. (Small wonder Mrs. Hines was voted Illinois Mother of the Year and later American Mother of the Year.) It was a miracle, parents and siblings agreed, that everyone in the Hines family returned home safely—no one even suffering a minor injury.[3]

During the fateful winter of 1944–45, the weather proved almost as threatening a foe as the Germans. Driving snow, freezing temperatures, frozen guns, and the lack of white camouflage suits and covers for their tanks compounded the frightful numbers of casualties incurred during the Germans' powerhouse drive in December, during the Battle of the Bulge. Morale was at alarmingly low ebb. One sergeant succumbed to the horrendous conditions and sought a self-inflicted wound as his only escape. Men by the hundreds poured into the first-aid units with frozen ears, frozen hands, and frozen feet. As Ted Thomas sought medical care for a frozen foot, once again his luck prevailed as his doctor studied the blackened foot and nodded, "I think I can save your foot, we won't have to amputate."[4]

The fighting on Leyte was vicious. Joe Brochin wondered how we ever won with untrained replacements, poor leadership, and ubiquitous mine sewn fields. One day, in an attempt to look over some tall grass on Leyte, Joe took a hit to his leg and was left for two hours unattended as he continued to bleed. When the medics finally discovered him and carried him to an aid station, Joe was chilled to the bone when he heard the doctor, after taking one look at him, dismiss his case saying, "Don't waste plasma on him. He's too far gone." Ironically, Joe watched as wounded Japanese were being given the precious plasma according to the Geneva Convention.

Eventually Joe received essential treatment for his wounded leg and was sent to New Guinea for further treatment. Surely his guardian angel had been watching over him yet again, for shortly after leaving Leyte, Joe learned that the Japanese had taken over the hospital where he had so recently been treated and killed most of the patients. At Hollandia, New Guinea, it looked as though Joe's leg would have to be amputated. This time, however, his degree in pharmacology came to the fore to save his leg. As his temperature soared to 104 degrees, Joe, knowing that this was a signal that amputation was imminent, surreptitiously took the thermometer out of his mouth, shook it down, and smiled innocently as the nurse came back to read it. "That saved my leg," he rejoiced.[5]

The men in Ted Thomas's unit saw their mess sergeant as an angel in disguise. When they were on patrol, Karl, a sergeant and the only black man in the squadron, was assigned the tiresome task of carrying clean water for the men who were wary of drinking from streams or from town wells for fear the water might be poisoned. As the men were about to cross the Rhine, out of nowhere three German planes zoomed in to strafe the convoy. The tanks and trucks were instantaneously divested of their occupants as everyone immediately jumped out and ducked for cover. Not so Karl on his water wagon. On the second flyby, Karl set his gun sights, and on the third attack brought the planes down single-handedly. Seeing that Karl had saved the day, the men simply mobbed him with hugs and salutations. Now and then justice prevails in a world gone terribly wrong, and in time Karl's courageous action was rewarded with a Silver Star.[6]

Billy Benton of Laurel, Mississippi was a veteran of submarine service in the South Pacific where he served as an electrician. He, like many 17- and 18-year-olds, "never thought about getting killed." Billy spoke for thousands of GI veterans. They would not take a million dollars for the experience but would never go through it again. Billy would never forget that while the Japanese were launching an aircraft carrier in Tokyo Bay, his submarine sneaked through the nets and lay at the bottom of the Bay. Although the Japanese, on the suspicion that there was an American submarine somewhere, dropped depth bombs and scoured the Bay, they searched in vain for Billy's submarine and finally gave up. When the Japanese opened the gate to let out a merchant ship, Billy's submarine went right out with it.[7]

Andy Andrews kept remembering being called up at 7:30 one morning for a special flight, whereupon he and his crew hurriedly dressed, ready for briefing. Suddenly there was a change in the orders, and their flight was canceled. Unfortunately, the pilot of the plane that took off in their place somehow became disoriented in a thick fog during take off. There was a tremendous roar just beyond the airfield as the doomed plane crashed, and its load of 500 pounds of bombs blasted away the entire crew as well as scores of English people living nearby. Andy and his men were shocked to think how easily that could have been their plane.[8]

Early on, seamen were cautioned about the hazards of carelessness and the possibility of falling overboard. Karl Legant remembered his departure from New York for Europe aboard an English troop ship. About an hour after leaving the New York docks there was an ominous announcement over the P.A. system. "Men, if you fall overboard, we are sorry."[9]

Not all ships' captains were as merciless as it might seem. If there were a remote chance of saving a drowning seaman, many captains would turn their ships around and engage in a desperate attempt to save the man. As commander of an escort ship, attached to a convoy transporting troops and supplies across the Atlantic, Eugene Pigg suddenly received an order to search the waters behind a French supply ship and try to rescue a crew member who had been lost overboard. Of course, there were no ship lights, and the chances of finding the man were slim indeed; however, the commander turned his ship around and repeatedly kept sailing for a few yards, then shutting off the engines and listening intently for any sounds of life in the murky water. Suddenly, there was the frantic sound of a man yelling for help. "You never saw a happier person in your life than that fellow we pulled out of the black Atlantic," the commander reported.[10]

As skippers for a PT boat, Roy Herbert, of Warren, Michigan, and his friend Martin Leupold took turns on 12-hour assignments during their tour of duty in the South Pacific. Attempting to catch a few hours' shut-eye before being awakened at midnight for his shift, Leupold was fast asleep on the fantail. Although the waters were calm, as he responded to the call and stood up to stretch, a mountainous swell suddenly washed over the deck, sweeping him overboard and into the dusky depths. The men went ballistic. They were only 100 miles off the Japanese shore and had been maintaining strict radio silence with no lights to reveal their presence. They were in an extremely precarious position, for turning on a light could easily alert the Japanese as to their location. Without a moment's hesitation Leupold's shipmates agreed: "To hell with the Japanese, were going back for Leupold." Radios came alive, a searchlight was turned on, and the ship made a 180-degree turn. In addition, four companion ships quickly joined the hunt. For half an hour they searched in the midnight blackness.

It seemed absolutely hopeless to try to find a man, without a life preserver, flailing about in the roiling waters. Suddenly, there was a shout, "ahoy, there to your starboard!" and sure enough there was Leupold floating in the briny waters. There was enough cheering to have awakened the Japanese as Leupold was quickly hauled aboard. It was a night to remember for Leupold and certainly for everyone else aboard ship. His friend, Roy Herbert, admitted that he was a good Catholic and had never prayed so hard in his life as those minutes involved in the search.[11]

As Humphrey Sears Taylor was engaged in the dangerous house-to-house fighting in the small towns and villages in Germany as the war was winding down, Hump cautiously pushed open the door of a house with the muzzle of his gun. The door might be booby-trapped, a die-hard German might be crouched in the room. His trigger finger was at the ready when suddenly there was a tap on his shoulder. Hump whirled around only to find that he had come within seconds of gunning down a nun, "complete with habit and headpiece." The nun was anxious to tell him to hold his gunfire when entering the basement for she had hidden a group of orphaned children there. It was a near miss for the nun and a near miss for Hump if the tap on the shoulder had come from a German guerrilla.[12]

One of his most stressful experiences, John Goodell confessed, came about suddenly one night when flying back at 15,000 feet from delivering his cargo across the Himalyas to his home base in Myitkyina, Burma, the crew ran into a violent storm with heavy rainfall. "Suddenly there was a blinding flash in the cockpit and all the electrical instruments were knocked out." Whether the plane was struck by lightening or whether there was a static electrical build up in the airplane John was never sure, but the windshield wipers would not work and there was no possible way of navigating. The crew panicked, convinced they would surely crash. Blindly, John held to what he desperately hoped was a westerly direction. Time seemed interminable, until "by sheer luck there was a break in the clouds and under us was the Irrawaddy River, the turning point to turn north up the River to our base camp. Swooping down through the clouds at 3 A.M. we saw the runway lights and landed safely... All in a day's work," John shrugged.[13]

On his first trip back over the hump (one of 18 trips), Jim Veen, co-piloting a B-24, underwent a similarly terrifying experience. Suddenly the crew found their plane in big trouble—they were totally lost. The weather was overcast, and with a new instructor, a new pilot, and a new navigator on board the situation looked hopeless. Finally, after what seemed a lifetime, the air tower located them and directed them in for a safe landing.[14]

What proved a disaster for some 1,500 men turned out to be the salvation of Dick Robinson. It was Christmas Eve, 1944, and after seven weeks on the coast of southern England, Dick was on his way across the English Channel on a troop ship. The bright moonlight apparently betrayed their position and suddenly there was a tremendous explosion announcing the torpedoing of the troop ship just two ships behind Dick's. The losses were catastrophic, some 1,500 men lost their lives or suffered injuries, and Dick and his buddies were sure their ship would be targeted next. Luck won out, however, and their converted cruise ship made it safely into Cherbourg. Because of the terrible losses, the powers that be decided against sending Dick and his men into the area of the horrific Battle of the Bulge. As a light machine gunner, Dick knew his chances of surviving enemy gunfire would have been slim indeed. Fate had surely played an important role in sending Dick home alive and unscathed after the war. Although he went into the war as a 21-year-old, he returned home a 25-year-old with a tremendous appreciation of life and his country and the conviction that he had certainly lived a "charmed life" during the war years.[15]

While Larry Hartman, a Coast Guardsman aboard the Coast Guard cutter the *Crocus,* was delayed in the Boston Harbor in 1943 awaiting a transfer of supplies, the *Escanaba* was sent out in the *Crocus'* place. Larry and his crew counted themselves extremely lucky not to have been on the *Escanaba,* which was torpedoed, and within three minutes, all hands, save one, were lost to watery graves.[16]

To survive one ship's sinking would call for great good fortune, but to survive two sinkings would border on the incredible. Gerald (Bud) Rogne, a farm boy from North Dakota, was the lucky survivor of the sinking of the *Lexington* and later the *Block Island.* During the momentous Battle of the Coral Sea in May of 1942, the *Lexington* took both torpedo and bomb hits that started internal explosions and fires that completely disabled the ship. With the call for "abandon ship," it was discovered there were not enough lifeboats, and as a result the wounded were lowered into waiting whaleboats while the able-bodied men made it down via ropes and into the water. As Bud struggled in the water, the suction of the ship kept drawing him closer and closer to the ship until finally he was able to swim away where after 25 or 30 minutes a boat from a nearby ship gathered him up.

One experience of having survived a sinking ship in the middle of an ocean was quite enough for Bud, but fate had yet another ship disaster for Bud. The *Block Island,* a merchant ship converted into an aircraft carrier, was attacked by a submarine in the Mediterranean Sea and once again Bud, leading a charmed life, was picked up by a whaleboat off a destroyer and was taken to Africa.[17]

Although Joe Spinosa, of Memphis, Tennessee and later Louisville, Kentucky, was somewhat ambivalent about his war experiences, he prides himself on having saved the lives of 12 of his buddies. One day during the fighting in Italy, Joe and his platoon were ordered to take a certain hill just ahead of them. It was daylight. There was absolutely no cover of trees, no rocks, and no protective gunfire. It was a suicide mission, and Joe, although only a PFC, refused to advance. "I'm not going on that hill," he shouted. In the background the officer growled: "Joe, you could be court-martialed for insubordination." "Go ahead court-martial me, you SOB, I'm not going," Joe retorted. With that, he and the other men stubbornly held their ground, and the raid was called off. The next night, the wisdom of Joe's decision was proven correct when scouts discovered an enemy machine gun nest that would have quickly wiped out Joe and his entire platoon. (Fortunately, the officer realized his faulty judgment and no court-martial was ever initiated.)[18]

Ray Young counted the two-week delay of his ship's departure from New York in early June of 1944 as one of his luckiest breaks of the war. The ship had been held up for repairs, and the late start prevented those men from being part of the first wave in the Normandy invasion. Again fortune was on his side when during the fighting near Troyes, France, his helmet took a sniper's bullet that pierced the metal and somehow miraculously circled around through the underside and came out the back. Ray was unscathed.[19]

In early 1944, as Dudley Rishell and his men were helping to set up a supply area in Mindanao, in the Philippines, one more truck was needed to transport personnel from the front area back to a "rest area," and sure enough Dudley Rishell was assigned to drive the truck. It was long past sunset, and it was dangerous territory from the standpoint of road mines and gunfire. There was only one way to make it, Dudley decided, and that was to floorboard it through the rough roads. His decision saved his life, for the trip turned into a race against death. His speed saved him from a shell that exploded directly behind him, a shell that would have sent him and his passengers into eternity. The next day he shuddered as he observed the masses of bullet holes that had perforated the canvas top of his truck.[20]

Call it divine intervention, luck, or fate, Wayne Adgate and his crew survived 35 B-17 bombing runs into Germany from his Air Force base at Bury St. Edmunds, located a few miles east of Cambridge, England. (It was an interesting sidelight that during their first few days at St. Edmonds, their co-pilot, who had remained behind with a severe sinus infection during a stopover in New Hampshire en route to England, rejoined the crew thus displacing the temporary replacement. The crew cheered his return, awestruck by his miraculously quick recovery, thanks to a brand new drug called penicillin.)

After two flights as a co-pilot, Wayne Adgate had been given command of his own plane and successfully flew his first mission over Germany. In celebration of their first mission, crews were traditionally awarded a 24-hour pass to go into London, and Wayne and his men jumped at the opportunity. As they emerged from the Underground in the center of London, they were greeted by the "Picadilly commandos" (the prostitutes) who were lined up eager for customers. Without hesitation Wayne's crew passed up the "girls" and spent their time in traditional tourist fashion, checking out Westminister Abbey and St. Paul's, taking in the theater, and looking over the Tower of London. It was a wonderful relaxing time, and 24 hours later the men reluctantly headed back to St. Edmunds.

At first it seemed like a letdown from their London trip, but for some reason, there was an ominous stillness about the base. Everything seemed almost deserted. There were no planes. All too soon came the sickening news that their squadron had suffered disastrous losses during the previous night's raid over Germany. Eight out of their twelve planes had been shot down. Wayne and his men were in a state of shock. How incredibly close they had come to death. While they had been cruising around London, having a jolly old time doing the town, dozens of their comrades had met death face to face. (From that moment on, close associations with other crews at the base came to halt. The death of friends rocked one to the core. Better to empathize with vague names on a roster rather than to suffer the gut-wrenching loss of personal friends.)

Wayne Adgate's crew suffered yet another death defying experience when on November 2nd, 1944, Wayne and his men took off from St. Edmunds on their twelfth mission over Germany. That day, "the pilots had the sky to themselves," and there was almost no anti-aircraft action. "It was a beautiful day, not a cloud in the sky," Wayne remembered. Coming down on their way to their target, the oil refineries near Leipzig, the crew watched in terror as the plane directly in front of them, Peterson's plane, took a direct hit and blew to pieces. They were flying in formation and, of course, there was no possible way to get in or out. Even so, the crew took what minuscule evasive action was possible in a supreme effort to avoid the flack from the Germans and the rain of debris from Peterson's plane. Thanks to prayers and grit, the crew finally made it back to the base where they counted 72 holes in their plane. Years later, crew members put in yearly calls to each other across the country in commemoration of their survival: "Remember what day this is—November 2nd?"[21]

Some of their most frightening experiences? On several occasions, Paul Niland and a patrol from the 10th Mountain Infantry who were inching their way through Italy were ordered to go ahead of the lines to reconnoiter. It was an overnight mission: first to secure positions in front of the lines; then to hole up overnight in the basement of a bombed-out farmhouse, and then to stealthily steal back to headquarters in the black of the following night. Scared? "You bet!" Paul responded. Actually the missions were more or less experiments to see if the men *could* pull it off.

As the fighting worsened during the battle of Castel D'Aino in the Apennines in March of 1945, and as the shells kept falling ever closer to his foxhole, Paul Niland was convinced he would never come out of the battle alive. Paul was sure that sooner or later one of those shells that was finding its deadly mark in the cold, muddy foxholes of one after another of his friends, would eventually have his name on it. As the fighting began winding down, Paul looked over to see one of his friends writhing in agony from a severe chest wound. But wait! If he could be given immediate medical attention there might still be hope for his friend. Almost without thinking and completely oblivious to the imminent danger of bombs and machine gun fire, Paul quickly commandeered two German prisoners of war, contrived a makeshift stretcher, and helped them to carry his fallen comrade back to the first aid station. Unfortunately, all the medical help in the world could not save Paul's friend. For Paul, there was the guilt of survival; for his courage, there was an unanticipated Bronze Star.[22]

A desire to see the world prompted John Joseph Murphy to enlist in the U.S. Navy in July of 1938. After eight active years of duty where he saw action at Guadalcanal, the Marshall Islands, Iwo Jima, Peleliu, New Guinea, Leyte, and at the Battle for Manila, John admitted upon his discharge that he had seen considerably more of the world than he had planned. As a Water Tender aboard the USS *Monterey* while the ship was engaged in a battle to destroy a major Japanese airbase on Truk Island, John remembered the Japanese strafing "the daylights out of us." Bombs rained down from the skies, and shrapnel flew everywhere. An involuntary movement of his hand to his face saved John from more serious injury or even death as a sizable fragment of metal hit his hand instead of his face or skull.[23]

John Gail McKane corroborated the heady feeling of danger expressed by carrier pilots as they attempted to takeoff and land on the pitching and yawing carriers. Carrier landings fascinated John McKane who saw them as a challenge "because they were tricky and dangerous. . . Even after combat experience, we carrier pilots considered carrier landings as dangerous as the missions. Of the 24 pilots in my unit, one other pilot and I were the only ones fortunate enough not to have an accident on takeoff or landing." There was always the problem of the movement of the ship. "When a pilot returned to where he expected to find his carrier and didn't, he had little time to search for it due to low fuel. Many ran out of fuel in that situation and had to ditch in the ocean. Some were recovered, some were not." Jay Sterner Hammond, two-term governor of Alaska, concurred with other pilots that their most stressful experiences in life were night landings on a rolling and pitching carrier.[24]

On his first mission while flying a new plane, a C-37, Air Force pilot Jack Shingleton was sometimes flying blindly with maps from the Royal Australian Air Force that read, "We cannot guarantee the accuracy of these directions to the islands in the Pacific. If you note an inaccuracy, please report it." (Planes at that time flew without navigators.) Other cards read: "We cannot guarantee the altitude here for we do not have the exact information. If you note an inaccuracy, please report it." Scary, yes?

Early during his wartime career as a pilot, Jack Shingleton and his crew had just unloaded a heavy cargo of parachuters with all their cumbersome equipment at Lae, the Army Air Force headquarters at New Guinea. The crew had scarcely time for a swig of Coca-Cola before they loaded up again, this time to transport five nurses to the front lines. Suddenly during take-off, when they were scarcely 400 feet off the ground, disaster threatened big time as the plane lost one of its engines. Hearts beat wildly as the plane neared stalling speed. Surely they were headed for eternity. With a good deal of luck and some skillful maneuvering, fortunately they were able to return to the base for a safe landing. The light weight of their five nurses made all the difference. Had the plane been loaded with the parachuters and their heavy supplies, there was no question but that they would have crashed. (In one of the most remarkable accomplishments of the war, Jack Shingleton and his five buddies flying out of Finschafen, New Guinea stayed together throughout the war. This meant flying 120 hours per month to scores of Pacific islands they had never even heard of before, surviving flack, typhoons, kamikazes, and enemy gunfire. An unbelievable feat!)[25]

Early in the war, Claude Fike was serving aboard a USS SC-102, a ship that was assigned to escort convoys from New York or Norfolk to Florida and then on return trips accompany other convoys northward. "The war came home to me for the first time with our second convoy," he wrote in his memoirs. It was a terrifying experience to see "a pall of smoke showing that a tanker had been hit by a torpedo." In a desperate attempt to help the survivors, Claude and his men "moved to the vicinity of the sinking tanker, with oil burning on the water around it, and approached an overturned lifeboat, which had not been launched properly. To our horror, when the crew got it righted, there were three or four survivors and eight or ten men who had died from burns or drowning. And while I would see many scenes of death during the next four years, this first one has stayed vividly with me. After that, submarine sinkings, usually at dawn or dusk, would occur with monotonous regularity in nearly all of our convoys. And there was little we could do at that time to prevent it. . . The winter of 1942 was a long and destructive time indeed. The dull thud of explosions, the pall of smoke and another sinking without retribution became a routine event on our convoy duty."

In the spring of 1942, Claude Fike's ship was struck broadside by a destroyer. Claude had been down in the small officers' quarters when he "had a sudden urgent impulse to go topside. Just as I reached the bridge I was thunderstruck to see looming directly over us on the starboard side the instant flash of running lights and the bow of an oncoming ship, only a few yards away. In seconds there was a tremendous crash and the sickening crunch of wood and metal as we were struck broadside. I was thrown across the bridge against the far bulkhead, and when I attempted to get up I realized my left arm was broken at the wrist." Finding himself trapped in the charthouse, Claude fortunately was rescued by one of the seamen, and he and his rescuer "made our way over the side to a waiting boat from the destroyer." From the deck of the destroyer, "we sadly watched the USS SC-102 go ignominiously to the bottom."

During a hearing at the Board of Inquiry, it was learned that the destroyer had mistakenly turned "prematurely, putting them on a collision course with the SC-102. The lookout had excitedly reported a submarine dead ahead and the forward gunners asked permission to open fire. The captain of the destroyer reported at the inquest that he had a strange, intuitive feeling that dictated him to delay the order to fire. Instead, he flashed on his running lights and at that instant, too late, saw the sub chaser under his bow. Had the destroyer opened fire at so short a range we all probably would have been instantly killed. Even so, the collision occurred in the one single spot where no casualties were suffered, namely the officers' bunkroom, which I had felt compelled to leave moments before the collision. Had it occurred a few yards aft it would have been in the crews' quarters and many would have died. So at least for me on that occasion there was something of extra sensory perception—as well as for the captain of the destroyer that hit us. The navy reported, without explanation, that our ship had been sunk off the Virginia coast, and this in turn fueled the report that I was killed or missing. In fact the rumor persisted until the end of the war."

On another occasion Claude Fike luckily escaped a torpedo that fortunately passed under his ship rather than blowing his ship and its crew to the skies. The enemy submarine commander could have surfaced and "sunk the lot of us with his deck gun . . . This was a close call, and its memory is forever etched on the minds of those of us who were on duty that night."[26]

Richard Jones was convinced that one of his luckiest moments was when a German fighter flying over their headquarters in Sudbury, England failed to successfully strafe the bomb dump just outside their quonset huts. (Equally fortunate were the two dozen or more bases in the area each with 72 B-17 planes.) One of Bill Noonan's most fortunate experiences was while he was helping unload ammo while his ship was in dry dock in Norfolk and finding a depth charge that had not exploded. Had it exploded in his hands it would have sent off 6,000 pounds of TNT and

blown the ship sky high. Bob Stern, aboard USS LCS(L)48, believed himself one lucky guy when he survived kamikaze attacks to his group of
ships that were providing a perimeter screen protecting Mariveles Harbor
in 1945. Three ships were decimated and another put out of commission
with a loss of 62 men.[27]

Instead of the customary cupful of water poured into his helmet for "bathing," Dudley Rishell was luxuriating in washing his face in a small creek
during his stay on Leyte. Thinking that a palm frond had brushed his
head, Dudley thought little more about the incident until back home a
physician examined his head and extracted five tiny pieces of shrapnel.
Another lucky day in the life of a GI![28]

While his ship was stationed at Guadalcanal, Joe Kish's executive officer
and several of the crew decided to go over to check out a Japanese ship
that had run aground. The ship should be a treasure-trove of souvenirs.
Somehow, at the last minute Joe had to beg off the expedition. And luckily he did, for the Americans had suddenly decided to use the abandoned
ship for target practice and every man in the little excursion was killed.[29]

Preparatory to the Normandy invasion as the U.S. Air Force began scouting for volunteers to be trained as glider pilots, Romayne Hicks' instructor at Pecos, Texas played caretaker to Romayne's crew. Calling them all
together he announced, "Any one of you guys who volunteers, I'll break
your arm. It's a suicide mission!" Obviously, the Air Force came up with
ziltch volunteers from that group.[30]

As the fourth-ranking naval ace, Lt. Alex Vraciu, pilot of one of the famous
Grumman F6F Hellcats, was credited with having downed 19 enemy aircraft and having destroyed 21 more planes on the ground during the war
in the Pacific. Six of those aerial feats occurred on June 19, 1944, when in
a single mission, Alex shot down six enemy aircraft in the incredible time
of eight minutes. Sent back to the States for several months, Alex became
bored with life as a noncombatant, and when it was rumored that he was
scheduled for a War Bond Tour, he set up a campaign to be sent back to
the Pacific war zone. Delighted to be back in the "action" once again, Alex
himself soon became the victim of enemy fire when his plane was shot
down as he was engaged in a strafing operation near Clark Field Luzon
in the Philippines in December of 1944. Anti-aircraft fire succeeded in
sending his plane spiraling earthward, and he was forced to parachute to
safety. Alex's luck continued to hold when a group of Philippine guerrillas rescued him, and together they spent the next five weeks maneuvering
around the Japanese in hopes of meeting up with General MacArthur's
American troops. Finally, their endeavors met with success, and Alex
walked into an American encampment bearded and dirty but very much

alive. Alex was gravely disappointed that regulations prevented his being involved in the raids on Tokyo. His accomplishments, however, did not go unrewarded, for he was the recipient of the Navy Cross, the Distinguished Flying Cross with two gold stars, and the Air Medal with three gold stars.[31]

The casualty rates for airmen flying A-36 dive bombers over Italy were high, almost 80 percent, Johnie Courtney remembered. The missions were particularly dangerous as the small planes flew at extremely low altitudes as they dive-bombed enemy railroads, tunnels, bridges, factories, and shipping installations in support of the Allies. While bombing the Campina airport outside of Rome, Johnie's plane was shot down, and as he bailed out and parachuted into a vineyard, he was hidden temporarily by the grape arbors. As the Germans combed the hillsides in a valiant effort to capture him, Johnie rolled down the hillside terraces and escaped while the Germans scoured a far end of the vineyard. After hiding out in haystacks and spending an overnight in a friendly Italian farmer's barn, Johnie finally neared the American lines and hailed a passing American scout car.[32]

On his first mission out of Italy as a B-29 bomber pilot, John Kennedy, of Shelbyville, Illinois, came off their target with three engines out and the fuel gauge verging on empty. A crash landing, fortunately without injuries, left the crew vulnerable for capture as they made their way through the woods. Thanks to an Allied truck that wheeled by, they were transported to a small recently captured town. There they watched in awe as the women (a significant percent) in Tito's army disassembled trucks and carried wheels, cannons, and propellers up through the mountains to the next day's battle.

Johnie, however, was not yet home free by a long shot. As the driver of the scout car rumbled along the bumpy terrain, they suddenly found the Germans were in hot pursuit. It was a race to the safety of the American lines with Johnie hanging on for dear life. Fortunately, they succeeded in outdistancing their pursuers, and Johnie's guardian angel had been hovering over him once again. After a brief R and R in the States in Miami Beach, Johnie put his good fortune to the test for the rest of the war flying P-51 Mustangs out of Iwo Jima as they escorted B-29s over Japan.[33]

Having survived intense fighting on Guadalcanal and at Cape Gloucester, New Britain, Marine Karl Leitz and the 64 survivors of his original company were waiting on a small island off New Britain for new orders when officials decided to make a random drawing of 15 men to be sent home on furlough. Slips of paper were placed in a helmet, most of them blank, but 15 were marked with the coveted number to entitle a lucky Marine to a trip back to the States. (On New Britain, the Marines had been left without air or naval protection while American planes and ships were battling the

Japanese at sea. The Japanese therefore could bomb the island incessantly and did. On one lucky day, a Japanese cruiser just off the coast was making ready to decimate Karl's company of Marines when a B-17 appeared out of nowhere and planted a bomb squarely on the cruiser. Karl recounted that "God was with them" or they never would have survived.)

He had, indeed, had an incredible number of lucky breaks. As Karl waited disinterestedly below deck for the drawing to conclude, his buddies urged him to at least go topside and draw a paper. With little enthusiasm Karl reached in the helmet, fished out the last number and stared in amazement at lucky number 15! Although there was slight hesitancy on Karl's part to leave his "band of brothers," home won out in the long run.[34]

As a science major at Hope College, Gradus Shoemaker, was deferred from the draft as the government endeavored to maintain a stockpile of talented scientists for work on the atomic bomb. Thanks to his background of math and chemistry, Gradus, following graduation, took the tests for Officers' Candidate School, passed with flying colors, and completed the training to become an Ensign. Waiting around for repairs on his ship, the USS *Henrico,* an attack transport, delayed his shipment to the South Pacific area.

And still Gradus' good fortune continued to prevail. A week before the invasion of Okinawa, Gradus and his shipmates aboard the USS *Henrico* were engaged in unloading troops to mop up Japanese resistance on a series of small islands on the outskirts of Okinawa. The fighting was minimal, and the men were able to secure an island and return to the ship in about a day's time. (The strategy no doubt saved hundreds of lives, for the Japanese were massing some 300 motorboats to use in suicide assaults against the invaders. Fortunately, they were obliterated in the island attacks.)

One particular evening, however, after dinner and the release from General Quarters, the men aboard the *Henrico* were horrified as they looked up to see two kamikazes swooping down from the sky, one headed straight for the demise of the *Henrico.* It released two bombs before striking the mid-ship. Luckily, one bomb hit an I beam and was deflected from the forward hold that served as storage quarters for thousands of gallons of fuel oil and munitions. The second bomb also was diverted, but as the plane exploded, loaded with gasoline, the fuel sent flames sweeping across the decks. Fires immediately engulfed the ship and tragically incinerated at least 50 members of the crew. (Trying to put out the fires and trying to rescue fellow shipmates conjured up painful memories that Gradus preferred not to go into.)

Minutes earlier, before the kamikazes struck, Gradus, who had been visiting with buddies, had for no apparent reason walked over to the port side of the ship. His walk saved his life. His General Quarters, the decoding room, was wiped out. Its occupants merely charred remains.

It was indeed a miracle that Gradus had not been killed. Had Gradus been in his General Quarters in the decoding room, had he been on the starboard side of the ship, or had he been in his bunk in the bowels of the ship, he would never have survived. Although the fires severely crippled the ship, there was not enough damage to sink the ship. However, Gradus suffered a concussion that sent him to sick bay. Luckily, on board ship there was a small supply of the new wonder drug penicillin, and Gradus was given all of it. Following his return to the States, Gradus was hospitalized in Oakland, California for several months and then sent for rehabilitation to—where else?—Yosemite National Park! Following his discharge, Gradus used the GI Bill to finish his PhD and afterward served for 39 years on the faculty at the University of Louisville. A charmed life? Divine intervention? Somebody up there liked him? Lucky breaks? Incredible good fortune? An angel on his shoulder? Whatever, it worked.

Not so lucky, Gradus remember sadly, was Lt. John Smith, the only Marine officer aboard, who "had been overjoyed to be assigned to shipboard duty rather than front line duty. Life expectancy in front line duty for Marine officers in the Pacific at that time was measured in months. The second bomb that hit us exploded in his room; we never found a trace of him or his belongings." (On the return trip of the *Henrico* to San Francisco for repairs, "one evening the officers' mess was served fish that unknowingly was spoiled," Gradus reported. "That night every officer was laid low—or more correctly seated in the 'head.' " The enlisted men had long claimed they could navigate the ship without help—that night they were right.)[35]

Medic Phil Montgomery was a party to one of the "miracles" being performed at an aid station in Luzon in 1945. Phil wrote: "On February 15 A Company was attacking across open fields against entrenched Japanese and two of my fellow Medics were shot through the thigh and brought into my aid station unconscious from loss of blood. The doctors were unable to get plasma into the collapsed veins of Bill Verlander while I was successful with Tom Parker." Later, Bill died, and Tom lost his leg, but not his life.[36]

During the horrendous fighting on Guadalcanal, Dan Kona figured he was one of the luckiest people in the world. Within a period of about 20 minutes, as his unit replaced some of the casualties on the front lines, Japanese snipers took out one of his comrades in the brush nearby, shot the corpsman who came to aid his stricken friend, killed the runner who had started back to the ship, and fatally wounded a fourth buddy.[37]

John Hoagland credited blind good luck with getting him through the war years. Early on he had been fortunate to have been sent for training at Harvard and at MIT and afterward to Hawaii for further study in radar.

Although he was requested to remain in Hawaii to train new recruits, John opted for further practical sea experience. In another great stroke of luck, John chose to serve on the USS *Louis Hancock,* where he became the radar specialist on a three-man team checking out airplane activity in various areas of the South Pacific. There was more good luck when he was transferred to the USS *New Jersey* and then to the USS *Brush,* one of the many ships engaged in the December 17–18, 1944, typhoon that took out three destroyers, heavily damaged scores of other vessels, and was responsible for some 790 casualties. Thirty-foot waves washed over the *Bush,* and John and his shipmates were beginning to think their time had come. Good fortune again prevailed, however, and the *Bush* survived the mauling, murderous waves to maneuver almost unscathed through the typhoon.

Whether one called it luck, chance, or God's will, almost every veteran agreed that choices, instinctive moves, and perhaps intuition played a vital role in one's survival. At Pearl Harbor, as they were completing their radar training, Lieutenant JG John Hoagland and some of his fellow officers were given a choice of the ship on which they wished to serve as they set out for the action in Pacific waters. Little did they know that their selection of a ship would eventually turn out to be a life or death decision. John chose the USS *Hancock* and was transferred to the USS *Bush,* which survived the December typhoon. John's roommate and special friend, Paul Harnish, had not been so lucky. Harnish had chosen to serve on the USS *Spence,* one of the three destroyers that capsized, broke in two, and went to the bottom during the typhoon.[38]

On an eventful Saturday evening in 1942, Claude Fike had a ship's stopover in Boston while en route from Portland, Maine through the Canal Zone and on to the Pacific. "I will never forget that particular evening," he wrote in his memoirs, "for Boston College had played Holy Cross that day and many football fans were in town. My fellow officers and I would probably have gone to the Coconut Grove Night Club, the most popular in town, had not there not been a large crowd of patrons ahead of us. You will remember the tragic fire that took some five hundred lives that night. We considered ourselves very lucky. Like Pearl Harbor, one does not forget that tragedy if they were in Boston that evening."[39]

Crews on planes were changed now and then, and Austin Hines and his buddies were stunned when one of the gunners on their plane was put on another plane, and word came back that the plane had crashed. Several days later the authorities came to gather up the gunner's belongings to send home to his family. There was almost a tug of war when Austin's crew refused to allow them to take his belongings. The said they *knew* he would get back to them—AND HE DID![40]

CHAPTER 11

The Softer Side of War

The wait seemed endless for the little group shivering as they waited alongside the railroad tracks. Earlier a telephone call from a benevolent conductor (perhaps with a son of his own in service) had informed the Hickses that their son Robert would be on a troop train passing near their home, and that if they could be at the railroad tracks in a few minutes perhaps they might be able to catch a glimpse of Robert as the train went by Harrison Road near the Trowbridge crossing. (Actually it had been Robert's casual mention to the kindly conductor that the train would be going within a mile of his home in East Lansing that had spurred the conductor into action to call Robert's parents.) The call, of course, generated a flurry of activity to hustle into coats, scarves, and mittens and rush in sister Helen's old car to the railroad tracks.

Had they missed him? Had the train been delayed or diverted? Would he ever come? Suddenly, there was a sharp whistle, and the black iron behemoth rumbled into view. The first car passed, and no Bob, a second car passed. The dirty weather-beaten windows framed round faces, fat faces, red heads, emaciated faces—and then suddenly there was the dear sweet face—Bob, with his nose pressed against the glass and his hands spread against the window pane. Just as quickly as he appeared, he was gone—a precious moment to be remembered for as long as life itself. (Fortunately he did return at the end of the war safe and sound.)

In his mother's memoirs she wrote, "As long as I live I'll always be able to see Bob's hands spread out on the window of the transport-train as it crossed Harrison Road." Jan Hicks (Ronk), about 10 years old at the time, confesses that she also remembers that vision, "and I shiver each time I recall that day. That was a day when the war hit close to home literally!"[1]

It was a joyous celebration at the Blackpool, England Air Force Base in 1944 when the co-pilot of John Haus' B-17 bomber received word that his wife, stateside, had given birth to a baby boy. It was a glorious day, and everyone shared in a new surge of energy and hope. Here was a ray of sunshine amid all the darkness of death and dying. Secreted champagne was dusted off, and toasts to the new young man resonated in the hereto-fore lackluster barracks.

It was scarcely three weeks later that the crew was called out for a dangerous mission over Berlin. As the minutes ticked away, however, the mission appeared to be too precarious to justify the potential loss of life. The Luftwaffe were out in record numbers, and the authorities decided to call the mission back. Unfortunately, as one of the lead planes, John's plane was too far out to get the recall notice to return with the rest of the unit. With little fighter protection the plane was surrounded by Luftwaffe who deftly took the plane out with a direct hit about 70 kilometers from Berlin. The pilot was killed instantly, and the other crew members struggled to bail out. Fortunately, John and two other members of the crew were able to parachute to safety, the only three to survive the hit. The co-pilot, the new father, had picked up a smoldering parachute and fell to his death. (One third of the 800 planes sent out that day were shot down.)

Lost in a forest and stumbling along on a wounded leg, John was quickly apprehended by the Germans and taken prisoner. His next 16 months were spent as a POW at Stalag Luft 1 near Barth, Germany. Feeling extremely fortunate to have survived both the plane crash as well as the miserable POW conditions at Stalag Luft 1, John, later, upon his discharge, felt conscience-bound to travel across the United States to visit and share his grief with the families of the seven men on the plane who did not make it back. It was at his stop to visit his co-pilot's widow and her young son that life changed dramatically for John Haus. In a storybook ending, John was immediately attracted to the pretty widow, and the attraction proved mutual. A short time later they were married, and thus began a happy married life with John bringing up the two-year-old boy as his son. In memory of his heroic father, John always insisted that the boy retain his father's name.[2]

Dave Anderson's service in North Africa and Sicily provided one of his most unforgettable experiences. As the Allied Forces inched their way through Sicily on their way to Italy, they discovered the Germans had destroyed an important road along a cliff overlooking the sea in northern Sicily. Orders were to rebuild that road posthaste. Dave, a noncommissioned officer of the Eighth Amphibian Force, and his unit fell to the Herculean task with nonstop exertion. Amid the perspiration and groaning,

Dave noticed one goof-off sitting smoking a cigarette. With the rest of the men working like tigers that was too much for Dave. With fire in his eye, Dave walked over to give the delinquent a dressing down. "Look, everyone else is working his butt off here. If you can't pull your weight around here, just get the hell out." The cigarette was immediately snuffed, and Dave continued his back-breaking work.

Thanks to an all-night work schedule, the bridge was repaired by morning, and as the lead truck crossed the bridge, Dave was in a state of shock to see that last night's cigarette smoker was none other than General Patton himself! As Dave was trying to make himself inconspicuous, Patton ordered his driver to stop. Knowing General Patton's passion for strict discipline and the complete submissiveness of his underlings, Dave thought, "Oh, boy, here goes."

"Which one of you was that private that chewed me out last night?" Patton roared. With both fear and alacrity Dave stood forward and saluted, "It was I, sir." Patton returned the salute, shouted, "Good work, young man!" and ordered his driver "Forward."[3]

Following a standoff with the Germans during the Battle of Ohlungen during January 24–26, 1945, John Walker and his men were ordered to dig foxholes. "For the next hour or so we worked feverishly to dig in among the pine trees. In the dark you could hear the clink of entrenching tools attacking the frozen ground to carve out the foxholes. An occasional German artillery round whined in to upset the peace and quiet with a tree burst and whizzing shrapnel."

"Strange things happen at times under trying circumstance such as this," Walker wrote. "A friend of mine, Mac McMurtrie, a BARman in one of our rifle platoons, was busy digging his foxhole in the dark. He was waist deep in his foxhole digging it deeper and had leaned his BAR against a nearby pine tree just out of his arm's reach. He heard a noise, looked up and into the eyes of a big German paratrooper standing next to his foxhole. The German had a machine pistol ("burp" gun) slung over his shoulder. Mac was stunned and paralyzed with fright because his BAR was out of reach. The German looked down at Mac and said 'Good evening.' At a loss for an appropriate reply Mac stammered 'Good evening.' At that point the German reached over, picked up Mac's BAR, handed it to him, then helped him out of his foxhole, and surrendered! How's that for luck?"[4]

Surprises? Millions of them. Stranger than fiction? Indeed so. On a bombing mission over Germany, pilot Owen Marmon remembered seeing a German pursuit plane off the left wing of his B-24. The German pilot, his plane emblazoned with the Iron Cross, was flying the same altitude and the same speed. Owen thought he must be hallucinating when in a friendly gesture, the German pilot smiled and waved. What to do? Why wave back, of course! This factual, although seemingly unbelievable scenario, in the middle of a war between two deadly enemies each seeking to annihilate the other, defies imagination.[5]

Jim Pyle had been 101 days on the front lines and for 18 months had drunk only creek water, had never had a clean bed, a glass of real milk, or a real egg. Each day Jim Pyle and his buddies wistfully dreamed of a little cold, a sore throat, a small fever that would keep them back from the next front line mission. Instead there were always the big pep talks by the commander and the forward push. After a day and a half of fighting, even as the men were claiming a victory, there was the gruesome duty of bringing the bodies, some 200 of them, back to camp amid the constant rain of gunfire. It seemed the perils would never abate. Morale was at low ebb. However, one day, out of the blue, a reassuring hand on his shoulder and a strange voice directed Jim to hold back "to protect the ammunition."

Minutes later an officer ordered Jim to the front lines to replace his fox-hole buddy who had been killed—the very foxhole where Jim, too, would have been the victim had he not held back. In one of those "out of body" moments, Jim had felt a hand tapping him on the shoulder that had saved his life. That extra-sensory touch had kept Jim from giving up. At home his wife was well aware his precarious assignments and was keeping a constant prayer vigil for him. In comparing notes later, at what must have been the same time, she, too, was tapped on the shoulder. "Prayer and divine intervention brought me home," Jim was convinced.[6]

Po Weatherford, a Mississippian, told of a similar experience. While standing in a ditch during the Battle of the Bulge, Po was doing his best to dodge the buzz bombs that were ominously sounding all around him. As the men struggled along through the hedgerows, their position had been spotted by the Germans, and their future looked grim indeed. During the worst of the fighting, suddenly Po heard a voice saying, "don't worry, you are coming home." So convincing was the voice that Po ceased to worry and has "given his life to the Lord ever since."[7]

Coincidences or ESP—one never knows. Austin Hines had formed a great friendship during his flying time in WWII with a buddy who later became a Catholic priest. For years they continued their friendship via the mail and visits. When his friend died, it was days before Austin was apprised of the fact. It turned out that at the precise moment of his friend's death, as Austin was taking a violin lesson, his violin suddenly slipped out of his hands and fell to the ground, an accident that had never happened before.[8]

In the 1920s, Charles A. Lindberg had earned a handsome reputation as one of America's most famous twentieth-century heroes for his solo flight across the Atlantic. Now, he came in for further hero worship, Carl

Tychsen, Jr. reported, when he appeared on a U.S. held airfield in the South Pacific and asked for a P-38 to be gassed up and ready for takeoff in 30 minutes. In a 12-hour flight, he instructed the pilots how to "lean out the plane's fuel mix" and thus enable them to provide fighter protection that had otherwise been thought impossible on the long B-24 runs on the Balikpapan oil fields. (Lindberg at that time was a consultant for Lockheed, maker of the P-38s.)[9]

Lieutenant Vincent Schumacher's PT 32 torpedo boat had been one of three torpedo boats that were escorting Gen. Douglas MacArthur and his men in March of 1942 on their evacuation of Corregidor. When engine trouble crippled Vince's boat it was left behind, a floating target for a Japanese warship or plane. About dawn the next morning a dim shape was seen amid the murky waters. Was it friend or foe? Knowing the USS *Permit* was shadowing the evacuation, Vince took a chance and with his blinker gun blinked out in Morse Code: *Permit. Permit. Permit.* A voice called out from the other ship, "What ship?" to which Vince answered, "PT 32. PT 32." "What's the first name of the skipper?" came the reply. "Vincent," the PT skipper responded. "Come alongside," the voice from the *Permit* called. A man on the bridge of the *Permit* had been playing tennis with Vince in Cavite the day before the Japanese attack on Pearl Harbor. Quick thinking, a bit of luck, and a friend indeed had saved the crew of PT 32 from being blown out of the water.[10]

As one will recall, the armed services were for the most part segregated in the early days. Blacks were put in separate units, often with a white officer in charge. Despite the system, the associations were at times most congenial. Bob Drake, a white officer in charge of training black troops, counted his greatest compliment of a lifetime the high praise professed by the first sergeant, the leader of the 200 to 300 black men in a company Bob trained at Fort Warren, Wyoming. As Bob was being discharged upon completion of his time in service, and as the troops stood in formation, the African American company's sergeant stepped forward and spoke with heartfelt conviction: "Sir, the men want me to tell you they'll send a substitute, but they'll never replace you." For the rest of Bob's life, any dark days or disappointments were relieved as he remembered that shining moment.

For Bob Drake, his service "as an officer with nearly all black enlisted men, was an enjoyable part of my life." There was great camaraderie as Bob and the men shared a love of music and a delight in good humor and fast repartee. At one time, Bob found himself in possession of $500 in the company fund, the accumulation of a regular monthly allotment to be devoted to "such needs as the company commander determined." How best to spend the money? In the spirit to true democracy, Bob decided to put it to a vote of the men as to how they would like to spend the little stockpile. The vote was unanimous: "Buy a piano!" A piano was purchased, and from then on there was scarcely a moment of off-duty time that some of the company's former professional musicians or even novices were not knocking out tunes for dancers or animated listeners.[11]

Wayne Adgate humbly admitted that his greatest honor in life had been his tail gunner's words at the end of the war. "Lieutenant Adgate, if you ever go again I'd like to go with you!"[12]

Early on, Dick Pearse had his sights set on being a "Hot Pilot" in the Air Corps. Things went along very well—he was the third in his class to solo and was doing extremely well in classwork and flight training. That is, until one day as he was practicing aerobatics, he simply was unable to resist the urge to fly down to buzz a cluster of grazing cows. That, of course, was a "no, no," but no one was watching, he thought, until suddenly off of his left wing there appeared the Commandant of Cadets in his plane flying almost wing tip to wing tip. Instantly, he knew the show was over. The next morning he was ordered to the Administration Building and eliminated from the Corps of Aviation Cadets.

That was a devastating disappointment, but it proved it was not the end of the road for Dick. Through a series of fortuitous events, he was assigned to a new Aerial Photographic Interpretation unit Oran, Algeria, North Africa. There he and a host of expert commercial photographers studied via a stereoscope the aerial photos to determine enemy positions and strengths. The unit was moved to Italy, and after locating for nine months at San Severo in the southeastern part of the country, they were relocated to Florence where they stayed for the balance of the European War. For a fortunate few, the war was not all blood and terror, certainly not for Dick Pearse. While in Oran, Dick was sure he had the best of all worlds by being designated an "Intelligence Specialist" (a flattering term he admitted), and this was generally a safe war time assignment. On days off he found it not too unpleasant to roam the streets of Florence and take in the historic towns of Pisa, Siena, and Bologna. A trip to Rome involved an audience with Pope Pius, where he was touched on the head and blessed. Talk about "the good life"—indeed, "It's an ill wind that blows nobody good!"[13]

Here and there colleges and universities made concessions for seniors entering the service and awarded diplomas to students who were within a few credits of graduation and who had satisfactorily completed a written comprehensive examination. Other schools waited for servicemen and women to complete their classwork at the end of the war, many, of course, taking advantage of the recently passed GI Bill. (The Readjustment Act of 1944, became generally known as the GI Bill of Rights.) Ensign Bob Stern had lacked two credits for graduation from the University of Michigan and thought little about it, until mail call one morning on the island of Samar where his ship was in dry dock preparing for the invasion of Korea. As he sorted through his mail, a flabbergasted Bob Stern opened up an official looking envelope and out popped his diploma, all signed and sealed. His friend Sue Sims (Schulze), a classmate at the U of M, had besought the Dean about the possibility of his eight credits earned at Midshipman's School at Columbia counting toward his degree. The Dean had followed through, and the credits gave Bob more hours than he needed. Thus, the diploma was granted, a document that later proved vital for Bob's post-war enrollment at Wayne Law School.[14]

BIG CITY HOSPITALITY OR "THE KINDNESS OF STRANGERS"

In January of 1945, Helen Deason rushed to Chicago to meet her husband who was on a brief leave while his ship was undergoing repairs in Seattle. As the men emerged from the train, Helen had never seen such a sea of white hats, and "then suddenly there he was!" On one of the evenings spent in Chicago before continuing on to see the family, the happy couple stood in line at the theater box office hoping for tickets for the hit musical *Oklahoma*.

No such luck, the show was sold out, but as they were dejectedly walking away, a man approached them asking "Sailor, would you like these tickets?" Of course, the Deasons were delighted, especially to realize there was no scalping involved, just the regular price for tickets that could have brought a king's ransom to a scalper "The man thanked Larry for serving his country and shook his hand." Dame Fortune continued to smile when it turned out the tickets were center aisle, 10 rows back![15]

Time in New York City was an eye opener for thousands of Midwestern and California servicemen. And surprisingly, the City, not principally known up until then for its warmth and hospitality, put out the welcome mat for servicemen. Even the most surly New Yorkers went out of their way for men and women in uniform. In theater or restaurant lines, very often the moment anyone saw a man in uniform, he was escorted to the front of the line. Broadway theaters sometimes slipped servicemen free tickets for sellout shows. Hotels gave suites of rooms to servicemen for paltry sums or even gratis. Policemen stopped rush hour traffic to allow military pedestrians to pass. As Dorrie and Paul Souder hesitated about crossing a busy New York City intersection, the policeman whistled traffic to a halt in both directions and with a cherry smile inquired, "What can I do for you?"[16]

New Yorkers turned out to be unbelievably generous to servicemen. Second Lieutenant Don Langworthy, a pilot with the Marine Corps, told about a time when "On a navigation hop to New York City for an overnight, we got downtown and had no room reservations, as they were scarce as hen's teeth. We went to the Waldorf and found that they had no rooms. However, the desk fellow said to me 'Tommy Dorsey's suite is not being used as he is out of the city for a few days. Would you like to stay there FREE of charge.' What a question! We did."[17]

On the spur of the moment while awaiting orders in Norfolk, Virginia, Ensign Gradus Shoemaker and three of his buddies decided to hop a train and check out Washington, D.C. As they expected, hotel rooms were booked solid with important military personnel, but undaunted, they kept calling one hotel after another deviously asking if their room was ready for their arrival. Hotel clerks searched the records and then realizing their ploy turned them down flat. A call to the famous Carleton Hotel, however, met with a fortuitous response. There was one luxury suite of rooms that was empty for the weekend, and they could have it if they wanted it. The guys held their breath and then erupted in ecstasy when the clerk announced that the charge would be $25 a night![18]

Although a curt bus driver had made her mother cry as she tried to cross town, Ginny Bennetts remembers a different scenario: the kindness of waitresses at the coffee shop where she and her husband breakfasted, who lovingly crocheted bonnets and booties for her newborn daughter.[19]

On weekend passes during the time her husband was stationed in San Diego, Rachel and John Jones did the grand tour of the Hollywood radio and film studios. It was a glorious day for Rachel when John's uniform netted him a ticket to see the Bing Crosby show, which he immediately turned over to Rachel knowing of her passion for the famous crooner. Insisting that she use the ticket, John promised he would join her were he able to secure another ticket. Within minutes John had his ticket when Bing Crosby himself, en route to the studio dressing room, approached him asking why he wasn't inside to see his show. John explained his generosity to Rachel with his single ticket, wherein Bing Crosby reached in his pocket, took out another ticket and "put the ticket in John's hand." Rachel, of course, was delighted to have John join her but, "I was so jealous, because I wished it had been my hand that he'd touched."[20]

It was a routine movie date, and as June Milks and her friend sat waiting for the feature film to begin, they both were giving careful attention to the Fox Movietone newsreel for pictorial documentation of the week's events on the warfront. There was news from Washington, a scene or two of Hollywood celebrities, and then a switch to the fighting in the Pacific. Suddenly, there among the soldiers on Iwo Jima a familiar face appeared—it was her brother! As June screamed out in astonishment, the entire movie theater erupted with her excitement![21]

Now and then the bartering that went on among the GIs achieved some rather altruistic ends. Carl Arthur Tychsen, Jr., of Edina, Minnesota, who had played baseball in the minor leagues before enlisting, thought a ball field for the men stationed on an island in the Admiralty chain would provide for a little recreation and a release of anxiety tensions. By collecting quotas from his nondrinking friends, Carl offered to trade a fifth of the whiskey to a Seabee bulldozer operator if he would bulldoze a baseball field for Carl and his men. The offer was too good to turn down, and in short order the men had their diamond.[22]

The lusty complaints that "We don't have dames" of the servicemen in the musical *South Pacific* brought back memories for thousands of veterans of those remote islands. Army nurse Alice Diggins serving in the Pacific remembered, "when the nurses and women arrived on the islands, of course, there was great excitement among the men, because what didn't they have? They didn't have dames! So the different units would get together with different hospital units and try to pair nurses and officers up, and I can remember one night I was with a pilot in their little Squadron Club, and we were dancing. And all of a sudden he started to shake uncontrollably. I thought, oh, my he's having a malaria attack or some kind of an attack. So I said do you want to go outside, so we went outside and he sort of collapsed on the steps. And he turned to me and he said: 'Oh, I'm so sorry. I haven't seen a white woman in three years,' and, he said 'you look so good, you smell so good, and you sound so good that I can't stand it.' And I said, 'now I'm shaking.' So we laughed and went inside and that was OK."[23]

Bob Overholt was serving in Paris as a dentist with the Navy in an office with an oral surgeon who had just accumulated enough points for a weekend pass. As he was leaving, he instructed Bob to simply take over. Throughout the weekend all was well as long as the patients came in for routine dental work. However, after a hilarious evening, a young GI came in with a broken jaw. Bob was stymied; this was not his field. The patient showed no dismay however. "I know just what to do. I worked with an oral surgeon before the war." The two worked together and while Bob wired the jaw, the GI made a splint that worked very well. Bob's co-worker returned with high praise for the procedure. "Great work, Bob, you knew just what to do!" Bob had indeed lucked out.[24]

After building and rebuilding bridges all across France and into Germany for Patton's Third Army, Lieutenant Kossie Akins's 529th Engineer Company had a welcome day off behind the lines (in 1944 about 50 miles west of the Rhine River) to work on their vehicles and equipment. As Kossie walked around superintending the clusters of men, out of the corner of his eye he noticed a file of his men emerging from a building across the way toting heavy wooden boxes. Kossie was curious. "What's with those men?" Kossie inquired of his sergeant. "Sir, it's an abandoned champagne factory. The men are 'removing' cases of champagne," the sergeant replied as he anxiously waited for Kossie's instructions. Kossie was of two minds over the "raid." "I ought to stop this," he thought. But on the other hand, the men had worked like demons in the past weeks and "if anyone deserved a little libation his men certainly did." There were a few more moments of hesitation and then "Ok, let 'em have it," Kossie responded. "But keep it under control." "Yes, Sir," the sergeant replied gleefully.

All day Kossie kept mulling over in his mind whether he had done the right thing. From a military standpoint, he probably should have forbidden the heist; but for a platoon of men who had put their lives on the line to build those bridges under constant enemy gunfire, welllllll. . . . The next day, still in torment over his decision, Kossie had to go back to his jeep for a wrench, and there, as he parted the canvas siding, was a case of champagne. His men in grateful appreciation had surreptitiously deposited the booty as a thank you for allowing them to plunder the factory. At that moment Kossie had his answer. He knew he had made the right decision.[25]

On Okinawa, Henry LaBrosse, although choosing neither to be a participant nor a recipient of the product, marveled at the consumption of "moonshine" concocted by several men in his battalion. The men, apparently "home schooled" in Tennessee, turned out to be experts at making moonshine out of pineapple juice and suffered little from any shortages of alcohol during their time on Okinawa. During the typhoon that hit Okinawa, the "distillers" holed up in the caves on the island and nursed their bottles, oblivious to the winds and rain outside. Less enterprising soldiers also hid out in the caves during the storm, seeking shelter among the hallowed bones of the deceased Okinawans.[26]

An interesting sidelight, Catherine Cross recalled, was serving as one of two nurses who assisted the doctors in treating some 100 badly wounded Japanese soldiers who had been holed up for days or possibly weeks in a cave on Okinawa and who in desperation had finally decided to surrender. Catherine and her fellow caregivers were completely taken by surprise when "One Japanese soldier requested that our chaplain marry him and a Japanese woman who had been taking care of the wounded in the cave. And our chaplain did. Our boys who witnessed the ceremony were intrigued by that. It seemed so hard to imagine that this took place in a war zone."[27]

Don Bancroft discovered he could do his bit to serve both God and his country in 1945 while he was stationed on Ie Shima, a small island off of Okinawa. (It was on the island of Ie Shima that Ernie Pyle was shot and killed by a Japanese sniper on April 11, 1945.) When, after repeated efforts, the Seabees were stymied in an attempt to put together an important piece of equipment, Don, thanks to his prewar experience in oil exploration in Venezuela, had the equipment in working order in no time. A grateful crew rewarded his expertise with two cases of whiskey. Later the priest of the local church sought out Don for financial help to build a church on the island. As his contribution, Don turned over part of the whiskey bonus, and the priest hired the Seabees to help construct the church, their payment in whiskey. Turns out there is indeed more than one way to skin a cat.[28]

Christmas Eve 1944 was a memorable evening for John Hoagland. "After weeks of continuous naval action our destroyer had arrived at the placid Pacific Ulithi anchorage. In previous days we had barely survived a terrible typhoon. It had been terrifying to be on the bridge of the destroyer and look up at massive waves towering above us. Our ship had rolled so much that, at times, it had been impossible for me to stay in my bunk. Frequently, I had to stand on one wall of my room then shift to the other wall as our ship was rolled by the waves. After hours of uncertainty, we finally reached calmer waters. Adding to our tension was our fuel problem. Prior to the typhoon, we were low on fuel but barely secured enough to make it through the typhoon. Our sister destroyer had not been able to take on fuel. It sank with all aboard. That Christmas Eve, as the sun was setting at the Ulithi anchorage, our ship's crew assembled to watch a movie. Spontaneously, someone started, then we all 'gloriously' joined in to sing Christmas carols. We were happy to be alive and our singing showed it."[29]

As a psychiatric nurse with the Army Nurse Corps, Hilma Wilcox spent her days helping administer insulin, cold packs, and shock therapy treatments to the patients at the Topeka, Kansas, General Hospital. One day, in the interests of putting a little sunshine into the ward, Hilma went back to her quarters after morning rounds and baked two small cakes for two of the patients who were having birthdays. The patients seemed pleased although slightly embarrassed by the extra attention. Later that day one of the men came in to thank her and admit that he had never had a birthday remembrance since he was seven years old. He was not getting any mail at all and wanted her to know how greatly he appreciated her kindness. It was just the token of appreciation that for Wilma made the long hours and difficult work all worthwhile.[30]

As the war progressed the Japanese were becoming much too successful in intercepting and decoding messages sent between American units.
Many of the strategists were specialists schooled in America who could
easily understand the English, assimilate the messages, and pass on the
information to higher-ups. Finally, the military came up with the idea of
employing Navajo "code talkers" to radio information from one unit to
the other in their native language. The Japanese were at a complete loss to
comprehend anything that was being said. A whole vocabulary of military
terms was invented to fill in for words for which there were no equivalents
in the Navajo language. For example, the code talkers used the Navajo
word for "eagle" to signify a "transport," a "whale" was a "battleship," a
"beaver" was a "destroyer." The code talkers, some 400 of them, were all
radio men, well-trained in all aspects of communication, who spoke the
language fluently. In some hours of crises, such as at Iwo Jima, as many as
800 messages were sent and received over a 48-hour period. Albert Smith,
a Navajo from New Mexico, who island hopped with the Marines through
the bitter fighting in the South Pacific, saw plenty of death and dying. Fortunately, he felt he was being watched over by "the spirits" and survived
to re-enlist in the Army in 1947. "I'm what we call a traditionalist in our
Navajo culture. I always sensed that I had the protection of our Navajo
spirits. When you don't know what the next minute can bring, it's nice to
know that you are not alone."[31]

CHAPTER 12

The Lighter Side of War

John Goodell found himself a long way from his Michigan home as a First Lieutenant flying C47 cargo planes on the China–Burma runs over the Himalaya Mountains. A recent graduate of the University of Michigan, John left his job as an insurance underwriter and enlisted in 1942, received his wings in 1943, served as an instructor at Randolph Field and then in Lubbock, Texas, and was sent to India for the demanding job of flying supplies "over the hump." "Naturally," John admitted, "the primary goal was to be able to live through each day." The crews were young men, however, most of them just out of high school or college and not above indulging in a little mischief now and then. John's recounting of "kidnapping an orchestra" illuminates the shenanigans that often served as a welcome relief from the stress and anxieties of a world convulsed by death and dying.

"The traffic was so heavy flying the hump during the spring of 1945," John remembered, "that the turn around time for pilots to head back to the base in Myitkyina along side the Irrawaddy River in Burma after having deposited their supplies involved a delay of several hours. Sometimes fifty to one hundred planes were lined up beside the runway waiting to make the return trip." On one particularly memorable night, the crew (John, his co-pilot, radio officer, and the crew's chief-mechanic) were waiting for takeoff, relaxing in their plane, possibly snoozing, reading, or reviewing the day's activities—the cargo door in back having been opened for ventilation.

"Suddenly an army truck drove up, braked to a stop, and the driver yelled to the crew chief who was standing in the cargo doorway, 'Is this the plane that gets the instruments?' " Scarcely drawing a breath, the savvy young crew chief, a brash New Yorker, yelled back, "'Ya, back her right up here.' And in minutes a complete band encumbered with all their instruments was loaded on our plane."

"Actually the band was supposed to go to India to play for a program for high ranking U.S. Army officials," John reported gleefully, "and instead we diverted the band back to the Burma base camp where they entertained us for two nights' running." The escapade was an absolute triumph for John and his men as John's base and the India base had long been in fierce competition. "We fixed them [the musicians] up with places to stay, provided an open bar and they hung around the camp until some pretty irate officers flew in from India to retrieve their kidnapped men. In the meantime soldiers, nurses and Red Cross girls from the six neighboring Air Force bases hopped on planes and came over for two days of gala partying." The crew, of course, were not unaware of the serious charges that they might incur, but (perhaps because of the levity provided in the midst of terror and chaos) "fortunately there was no discipline meted out." And thus a good time was had by all—except, of course, the angry, bested Army Air Force officials.[1]

At least for a few minutes democracy prevailed even in Shanghai—thanks to some fairly well-oiled Army Air Force men. Following the war, John Goodell's squadron was deployed to help move Chinese airmen from Shanghai to Peking. One evening after becoming somewhat bored with the nightly routine of carousing in the bars in Shanghai, John and four friends went scouting for a little more excitement. After stops at several bars and liberally sampling the offerings, the airmen finally decided to call it a night and head for home.

Out on the street the rickshaws were lined up patiently awaiting passengers. One look at the poor devils forced to push heavy loads for a pittance drew immediate sympathy from the slightly inebriated officers. Surely the rickshaw "drivers" deserved at least a momentary respite from their labors. And in the spirit of the evening (and in the spirit of democracy and equality), the officers immediately ordered the drivers into the rickshaws, got into the traces themselves and gave the drivers a joy ride. The drivers were immensely amused, but not so the high ranking officers housed at the large, swank Peking hotel as the little convoy pulled up to the front door. The fun was suddenly over as the pranksters were admonished for conduct decidedly unbecoming Army Air Force men. Whereupon the revelers returned the drivers to their livelihood, and jovially wound their way back to their own hotel.[2]

Car drivers can get in deep trouble for forgetting to fasten their seat belts, so, too, did one civilian flight instructor at Corsicana Field, Texas. Don Van Gorder told of a buddy's terrifying experience while on a training flight in an open cockpit plane when he was ordered by the instructor to do a "slow role" practice maneuver. Suddenly, the pilot trainee found himself alone in the plane. His instructor had carelessly forgotten the cardinal rule of airmen to "Fasten your seat belts" and suddenly found himself plummeting toward earth. He had fallen out of the plane! (Fortunately he had remembered to strap on his parachute!) For the inexperienced PT-19 pilot, however, it was the first solo landing of his career. With the adrenaline running high he made a perfect landing—a source of pride for the pilot and a source of considerable embarrassment for the flight trainer.[3]

One night while out on patrol in Germany, Paul Niland looked up to see a chicken crossing the road not more than 10 yards in front of him. He and his comrades, having subsisted on crackers and K rations for over a month, were convinced that a tasty dinner loomed just ahead. In an instant every gun hit a shoulder and every gun fired—and every shot *missed*—as the bewildered chicken blithely continued to strut across the road and into the underbrush. And so much for expert American marksmanship![4]

In moments of slack there were usually eruptions of mischief or perhaps just high spirits that would relieve the angst of battle. Somehow, during a lull between assignments in the Philippines, one of Bud Maner's men either bought—or was given—a fighting cock. And naturally what would one do with such a possession but arrange a cockfight? Betting rose to a fever pitch; everyone got into the action. It was difficult for Bud as commanding officer of the day to know just how to react. The training manuals had no instructions about cockfights, and the men were having such a grand time. Best to just ignore the situation Bud finally decided. It was not long, however, before someone called "fowl!" and Bud's superior officer took the opportunity to give him a royal chewing out. That, of course, put an end to the cockfights—and to the fighting cock. "So," Bud related, "we boiled up that chicken and ate it. And boy, that was one tough chicken!"[5]

Just before setting sail for the Pacific in March of 1943 from the Canal Zone, Claude Fike, the new commanding officer of the USS APc-5, noticed that "One of the ship's crew brought back two small monkeys as ship's pets for our long forthcoming voyage. As the new captain I decided to indulge their whim, and against my better judgment remained neutral and let them remain aboard. I need not have been overly concerned. The monkeys lasted about forty-eight hours. The first one met his fate when he curiously looked into one of the ship's blower fans and was instantly decapitated. The second monkey was caught on the bridge urinating on the ship's charts by the irate quartermaster, who simply tossed him over the side."[6]

There were ecstatic cheers when Ensign Joe Foster's crew aboard the U.S. Navy PCER 858 were informed that they had successfully cleared the mines outside of Kure, Japan, in preparation for the occupation troops and now would be sent home to the States. In their exuberance, as they made ready to depart, the pranksters aboard ship wanted to leave one final memory of their heroic mine-sweeping action that paved the way for the safe landing of the Allied troops. Why not advertise their coveted treasure of a hot new Humphrey Bogart film and sell to the nearest ship making the highest bid? The signaling between ships heated up until finally the highest bidder agreed to trade five of their own movies for the one Bogart film. The transaction was completed, the films exchanged, and Joe's ship headed out to sea, the crew smug with the acquisition of five movies to relieve the boredom of their upcoming weeks of travel to the States. They suffered no guilt, however, in the fact that their little ship had pulled a fast one on the largest ship in the harbor. Actually they had no hot Bogart film, but had traded a spliced training film (even one section on venereal disease) instead. As he stood on the bow of the PCER as the ship lifted its anchor, Joe wondered aloud just how far the guns of the loser might be able to fire. (Years later, in Naples, Florida, as Joe and a friend were discussing their war experiences, Joe learned that his friend had been on the ship that had so eagerly traded five films for the prized Bogart film. However, in the embarrassment over the chicanery, the "wheeler dealers" on the duped ship kept the "deal" a hush-hush secret from the crew, and the deception was never revealed.)[7]

The news of D-Day sounded loud and clear over the PA system as Doug Dunham was sailing on board a ship heading for he knew not where. (The noise of the zigzagging through the waters to avoid enemy submarine attacks still drones in Doug's ears.) As it turned out he was headed for Puerto Rico and assigned to teach Puerto Rico draftees to speak English. From Puerto Rico he was sent to the Virgin Islands, Aruba, and Curacao. Fortunately, his students were eager to learn to speak and write English, an enthusiasm that, of course, made for apt students. Some Puerto Rican draftees had wives who could read and write English, and they begged Doug to write romantic letters home for them. Doug laughingly says he "made love to scores of women via the mail." Interesting though his work teaching English proved to be, it was not always the easiest of assignments. There were also scary moments such as when as a passenger on a C-47 troop plane half way out in the Caribbean Doug heard the announcement: "Well, men, we've got to go back, we've lost one of our engines." Fortunately, the plane made it safely back to Puerto Rico, the men changed planes, and headed out once again.[8]

The zealous German interrogators were consistently frustrated in their attempts to obtain more than name, rank, and serial numbers from captured American prisoners. Especially irritating to the enemy were saucy answers to questions about how many American paratroopers made a particular jump. Replies such as "millions and millions" or "just me" brought down the wrath of the thwarted questioners.[9]

It was 1:30 in the morning when Roger Dunham (Doug Dunham's younger brother), stationed at Prestwick Field in Scotland, was roused out of bed. A terse message had arrived at headquarters: "Sledge Dog coming." As this was the code name for President Roosevelt, this indeed would be a momentous occasion. It was frightfully short notice, and there was a mad scramble as the order went out for all men to dress at once and be ready to appear in uniform and standing at attention to welcome the President's plane as it taxied down the runway. There was mass confusion as half-awake men dusted the sleep out of their eyes, hurried on their uniforms, and raced to the airfield. Suddenly, the plane swooped down from the darkness and braked to a stop. All hands were raised to a salute as the door opened—and 12 furry Alaskan sledge dogs leaped out onto the tarmac.[10]

Helen Brush (Hiscoe) remembered one of her first jobs as a graduate assistant teaching physiology at the University of California at Los Angeles. The day for the dissecting of frogs had arrived, and the distribution of huge Brazilian bullfrogs had met with a resounding chorus of "YUCK!!!" from all of the would-be scientists. (The class consisted entirely of females, the men were all off at war.) Suddenly the air raid sirens blared forth, and the girls gleefully dropped their frogs mid-air and headed for the air raid shelter. The frogs, equally gleeful to be freed from their ominous looking "pokers" and "prodders" outdistanced Mark Twain's "Celebrated Jumping Frog of Calaveras County" as they leaped to find refuge in wastebaskets, under sheaves of paper, in open drawers, in the drinking fountain, under lab tables and stools, in the bookshelves, and in nearby classrooms. Fortunately, the alarm proved to be a false alarm, and Helen and her assistant spent the next 45 minutes trying to round up the illusive amphibians.[11]

As a former junior high school teacher, Doug Dunham was inducted into the army, given corporal stripes, and assigned by the army officials at Ft. Leavenworth to teach a 12-week course for illiterates to bring them up to fourth-grade reading and writing abilities. (Up until 1942, functionally illiterate men were usually deferred. There were changes, however, and by 1943, illiteracy did not preclude induction.) The task was a daunting one, and the men were first taught to write their names and then read items on a laundry list to enable the men to be able to identify their own laundry. Surprisingly there was considerable progress, and former grade school dropouts advanced with basic reading and writing skills.

In many respects it was also an education for Doug. He learned that some of the men were married men, some married to wives who were literate. When Doug queried one of his illiterates about whether his wife knew he could neither read nor write, he immediately confessed that she had no idea he was illiterate. By listening to the news programs on the radio all day at work, he explained, he was always up on the news. He could come home, open the paper, and pretend to be reading in his easy chair as he discussed the day's news with his wife.

Years later, following army service and completion of a PhD degree at the University of Michigan, Doug was teaching Social Science courses at Michigan State University in 1947 to classes overflowing with returning servicemen. One afternoon, in an attempt to liven up a class session on World War II, he recounted some of his experiences with teaching illiterates at Ft. Leavenworth. His class apparently was duly impressed and at the end of the lecture one pretty young co-ed queried, "Well, Dr. Dunham, whatever became of those illiterates?" There was not a second's hesitation before a hardened WW II veteran from the back of the room, shouted out: "Oh, what the Hell, they sent them to Officers' Candidate School."[12]

It didn't take long for Karl Legant to lapse into the profanity that had so pervasively infiltrated the language of the military personnel at Camp McCoy, Wisconsin, where he was busily engaged training new recruits. In an off moment one day, Karl began thinking about the negative effect these expletives might be exerting on his young instructees, their psyches, and their speech. The more he thought about it the more concerned he became—and cold turkey he dropped his profanity and gross language. Karl had four weeks of intensive training with these men before they would be sent to other army posts where they would be turned into cooks, bakers, clerks, or military policemen. On the last day of one of these month-long sessions, as Karl was beginning to feel much better about himself and his teaching, he walked into his room in the barracks and there on the bed lay an envelope containing $35.00 in bills and loose change. Where had the money come from? Karl was at a loss to know how the mysterious envelope had landed on his bed. Seconds later there was the sound of footsteps in the hall, and as Karl glanced up two grinning recruits were sheepishly shuffling about in the doorway. "You guys know anything about this money?" he queried. There was an embarrassed pause and then a heartfelt smile: "Well, sir, we appreciated the fact that you did not swear at us. We took up a collection." (Boot camp anywhere, but especially for Marines, was certainly no bed of roses. Gene Cornelius sadly remembered two men during his training at Camp Pendleton who committed suicide rather than continue with the demeaning treatment handed out by their instructors.)[13]

Henry Nelson knew he had one of the greatest jobs in the Air Force, playing flute in the Air Force band at Seymore Johnson Field in Goldsboro, North Carolina. An added bonus was sitting next to another talented flute player, the famous Henry Mancini. Not only was the "duty" enjoyable, but Henry believed it was "musical education" playing with professional musicians such as members of the Glenn Miller Band. When his band was transferred to the Army Service Force where they made the rounds of the "hospital circuit," it was a rewarding experience helping to comfort battle scarred veterans and help ease them back into "wellville" once again.[14]

In the Battle for the Philippines, Infantryman Joseph Victor Brochin, of Minneapolis, Minnesota, explained, "As we approached Leyte, Japanese Kamikazes hit some of our transports, and we took many casualties. . . . Once on the beachhead, it was mass confusion. The firepower on both sides was fierce. While I was ducking behind a palm tree, a GI who was also hunkered down about 20 feet from me yelled out, 'Soldier, what's the situation?' I responded quickly with the reply, 'How the hell should I know?' When I looked over at him after my reply, I saw a brigadier general's star on his helmet so I added 'sir' to my smart remark. It was a time when the GI's term FUBAR applied—Fouled Up Beyond All Reason."[15]

Legrand Johnson and the troops on his ship worried they'd be too late for the war when it took 43 days for them just to cross the Atlantic.[16]

The enemy took many forms during the war. Diseases such as malaria and the hosts of jungle fevers, rodents, infected blisters, jungle rot, hookworm, and Mother Nature herself in the form of typhoons and even less virulent storms wrecked havoc on the hapless GIs. As a medic, Ken Springer, while at Huggins Road Block in New Guinea (where the Americans were fending off the repeated Japanese assaults) attempted to treat a soldier eaten up with a resistant fungus. After administering a shot of morphine and then a second shot, Ken was making no inroads on alleviating the man's frantic itching. The soldier was scratching himself raw and in great danger of contracting a deadly infection. Finally, Ken queried, "Are you a good Christian?" "You're damn right I am!" came the reply. "Well, then, you might want to start praying" Ken suggested, "for the nearest doctor is about three days' away."[17]

There were always problems with the officers who vigilantly censored the letters to loved ones at home. Some men had devised secret codes for letting their wives or parents know vaguely where they were. Careful not to reveal important information, the writer might surreptitiously note: "That blue book on the second shelf of the library has some of my favorite poems that I'd love to read again." (The blue book was actually a romance novel set in Italy and gave the reader a general idea of the whereabouts of the soldier—and got the information by the censor.) Frank Bourke was incensed when a universally disliked censor summarily cut out an innocuous portion of his letter to his wife and admonished Frank: "You told your wife where we weren't."[18]

Staff Sergeant Frank Young laughed as he remembered the censorship that took place as officers read their men's letters home, searched them for security leaks, and cut out telltale parts. He remembered one officer penning a note to a mother whose letter from her son looked like a paper doily after he snipped out security risks. "Your son still loves you but he talks too much," the officer added and sent the letter on.[19]

A supply officer's mistake in ordering 10 times more toilet paper than Bob Stern's ship needed was actually a stroke of luck. Instead of being reprimanded, the officer turned out to be a hero as the extra toilet paper turned out to be pure gold to be traded with other ships for fresh meat, cigarettes, candy, and vegetables. "You could barter toilet paper for anything!" Bob remembered.[20]

Trading was the order of the day for servicemen. Bill Noonan remembered seeing a ship unloading supplies at Tacloban. Asked if he had any beer, the supply ship officer cut a deal to trade beer for a half case of cigarettes. When Bill and his men produced a whole case of cigarettes, the ecstatic officer rewarded them with beer up to their ears.[21]

Frank Feeley was proud of his promotion to Private First Class and immediately sought the first opportunity to take his new stripe into a tailor in London. When he returned to headquarters and joined his buddies for dinner, the dining room was suddenly convulsed with laughter. The tailor had sewed the insignia on upside down (as was English custom). An embarrassed PFC quickly made a return trip to back to London.[22]

It would take time for the mushrooming of gambling casinos like the glitzy Las Vegas, Atlantic City, and Biloxi casinos to develop into billion dollar enterprises, but gambling for vast numbers of GIs provided entertainment or perhaps an opportunity to fill in the long hours of "hurrying up and waiting" so characteristic of the military. For some, gambling had become a sport, and addicts threw caution to the winds when even life itself appeared a chancy game. Lee Conley remembered that the first night out on the trip across the Atlantic one of his fellow Marines immediately made a beeline for the "head" and started a crap game on the floor of the "john." Despite the loss of sleep, his friend's all-nighter netted him $1,500 (which the authorities immediately ordered him to turn over to the purser for safekeeping). Lee, himself, wanted no part of the crap game but lost his money anyway when he naively left his wallet in his trousers on a hook as he swung into his berth (hammock) for the night. The next morning there was no sign of the billfold or his $90 departure pay. (The crossing was not without excitement for everyone aboard, however, when a sudden lurch of the ship threw Lee and his bunkmates out of their beds in the middle of the night. A Japanese sub had fired two torpedoes, that had fortunately missed their mark and everyone aboard ship was awarded a battle star "for escaping torpedoes.")[23]

One GI remembered a comrade's waiting in the long line for his pay, taking a few steps, and tossing the money on the ground. Any and all were invited to gamble for the full amount. After a heated bidding, one lucky bloke walked away with the greenbacks, as the recent payee nonchalantly trudged off sans funds for the rest of the month. Any further interest in gambling ever came to a screeching halt when on his first payday, Dick Bacon lost his entire pay in 10 minutes in a blackjack game.[24]

One night, while stationed on Leyte, Artillery Captain Bob Wilcox was awakened about 2 A.M. by his extremely nervous jeep driver who was clasping a huge wad of money—$2,400 to be exact. "He begged me to find a safe place for the money because sore losers, after drinking, could become violent and seek satisfaction toward getting some of their money back. We worked out a safe place with the first sergeant to 'hide the stash,' and with the understanding that officers were never to be used to process gambling debts." A few weeks later, as Bob was heading north to Manila with another unit, his driver surreptitiously appeared with two bottles of stateside whiskey for Bob. In deep gratitude he confessed, "You saved my life!"[25]

Milton Ames considered himself lucky to be aboard the *Queen Mary* for the Atlantic crossing. On the plus side, it was a faster ship than most troop ships. On the negative side, he insisted, GIs were squeezed into every square inch of space. There was scarcely room to breathe. There was a surprise in store for the troops, however, when on the second day out there was the announcement: "All hands and Soldiers Attention." If anyone missed it the first time the third repetition got everyone's attention. The announcement continued: "We are very proud to have aboard Prime Minister Churchill [returning from the Quebec Conference] who would like to say a few words to you." The men were awestruck as Churchill thanked the Americans profusely, saying there would be no England without the Americans. It was a never to be forgotten moment. Spirits soared, and the war took on new meaning—despite the fact that D-Day loomed ominously ahead.[26]

In June Milks' hometown, Battle Creek, Michigan, setting for one of the country's largest hospitals, Percy Jones, there were soldiers and more soldiers before, during, and after the war. June and the town's residents well remembered the generosity of Hank Greenberg, the famous Detroit baseball player, who had enlisted in the army and was stationed in Battle Creek. There, every Friday and Saturday evening, Hank drove his big shiny Cadillac down to the gate, crammed as many soldiers as possible into it, drove into town with them, and treated everyone to dinner that evening.[27]

In 1942, while his submarine was being refurbished, Vince Schumacher got a seven days' pass to marry his ladylove on Mare Island (near San Francisco). The wedding was celebrated in style at the Officers' Club with Vince's crew members as guests, plus some rather unruly crew members who emerged from two Russian subs that had come to the island for repairs. To the surprise of the bride and groom, what should have been a staid, formal reception, was eventually turned into a three-day orgy of liquor and food by the spirited Russians.

After the cutting of the cake, however, Vince and his bride succeeded in extracting themselves from the raucous partying and headed for a honeymoon at Yosemite. In a not too unhappy turn of events, they found they had the place all to themselves. Because of gas rationing, tourists could not obtain enough gas stamps to drive to Yosemite—at least not that weekend anyway. Actually it was thanks to Vince's mother, whose job with the state of California allowed her extra gas coupons in connection with her work, who had saved her stamps and given them to the happy couple for their honeymoon trip.[28]

During her assignment in Corpus Christi, Texas, Lenore Moe was busily engaged teaching instrument flying to flyers who had successfully made their runs in the Pacific but were now enjoying a little R&R as they readied for advanced in-depth training with new, more modern instruments. The men, temporarily free from the rigors of combat and routine, found time hanging heavily on their hands and simply ended up each day lounging in Lenore's office with nothing much to do. An avid knitter herself, Lenore soon found something for them to do; she taught them to knit. Providing the yarn and a few simple directions, she discovered using their hands with no mental exertion required was the perfect therapy for the seasoned veterans. There were no fashionable scarves or warm mittens produced, but the relaxation and sheer enjoyment proved to be miraculous.[29]

There was savage fighting on Guadalcanal with Japanese planes harassing the Allies by day and Japanese ships bombing them at night. Finally, the last Japanese had finally been evacuated, and Norm Pierce and his Marine unit were shipped off to New Zealand for some badly needed R and R. (Norm remembered they had spent more time in foxholes than in their tents.) The New Zealanders gave the GIs a warm welcome, and the men reveled in free time to check out the nearby towns. One afternoon, as Norm and two of his buddies were ambling along the street looking for a little excitement, they noticed a beauty shop, and peering in the window glimpsed three attractive beauticians apparently at liberty. Why not get acquainted? The girls were really good looking! Norm and his buddies got acquainted all right; more than that they emerged two hours later with curly permanent waves. Although they were rather pleased with themselves, their sergeant was furious when they returned to the base and immediately ordered them to shave their heads. Well, so much for an afternoon's escapade.[30]

Complaints about food were almost universal. Bill Noonan told of some of the men on his ship holding up a piece of bread to the light and informing the cook it had weevils, and "this is Friday and we're not allowed to eat meat on Friday."[31]

As he was waiting in line at Great Lakes for his discharge from the Navy, John Rodgers almost had a heart attack. As his turn finally came, the officer at the desk looked up, smiled and congratulated him with, "You sure made the right decision!" "What do you mean?" John asked quizzically. "Why this is the re-enlistment line," came the answer. John practically hit the ceiling, that is, until the officer winked and responded, "Just kidding, just kidding."[32]

Universally, the GIs were wild about Bob Hope's shows for the men overseas. Paul Souder particularly remembered one evening in Honolulu when Hope and his entourage were performing. Hope, naturally, drew a huge crowd, including Admiral Halsey in the front row that night. Bob, true to form, had his audience convulsed with his one-liners, but it was when Frances Langford appeared in her sexy hot pants that the crowd went ballistic with applause and cheering. A bugler tried to get the men to calm down; however, during a moment's pause a voice in the rear rang out, "You don't have to do a thing, baby, just stand there!" Once again the audience erupted into tumultuous laughing and screaming. Obviously, it was some time before the audience could be calmed down and the show could continue.[33]

CHAPTER 13

The Home Front

WEEKEND PASS WEDDINGS

All across the nation, young couples were deciding that a weekend pass was a perfect time for a wedding, rather than waiting for who knows how long until the end of the war. "I now pronounce you" resounded at formal church ceremonies with brides replete with flowing trains and the traditional elbow length lace gloves. Vows were also repeated before improvised living room altars; in tiny, far away chapels following a fiancée's grueling cross-country train ride; in austere, no-frills small town courtrooms; in the parlors of a convenient clergyman, his wife in attendance as witness.

Ginny Rath (Bennetts) kept her promise to her parents to finish college before marrying, but immediately following graduation she was off to Miami where her fiancé, Fritz, was stationed and where they were to be married. The train trip, however, proved daunting. Although they were proud holders of reservations inveigled somehow by her mother-in-law, who accompanied her, both women panicked when the trainmaster announced that Ginny and her mother-in-law-to-be had tickets for a train that did not exist. The only alternative was to wait in line and hope for coach accommodations on another train.

As they squeezed their way into two sooty, threadbare seats on a train that looked promising, they looked around and saw there were no other seats to be had. For two days they sweltered on a train that surely had been dragged out of mothballs; a train that stopped every few stations to take on more and more passengers who would be destined to sit on suitcases or stand in the aisles. They felt themselves lucky to snag a vendor passing through the cars with sandwiches; liquids were almost an impossibility to come by. At Jacksonville, on a transfer of trains, they peeled off their hosiery, only to find their legs jet-black, and no opportunity for soap and water bathing. Early on, Ginny had had to abandon her white gloves and fashionable straw hat. At the station in Miami the two were so grimy and disheveled that Ginny's fiancé walked right by his mother and bride-to-be without even recognizing them.

Fritz had assured Ginny that everything was in readiness for their wedding. As it turned out, Fritz had casually mentioned to the chaplain as they passed in a hallway one day that he would like him to officiate at his upcoming nuptials. It was left to Ginny to procure the licenses and make the arrangements for a reception at the Officers' Club. Attention to a few more important details and all was in readiness. It was a beautiful wedding with full military flourishes, Ginny remembered, other than that she had never even seen the members of her wedding party before the ceremony. As was the case for many newlyweds, there was no honeymoon. Ginny returned home, and Fritz took off for his assignment at Staten Island in New York Bay.[1]

No telling how many millions of letters were lost in transit, but one missing letter in particular caused Maxine Hari (George) real problems. The letter from her fiancé, stationed aboard the USS *Eastland* in the South Pacific, telling her of her of his good fortune in getting a leave two days after V-J Day and urging her to make all the necessary arrangements for their wedding never reached Maxine. Instead, an out-of-the-blue call from San Francisco sent Maxine into a state of shock. Harry had arrived on the West Coast on leave and he would be home on the first available means of transportation. His leave would be short, only while the ship was in dry dock awaiting repairs. And how were plans coming for their wedding he inquired anxiously. The news, of course, was wonderful, but without a shred of advance notice Maxine put in some frantic hours finding a wedding dress, borrowing a veil, arranging for a church, a minister, and a reception, and getting the license and necessary blood tests. All this complicated by the fact that many offices and shops were closed in celebration of V-J Day.

It was no small task just to get to Mt. Union College in Alliance, Ohio from Washington, D.C. where Maxine was living with her parents during the war years. Maxine and Harry had met while in college, and that was to be the setting for their wedding. Their friend the college chaplain was contacted to perform the ceremony, two summer school students agreed to serve as groomsmen, and Maxine's Alpha Xi Delta sorority house was decided upon for the reception. Both Harry and Maxine agreed it could not have been a more hectic time. A common ordinary cake served in place of an ornate, tiered wedding cake. The woman who was to help with serving the guests made a huge urn of coffee and then left the house. By the time the wedding party and guests reached the sorority house the coffee was stone cold. If that wasn't enough, after the reception, the young couple were informed that Harry's grandmother had died that day. Much of their brief honeymoon time was spent borrowing a car from his uncle and driving to the funeral.[2]

HOUSING SHORTAGES

In the summer of 1942, Bev Doane (Marshall) remembered being left at home admiring her pretty diamond engagement ring as her fiancé went off to war. In short order the nightly telephone calls became more and more persistent with Gary's pleas for Bev to hurry down to Fort Sill to marry him in the Old Post Chapel. Decisions, decisions—and such important ones! Despite her family's reluctance to have her wedding take place hundreds of miles away from home, Bev and Gary were married on September 5th.[3]

The ceremony over, the newlyweds were immediately confronted with the formidable struggle to find living quarters close to the groom's military base. Not only newlyweds, but wives of servicemen everywhere trudged the streets knocking on doors, posting signs, running newspaper ads, and chalking up astronomical phone bills in a desperate search for housing. Everyone was on the move. Army bases were crowded to overflowing; hotels and motels were pricey and filled to capacity. Finding an apartment near a military base was almost an impossibility. Young wives were hard put to find even a tiny room for themselves and their husbands. Thousands of kindly, patriotic women opened their homes in an attempt to provide housing for the young people; nevertheless, most living quarters proved to be expensive, uncomfortable, and all too often just plain miserable. (At one time in Texas Peg Higbee shared a single bedroom with five other servicemen's wives.)

Janie Boyd (Tabler) and her husband considered themselves lucky to find lodgings, such as they were, in a variety of incommodious quarters: first in a chicken coop, later in a bedroom atop a fire station, and still later in a room in a motel that turned out to be in the center of the town's red light district. Their "chicken coop" residence was thanks to an enterprising landlady who rented out every room in her house, including the barn and chicken coop to soldiers and their wives. Ten couples shared the tiny kitchen, and an outhouse served as the community bathroom. Despite the deplorable conditions, the chicken feathers here and there, and the somewhat odoriferous reminders of the former occupants, the "coop" was expensive. In exchange for a cut in the rent, Janie struck a bargain and agreed to do the laundry, 20 sheets and pillowcases each week, for the landlady and her tenants. Iron-rust water, a prehistoric washer, and a hand-cranked wringer, combined with temperamental clotheslines and inclement weather, all added to the challenges of washday. At a later abode, Janie agreed to help deliver the morning papers for a decrease in the rent.

Things got even more hectic when Janie found she was pregnant, and several months later she gave up the washtubs and paper route and returned home to her parents to deliver baby Johnny. It was a short visit with her parents before an opportunity arose to hit the road again and rejoin her husband. The train trip with a three-week old baby was memorable in itself, but fortunately Red Cross women met every train, passed out coffee and donuts, and even held the baby for a few minutes' respite for the weary mother. This time Janie's husband had secured an apartment for them—with a real bathroom! It was above a fire station, and as Janie said "the firemen got to know Johnny rather well." Now and then they would even babysit for an hour while Janie did her weekly grocery shopping. Young Johnny's bed was a bureau drawer in their room and his diapers were stretched across a line from their bedroom to a pole attached to the fire station, a line that the ever-attentive firemen helped her rig up. (Those were the days long before the introduction of disposal diapers, and the shortages of ready-made baby diapers sent new mothers to the department stores for flannel to hem up and make into diapers for their newborns.)

Their next accommodations in a room in a motel appeared to be a great improvement, that is until it became abundantly clear they were located in the center of the town's Red Light district in Laurel, Maryland, where "ladies of the evening" plied their trade just outside their door. It quickly became obvious that Janie and her husband were the only residents not involved in "the business." Actually, Janie had no real complaint about their surroundings, for the ladies were most attentive to little Johnny and often came to see and hold him.

Despite the deprivations and sacrifices, there were few complaints from Janie and the thousands of young wives like her. They were happy not to have to sleep in their cars at night as some of their friends were doing. All seemed to take the inconveniences in stride; everyone was in the same boat.

When it came time to return home as her husband was readying to be sent overseas, Janie's parents were sure Janie and her husband would never make it 50 miles, to say nothing of 1,000 miles, in their old, beat-up car. Tires were impossible to come by, but somehow Janie's father inveigled four tires on the black market and sent them to Janie and her husband in Waco. Fortunately, they arrived the day before the Boyds left for home. With the back of the car loaded with tires, Janie, her husband, and baby Johnny started for home. One by one each of the tires was replaced with a new one and finally, just about 100 miles from home, the car was jacked up a final time and the last of the four tires was put on for the final stretch.[4]

During her husband's assignment in Williamsburg, Dorrie Souder had about given up on finding a place to stay in order to be with her husband. At one temporary rental Dorrie was considerably underwhelmed with the tradition of "Southern Hospitality" when the landlady at Camp Peary charged them 10 cents for every shower, 10 cents for a clean towel, and 10 cents for a clean sheet. After more days of walking the streets and knocking on doors, finally an angel lady (actually the Registrar) took pity on her. "Why, honey child, you and your nice husband come live with me." What a happy day!

At Quonset Point, Rhode Island, another angel lady, who had already lost a son in the war and somehow felt it her duty to take in soldiers' wives, had converted the top of her garage into an apartment and there the Souders found a happy home until Paul's reassignment.[5]

Hattiesburg, Mississippi's proximity to Camp Shelby ushered in congestion and an incredible demand for rooms for soldiers' wives, many of whom were there to see their husbands for a few precious moments before the men were shipped out. Even the most elite families rented out spare rooms to servicemen's wives. Ruby Martin (Bancroft), who was busily employed working in the camp hospital, came home one evening shocked to find her mother had rented out all three bedrooms in the house. Ruby, her sister, and her mother moved their beds into the dining room for the duration. This indeed complicated matters for Ruby and her sister who were constantly bringing home guests for Sunday dinner. Homesick soldiers from Camp Shelby or servicemen who had found a Sunday sanctuary in their Petal, Mississippi Methodist church found a few hours of relaxation and good old-fashioned, home-cooked meals thanks to the caring Martins.[6]

THE BIRTHING OF BABIES

At 2 A.M., Ginny Bennetts awoke suddenly with the first labor pains of her pregnancy. Quickly she roused her husband, and in minutes they were standing in front of their apartment hotel, their "home" in New York City from which her husband Fritz, a Lieutenant J.G, commuted each day to his base on Staten Island. There was another stabbing pain as Fritz frantically sought a taxi that would rush them to the Brooklyn Naval Hospital. His search was in vain, however. Although the cab drivers were most sympathetic, they were unwilling to take the chance on having enough gas to make the return trip back to their regular route. (Gas shortages, remember!) Fritz could scarcely meet Ginny's eyes as he announced in desperation, "We're going to have to take the subway." "We're what!" Ginny shrieked, between ever-sharper labor pains. "You've got to be kidding. There is no possible way we can take the subway!"

The good news was that the subway entrance was only a short distance away. The bad news was that the train was a local to Times Square. Things began looking up with an express train to Brooklyn, but it was another downer at the hospital where all was in darkness, not a soul to be seen anywhere.

Fortunately there was a bell that summoned a seemingly indifferent attendant who cleverly observed, "Oh! you're going to have a baby. Ok, come in, and goodbye lieutenant! We'll give you a room, lady, but please don't bother us as we're far too busy."

Ginny remembered little else other than minutes later crawling on her hands and knees to the door of her room for help. Early afternoon, she was awakened when her husband's superior officer appeared at her bedside. "Where the Hell is Fritz?" he bellowed. The anesthetic was beginning to wear off. "Do you know you have a baby girl?" No one had told her a thing!

The frenzied search for Fritz took several hours. Delayed by a lengthy subway tie-up and further held up by a blackout, the proud father breathlessly appeared at Ginny's bedside for two kisses, two hugs, and a speedy return trip back to Staten Island. The next day, Fritz and his ship left for his assignment to serve with the 7th fleet in the South Pacific. That would be the last sight of his wife and baby daughter for 12 long months.[7]

Accommodations for soldiers' wives were particularly scarce in 1945 in Fort Pierce, Florida, where Jamie Goodell Iddings (Haley) was attempting to find housing accommodations in order to be near her husband, Bob Iddings, for the birth of their first child. Although eight-and a-half months pregnant, Jamie walked the streets of Fort Pierce desperately seeking a place to stay, even temporarily. Heads shook sadly, women threw up their hands in desperation; no one even knew of a home where Jamie could even rent a room. Finally, almost miraculously, a Mrs. Hart at the Chamber of Commerce took pity on the very rotund mother-to-be and led her to the top of the family's garage where she had converted limited space into a tiny apartment. Jamie could stay with her husband, and the new baby would have a home.

Not every woman gives birth to a baby in a hotel room, but during the war that's exactly what Jamie Iddings did. It wasn't that they couldn't get to the hospital on time, it was that there *was* no hospital. Fort Pierce, where her husband, a Lieutenant in the U.S. Navy, was temporarily stationed, was a minuscule operation in 1945. In the absence of a hospital, one floor of the town's hotel (the other floors having been converted to army offices) was made into a makeshift hospital and there, amid cancer and pre- and post-operative patients, Jamie's daughter was born. Alone in a strange place, with no TLC from family or friends to see her through, it was not surprising that the new mother was feeling terribly lonely. Gasoline, of course, was strictly rationed, but in a supreme gesture of

unselfishness, neighbors of Jamie's parents came to the rescue. By deny-
ing their own needs they generously pooled their gas coupons to enable
Jamie's parents to drive to Florida to welcome their first grandchild.

Once the baby was born and old enough to travel, getting the baby back
to Jamie's Michigan home was yet another memorable wartime experience. The train north was crammed with servicemen. The aisles of the
train were jammed with women uncomfortably perched on suitcases
struggling to get somewhere to join a loved one in service. Necessity being
the mother of invention, a can of sterno served to heat the baby's bottle
and diapers were washed out in the sink in the women's lavatory and
hung out on the back of the train to dry. Surprisingly, mother and baby
survived the trip in style.[8]

THE COLLEGE SCENE

Pearl Harbor rocked the college campuses, and numerous colleges immediately reorganized and condensed semester and term schedules to enable
the men to more quickly enlist without losing too many credits. As a
result, classes were held at the University of Michigan on New Year's
Day in 1942, for example, and profs took attendance! (A huge New Year's
Eve dance at the IM building helped soften the blow at having to attend
classes on New Year's Day; however, at least one celebrant arrived in class
in his "white tie and tails," shrugging off the fact that he had not had time
to change into more casual attire, having partied all night.)

Young professors were drafted or, having enlisted earlier, were called up
with little prior notice, and a student might have three different instruc-
tors during one semester. It was somewhat disconcerting to arrive in class
and find yet another new face behind the podium. At many universities
there were three different graduations: spring, summer, and winter. As a
result of varying times of graduation, the U of M yearbook, the *Ensian*, for
example, was published in three different sections and sold with a loose-
leaf binder. Many other universities, colleges, and high schools adopted
the same yearbook solution.

During the war years, female college students watched the civilian male
population disappear from campuses as boyfriends and fiancés enlisted
and headed off for the various services. Soon, however, thousands of V12
and ASTP servicemen arrived to take their place.

The exodus of males during the war made a profound impression on
Dell Boettcher, a student at Western Michigan College (later University).
Each day, it seemed, there would be at least one fewer male student in her
classes. One year, the college evicted the women from the college dorms
and made them into living quarters for servicemen. To accommodate the
women the college bought up five houses and turned the rooms over to
them. There was considerable confusion involved in the switch, for the
rooms in the "dorm homes" were allotted by draw, and when one of

Dell's friends could not get a room she punished them and signed up with the WAVES. Many married women who returned to college while their husbands were serving in the military were carefully screened and not allowed to live in the dorms or sorority houses. One wonders what sexy secrets might they share with their dorm mates?[9]

Dick Bates, a medical student at the University of Michigan, described the campus scene in Ann Arbor in his diary.

The war pervades a good deal of our lives. The campus is almost taken over by soldiers, sailors and Marines who can be seen marching to class at any hour. Ann Arbor is only seven miles from the Willow Run bomber plant, so that there has been an influx of workers, doubling the population of the county in the last year. This taxes all laundry, eating and entertainment facilities. Prices are as high as the government limits allow: eggs, 5 cents apiece; fresh string beans, 25 cents a pound; milk, 15 cents a quart, etc. All meat, butter, lard, sugar, gasoline, fuel oil, shoes, canned goods and (but recently) coffee are rationed, so that one must present little paper stamps issued by the Government when buying these items. The roar of big bombers is almost constant over town, as is the noise of freight trains in the valley.[10]

The popular college hangouts were alive with servicemen. Dick Bates recalled taking a date to a movie, then to the Pretzel Bell (U of M's most popular hangout). "The place was crowded with servicemen and officers in a galaxy of summer and winter uniforms mixed. From time to time the whole room would burst into 'Anchors Aweigh' or 'The Caissons go Rolling Along' or some other song. Quite a thrilling sight and sound."[11]

As a result of a dearth of maintenance men on campuses, many a co-ed waded through knee-high snow drifts on her way through the snowy walkways to her seven A.M. classes. Girls on every campus throughout the country took on paid or volunteer work to help out with the war effort. At Michigan State College some girls worked the dormitory switchboards, and some worked at the forge plant on campus or in the heating facility. Some helped with the mowing; some worked in the fields where vegetables were cultivated for the dormitory menus. At least one worked in the prophylactic center on campus and came in with wild stories for her roommates about the activities of the soldiers stationed on campus who had their fling on weekend passes spent in town. Apparently the town girls were more popular than the co-eds who had to "keep hours."

Big proms and dances were abandoned at many of the colleges and universities during the war, and often a big Saturday night for a dateless co-ed involved hitchhiking downtown, purchasing a 15 cent movie ticket at the theater (for a double feature!), and spending the remaining 10 cents left over from one's "two bits" for a bag of popcorn!

The theater departments of most universities and colleges suffered a dearth of male actors. Plays with predominantly female casts such as *Ladies in Retirement*, along with classics such as *She Stoops to Conquer* (with females dressed as males in period costumes) proved popular offerings. The male drama students remaining on campus got a real workout as they were often engaged in playing several parts in a single production. Ted Kennedy recalled playing three different roles in *The Skin of Our Teeth* in a production at the University of Iowa.[12]

At the University of Michigan, Monna Heath remembered that as a result of the labor shortage co-eds were recruited for a variety of work including waiting tables at the Michigan Union for the faculty club diners, pressing hospital gowns for the U of M hospital patients, helping out in the hospital laundry, and even setting up pins in a bowling alley.[13] As a result of the shortage of nurses, college students at countless universities were asked to take Nurses' Aid classes and volunteer at the hospitals. Even those without Nurses' Aid training were welcomed, especially during the dinner hour to help feed infants in the pediatric wards. Student War boards were elected to help facilitate the war effort on campuses. In the dormitory and sorority houses residents served themselves cafeteria style and bussed their own dishes. A most important requirement involved students bringing their food ration coupons from home to enable the dorms and sororities to obtain sugar and meat for their needs. Fraternity houses were left half-empty or turned into housing for servicemen.

Hitchhiking was fairly safe traveling for girls during the war years and, furthermore, because of the gas rationing it was about the only way to get someplace—or almost anyplace. (The girls remembered always carrying a pair of scissors in their pocketbooks for protection!) One summer, when a roommate of Jane Leipprandt (Scandary) was getting married in Detroit, Jane and one of her friends at Michigan State College (later University) were bound and determined they were going to get to the ceremony. Dressed in their Sunday best, including high heels, fancy dresses, white gloves, and be-flowered hats, they stood on the main drag with their thumbs held high until the chauffeur of a huge black car pulled to a stop to ask their destination. "Detroit, our best friend's wedding," the girls explained. A voice from the interior of the car apparently signaled approval, and the girls hurriedly stepped into the car. Inside, as they were smoothing out their finery, lo and behold, they looked up to find their benefactor none other than the conductor of the Detroit Symphony on his way back to Detroit. The girls were then whisked off across town and deposited at the appointed church just in time for the wedding march.[14]

Everybody was hitchhiking. What would be unthinkable today was commonplace during the war years. At 12 years of age, while she was visiting relatives in southern Michigan, Jan Sullivan (O'Leary) remembered her aunt's standing at the roadside, sticking out her thumb, and critically surveying the couple who pulled up and offered a ride. Deeming the couple responsible, Jan's aunt casually deposited her in the back seat for an 80-mile ride to Lansing to see her mother. Such was the way of life in those days.[15]

THE HIGH SCHOOL SCENE

It was during her senior year of high school that Sue Coleman (Johnson) and crowds of her classmates cut classes and went down to the train station to see their friends leave for military service. It was indeed a win-win situation. For parents of the departees, it was a diversion that helped turn tears into smiles. For the inductees, there was a vote of confidence from their peers as they headed out into the great unknown. For the bon voyagers, it was a devout expression of caring, doing something to make the pain of parting a bit more bearable. The high school principal surely deserved honors, for even if it meant interrupting classes, a send-off was permissible on the condition that everyone return to classes that day. And everyone did.[16]

Senior Proms in many high schools and colleges were disbanded or moved ahead, as in East Lansing, Michigan, in 1943, to accommodate seniors who were leaving school before graduation to embark on their military service. It was a happy evening in East Lansing, yet one tinged with sadness, for as the couples gaily danced the night away, in the backs of their minds lurked the ominous reality that very soon their numbers would be diminished and the reality of war would set in. As the evening was winding down, and the band readied for the last set, Evie Wolfram, one of the area's most talented vocalists (she later became a professional singer), stepped up to the microphone and in soft, heart-wrenching tones sang "I'll Be Seeing You," to her date, her steady boyfriend through high school. Needless to say, there wasn't a dry eye in the room.

One tends to forget that families of career military officers were routinely moved about the country as new assignments involved new homes, new friends, and new schools. Bunny Brunner (McComb) attended 18 different schools! Undismayed when a new school proved a big disappointment as to teachers, classes, or friends (or all of the above), Bunny always assured herself that a change would be coming soon. And it always did! She was particularly pleased when she was moved to a new school during the school year and not in the summer. Searching for new friends during the summer months when everyone was scattered proved a trial. When school was in session there were new acquaintances and scores of school-related activities from day one.[17]

Most schools had War Bond Drives that encouraged students to solicit neighbors and relatives to buy War Bonds. Not many schools, however, had the good fortune to have movie stars Gene Tierney and Anthony Quinn arrive to deliver a personal thank you for the school's having gone over their $25,000 goal in selling bonds. Shirley Dean (Guider) and her fellow students in the Normandy High School in the St. Louis suburbs went wild with excitement. The school's 1944 yearbook *The Saga* noted: "Autograph hunters by the hundreds swarmed in on the stars, who were nearly drowned in a sea of pencils, bits of papers and outstretched arms. Even after the big Cadillac had whirled the pair away the impact of concentrated glamour left the school in a delighted daze that textbooks could not destroy." A postscript added: "Antidote for glamour—final exams!" A few days later exam blues were past tense, and it was back to jubilation as everyone joined in the Victory War Bond Dance in celebration.[18]

RATIONING

Rationing of shoes, coffee, meat, sugar, butter, fuel oil, and gas was certainly irksome, but most people felt it also served to help remind people of the huge sacrifices the men and women in uniform were making. Most felt the morale was greater than at any other time in our history, that at last the country was experiencing a sense of community.

Much of women's shoe fetish and probably much of women's later foot troubles can be attributed to wartime shoe rationing. Thousands of women vowed that if shoe rationing ever ended, they would buy every pair of shoes that fit—and maybe even a pair or two that didn't fit precisely. No matter how comfortable a new pair of shoes (for which one had to cough up one precious coupon) felt in the shoe store, then and now, shoes could grow uncomfortable when subjected to rain and snow—and too much walking. Not all shoes age comfortably. Of course, now and then someone would pass along a pair of shoes that were really an impossible fit, and although they were not quite the right size for the recipient either, they were perfectly good for sit-down or go-to-the-movies evenings. Nylons were pretty much nonexistent, other than the treasure of a pair saved from prewar days. Most women wore lisle or rayon hose that never seemed to get thoroughly dry. Leg make-up, of course, was an alternative for real hosiery. Leg makeup—messy, smeary, and easily shared with upholstery, velvet dresses, and car seats—however, was not always a happy choice. Clothing, shoes, and hosiery, all came under the heading: "Make it over, make it do, or do without."

One youngster, while out grocery shopping with her mother, was dismayed when she saw her suddenly burst into tears. She had never seen her mother cry before. A thief had somehow stolen a package of hamburger from little sister's baby carriage where her mother thought she had carefully sequestered the package in the folds of the blanket of the buggy. It had taken precious food stamps to obtain the meat, and now the family's entire week's meat ration was gone.

Sue Sims Schulze was disappointed that her family could never make use of their summer home at Harbor Springs—gas rationing prevented all but the most necessary travel. One girl remembered that their last trip to their summer home in northern Michigan was in 1943. It was three years before they could get back again.[19]

The fact that her mother had tuberculosis enabled Bernice "Bunny" Roe (Smith) and her family to obtain extra gas so that the family could go to their summer home in Charlevoix during a few of the summer months. (Their yacht, the REOMAR, was taken over by the government and returned at the end of the war stripped clean and abandoned, for it would be far too expensive to refurbish.) At best living in Charlevoix was no picnic; residents spent anxious days fearful that the Germans might have their minds set on bombing the Straits of Mackinaw.[20]

During the winter months, oil to heat their "country home," some seven miles outside of Lansing, Michigan, was so scarce that Bunny, her parents, and her brother were forced to move into the Hotel Olds (which they owned and where their uncle served as manager) in downtown Lansing. Because they ate all of their meals at the Hotel (a distasteful experience for Bunny) they never had to part with their precious food coupons. Christmases, however, they splurged big time, heated up the "country home," and made a truly Merry Christmas of it. During the war the Oldsmobile plant (Bunny's grandfather was R. E. Olds) was, of course, converted into a factory making war materiel.

Living in a rural area meant that farmers could often get gas. It was tempting but unpatriotic to use tractor gas in one's car. There were of course those who could not resist temptation. (It was wise to date a farmer's son one teenager confessed.) Most farmers, however, deplored the use of tractor gas for cars. Rex Shugart remembered that there was "not a single person I ever knew of that used agricultural or tractor gas in their car."[21]

Liquor was hard to come by, and there was a considerable dry spell for many civilians. In 1943, while her husband was stationed at Camp Peary, Dorrie Souder had taken a job as a secretary for a faculty member of a nearby college. Now and then during her tenure, Dorrie and her boss found a few moments to chat about the college, their families, and the war situation. One day her boss brightened up with a splendid idea. "By the way, Dorrie, what does your husband do with his liquor quota? I'd be glad to pay Paul for his allotment."[22]

The idea had great appeal for Dorrie, too, for neither she nor her husband had ever even had a drink of alcohol. "Well, I could bring it to the office," Dorrie suggested. "Oh, no!" her boss declared. "That's not a good idea. I don't dare risk it here. It would be too dangerous."

Within minutes Dorrie and her boss concocted a plan whereby her husband, Paul, would regularly purchase his allotment of one bottle of liquor each month. It was then up to Dorrie to camouflage the bottle in newspapers, go to the Post Office on the appointed day, surreptitiously stir around a few newspapers, leave the package unattended on a table and exit the building as she saw her boss approaching the Post Office to pick up his package. It was a neat setup; a clandestine operation that could have rendered them candidates for the Intelligence Services.

Although O. H. Barnett, of Leake County, Mississippi, had been too young for World War I, he was too old for World War II; however, he was appointed to the rationing board of Leake County, where they rationed everything from sugar to automobiles. He insisted that "all the battles were not fought overseas." There were never ending battles "whether a man could get gas, or whether he could get sugar, or whether he could get shoes, or whether he buys an automobile or tires." (There was always the fear that one's gas might be siphoned off if a car were left unattended in a strange neighborhood or in a dark parking lot. The exchange of stamps for merchandise or services was prevalent everywhere. Some women even succeeded in trading sugar for doctor's bills.)[23]

WIVES' CLUBS

Because there were few alternatives, most wives were resigned to their separation from their husbands and took their absence in stride. Many returned home to live with their parents. Many enrolled in Nurses' Aid courses and volunteered at local hospitals. Many formed "War Wives" clubs and joined bridge clubs as an opportunity to socialize and to share news of husbands and brothers stationed overseas.

Several women from Lansing, Michigan will never forget their Wives' Club outing in Detroit. While their husbands were in service, a small coterie of women formed a support group for each other, designating one night each week to meet at each other's homes for bridge and gossip. Mary Sharp remembered five friends from their so-called Wives Club arranging for baby sitters, pooling their gas coupons, and heading for a day in the "The Big City," 90 miles away. (One must remember that in the 1940s, a day's trip into Detroit with its big department stores, fashionable hair styling salons, and elegant restaurants was for Lansingites like a day in Chicago or New York City for women a generation later.).[24]

Suffering a twinge of guilt about a day of hedonistic pursuits, the women first gave blood at the Red Cross Headquarters and then set off on a gala day of self-indulgence. A mandatory stop, of course, was the famous J. L. Hudson Store (occupying a whole city block, mind you!) with its impressive beauty salon and popular penthouse luncheon room. Then it was a hurried tour through the myriad downtown fashion centers—not much buying but plenty of sallies of imagination and desire. By six o'clock the stores had closed, and at the appointed hour the little group of friends gathered for dinner at Detroit's poshiest restaurant—The London Chop House. Dinner plans changed quickly, however, when a haughty maitre d' surveyed them suspiciously. "Ladies, where are your escorts?" he queried in an icy tone. With understandable indignation, the ladies proudly informed their inquisitor that their escorts were in uniform busily engaged in flying missions over Germany and in serving their country in Italy and North Africa. Unmoved, the maitre d' summarily waved them off. "I am sorry ladies, but we do not serve unescorted women here." With equal disdain, the ladies turned on their heels and sashayed over to the Book Cadillac Hotel dining room—there perhaps even ordering a glass of wine to cool their outrage.

TRAIN TRAVEL

Train travel was frenetic during the war. Every wife or fiancée making her way across country had a tale to tell—about perching atop suitcases in the aisles for days at a time, about the dining cars closed to patrons other than servicemen, about prolonged delays and rerouting—all of which were common occurrences. As Helen Deason accompanied her husband back to his ship in Seattle after his short leave at home, her husband, by resting his head on her shoulder, was able to catch a few winks' sleep during their three-day cross-country trip. Looking down at the dear sleeping head on her shoulder, Helen leaned down and gently kissed the dreamer's forehead. At that moment a conducter strode by and reprimanded her: "No more of that, Girlie!" Helen was furious that the man could have so grossly misjudged her innocent, caring gesture.[25]

Travel by car necessitated ration stamps for gas; travel by train necessitated stamina, perseverance and, at times, a good measure of lunacy. The trains were bulging with servicemen, and to get something to eat involved a friendly GI who might bring something back from the diner (open only to service people) or bringing along prepacked sandwiches and snacks. Civilians were forced to stand or sit on suitcases in the aisles or on the back platforms, and a cross-country trip to visit a loved one in California immediately excluded the fainthearted and the irresolute.

Following a visit with her in-laws in Columbus, Ohio, Carolyn Talbot Hoagland wrote to her husband, John H. Hoagland, stationed in Pearl Harbor, with details of her trip back to Dayton where she was spending the war years with her parents.

I was herded like cattle onto an already over-crowded train. I sandwiched myself on the platform between two steaming coaches. They were the kind that had all the windows open to let the soot and *some* air in. People were sitting on suitcases all thru the aisles. So I shared my big bag with another woman on the platform. (You know most times people aren't allowed to stand there between the cars. But today there were about eight of us there.) The dirt came rolling in. Since there was nothing else to do, I sat there and enjoyed it. I kept my eyes closed to keep cinders out. So to keep from being bored I pretended I was sitting in a covered wagon back in '49 with my eight children around me bouncing along out west.

However, from Springfield on—my imagination went into competition with "life" and facts. The trip became really exciting. Result I descended the train in Dayton with a dress spattered with blood. Curious—? Wanna hear more—

There had been a lad (in civvies) walking thru several times—quite high. When we stopped in Springfield the conductor wouldn't let any passengers on where we were. He called to someone to get a doctor—and to get "that boy off the train." I decided that the drunken lad had really got sick. They brought him thru to the platform where we were standing. Then I saw a very vicious looking gash on his right wrist. Blood was just streaming forth—really a stomach turning sight. (Apparently he was bleeding from a wound acquired when he thrust his hand through the mirror in the men's john.) He had sobered up some and was begging not to be put off. Said he had just received his "Greeting" from the government and had just a day to see his mother before reporting to the army. Maybe I'm just chicken hearted, Johnny, but when that crying kid was standing there begging to be permitted to go home and holding that blood soaked wrist, butterflies started dancing in my tummy. No, I'll never condone his getting sky high like that but I can almost understand how a boy would want to get in that "trouble killing state" when heading to the army. I say I can understand it in a person like he probably must have been . . . Just the same it was pathetic.

Then as calmly as anything an army boy saw what was going on (he didn't even have PFC stripes) and took over. The kid brushed by me getting some of the blood on my dress. The soldier took him to the nearest john (which happened to be WOMEN) and washed his wrist—then sat him down and proceeded to pull handkies and towels from his dufflel bag—tore them into bandages. He acted as calm as tho it were an every day task of his. He himself couldn't have been out of high school long. Even after he was bandaged the lad went out cold for a few minutes.

After it was all over . . . I was talking to the army kid and mentioned how professional he had seemed. He smiled and said, "It's what they teach us—good practice for things to come, I guess."[26]

Ticket lines for buses and trains wound around for blocks as servicemen sought transportation home to families or back to bases. Civilians were, of course, second class citizens and as noted found travel a veritable challenge. One poignant memory for Christy Clark (Nichols) was returning home from Randolph Macon College one Christmas during the war, balanced uncomfortably on a suitcase because of the crowds of servicemen. Suddenly, in the middle of the night on the train journey, which seemed interminable, a serviceman began whistling "Silent Night," and the whole car lulled to the soft whistling. The melodic airs were a mesmerizing touch, and somehow the long journey took on a much happier dimension for both standees and suitcase sitees.[27]

CHAPTER 14

The Home Front: The Good and the Sad

DEFENSE WORKERS

With most of the young male population engaged in serving their country with the armed services, women emerged from their kitchens and their "cult of domesticity" and took over men's jobs in factories. As the war wore on, thousands of factories converted to making planes, ammunition, guns, and war materiel. By the end of the war, women working the defense plants were credited with making a vital contribution to the war effort. Although many of the women capably took over clerical jobs, tens of thousands worked long hours on assembly lines in noisy, overheated buildings, under far less than desirable conditions.

"Rosie the Riveter" had won a place deep in the hearts of Americans during the war years. Rosie posters captioned "We Can Do It" were ubiquitous. Millions of pictures on storefronts, in newspapers, on stamps, T-shirts, and on signposts depicted Rosie, sleeves rolled up, arm raised, and exuding energy and enthusiasm, as representative of women's role in contributing to the war effort by taking jobs in factories and defense plants. By stepping into what had heretofore been primarily a man's world, she became a heroine, a boon to the war effort, by releasing a man for service with the military. For the more than 6 million women who joined the workforce during the war years, World War II marked a time of immense change—a change that in many respects helped to initiate the Women's Liberation Movement. In addition it also marked a time for the growth of unions.

While her husband was overseas helping settle the war in the South Pacific, Ilah Meyers took a job in a local factory (Abrams' Instrument

Company in Lansing, Michigan) making controls to facilitate torpedo accuracy. Work on the assembly line soon led to her promotion to a machine operator first class. Although her pay never equaled that of a male operator's take-home pay, the remuneration was a considerable improvement over that of many other jobs. The work required considerable digital dexterity, and as a result, Ilah discovered that many of her co-workers had formerly been craft teachers, musicians, and women with extremely sensitive hands. Since most of the men were in service, the work force numbered 200 females and 150 "old men" or 4Fs. Fortunately, there was a good deal of camaraderie in the factory, and Ilah sensed no great antipathy from the men toward women taking factory jobs. The work was hard, however, involving nine hour shifts, six days a week.

Later Ilah's work at the plant consisted of making control shutters for the cameras employed in the nose of the bombers and used to take pictures before, during, and after the plane dropped its bombs. Increasing production was the name of the game, and Ilah was pleased to feel she was doing her part to help when she was rewarded with a war bond bonus for her suggestion on how to speed up production. The unions were beginning to make themselves felt in the factories, and many women, including Ilah and a fellow female employee, took the heat from many of the men for refusing to join the unions that were forming.[1]

Maxine Grissett, of Andalusia, Alabama, worked in a jeans and overalls factory making khaki work pants for the army. Starting at 13 cents an hour, Maxine finally worked her way up to the munificent sum of 50 cents an hour. There was a special kinship among women working in factories, perhaps because most of them held similar interests and concerns in husbands serving in the armed forces. The whole Andalusia factory came together to share in Maxine's anxiety when it was learned her husband, Cleb, accidentally tripped a cord as he stepped on a land mine in the Philippines. The man next to him died, but fortunately Maxine's husband suffered only minor injuries all over his body from the shrapnel. Her fellow workers joined in her rejoicing when, after six months in an American hospital, her husband was pronounced almost good as new again.[2]

During the war years, Marjorie Pearson worked at the Burroughs Adding Machine Company in downtown Detroit, a declared defense plant that made parts for the Norden bombsite, as well as other small parts needed by the government. She was proud to be replacing two men, who could then be freed for military service. Her work as "stock chaser," seeing that the right part got to the right stock room, involved long hours. "We worked 54 hour weeks, 10 hours a day, except Friday which was an 8 hour working day and 6 hours on Saturday." Even so, her hours were far fewer than those of her parents who worked at the Willow Run plant in

Ypsilanti, Michigan. "Father worked twelve hours a day, sometimes every day of the week."

"We were instructed not to talk about our jobs to others as 'Loose Lips Sink Ships,'" Marjorie continued. Workers in the plant and elsewhere were told "to watch for any suspicious activity or strangers in our neighborhood." Single women at Burroughs were urgently encouraged to join the services, and supervisors and department heads intimated that "if they didn't join the service, they had to work two more years before they could quit after the war was over."[3]

Alice Haber, who worked in the main office of the Buick Division of General Motors in Flint, had a far different story to tell about employers' attitudes toward women enlisting in the services. The president of the Buick Division sent his secretary to her office "to tell me he didn't approve of girls in the service." Alice shrugged off his disapproval and told him she was going anyway. "So they severed me, and they gave me severance pay and told me I would have no longevity with Buick. Well as it turned out, that became a national law, that anyone who went in to service had to be given his or her job back. And so they had to give me my job, but they couldn't get the money back because I'd already spent it," she laughed.[4]

While her husband, a sergeant doing psychological testing with the Army, was stationed in Long Beach, California, Muriel Rokeach undertook her own crusade for the good of mankind, in some respects a bit different from the ordinary defense worker. "Muriel the Riveter" wasn't desperate for the money, although 40 dollars a week was pretty good pay in those days. Actually she wasn't primarily motivated by the goal to serve her country, although that was certainly not an unwelcome bonus. She wasn't required to work the graveyard shift, midnight to 7 A.M., even though the pay was better. However, Muriel was, by her own admission, a flaming liberal fresh out of the University of California and fervently committed to changing the world—well, at least life for underpaid, blue collar workers—well, at least workers in California—well, at least workers in Long Beach.

Working to unionize the defense workers at the Douglas Aircraft factory making C-47 cargo planes in 1942 seemed a sensible place to start. Getting a job was easy; demonstrating the manual dexterity required to work as a riveter was not. Muriel, despite her college education, was somewhat humbled by the fact that she could not qualify as a skilled worker. (Lesson learned: "No matter what job you have, if you're not good at it, it makes you feel terrible.") Despite her lack of dexterity, Muriel qualified to work inside the planes maneuvering the little metal bar that helped hold the rivet (driven in by a woman outside the plane) in place. Her commitment, she wanted it remembered, doing an exacting job on the planes that would help save lives, was her first concern. Working as a union organizer was an added dividend. Lunch times Muriel spent enticing workers to sign cards indicating an interest in seeing the plant unionized. (If enough people expressed an interest in a union then the UAW could call for a vote.)

Her co-workers, from 65 to 75 percent of them women, proved to be an interesting group. Many of them were migrants from the "Dust Bowl" depression areas (shades of John Steinbeck's *Grapes of Wrath*). During the war those women flooded to the aircraft industries for there at last was a paying job, an escape from the depressing migrant workers' camps. When asked about possible problems of sexual harassment, the women defense plant workers pointed out that the proportion of women to men in a wartime factory made it difficult for men to get too far out of line.

Would she do it all over again? "Of course, were I twenty-two years old," Muriel Rokeach smiled. (The union did win, she later learned, after she left to follow her husband to his new assignment in Denver.)[5]

During the war, Doris Warden enjoyed her two years' work as a riveter in a defense plant. She was serving her country, and, of course, the pay was not an unwelcome feature. However, Doris later discovered serious repercussions from her years in the factory. In 1944, when her fiance returned home from serving in Australia, they were married and Doris soon became pregnant. Giving birth to a beautiful daughter was a dream come true, but the days following turned into a nightmare. From the moment she was born, baby Linda screamed day and night at the top of her tiny lungs and adamantly refused to feed. Her parents were frantic as each day the situation grew more ominous. In a desperate plea for help, a specialist was called in who examined the infant and then instructed the distraught parents to check the baby's diapers for metal shavings ingested during Doris' employment at the defense plant. Sure enough, there were the tiny filiaments that were responsible for the baby's anguish.

Safety measures were notably absent in defense plants during the war: there were no masks or ear plugs. Doris had inadvertently inhaled tiny particles of aluminum during her work at the factory, and they had filtered through her body, passed into the womb, and into the intestinal track of baby Linda. Fortunately the baby succeeded in passing the filings and soon became a model, healthy baby. The story was difficult to comprehend, and over the years Doris' mother insisted on sharing the story with neighbors, friends, and anyone who would listen. As proof of the story, the grandmother stuffed some of the filings into a little snuff bottle and showed them off to give veracity to the account. (One wonders how many other babies of factory working mothers might have shared a similar problem and died from lack of an expert diagnostician.)[6]

Saddled with three young children to feed and clothe following her separation from her alcoholic husband, Jan Sullivan's (O'Leary) mother moved from South Orange, New Jersey to Lansing, Michigan where she obtained a job with Fisher Body making war materiel during the war. In order to keep up with the long hours and to provide some degree of adequate home life for her children, Jan's mother farmed them out with her parents in Remus, Michigan, some 78 miles from Lansing. As noted earlier, as a result of the wartime shortages of automobiles and gas, hitchhiking became one of the most effective (and often the only) means of transportation. Each week, Jan's mother hitchhiked to and from Remus in order to be with her children on the weekends.[7]

LABOR SHORTAGES ON FARMS

Labor shortages were felt everywhere—in industry, in restaurants, in stores, in hospitals, in agriculture. Annie deVries (Robinson), a high schooler, remembered, "One fall, the sugar beet farmers hired us to harvest their crops. The usual Mexican Labor couldn't come up here [Michigan], so the farmers were stuck with no help. They let school out and hired as many of us that would work. I always thought it ironic that the guys got to drive the tractors and we girls had to top the beets with huge knives-then throw them in the trailer. Beets were not small. They were sometimes a foot across. I don't believe I have ever been so tired and sore in my life! We worked three days and got the job done! I can't remember how much money we made. It rained all three days, so we worked doubly hard as the mud was mostly clay and we carried it around in big chunks on our boots."[8]

In the absence of migrant workers, not only school kids but thousands of soldiers were bussed to areas devoid of the usual seasonal help. Lieutenant Harold Cunningham and scores of his buddies, for example, were sent from their base at Camp McCoy, Wisconsin, to North Dakota for three weeks to help harvest the wheat crop.[9]

As older brothers went off to war, younger brothers and sisters (and wives) took over the work on the farms. After her brother left, when she was about 12 years old, Iona Shugart's father took her out one day and said, "'Here's the tractor, and this is how you run it.' And I dragged, what they call dragged the land, planting. And after that I kind of took over the things on the farm that my brother had done for my dad, which I enjoyed." Work for many farm children included breaking open the milk-weed pods from the fields, the contents which were processed, the seeds separated, and the feather-like material used like kapok in life-jackets.[10]

EVERYONE WAS INVOLVED

Dan McHugh credits his mother, as well as other mothers, with being the real heroes of the war. Dan had two sisters in the Red Cross and three brothers in various branches of the service. Each week Dan's mother wrote to each of her six children, and every Thursday she walked a mile to say a novena at her church. In the meantime she rolled bandages, collected salvage, and did other volunteer work. Both parents volunteered for the gruesome task of calling on parents who had lost a son during the war. Helen Hines, of Springfield, Illinois, also kept the post office busy with letters to her seven sons and two daughters who were all serving their country.[11]

Even young teenagers got involved in war work. Jane Hootman (Drake) helped harvest vegetables from the Michigan State College Victory Gardens—and got paid for it. There was patriotism and extra spending money involved in helping at Michigan State College's canning "factory." Actually, the "factory" was a shed set up on the south side of the Red Cedar River to process food from the College's Victory Gardens for use in the college dormitories. Jane liked the remuneration, albeit minimal, derived from sitting on a stool making sure there were no malformed or imperfect beans as she watched the beans flow by on a conveyor belt.[12]

Sue Coleman (Johnson) told of a friend of her father's who set up three mini assembly lines as part of his small defense plant in Lansing. There she and several of her friends during the summer of her junior year put together tiny packages containing three or four cigarettes, gum, two or three matches, water purification pills and a couple of other basic necessities that were sealed in khaki colored packages and tucked in between C rations for the servicemen. Years later, she met a veteran who remembered and appreciated those tiny parcels. "They were great!," he insisted.[13]

Everyone who could sew, knit, or crochet was implored to do her bit for the war effort. Rarely was a serviceman allotted a uniform that fit perfectly. There seemed to be only two sizes—too large or too small. Jane Drake remembered her mother sewing for the disgruntled ROTC and ASTP soldiers who came to the People's Church, across the avenue from the Michigan State College campus, beseeching the female members of the congregation to please tailor their uniforms to fit. Grade schoolers were urged to "Write to a Fighter." In many schools the young "scholars" knit blocks for afghans to be sent overseas.

While working as a secretary at the Bradford Hotel in Boston, Agnes Parsons (Pulling) responded to the call from a housekeeper in the hotel who was asked by the Red Cross to recruit women who would be willing to knit scarves, sweaters, mittens, or gloves for servicemen. Agnes volunteered and was given a pattern for a "helmet" of sorts with holes for eyes, nose, and mouth. Sometime later, when they had finished their work, it was suggested that each girl, as a personal touch for the recipient, attach a label to her handiwork that listed her name, address, and telephone number. Thinking little of it, Agnes went along with the others and attached her name and address to the "helmet."

About a year later, Agnes was surprised to open a letter from the recipient of her "helmet" (a young GI named Malon stationed at Fort Ruckman, just outside of Boston) thanking her, enclosing a small picture of himself, and suggesting that they should meet one day. The handsome picture and the idea of a meeting were not too displeasing, and on Malon's next leave Agnes drove to Boston, met Malon, and took him back to her home to have Malon meet her family.

Following their original meeting there were there innumerable movie and dinner dates, and the reader can quickly surmise "the rest of the story." At the time, however, money was scarce and there were serious talks about whether they really should get married then or wait until after the war. "We'll do ok," they decided, and 63 years of happily married life proved them right.[14]

"THE ENEMY"

For some Americans, the "enemy" had special ramifications. Civilians, and there were many, with strong ties to relatives living in Germany suffered immense concerns about the welfare of their families and friends. Lillian Lockwood had a special reason to be worried about the war—her grandparents and several aunts and uncles still lived in Germany. Following his capture during the European campaign, her mother's only brother was sent to a POW camp at Ft. Lawson, Oklahoma. "Mother and I took the train to see him, an unforgettable experience. The train was packed with soldiers, wives with children and nurses. In Chicago I remember seeing a train car filled with wounded soldiers and nurses attending them. That really made an impact about the war and affected me deeply. Upon seeing my uncle his first words to mother were 'Do you hate me?' I felt so sorry for him because we had heard from him before the war in Europe started that he wanted to leave Germany but his wife refused to come. He was drafted in 1942 and captured in 1943. He was sent to Russia after the war and died shortly after returning home. My grandfather was killed during an air raid and my grandmother and aunt had to move twice because of the bombing. Grandmother died in 1945. My father's sister strongly objected to Hitler and wrote many letters berating him. The letters stopped coming in 1942 and we later found out she had joined resistance fighters in or near France. We never heard from her again."

Lillian Lockwood continued: "The suffering of so many innocent people has stayed with me through the years. My grandparents wrote so many letters about how puzzled and unhappy they were about their situation. They were too old to try to move and wouldn't have been allowed to anyway. I have never forgotten the troop train with all the wounded men, row upon row of bandaged bodies."[15]

Signe Hegge (Bates), whose father served as director of the Wayne County Training School in Detroit, remembered the sad plight of two psychiatrists who came to join the staff. Both were Jewish and had escaped Hitler's purges with little more than the clothes on their backs. They and their wives and children occupied a single room in the teachers' quarters at the Institute. Despite their cramped quarters, they knew how fortunate they were and grieved for family and friends who were unable to escape and who they knew were suffering some terrible fate. The psychiatrists had made their escape first going to France, Switzerland, Spain, and then out of Portugal to the United States with a suitcase each, most of their belongings having been sold to pay the expenses of their escape and travels. Even in the safety of America, a feeling of discrimination prevailed among their children, who now and then would burst into tears in hurt feelings as they questioned their new acquaintances: "Don't you like me because I'm Jewish?"[16]

As a newly hired "government girl" working in the typing pool in Detroit's Union Guardian Building in August of 1942, Mary Saltzman (Baron) was asked by her supervisor if she would be willing to leave that afternoon to go to Washington, D.C. to work on a temporary assignment for the Office of the Chief of Ordnance? "Why Not?" Mary thought, and by 5 P.M., clad in a newly purchased business suit and carrying a brand new suitcase, Mary was on the train to Washington with 12 other volunteers.

In Washington, Mary quickly learned some important lessons about discrimination as 4 of the girls, including Mary, were advised to keep the fact that they were Jewish undercover. "Anti-semitism, according to the chaperone, was alive and well in Washington. But then so was racial segregation as they soon noted."

Life in Washington, D.C. had its plusses, for during their lunch hours Mary and a couple of her friends could walk to the Smithsonian cafeteria, take in a brief tour of it or the Mellon Art Museum, and still make it back to work within their hour's break. It was a bit of a letdown to return to the routine of Detroit metropolitan living.[17]

THE TERRIBLE TELEGRAM

Anxiety, of course, was a constant companion on the home front. No family was fortunate enough not to have a member, a relative, or a friend in harm's way overseas. The appearance of a Western Union messenger, a telegram in hand; a strange officer in uniform at the door; an official military vehicle in the driveway—all could herald tragedy. Scenes similar to Mary Jane Schmierer's devastating experience were re-enacted throughout the country. Not all stories, however, shared Mary Jane's eventual denouement.

While her husband was serving with the U.S. Force in Italy, Mary Jane Schmierer and her two-year-old son were making their home with her parents in St. Paul, Minnesota, where she had grown up. That particular day, October 17, 1944, was a day pretty much like any other as Mary Jane smoothed on her lipstick and gave a final pat to her hair in readying to leave for another day of teaching St. Paul's young scholars. For a moment, the ringing of the doorbell so early in the morning caught her by surprise. Oh, probably a neighbor short of milk for cereal that morning, she reasoned. Instead, the door opened to the spine-chilling sight of a Western Union man with a telegram in hand. "I'm afraid I have bad news for you. May I come in for a minute?" Mary Jane beckoned him in, opened the envelope, took a deep breath, and read: "The Secretary of War desires me. . . ." Mary Jane's husband, Ray, had been killed on October fifth in the fierce fighting in northern Italy.

Mary Jane and her parents were well aware that Ray was involved in heavy fighting when he had written earlier asking them to "pray for me." In his last letter home, a V-mail, Ray wrote lovingly to his two-year-old son: "How is my little boy getting along these days? Maybe I should call you my big boy. Mommy says you are growing up so fast, so tall and strong . . . I hope too that I can come home soon. There are lots of things that I have planned for us to do, you and Mommy and I . . . Be a good boy for me and help keep Mommy happy all of the time. Give grandpa and grandma a big hug for me, 'cause I like them lots too. Love and a big Kiss, Your Daddy." "I will read you lots of stories when I come home," he had promised.

Unfortunately, the shock and devastation of that moment was a scene that mirrored tens of thousands of homes across the country. A blue star in the window signifying a family member in the service of his country could overnight became a gold star, indicating the loss of a family member. For Mary Jane and the multitudes of other wives and mothers suffering the tragic loss of a loved one, the weeks and months dragged on in seemingly endless gloom and despair.

For Mary Jane, however, there was consolation in her friendship with Don Gregg, who had been an ardent suitor during her high school and college days. The two had kept in touch over the years, and in a miraculous coincidence, the very day the fateful telegram arrived there was a bottle of perfume in the mail for Mary Jane that Don had purchased in Paris—"one for his mother, one for two aunts and one for her." "Did that just happen or was it a gift from the Lord?" Mary Jane wondered. A year later, following Don's return after V-E Day from his wartime service with the Air Force, their earlier relationship blossomed into a serious romance and a wedding in 1947. Two sons were born of the marriage, and although Don raised young Johnny as his own, he never let the boy forget his father, Ray. Years later, at Don's suggestion, the family visited Ray's grave in Italy, where he had been laid to rest among the people for whom he had given his life. The maple leaves they picked that day were later pressed into gold frames to augment the pictures that were etched into eternity in Mary Jane and Johnny's hearts.[18]

At the Air Force Base at Big Spring, Texas, later known as Webb Air Force Base, First Lt. Don Swope, who was busily engaged in training pilots and bombardiers for overseas service, became involved in the most devastating experience of his life. For 24 hours a day some 180 planes roared through the skies as their pilots continued to hone their skills in bombing targets marked on the fields below. Sometimes there were live bombs, other times there were practice bombs. Sometimes there was a payload of 30 live bombs to be dropped. The Air Force needed experienced men, and the practice continued day and night. One night, during the darkness that seemed not too different from any other night, there was a terrific explosion that rocked the base—two planes with live bombs had collided in midair. There were no remains, both pilots, co-pilots, and their planes were dust. Surely every wife with a husband out that night shuddered at the sound. It was Don Swope's heartrending assignment to knock at the door of a lovely young bride of one week, to tell her that her husband had been one of the men killed that night. General Sherman was indeed right—"War is hell."[19]

In Baltimore, Maryland, tragedy struck home for Sonia Dudek who was living with her mother while her husband, Ed, and her three brothers were serving with the military. Sonia had just come from the hospital with their newborn daughter, Constantina, when she answered the door to a solemn-looking soldier who handed Sonia her husband's dog tags, wallet, and a Purple Heart medal. "I hate to bring this news to you but your husband has been killed in action." The news was devastating and immediately sent Sonia into a coma. How long was she traumatized? She only remembers that when she recovered she had downsized from a 24 and a half dress size to a size 8.

Several months later, Sonia was stunned when a postcard arrived from Ed saying that he was alive, but slightly wounded. The postcard must have been written sometime before his death; the dog tags and wallet were certain testimony to his demise. It would be insanity to think that he could still be alive. Yet, the next day a second soldier came to apologize for having given out misinformation. Sonia's husband was indeed alive and would be home soon! In time a third soldier, a medical doctor, appeared to reassure her that Ed was alive and would be coming home. Reality finally settled in, and miracles turned life around for Sonia.

Several months earlier on the battlefield during the Battle of the Bulge many of Ed's buddies had been killed, and when the gunshot wound to Ed's upper thigh left him prostrate on the ground, the Germans had thought he was dead and passed him by. A short time later, two fellow GIs dragged Ed to safety in the nearest field hospital. His wound had been so severe that he had little memory of his being sent from field hospital to field hospital, unable to identify himself. His dog tags and wallet lost on the battlefield gave rise to the conviction that he was dead.

Months later, Sonia was seated in church listening intently to the pastor's sermon when suddenly she turned her head and there in the back of the church beamed that dear face. Her most fervent prayers had been answered, and the whole church suddenly erupted in exuberant celebration.[20]

CHAPTER 15

The Atom Bomb and V-J Day

By August of 1945, a few optimists thought the end of the war with Japan was perceptibly imminent. For the less sanguine, however, news of the atomic bombs and the surrender came out of the blue. Tens of thousands of troops were already poised, ready for the invasion of Japan, an assault that everyone knew would be extremely costly for both sides. Estimates ran to at least 800,000 to 1 million Americans who would die in the operation. And that would say nothing of the millions of Japanese, both servicemen and civilians, who would lose their lives defending their country. The dropping of the atomic bomb was to forever after transform the dimensions of war and peace throughout the world. The war was over at last, and many of those on the home front who were not cheering, and shouting, and dancing, and kissing, and hugging found themselves weeping with uncontrolled tears knowing that the sacrifice, the separation, and the suspense was at an end.

Early in the summer of 1945, Pilot Romayne Hicks and his B-29 crew waited for orders (most likely to the South Pacific) at their base in Lincoln, Nebraska. Somehow there was an ominous tone to the officers' repeated questioning them about whether they had any qualms about being involved in a bombing mission that might be disastrous to large numbers of civilians but would save thousands of American lives. Romayne and his crew had read stories about the Japanese atrocities, and any reservations they might once have had were long gone. Clearly, Romayne and his men were in line for the bombing of Japan preparatory to the expected invasion—or perhaps they were even being tested for a future atomic bomb delivery. A few weeks later, the dropping of atomic bombs on Hiroshima and Nagasaki ended the war, and Romayne's crew was disbanded.[1]

During the late summer of 1945, Howard "Gov" Miller, navigator with the 505th B-29 groups who were flying missions from Tinian over Japan, became curious about a special group of men who were segregated from the other groups. Their headquarters were tightly secured; they had their own mess hall, separate barracks, special training, and different plane armament. Miller told of his flight engineer who loved to drink beer and in the course of his "downing a few" found some of the guys he trained with were in this new, secret group. One night, the flight engineer returned with the report, "Those guys in that new group said they have a bomb that will end the war—what a crock." Rumors abounded, and Miller's crew tossed off the announcement as "latrine humor." Little did they know this was the atomic bomb the secret group was talking about! The men of the 509th were being groomed for the dropping of the "A bomb." (Had their commander known of this breach of security one suspects they might have been court-martialed or certainly demoted for passing on such vital information.) Much earlier, when Greg Deliyanne had been stationed in Texas, he had heard rumblings from some liquored-up airmen about a new sophisticated plane that could drop an incredibly huge bomb.

Gov acknowledges the atom bomb's effect on ending the war. However, he and many of his comrades believed that "those thousands of bombs we dropped over the last six months already had those Japs on their knees— long before those guys got here!" On March 9–10, 1945, Superfortress bombers dropped some 1,665 tons of incendiary bombs on Tokyo that killed some 84,000 to 120,000 people, injured from 40,000 to 125,000, and destroyed 267,000 buildings and homes. The M69 incendiary bombs (specially developed to blast through the roof of wooden Japanese houses and explode exuding a burning gel that inflamed the surrounding area) were indiscriminately leveled on Japanese nonmilitary bases. Some 40 square kilometers were destroyed by the fires. The March 9–10 incendiary raids on Tokyo accounted for at least 84,000 deaths—Hiroshima deaths were some 70,000, Nagasaki deaths about 20,000. In other words the incendiary raids cost almost as many (or perhaps more) Japanese lives as the two atom bombs.[2]

During his watch aboard the USS *Buckingham,* en route from Eniwetok to San Francisco, Claude Fike (APC5) was handed a news bulletin that announced that "a new and powerful bomb had been dropped on Hiroshima, Japan, that had the explosive power of 20,000 tons of T.N.T. I was familiar with the 'blockbusters' and assumed that this was another bigger and better one of those. I also realized that the radioman had put down too many zeros, so sent him back to get the right number, thinking that the explosive power of 2,000 tons would be some big bomb indeed. When he returned shortly thereafter and stated he had checked three times and the number was right, my expression was, 'My God.' I was left to speculate as the word 'atomic' was omitted from the newscast. Only later did I realize the monumental impact of that night that launched us into the atomic age."

With no radios and scanty information on bulletin boards, many servicemen read only that the United States had dropped two bombs on Japan. Days later, as did Claude Fike, they learned that this was the dropping of the atomic bombs and now at long last the war was over.[3]

One evening, while stationed on Leyte preparing for the invasion of Japan, Captain Bob Wilcox and several officers from his artillery battalion were invited to an evening party at the 8th Army Officers' club. It was a relaxing evening enhanced by the company of a group of Army nurses and Red Cross workers stationed nearby. Suddenly the music came to an abrupt halt as the Officer of the Day solemnly crossed the dance floor and approached the bandstand with a large piece of paper in hand. The suspense was awesome. Something big was clearly about to happen. The announcement electrified the club. The Japanese had surrendered! This was official. Anyone who had a pistol shot it off; machine gun fire resounded throughout the night; blasts from ships in port rent the night air. The scene was a wild combination of bedlam, chaos, and mayhem. To be sure there were some headaches and hangovers the next morning as life assumed a more normal routine. Unfortunately, there were still pockets of Japanese resistance yet to be subdued.[4]

As for the dropping of the atom bomb, Dave Ruff and his comrades breathed a big sigh of relief for they, as were tens of thousands of troops, were being readied for the invasion of Japan. They had already observed first hand the Japanese disregard for life and knew the Allies faced a monumental task ahead. Without a doubt the Japanese would fight down to the last man standing.[5] Aerial photographs they had taken of a massive array of Japanese planes parked behind almost unassailable bunkers at various Japanese airfields quickly convinced Louis D'Valentine, his crew, and his comrades on the base that the Japanese expected an invasion and were ready for it. First hand knowledge of the build-up of arms and planes with which the Japanese intended to ward off any Allied invasion of their homeland had also persuaded Miller Perry that the carnage of an invasion of Japan would be far, far worse than the Normandy invasion.[6]

On a troop train en route to the port of embarkation and scheduled to be in the first wave of troops to invade Japan, Dave Anderson and his unit first heard the news of the dropping of the atomic bombs. Not surprisingly, they were overjoyed, for the projection of 1 million casualties in Japan had ominous prospects for everyone on the train. Bob Drake and millions of others realized that the atomic bomb had to be used to end the war. There was universal agreement that many of their friends and perhaps they themselves would not be around today, had the bomb not been dropped.[7]

V-J Day refocused doubts for Gus Ganakas about "Will I ever get back home?" to joyous certainty that "I AM going to get back home."[8]

Following the 14-week boot camp training that Marine Gene Cornelius and his unit took in 9 weeks (shortened because of the desperate need for replacements in the South Pacific), the men spent unending days and nights in preparation at Camp Pendleton, California for the invasion of Japan. There were more than 50 movies detailing Japanese fighting tech-niques, daily physical routines, extensive training with LST landing craft, repetitive target practices, and emergency medical procedures—until at last they were deemed ready for the assault. There was a quick trip to San Diego where they boarded their ship ready to leave when out of the blue—a miracle—the announcement of the dropping of the atomic bomb and the Japanese surrender! Cheers rang out, horns tooted, and liquor mysteriously appeared from below deck lockers. Gene and his comrades were numbed by the news. It had been a very narrow escape from what would certainly have been the bloodbath of the century.[9]

There were those, among them Mary Moir (Groves), who felt then and now that we were wrong in dropping the atomic bomb, that it was cruel and inhumane punishment vented on civilians. Despite having two brothers in the service, Mary thought church officials should have been consulted and that once we had invaded Japan their people would have agreed to a negotiated peace.[10]

Henry LaBrosse thought the dropping of the bombs a wise decision. "We wanted an end to the war; furthermore it took two bombs to convince them."[11]

"Thank God for President Truman's decision to use the atomic bomb." Bill Ewing's words echoed the feelings of most Americans. The 1 million projected deaths of the allies "would not have been a drop in the bucket compared to the Japanese losses," Bill pointed out.[12] Roy Herbert, as no doubt most servicemen, wished the atomic bomb had been created and dropped sooner.[13]

Asked about his feelings concerning the dropping of the atomic bomb, Wayne Adgate's answer was succinct and to the point: "I felt like Harry."[14]

THE CELEBRATIONS

It was the last mission of the war, one forever engraved in the mind of Louis D'Valentine, a gunner on a B-29 bomber, who was on his 31st mission over Japan, completing his tour of duty. Right on schedule the crew had dropped their bombs over their Osaka target and were headed back to their base on the island of Saipan when they received the radio message "Chicago," the signal to abort the mission and return to base.

Suddenly, radio silence was broken with the incredible news that the Japanese had surrendered. The war was over! No more terrifying kamikaze attacks, no more flack, no more landing with a fuel gauge reading empty, no more counting 136 holes in the plane following a dangerous mission.

To say the crew was ecstatic was putting it mildly. It was almost unbelievable! They were safe, and all the days and nights of gut-wrenching fear and dread were behind them! For the rest of the trip back to base, radio silence exploded into a cacophony of voices from radio stations all over the world, exulting in the news.[15]

Victory over Japan brought with it celebrations, wild parties, and drunken euphoria. Lee Conley had a hard time forgiving some fellow Marines who embarked on a shooting spree and "accidentally" killed 10 Philippine civilians. In another instance, Bill Pace reflected sadly, that in their exuberation "the American soldiers shot off anti-aircraft guns and inadvertently killed some twenty men." (A few months earlier the celebration of V-E Day in Jim Pyle's outfit was similarly marked with tragedy, as men who had survived the horrors of battle grew careless with guns and alcohol and died celebrating the Allied-Victory in Europe.) In a less violent celebration, Bill Pace told of being stationed on Okinawa on V-J Day, "and that night a big sailor ran up and kissed me right in the face and said 'the war is over!'"[16]

People went ballistic with the news of the Japanese surrender. Downey Milliken Gray, Jr. was waiting out a new assignment (probably involving the invasion of Japan) in Long Beach, California, and in joyous celebration he and his navy comrades took the opportunity to party nonstop until dawn the next day. About 11 A.M. there was a knock at his cabin door reminding him of his approaching appointment for a physical exam. It was a supreme effort to struggle out of bed and make it to the medical office where the doctor, clearly hungover himself, took one look at the bleary-eyed Downey and queried, "How do you feel?" "Probably like you do," came Downey's reply. Without further examination the doctor smiled sheepishly, "That's ok, you pass," and stamped Downey's papers.[17]

Just before leaving for overseas, Dave Anderson and a date visited one of New York City's ubiquitous tea rooms where the fortune teller had good news for Dave's date, but she had bad news for Dave. In an ominous voice, she solemnly predicted that he would be dead before he was 21. On V-J Day, Dave rejoiced in proving the fortune teller wrong.[18]

Amid the wild celebrations there were tears for those remembering lost sons, or fathers, or brothers, or sisters. Dorothy Schieve had returned from her service in Europe and was with her mother at home; both were weeping remembering the son and brother lost over Alsace Lorraine.[19]

News of victory announced over the loudspeaker aboard Fritz Bennetts' transport ship in the South Pacific touched off some 30 minutes of delirious "hollering, yelling, and cheering" as each seaman vented relief and gratitude that he had made it through the war alive. The fact that each man would very likely need to serve additional time in the cleanup operations and in occupational duties failed to quell the celebrating. The war was over; the terrible fighting was at an end.

Several days after V-J Day, a sister ship that had been through some of the most savage fighting of the war pulled up alongside Fritz Bennetts' ship and enjoined the men to stop at a small island nearby and hold a party in celebration of the war's end. It took little persuasion to get the men to comb their lockers for libation, and the party soon became an orgy, a wild outpouring of pent-up emotions that revelers could release without landing in the brig. How long did the celebration last? Apparently until the last unaccounted for sailor could be cornered and dragged back to his ship.[20]

For Dave Ruff and his fellow Marines there was quiet reflection and relief. Dave remembered hearing a few guns being shot off, but most of his buddies just sat quietly reflecting on their survival and the carnage they had witnessed.[21]

Amid the joyous celebrations on the home front, one man remembered being in the stands and catching a ball in Comiskey Park on V-J Day. Unfortunately, his precious souvenir of the game on V-J Day was quickly confiscated by the officials who insisted that it must be held among the Park's important World War II memorabilia.[22]

Barbara Brown will never forget the lights being turned on in Washington, D.C. after the war. There was a tug at the heartstrings as the lights on the capital dome suddenly illuminated the night, and hearts everywhere rejoiced in the hope that the darkness that for so long had shrouded the world might now be lifted forever.[23]

With the news of the surrender, the staff in Elizabeth McIntee's Office of Transportation in London at first quietly expressed sheer relief, but within minutes London exploded in wild revelry. Everyone hit the streets, conga lines wound through Hyde Park, and traffic jams clogged the thoroughfares. Elizabeth's group ended up in front of Buckingham Palace in time to see the Royal family step out on their balcony to wave to the throngs of joyful celebrants.[24]

For some, the enmity would continue. Back in the States, on V-J Day, Mel Buschman, recuperating from his wound and completing his physical therapy at a hospital in the United States, joined the throngs in Annapolis jubilantly celebrating the end of the war. Innocently, he and his friends parked near a Chinese restaurant and soon became privy to a gang of wild teenagers who were savagely beating up anyone who looked even slightly oriental. When they took on the owner of the restaurant, Mel, even though on crutches, and his friends, fought off the young thugs. A few savage swipes with his crutches forced the thugs to back off and saved the Chinese owner and his restaurant from further deviltry.[25]

The battles were not over for many thousands of men, such as Andrew Leech, who wrote, "When V-J Day arrived it found me in the 98th general hospital fighting a battle all my own." For two months after the end of the war Andrew Leech struggled to regain his health. The physical and mental strain of having served for two years in six Theaters of Operation, his diet of cold C rations, his exposure to the extremes of intense heat and frigid temperatures had left him "rundown and in a pretty bad condition. So I am fighting my own battle and by the help of that same Creator that brought me through the war I hope to regain my health once more."[26]

The submarine USS *Tigrone*, skippered by Lt. Comdr. Vince Schumaker, had been routinely patrolling the South Pacific when word of the Japanese surrender came over the loudspeaker. (Actually, the crew claimed to have fired the last shot on Japan by having bombarded Mikomoto Island shortly before the surrender.) Although home was foremost in the crew's thoughts, the *Tigrone* was dispatched to Tokyo Bay for the formal signing of the Japanese surrender papers.[27]

The air was heady with anticipation and excitement on September 2, 1945, in Tokyo Bay as some 242 Allied ships anchored around the USS *Missouri* for the momentous occasion. At first, Skipper Vince Schumacher was extremely dismayed to find his submarine, the *Tigrone*, was moored alongside the submarine tender the USS *Proteus* in a way that would completely obstruct his view of what would surely be an awesome sight. It took only moments, however, for Vince to realize that he could use his elevated periscope with its 65-foot reach to great advantage. By focusing his periscope over the top of the *Proteus*, Vince and his crew members had a perfect view of the *Missouri*'s quarter-deck with its full assembly of VIPs. As the ceremony continued, a thoughtful Vince beckoned each crew member up to the periscope to have a look. Surprisingly, there were a few who casually "ho hummed" the offer until Vince made it an order. "Gentlemen, this is an historic event, something you will want to tell your grandchildren about." And indeed it was!

In the skies above the battleship *Missouri* were some 30 to 40 B-29 planes, one of them carrying navigator Howard "Gov" Miller, who noted: "We were "flying a symbolic show of force to impress the men of Nippon that they had been defeated after nearly four years of a long and bitter war. We flew at 3,000 feet and could readily observe the havoc we had wrought on the Japanese capital after dozens of repeated raids by thousands of Superfortress bombers. There was utter devastation."[28]

The final surrender of the Japanese on September 2nd was made even more memorable for Bill Emerson and the crew of the USS *Buchanan* when they were assigned to escort General MacArthur and members of his staff to the scene of the signing on the battleship *Missouri*. The fact that they were then anchored close to the *Missouri* provided them with an eyewitness view of the surrender ceremonies. Following the completion of the historic signing, they returned General MacArthur and his party to dockside. (A day earlier Bill and the *Buchanan* crew had had two other important Generals aboard ship when they had taken General Nimitz and General Halsey to the Yokohama dock for a meeting with General MacArthur and later back to their respective flagships.)

Four days later after arriving in Honshu, Japan, the *Buchanan's* passengers were a far cry from the prestigious generals at the *Missouri* signing. Instead they took on 197 emaciated, half-dead prisoners of war from Gosselin and took them to ships waiting in Tokyo Bay.[29]

As the first troops to land in Yokohama after the war, Harry Hedges (Technician 5) and his unit were awestruck at the devastation that had been wrought by the American bombers. In Yokohama and the surrounding areas, they observed the people struggling amidst the burned-out ruins to create tin and tarpaper shacks from the debris that had once been their homes. Surprisingly, the Japanese people they encountered evidenced no hostility toward the Americans, but seemed submissively resigned to their fate.[30]

A JOURNEY BACK IN TIME

Forty years later, in August of 1985, Paul Nielsen reflected on his memories of that eventful day in the August 1985 issue of *Today's Seniors*— observations that bear repeating:

Every year on the 6th of August it all comes back. It was August 6th, 1945, and we were at Iloilo, Panay, Philippine Islands. There was an announcement about a bomb—some kind of special thing, but no one paid attention. We had heard about a lot of bombs in the last three years or so. Another bomb—ho-hum. The war goes on.

I had been in the Western Pacific approximately 24 months, and the word in those days was "duration plus six months." Whenever time was discussed the word was "duration." At this point "duration" seemed a long way off.

For a month we had been training the First Cavalry Division in amphibious landings. This duty was a "reward" for our time spent from April 1 to June 21 during the invasion and the Battle of Okinawa.

The duty was preferable to Okinawa, but the loading, carrying, and unloading of Army tankers and their crews every day six days a week was growing boring to the extent that combat might even be preferable—maybe.

The routine went on and on. Take on tanks in the evening, show a movie almost every night while we lay at anchor in the bay. At 4:30 A.M. all hands on deck and prepare for landing tanks at dawn. After landing the tanks and securing from General Quarters get underway and return to Iloilo and take on new tanks and new tank crews.

We had our ups and downs. There were some sorry moments at Okinawa—it was a sobering thing to see the Kamakazis hit nearby ships, and, even worse was the carnage we saw each dawn as the Destroyers and Destroyer Escorts limped by with guns and superstructure twisted like a bunch of paper clips due to suicide bombers which took the greatest toll in men and ships that the U.S. Navy had ever experienced. Those sailors, who served on what the Navy called picket duty—a ring of ships around the entire island—paid a dear price for the comparative safety of the island and the anchorages.

Of course, we had one other anti-climax in May. The war was over in Europe. Big deal. No one celebrated in the South Pacific. Most felt a little better . . . maybe the "duration" would come a little sooner. Maybe even home.

But we all knew what lay ahead—the invasion of Japan. Everyone assumed that the losses would be fantastic—the estimate for casualties in "Operation Olympic" was one million.

For me, I secretly rejoiced for my family in Denmark would at last breathe in freedom after five years of occupation by the Nazis. It was a big, big moment. But one learns not to rejoice when your shipmates are blase about what may be thrilling to oneself.

Now to top this off, the Admiral called for an inspection of our Flotilla. It was a bitter pill for a bunch of sailors who looked on themselves as "old salts" whose experience should qualify them not to be treated like raw recruits in boot camp.

The inspection was on regardless. Get out the swabs. Chip paint. Paint. Shine bright work. Break down the guns. Clean, oil, and assemble everything. "Make everything ship shape. The Admiral and his staff are coming (and they will all be wearing white gloves)." What a bore. And then the 9th day of August dawned. The inspection was to be this day—what a day to stand inspection in this tropical climate for a bunch of seasoned "salts."

And then it happened. All hell broke loose! Japan had offered to surrender provided the Emperor was allowed to keep his throne. The second atomic bomb—the same kind we assumed was just "another" bomb that had destroyed Hiroshima—had fallen on Nagasaki. As we learned later, the utter destruction of the bombs forced Japan to make a decision.

Needless to say, the inspection came off all right, but it was passe. No one took anything very seriously from the moment of the announcement of the surrender.

The inspection was the doldrums. The Admiral's staff went through the motions. They looked at everything, but the dirt on the white gloves, wherever found, meant little. Every mind had one thought—HOME. It was over.

We had been out there a long time. Personal liquor and drinks of all kinds on the ship were in short supply. No one had anything left for celebration after all this time. We were all in high spirits, and after dinner we relaxed in a way we hadn't relaxed in many, many months. Yes, it was over.

Anticlimax though it was, a miracle happened. From footlockers, lockers, and many secret storage compartments, Scotch, Bourbon, beer, and all kinds of other refreshments were put on the table. I had kept a bottle of Johnny Walker for this very moment, but I figured it would be at least 18 more months before it was consumed in rejoicing over the end of the war.

It was a minor miracle that I had kept it as long as I did.

It was a night to remember. No one went to bed. Only the Chaplain's Assistant was sober. Alcohol was in the air and the excitement of the moment overwhelmed me.

Sometime around 1 A.M. I left the party below decks and went topside. The night was beautifully cool, and I was all alone with the millions of stars shining brightly. As the cool air cleared my mind I tried to comprehend this gigantic moment for all mankind. As I looked up moisture filled my eyes, and from somewhere deep in my throat the word "Thanks" fell on my ears. The agony had ended.

Within a few days we were on our way to Tokyo. The peace was complete on August 14, 1945 when the Japanese accepted the terms. On September 2 the formal surrender took place on the *U.S.S. Missouri* in Tokyo Bay. We didn't get to see the signing, but we could see "Big Mo" out there in the stream—and that was plenty good enough. And we were walking around on the island of Honshu and no one was shooting at us. The killing had stopped, the price was high but now those of us who remained looked only to the future.

Those are my memories of August. On August 9th as I raise my American flag in my front yard, if my lips don't say "thanks" my heart will.[31]

CHAPTER 16

Home at Last

HE'S HOME!

With the return of her husband, Lois Ella Gill's whole world changed. Although everyone else in town seemed to routinely return to "business as usual," Lois secretly harbored thoughts of making a banner for the top of the car and then parading through town blowing the horn at full blast so people would realize the dawn of her bright new world. "My banner," she fantasized, "would read 'Look, he's home, he's home!'"[1]

There was a moment's hesitancy involved in one young man's long anticipated homecoming. As he stepped off the train into what he expected to be the open arms of his loving wife, he was a little unsure about whether the woman waiting on the platform bundled up in a voluminous silver fox coat was really the beautiful bride he had not seen for three and a half years. In turn, his bride was shocked to see a bronzed, emaciated young man emerging from the train who looked so amazingly different from the robust husband she had bid goodbye to so many months ago. In seconds, however, the 51 pounds she had taken on in his absence and the 45 pounds he had lost thanks to Atabrine and the heat during his service in the Pacific, were insignificant distractions amid their joyous reunion.[2]

After three years of service, Po Weatherford was mustered out at Camp Shelby, caught a bus to Meridian, Mississippi, and walked the mile from the bus stop to his home. His father was almost hidden as he worked in the midst of a giant patch of sorghum. "Hey, Dad!" Po yelled. "That you, son?" his father's voice trembled. His father's hug had been so smothering, Po remembered, he was afraid it would kill him. At the farmhouse, his mother took one look and became hysterical.[3]

Jim Pyle well remembered his homecoming. Jim was one of the few men interviewed who did not think he would be coming home. "I was sure I'd never make it out alive." During the fighting in Italy near Bologna, his outfit lost one-third of its men. It was a sickening experience to see 25 to 30 dead comrades stretched out on the ground around him. Foremost in his mind as the shells were "bouncing like popcorn" around him were images of his wife and infant daughter, five days old at the time of his last leave at home in Mississippi. A constant companion throughout the war was a tiny candle that had topped his daughter's first birthday cake. (A talisman that his daughter retains to this day!)

Now at last the devastating war was over, and Jim was on his way home. Days seemed to last for eternities—at last Mississippi, and finally Petal. As he pulled into the driveway, a tiny girl paused at play in the yard. His voice quivered as he swept her up in his arms. "Are you my little girl?" "Uhhuh," came the answer as she snuggled closer. "Are you my daddy?"[4]

After picking up stragglers (people who had been trapped by the war in China and various other Pacific spots), Frank Bourke, who had so often stood on the bow of his ship realizing that he was thousands of miles from his home and family and headed in the wrong direction, finally in mid-November 1945, breathed a sigh of relief as he saw the sun sink behind the ship. At long last he was headed east.

Offers to take a leave and stay in the Navy were turned down flat, and homeward bound trains couldn't eat up the miles fast enough for Frank Bourke. Slowly the train whistled to a stop in Escanaba, Michigan, and there eagerly pacing the station platform was the love of his life. It was a short ride home, and as he opened the door there at the top of the stairs stood his mother, his eight-year-old daughter, his five-year-old son, and the little one-year-old he had never seen who was clapping her hands and calling, "Goodie! Goodie! Goodie!" It was a dream come true, for many were the times he thought he'd never ever see them again.[5]

OH HAPPY DAY!

For aerial gunner Jim Clark, who had been shot down in May of 1944 and imprisoned in Poland and Germany, "The highest point was when I saw the American flag after being released from prisoner of war camp. That's the highest point. I don't believe I have every appreciated anything like I did the first time I said, 'Well I'm back at it.' They were flying the flag over camp Lucky Strike [an embarkation camp for servicemen about to be sent home] when I pulled in, and I cried like a baby. But, suddenly I was home, it felt like. It was just a big experience. . . . I'm thankful for all the experiences I have had. I have known fear, and even though I'm more of a coward at heart than anybody, I still wouldn't take a thing for the experience. God's blessed me in a lot of ways. The people I have known, the units I've flown with, and the things I've done through the years. There's just no way to explain it. If I wanted to buy it, I couldn't buy it."[6]

Upon her discharge and return home, Elizabeth McIntee hurried off the train in Tallahassee, hailed a cab, and dashed up the stairs to "home sweet home" only to find the door locked, as yet unopened to the morning light. As she knocked on the door inside she could hear steps approaching and the voices of her parents clamoring: "Let me go first. I saw her first." "Oh, no you didn't. I saw her get out of the cab." "Oh, please let me be first!" There was the click of the lock, then rib crushing hugs—and tears—lots of tears. How could there be a better homecoming? Tell me about it![7]

Ralph Moulton remembered that his ship, the USS *San Jacinto,* was "all dolled up" for its homecoming in San Francisco with "flags aloft from stem to stern. Our first sighting was the towers of the Golden Gate Bridge rising above the horizon. My skin crawls even after all these years just recollecting the sight."[8]

It was a glorious return to the States for Lamar Rodgers. On the ship coming back from England to New York, the 20 dollars paid the men in France was circulated and recirculated as the men spent much of the time during the long journey across the Atlantic gambling. As the trip was winding down, Lamar Rodgers was busily engaged shooting craps. "I had about seven hundred dollars laying there, shooting it, and I lost it all in one roll of the dice, when somebody said, 'There's the States, there's land.' I got up and left that and went running up top. I just said the heck with them. I didn't care anymore because I was home free."[9]

Following surgery on his leg after his tank hit a mine during the Battle of the Bulge, Ted Thomas returned on crutches to his unit, and after yet another accident and further injury to his leg, Ted was finally on his way home on a ship with a dining room that had white tablecloths and silver eating utensils. For the first few days of the 30-day trip home, Ted and a group of ambulatory patients were quartered across the passageway from the padded cells of men who were suffering severe psychiatric problems as a result of the war. As the deranged men clawed at the bars and shouted obscenities at them, Ted and his comrades, happy that they had survived mentally intact, begged to be quartered elsewhere on the ship. As it was, each man was struggling with his own emotional baggage, memories that would continue to last a lifetime. As the ship sailed into port in

Charleston, South Carolina, Ted admitted that he was never so happy in his life to hear the band strike up "Sentimental Journey." The war in Europe was over, and "I was still alive."[10]

After 37 months in the army, John Walker was "a very happy guy" to become a civilian once again. "In those three years I had seen a lot of the U.S., a lot of Europe, had experienced months of unforgettable events in combat in France and Germany, and shared the army life and discipline with many fine young American men, and returned from it all in one piece, something denied to so many of my friends. Now it was time to return to civilian life and my family and I eagerly boarded the train in New Brunswick, N.J. to do just that—return to my parents and sisters in Little Neck, Long Island, New York who had supported me so staunchly in all those months with letters, packages, snapshots, and prayers."[11]

"Greetings" from Uncle Sam; voluntary enlistment in order to have a choice of which branch of the services one wished to serve in; signing up because all of one's friends were enlisting; family pressures; sudden bursts of patriotism; guilt over not contributing enough to the war effort—those and hundreds of other reasons prompted young men, and older ones as well, to enlist in the armed services. William Horton had romance on his mind as he bought a new Ford car and proudly headed out to pick up his girlfriend for a night of dancing. The new car counted for nothing as Bill rang the doorbell and was icily informed by his ladylove that she was going to the dance that night with someone else—Phil to be exact. "Sorry buddy"—or was she even sorry? Understandably angry, Bill turned on his heels, headed back home, turned in the car the next day, and enlisted in the Navy. (Two years later, Bill's anger had subsided and when on a pass, he made a special effort to visit his former girlfriend, who by this time had tired of Phil. Cupid sent his arrow straight this time, and soon the two were making wedding plans that culminated in their marriage on January 31, 1944.)[12]

There was a less happy ending for the boyfriend of Genevieve Luckey. Over a period of months, Genevieve had been steadily and seriously corresponding with a young man she had been dating, until one day she was stunned by the return of her letter indicating that he had been killed in action. It took months for Genevieve to even partially recover from her devastation, but in time she met, fell in love with, and married a young Marine. In a shocking turn of events, apparently the KIA information had been in error. "He came back, just after we had gotten back from our honeymoon, and he called me and I had to explain to him that I had gotten married. It was hard."[13]

For three years, while Barbara Brauker's husband, Wayne, had been serving in the South Pacific, their dog, Queenie, had been a faithful watchdog, protecting her mistress and barking her lungs out at every strange person or sound around the Brauker's home. Queenie's barking could have scared off any potential thief within the radius of two miles, and when Wayne returned home, his heavy footsteps on the porch set off Queenie's personal alarm. However, in seconds Wayne had dropped his duffel bag, and the ferocious barking stopped as Wayne inquired, "Hey, Queenie, what's the matter?" Whereupon Wayne faced his second life threatening experience, that of being licked to death.[14]

There was still a wildness in some of the returnees after the war. Perhaps there was an ecstasy in the relief of survival that still made some veterans thrill seekers. Accustomed to living dangerously during the war, Don Bancroft's crew took a vote whether to fly under or over the Golden Gate Bridge. Fortunately, all but one voted "over."[15]

For one "adventurer," the return trip home aboard an aircraft carrier en route to San Francisco apparently was boring after all the tumult of war. The entire ship chilled to the shout of "Man Overboard" as the captain quickly ordered the ship to turn around. All hands were on deck, Paul Souder remembered, vigilantly searching the gigantic waves for a head, a hand, a cry for help. Following a lengthy search, miraculously the "victim" was spotted and quickly hauled aboard. Everyone, particularly the captain, was considerably annoyed when it turned out the guy had made a bet with his buddies that if he jumped overboard the ship would turn around. He won his bet alright, but it was also accompanied by a court-martial.[16]

Good-byes were often tearful episodes, and not a few returnees asked their girlfriend or wife to meet them at the same spot, wearing the same dress that she wore when they said goodbye. There was something of a penchant, perhaps an attempt to obliterate time, for couples to meet after the war at the precise spot of their last date or the exact doorway where they parted. Perhaps it was the front steps of the Kappa house at UCLA, the same hotel room where they honeymooned in '42, the waiting room in New York's Grand Central Station. Carolyn Hoagland's father arranged space on a train to enable her to meet her husband, John, at the same place in San Francisco and wearing the same dress as when they said goodbye a year and a half earlier. Ah, romance![17]

A TIME TO BOND

For some fathers, homecoming involved getting acquainted with a new addition to the family, born while the father was overseas. Fritz Bennetts had had a brief, precious meeting with his daughter the day she was born at the Brooklyn Naval Hospital in July of 1945. Early the next day his ship left to join the 7th fleet in the South Pacific, and it was a year before he would see young Stephanie again. Following his discharge in 1946, there was a long, tedious train ride to Ann Arbor and finally a glorious reunion with mother and daughter. By then the precious bundle had grown into a lovable one-year-old who seemed extremely perplexed at this big strange man getting into the car with them and smothering her and her mother with kisses. She had been living with her mother and grandparents while her father completed his time in service, and for the first few days would having nothing to do with her adoring father. Little by little Stephanie would inch one step closer to her father until finally one day he caught her up in his arms and a bonding for a lifetime began.[18]

Wartime mail was slow, very slow. About the middle of December, 1944, after almost two anxious months of waiting, Bud Maner finally received the telegram from his wife, sent eight weeks earlier, announcing the birth of their son, "Watsie." Phyllis, thousands of miles away, could almost have heard the cheering and jubilation that resonated around the headquarters at Biak, just north of New Guinea. Upon Bud's return home, the elation of seeing his firstborn soon took on a more serious tone, however, when wife, Phyllis, in the interest of bonding father and son, directed him toward the bedroom and instructed him to change baby Watsie's diaper. Thirty minutes later Phyllis came in to rescue the baby and finish the job. Typical of many infants, who had never seen their fathers before, there was a period of adjustment, almost traumatic at times. There was wide-eyed amazement from young Watsie for this strange man who seemed to have such an affinity for his mother—and for him.[19]

It was going to take some time, Ray Young discovered, to get acquainted with his three-year-old daughter who had been living with her mother and her uncle. Her uncle was "Daddy" to her, and she was a bit confused by a second Daddy appearing on the scene. Don Bancroft remembered that his young son, Rusty, born while he was overseas, would have nothing to do with him upon his return home. His wife had gone to live with her parents while he was overseas, and to Rusty his grandfather was his "papa." Joe Spinosa experienced the same problem of many returning fathers in bonding with a child he had not seen in four years. Naturally, the child did not know him, and as he had been staying with Joe's wife's parents, whenever things went the wrong way he immediately called for grandfather.[20]

One vet was able to keep in touch with his young daughter in frequent furloughs. However, he laughs now, recalling that when forced to give even the slightest reprimand to his beloved daughter, she would quickly turn and implore her mother "to put Daddy back on the train."[21]

SOME UNUSUAL HOMECOMINGS

Feeling deservedly proud of themselves after having successfully completed the dangerous job of mine sweeping the Inland Sea to the harbor at Kure, Japan that would facilitate the landing of the troops of occupation in Japan, Ensign Joe Foster and the crew of PCER 858 had been commended and returned to the States. At the entrance to the San Diego harbor two huge signs: "Welcome home" and "Well Done," had greeted them and augured well their long anticipated heroes' homecoming. Adding to their triumphal entry as they made ready to tie up at the quay at San Diego, a small band was playing on the dock. All in all they were feeling rather like conquering heroes.

The three Navy ships ahead of them had already docked, and now it was up to an unfortunately inexperienced officer who had never docked a ship in his life to tie in beside the others. A stiff breeze served to complicate the docking, and the novice officer, eager not to smash into the other ships, turned off the engines too abruptly, and suddenly the breeze was carrying them back out into the harbor. The embarrassed officer quickly restarted the engine and came in for a second try that was also aborted. (Each try involved about a 45 minutes turn-around.)

On the other ships, the men were convulsed with laughter, and by this time the band had given up, packed up their instruments, and departed. The third try made it, and as the crew stepped onto the mainland, instead of crowds of well-wishers, only two stalwart Red Cross ladies were there to greet them. The good news was that the women were distributing half-pint containers of ice-cold milk, a treat that had become almost a distant memory for the crew.

If the docking debacle had not been humiliating enough, there was more to come for Joe Foster. How to celebrate being on home territory once again? Why naturally the first thing to do would be to head for a drink at a bar. In short order a bar was located, but Joe being the last one through the door, was forcibly stopped by a diminutive woman bouncer who put her arms up with a one word command: "Wait!" One look at his Navy ID and there was a second order, "Out!" (Joe was not 21 yet.) Joe's pleas to be allowed to come in "for just a coca cola" met with a repeated order: "Out!" A veteran of months of service to his country, and yet Joe could not even enter a bar. As Joe shuffled around on the sidewalk outside, his buddies unaware of the problem stepped to the door to find out why he wasn't joining them. In a fit of pique, Joe and his friends quickly left the bar and headed for a hotel where the bartender was less precise about age limits. Some homecoming![22]

Donald Strand, of Seva, Minnesota, was less than impressed with his homecoming at Boston Harbor in June 1945. His shipmates (returning veterans from harrowing service in the North Africa and Italian campaigns and in the push through Germany) were speculating about the heroes' welcome of bands and cheering crowds that would be lining the docks. It turned out to be a great disappointment when only a handful of Salvation Army people met them "with orange juice and cookies. So, Don mused, contrary to what we have heard otherwise, not every returning bunch of men coming back from the War had a big welcome."[23]

Homecoming for Jim Perkins was not the carefree trip that he had envisioned. What should have been some of the happiest moments of Jim Perkins' life, his return to the States (for a furlough and supposedly for retraining in B-29s, pre-Hiroshima), turned out to be "the most memorable journey of his life." En route home, their plane, a "beaten-up hundred mission plane," ran into storms that threatened to devour the plane plus multiple engine problems that forced them into an almost disastrous landing that ended 20 yards away from the end of the runway. All in all the problems that had confronted Jim during his war missions seem minimal compared to the horrors involved in making it home safely.[24]

After completing his required missions over Germany, Lieutenant Al Jones was ecstatic about the opportunity to return home. Aboard his ship were 1,500 German prisoners of war who were being sent to American POW camps. Not surprisingly, some of Al's fellow officers were incensed when they were given tourist class accommodations while the German POW officers were given poshy First Class accommodations. Most of the prisoners, Al remarked, were contrite and well-behaved; however, a group of former SS Troops were boisterous and unruly in insisting that New York City had been completely leveled by German bombers. Hitler had told them so. As they docked in New York harbor, Americans smiled at the shock registered by the POWs to see the city thriving, its skyscrapers and congested streets intact.[25]

Paul Souder, as did many returning veterans, found it difficult to find the words to express his deep emotions about returning to San Francisco under the Golden Gate Bridge. However, he still recalled the feeling of exhilaration as the prisoners on Alcatraz floated a banner, "Welcome Home." Extremely proud of his four battle ribbons when he returned home, Paul suffered great humiliation when he realized that he had fewer ribbons than anyone else he met as he walked down the streets of San Francisco.[26]

The sight of the Golden Gate Bridge and the hillside sign "Welcome Home, Job Well Done" provided Willis Libolt and his fellow GIs with a deep emotional surge of elation and pride as their ship docked in San Francisco. As they got off the ferry at Camp Stoneman, Willis remembered an arch that they had passed through during their departure: "Through these portals pass the best damned soldiers in the world." Willis turned to check out the arch. It was still there, and "the best damned soldiers" were now return-ing. Willis breathed a sigh of relief: "My prayers had been answered. I was going to see my wife and family. I was thankful to the Lord for keeping me safe and unharmed."[27]

Irv Nichols' mother gave her returning son a barrage of hugs and kisses in the doorway, and then, fearing the potential of lice and bedbugs, issued orders, "Don't bring that stuff in the house." Accustomed by now to obeying orders, Irv dropped his duffel bag on the porch and entered the house unencumbered for a wonderful welcome home celebration.[28] In another homecoming, Wayne Adgate and his brother were absolutely shocked to see that their mother's dark hair had turned pure white in their absence.[29]

Bill Noonan's homecoming at Long Beach, California ran headlong into a serious problem. As Bill's ship pulled into the dock, the crew discov-ered that the longshore men were on strike, and the union men threatened not to allow them to unload. Some welcome for a shipload of men who had risked their lives for months to secure the safety of those at home! The crew members' anxieties were short-lived however, when several Marines aboard Noonan's ship changed the longshoremen's minds for them.[30]

Coming home through the Golden Gate Bridge was the thrill of a life-time for thousands of Pacific veterans, but not so for the crowd of ambula-tory casualties aboard Claude Fike's ship who had gathered on deck for "their first glimpse of home." Their "spit and polish" captain "ordered the decks cleared for a 'trim ship' entrance to San Francisco. Officers' protests were to no avail, and a growing resentment grew for yet another example of the captain's "petty tyranny." As they were approaching San Francisco, the glorious news of V-J Day reached Claude Fike and the men aboard the USS *Buckingham*. There was celebration aplenty aboard ship; how-ever "the celebration in San Francisco had been so wild and boisterous that the Navy canceled liberty for the ships' crews and the message was received with great disappointment aboard ship. However, normalcy had returned and the order was revoked by the time we arrived on August 17th."

   Claude Fike and his fellow officers aboard the *Buckingham* were furi-ous when their captain announced to the ship's officers that he would refuse to honor the government's point system, whereby the men with the longest period of service would be discharged first. Aware of the provi-sion that indispensable personnel could be "retained at the pleasure of their commanding officer," the ship's captain was unwilling to part with his experienced officers. The *Buckingham*'s officers were furious. Most of them had well over the required points and were eager to secure their discharges.

While the captain was on leave visiting his wife in San Diego, Claude surreptitiously went ashore. At the headquarters of the naval district in San Francisco, Claude presented an "academy award" plea to a secretary in the Admiral's office for detachment orders for Claude and eight of his fellow officers, all of whom had the necessary points. Insisting that he represented his commanding officer in applying for the detachment orders, Claude secured the necessary papers leading to the men's honorable discharge. His return to the ship met with near disbelief over his success story and a whirlwind of packing up and ship departure ensued before the return of the captain. Wonderment over how the captain would find replacements was lost in the drama of a return to home and the resumption of civilian life.[31]

The Tuskegee Airmen, the African American P-51 fighters, one of the most decorated fighting units in the war, earned "150 Flying Crosses, one Legion of Merit, one Silver Star, two Soldier's Medals, fourteen Bronze Stars, eight Purple Hearts, 744 Air Medals and three Presidential Unit Citations." John Kennedy, of Shelbyville, Illinois, was merely one of the myriad of B-24 pilots who sang the praises of the Airmen who had so often and so successfully protected them in their flights over Italy, France, and Germany. The Red-Tail Angels, identified by the custom painted red tails on their planes, were further distinguished for "never having lost a single bomber to enemy aircraft." "They were super fighters, super good guys," Kennedy professed.

At the end of the war, John and his unit were proud to have the Airmen fly home with them; however, as they were waiting at the railroad station in Atlanta for transportation to their homes in the North, an ugly scene of racial bigotry broke out. White citizens were incensed that African Americans were being accorded sleeping car accommodations and they were not. John and his men were aghast as pushing, shoving, and loud denigrating language took place on the part of the whites and finally erupted into a near riot. How sad that the white Americans did not comprehend the tremendous contributions and sacrifices the black Americans had made for their country.[32]

After the war, Bill Noonan was giving serious thought to perhaps remaining in the Coast Guard. A little incident changed all that. Having served in the South Pacific for most of the war, Bill had almost no winter clothing and not a complete uniform, winter or summer. In California, he had been given an official letter permitting him to return home out of uniform. All was well until he arrived in Detroit when a self-important Ensign challenged his letter, authoritatively asserting that Detroit was the 9th Naval District, and his letter of permission was not valid for that District. After a few days at the Detroit Separation Center, Bill was called up for a "Captain's Mast," and queried about his being out of uniform. With the reading of his letter, the Officer in Charge dismissed his case with a curt, "Ensign why don't you leave these guys alone?" Enough was enough, and no way was Bill going to re-enlist.[33]

It was a different scenario for Robert Flores. Following the bloody fighting on Okinawa, Robert Flores (see Chapter 1) and a number of his shipmates were assigned to an Army transport ship to return to the States. Away from the devastating fighting on the island, life was not too distasteful aboard the transport, and as it turned out, the battle-scarred seamen relished a golden opportunity to seek a modicum of revenge upon the enemy who had taken such a fearful toll on so many of their buddies in recent weeks. Some 100 cages of Japanese prisoners were secured above the hatches, and Robert and his fellow veterans of Okinawa were assigned to guard them on the long trip across the ocean. "Actually we were not too nice to them," Robert admitted. Now and then the irresistible urge to hose them down with saltwater was answered with a thorough dousing of the prisoners. Now and then the cook's specially prepared meals of rice and vegetables for the captives got dumped overboard, the GIs being convinced that "that food is too damn good for those S.O.B.s." Although the navy men were supposed to feed the prisoners, now and then the Japanese were forced to scramble for their food, which was tossed—or even thrown—at them.

A survivor's 30-day leave found Robert at home on V-J Day, and upon his return to Portland and a new ship, he was greeted with the news that he actually had enough points to return to civilian life if he desired. Decisions, decisions. Once the bloodshed was over, life in the Navy might not be too bad a deal. On the other hand. . . . "Well," he pondered, "Where is *this* ship going?" The reply was succinct: "China." It took just moments before, "Oh, well what the hell!" Robert decided. "I've never seen China." And for the next two years most of his duty consisted of the not too unhappy assignment of hauling Marines out of China and bringing them back to the United States. Robert had found his niche for the next 27 years with the Navy.[34]

Following their discharges, some men were flown home, others took trains or buses. Albert Fine took the subway to his home in Brooklyn. En route, a complete stranger saw he was a veteran, grabbed him, and hauled him into the nearest bar for a celebratory drink. One drink, a thank you, and Albert was headed home for good.[35]

CHAPTER 17

The Aftermath of War

War changes the lives of everyone—there could scarcely be a greater truism. Naturally, it decidedly marks the lives of the participants. For them especially, life would never be the same again. For many, their physical and mental scars would remain with them for as long as life itself.

For some veterans it took as much or more courage to face the "tomorrows" after the war than it did to face the enemy on the front lines. Thousands were plagued with the "guilt of survival," remembrance of things past or post-traumatic stress syndrome. For some the battle continues as they live their lives in whiskey bottles, or in veterans' hospitals, or on the streets among the homeless.

Claude Fike expressed it well when he began his memoirs: "The old adage that memory is fleeting ignores one universal exception among men, namely, those wartime experiences that forever brand their events on everyone who has lived through them. The more horrible the events of war are then the more indelibly the imprint is, despite all efforts to erase them. This explains why veterans, after years of trying to blot out these searing memories, can still recite them in detailed word and print forty or fifty years after the fact. And so it is with me as I summon up these remembrances of things past."[1]

Although thousands of GIs were, and still are, reluctant to talk about their war experiences, for others their war years were some of the most significant years of their lives. No subject is more interesting to many GIs than recalling and sharing their experiences with fellow veterans. "Participating in a war," Hall Tennis noted, "gives many people a reason for being, short-lived as it often is. The shock of confronting your own imminent mortality establishes an immediate bond between people."[2]

Did their experiences change them essentially? To a man, every male interviewee agreed that he grew up in a hurry during his time in service. It was a time of "growing up and learning how to get scared," Johnie Courtney admitted. Paul Van Oordt quickly found that war was no Boy Scouts and flashlights. Van felt it changed him from a naive young man who learned early on what it was like to lose best friends. He saw his best friend shot down in July of 1943, and for months afterward, Van would wake up sweating, sitting on the side of the bed, and screaming. Eventually, and thankfully, the nightmares subsided. Sixty years later, however, the sudden sound of a truck backfiring still gives Dudley Rishell goose bumps.[3]

Thankful to be a survivor, William Summers believed his experiences as an Ensign with the Navy in the South Pacific were the greatest experiences of his life. "Nothing else can begin to compare with those events," he and his comrades agreed at a recent reunion. Larry Von Tersch considered his war experiences an all expense paid tour of the Pacific that provided an important education and a new perspective of world affairs.[4]

CHANGES IN PERSPECTIVE

For millions of servicemen their experience in the military opened up new worlds for them and awakened an appreciation of the blessings of freedom and the opportunities America has to offer. Walt Woodhouse, during his service in India, was appalled at seeing dead bodies littering the streets until someone could claim them or their bodies could be removed and placed on the burning barges. Street children with sore eyes bespeckled with flies, begging for a handout of food or spare change; the filthy Ganges with its launderers and bathers; the ubiquitous poverty and squalid living conditions of the people were everyday scenes that chilled Walt Woodhouse and his fellow GIs to the bone.[5]

"You'll smell Calcutta before you see it," Ted Bauer remembered sailors on another ship previewing his landing in India. The stench from dead animals, the dead bodies floating in the Ganges, the lack of a sewage system, and the hordes of beggars gave Ted a new appreciation of life in the United States.[6]

As they reflected on their war experiences, veterans sought to define the profound impact the war had on their lives. Following his company's liberation of Hitler's concentration camps, Walter Adams' hatred of ideological bigotry and racial intolerance soared to new heights. "After seeing—first hand—the ultimate in man's inhumanity to man, I vowed that for the rest of my life I would stand up and speak up against injustice. Looking back, I hope I have been true to that pledge."[7]

Asked if his wartime experiences had changed him in any way, Paul Niland admitted: "I think it broadened my experiences a great deal. One example of that," he continued, "was when I got to Fort Sheridan [for basic training]. We were thrown in with all kinds of different people. The fellow on one side of me was illiterate, and the guy in the next bunk was receiving treatment for syphilis. I just couldn't imagine this," Paul confessed.[8]

Irv Nichols found his limited childhood experiences in a small Atlantic Coast town had ill-prepared him for the diversities of Navy life. His military service had considerably expanded his limited worldview. Rocky Mount, North Carolina, at that time was a small town on the Atlantic Coast where textile mills, the railroad, and a brisk tobacco business constituted most of the town's commerce. In the service, Irv was exposed to a completely different element as compared with his hometown friends. He became a hero to his illiterate comrades in the service for whom he helped to conduct an extensive correspondence, reading letters from girlfriends and composing romantic missives in return.[9]

Was Lee Conley changed by the war? Yes, indeed! From being a naive acceptor of America's bounty, Lee had become an observer of life at its worst, and his experiences led him to a far greater understanding of the vital importance of freedom and democracy. It changed his whole outlook on the world. After the war he took advantage of the GI Bill, earned his teaching certificate, and for 41 years devoted himself to teaching in the public schools. His free time has since been spent doing extensive volunteer work for the Red Cross.[10]

Mel Buschman firmly agrees that his war experiences changed his perspective on the world. The war had added dimension and insight to his otherwise limited point of view. Following the war and his post-graduate education, Mel taught in 33 different countries for Michigan State University. In one year he taught in four different countries.[11]

Had his army service in any way conditioned him for a career in medicine? Paul Niland, later to become a prominent radiologist, thought for a moment and then responded, "Well, I think the experience of having seen death and people dying made it easier to accept that as far as medical school was concerned. There was a pause and then: "Of course, one of the first classes you have in medical school is anatomy and you have to dissect a cadaver." After the first anatomy class, one of Paul's classmates failed to show up the next day. The second day and the third day he was still noticeably absent. Shortly thereafter it became clear that the cadaver experience had brought the young man's medical career to an immediate halt and "he had joined the Trappist monks."[12]

At the end of the war, Anita Johnson Dean met and later (in 1946) married the love of her life, and for a short while their time together was idyllic—that is until her husband, who had decided to make the army his career, returned to more death and carnage on the battlefields in Korea.

Within four months following his departure, on what had been a perfectly ordinary day in East Lansing, Anita returned from classes at MSU, where she was continuing her studies in food and nutrition, to find a letter with the ominous return address of Dick's best buddy overseas. Dick had been killed, and she was now a widow. Two weeks later there was the official knock at the door as two army officers delivered the news officially. For a year she dropped out of college and returned home to live with her parents as a basket case. Finally, with time and support from family and friends, she re-enrolled at MSU and completed her MA. After completing her degree, she resumed her career, which she knew would have pleased her husband.[13]

After the war, physician Mike Sharp returned to his residency at Woman's Hospital in Detroit. At first, however, the officials were hesitant to allow him to resume his residency. He had to go through a battery of tests to determine whether he jerked his head or trembled or shook as a result of combat fatigue. Once he assumed his duties as a resident physician, Mike soon discovered a lack of bonding with other physicians. He had become so accustomed to giving brusque, dictatorial orders during the war, that his officious manner was alienating his fellow physicians. He was soon made aware of the error of his ways when one of the interns habitually replied, "Yes, Massa!"[14]

One would-be physician's application for medical school was turned down for two years because the authorities thought he would not make a good doctor because he had eaten rats and bugs as a Japanese prisoner of war. The members of the Medical Board were oblivious to the fact that the willingness to eat caterpillars, horsemeat, rats, and worms often meant the difference between life and death for gravely emaciated POWs in Japan.

Before the war, Paul L. Curry had been interested in becoming a mortician. While Paul was in his teens the local undertaker had agreed to Paul's working as an apprentice to him. It didn't take long for Paul's experiences with death and grief during the war to effectively change all that. He had already seen too many dead people.[15]

During his service as a cryptographer, coding and encoding messages for the 20th Bomber Command in Kharagpur, India, Al Boettcher was shocked at the seemingly ubiquitous poverty that pervaded much of the country. Small children their eyes weepy from infections yet hosts to giant swarms of flies; clay lean-to one-room hovels sans running water and stoves; the abominable caste system; herds of shoeless children with grimy outstretched hands beseeching a penny or a crust of bread; the casual indifference toward the dead and dying left abandoned in the streets—all gave Al Boettcher a far greater appreciation of his own country than ever before.[16]

The war did indeed mark the survivors in many diverse ways. One veteran, overjoyed that he survived his 50 or more B-18 missions over Germany, vowed never ever to go up in an airplane again—and never did. Phil Brain promised never ever to buy a car made in Japan—and he never did.[17]

The war, Bob Stern believed, made him a much more responsible person. Having been accountable for the men in his crew, Bob, after the war, looked at his responsibilities to his fellowman with far deeper commitment. As did thousands of servicemen, the war considerably widened Bob Stern's knowledge of the world and its inhabitants. Diverse people and their cultures made a profound impression on young men who had never been more than 50 miles away from home. Later in life, this taste of other worlds manifested itself in a tremendous interest for Bob to travel the globe.[18]

Was Bob Drake changed in any way by the war? It made him vow to try in the future to do everything in his power to end man's inhumanity to man, to work to peacefully solve differences rather than to resort to violence. This vow was later translated into his efforts as a Probate Judge to help people resolve differences amicably, rather than through violence. Violence, Bob Drake insists, begets violence—in the home, in the community, and in international relations.[19]

The war made Alan Suits ever alert for any possible signs of totalitarianism and discrimination in America that could lead to the evil that had so completely engulfed Germany. A year after the war, Alan and a buddy were outraged at the sign posted at a swimming pool near their home that read RESTRICTED—NO JEWS. The next night they came out with buckets of black paint and blackened the offensive sign.[20]

For Leroy Schroeder, his war experiences served to intensify his hatred of the insanity of war. Thousands of young men's lives were cut short, and quickly was the blurring of past atrocities and the casual drift into forgiving and forgetting.[21]

Henry LaBrosse concurred that most people in the United States don't realize how fortunate they are. "Unfortunately, young people take too much for granted," he maintained. Many interviewees thought it a good idea for young people to serve a year or two in the military after high school before going on to college. The lessons in discipline and responsibility, they believed, could be invaluable.[22]

Had Elizabeth McIntee's 17-month WAC Service in London changed her? "Well, people say it did!" Elizabeth reported mysteriously.[23]

John Key acknowledged that the war had indeed changed him. His experiences made him "determined to make something of himself, to get more education." Jane Weatherford believed that the terrible grief suffered by friends who had lost sons and brothers to the war changed her ideas about human rights, how people were treated, and brought forth a new sense of compassion. At the time, and ever since, Jane strenuously objected to those who could have volunteered for service but who "had to care for business" or professed other "ridiculous excuses."[24]

After three years of separation, not a few couples realized that their marriages needed some re-adjustment. For some couples their paths and interests had so radically changed over the years that divorce appeared to be the only answer. Don Swope had been quite smitten with a girlfriend in high school. They corresponded in loving terms throughout the war— although he was casually dating a girl in Texas. At the same time, Don's Texas girlfriend was more-or-less committed to her longtime boyfriend overseas.

   After the war and two-and-a-half years of service as a pilot with the Air Force, Don returned home to discover the high school girlfriend was a bit too juvenile, and surprise, surprise, the Texas friend was disappointed by what she had earlier thought to be true love when he returned from service.

   Don and Myrle Barron's feelings turned out to be mutual, and following a marriage proposal by mail and a short but romantic long-distance courtship, the two were married. Perspectives can indeed change.[25]

A wartime romance turned sour for Wayne Lesher even though he married "Miss California." A couple of years later life had taken different turns for each of them.[26]

The shutdown of the WASPs program after the war disappointed many of the women who had so greatly contributed to the war effort by devotedly ferrying planes and supplies around to various localities in the United States. (Actually, the WASPS were not officially in the military during the war, and it was 1977 before they were accorded military status.) Once the war was over, the authorities decided they had too many pilots and that it was too expensive to train the women. (More expensive than to train men??? Come now!) After all their commitment and long hours of service, Dorothy Dodd Eppstein and thousands of her comrades were summarily dismissed to accommodate male pilots.[27]

In the spring of 1946, the war was over, of course, but Americans were still engaged in bringing their fellow Americans home from overseas. As a member of the Foreign Claims Commission, Bob Fisher was stationed in Shanghai, China, where his job was to interview Chinese men whose business or whose person had been injured by U.S. servicemen. Usually, there was no malice involved in the incidents. Instead a few liquored-up Marine or navy men bent on mischief got carried away with deviltry and tossed bricks through windows, stole merchandise in stores, or created mayhem as they hurtled through the countryside in their jeeps. In one case, a handsome elderly bookseller clad in his exquisitely embroidered mandarin coat came in to Bob's office requesting restitution for damages to his bookstore and the theft of many heirloom volumes, the work of a gang of intoxicated servicemen "on liberty." Fortunately, Bob helped secure a 700 dollar compensation for the distraught owner. On another occasion, a wrinkled, weather-beaten farmer sought reparation after an American Marine had driven his jeep into the man's horse and wagon, killing the horse and the man's wife. The Americans were astonished when the farmer settled for repayment of $1,200 for his horse and only $600 for the loss of his wife.[28]

Two girls from Italy, Inez Flanders and Louise Cullefer, recalled how when they were youngsters and living in Italy, they were indoctrinated to think that Mussolini was all but divine. Both girls married American servicemen, and made a comfortable adjustment to life in America. Both girls insisted that they had never heard a word about Pearl Harbor before they came to the United States.[29]

Frank Feeley was one of the thousands who found readjustment difficult. After changing jobs several times, he could never quite find what he wanted until he decided that after all of his traveling what really seemed his right niche was the military, whereupon he re-enlisted and made the Air Force his career. After months of having been directed "what to do and how to do it and when to do it," Alice Diggins felt a little disorientated upon her return to civilian life. For a while it seemed strange to be on one's own once again.[30]

The horrors of the war were still raw memories for many veterans who were secretly annoyed as they saw civilians enraged over a piece of burned toast or angered by a driver holding up traffic in the turn lane. Life for them was too fragile to be spoiled by trivialities.

Haunting memories still return for Chuck Larrowe of the bloody fighting on Okinawa when his Captain kept urging the men to keep moving up.

Chuck's men were being picked off like flies. The carnage was sickening. Finally, Chuck exploded: "Capp, God damn it, if you could see all the men in my platoon getting killed, why don't you just come on up here and show me how to do it?" Captain Capp did so and was immediately shot and killed. For Chuck Larrowe, that was the most unfortunate event of the war. A moment he can never ever forget.[31]

After 34 months in the Marine Corps, spent mostly in the South Pacific, Hall Tennis was concerned about the damage war does to the person. "I cannot imagine it makes for a better person." In a personal evaluation, however, he humorously concluded that he did not believe "that experience made me any more neurotic than I already was."[32]

It was difficult for Joe Kish to talk about the places he had served during the war—there had been so many of them as he "island hopped" with the Navy across the Pacific. Had he really been at a certain place or had he just heard his friends talking about being there? Places and landings and beaches tended to run together in his mind. Finally, at one of the reunions, as his buddies opened the logbook and pointed to his name, he realized he really had "been there and done that."[33]

Time and again during his tour of duty Hall Tennis, had told himself: "Nothing that ever happens to me can be as bad as this (can be worse than this?), and if I get back to the States, nothing is ever going to bother me seriously again. I'm going to call it all my way." At the time of his discharge, Hall seriously considered staying in. "It was an accustomed place, but I wanted to learn about the larger world. And, threatening though it was, I decided to take the harder road. Be a civilian."[34]

PSYCHOLOGICAL SCARS

Following the war, men donned civilian clothes, returned to their jobs, found new ones, or went to college. The past was past; nevertheless, terrifying nightmares could still jolt a sleeper into reliving the numbing fear of an enemy assault and the appalling scenes of death and destruction. A car's sudden emission, a surprise tap on the shoulder, even innocent Fourth of July firecrackers all could trigger a momentary panic attack. But why dwell unnecessarily on battlefield horrors? Why upset one's family with ghostly memories? Get on with life, they determined.

When Philip Montgomery dropped out of the University of Michigan in 1942 after his sophomore year to go to war, he learned that the newly formed parachute infantry paid 100 dollars a month (twice the pay than that of the ordinary soldier). Intrigued by the idea of parachute jumping (and the pay), Phil thought it sounded like a good deal. He volunteered and was assigned to the Medical Detachment of the 511th Parachute Regiment, 11th Airborne Division. After extensive training, jump school, and maneuvers he was sent to New Guinea and from there in November of 1944 into combat at Leyte. "The second day in we were ambushed by the Japs and one of my fellow medics was killed. I gave up my poncho to bury him in so that I slept in the mud with no cover for the next three weeks. (The guys with ponchos were only a little better off.)" After completing their mission at Leyte, the men spent a month regrouping for a jump on Luzon and then on to the southern outskirts of Manila. During combat on February 15th, entrenched Japanese shot two of Phil's fellow medics through the thigh, and the men, unconscious from loss of blood, were immediately brought to his aid station. "The doctors were unable to get plasma into the collapsed veins of Bill Verlander while I was successful with Tom Parker. Back at the field hospital Bill died and Tom had his leg amputated. I could not get Tom out of my memory after the war."

The emotional scars ran deep, and for 40 years afterward Phil would never discuss the war with his wife or anyone. After all those years of wondering what had become of Tom Parker, Phil suddenly decided to look up his friend. As they reminisced, both men found a release for their long suppressed emotions and finally could talk about the war with family and friends. From that time on, each year Phil went to see his friend who years earlier had credited Phil with saving his life.[35]

The memories of all those killed, Dave Ruff insisted, "were the worst part of it all." The trauma experienced in seeing friends—and even complete strangers killed—was horrendous, but it was a double whammy when the casualty was a member of one's own family. It was a gut-wrenching moment when Dave picked up a pile of letters and discovered that his brother had been flying a hospital plane of wounded men to U.S. hospitals when the plane crashed in Oakland, California, and he and 23 other men were killed on February 13, 1945. "It was hard to figure out," Dave reasoned, "why you came home and so many others didn't." Dave found comfort in his religion, but he still chokes up and remembers things as though they happened yesterday.[36]

Joe Spinosa has never been able to divorce himself from his war experiences. The sights of dead bodies, screams from wounded buddies, and the numbing fear of attacking or being attacked have haunted Jo Spinosa for 60 years. Frequent trips to veterans' hospitals and psychoneurosis specialists still punctuate Joe's postwar life. (The term *shell shock* was used in World War I and Post-Traumatic Stress Syndrome after the Viet Nam conflict.) "War is hell," Joe echoed General Sherman's assessment during the Civil War. It was a hell for Joe as well as his wife, who received two telegrams informing her that "her husband had been wounded," but not saying whether he was an amputee, had been blinded, or was otherwise incapacitated. "People don't really understand that war is not just a John Wayne movie," Joe surmised. "The bullets are real! Even the bravest finally can take it no longer," he explained.[37]

Robert McCollough was absolutely devastated by the death of two of his buddies as they flew off into the sun one day while flying the Hump. Their wings locked and the two planes exploded, killing both of the pilots. Never to be forgotten was the heart-rending task of gathering up their clothing, cutting the rings off their fingers, and struggling for words to relay the news to the families.[38]

Leo Chick came through the war with some psychological scars but fortunately no physical scars. He keeps living and reliving his days in the field artillery during the fighting in Germany, especially during the Allied crossing of the Rhine River, and still suffers terrible nightmares. Even so, he thanks God he did not suffer the mental breakdown after the war of two of his buddies who were unable to shake the trauma of their experiences in the military and finally gave up and committed suicide. Yet another buddy endured emotional disorientation, left town for a week, came back, and had no idea where he had been.[39]

On the verge of a nervous breakdown after the war, Lloyd Hamlin decided, "There were only two people who could do anything about this—me and the Almighty." Together they made the transition to a successful civilian life.[40]

"The sadness came years later," Phil Montgomery explained. For years after the war the slightest sound would awaken Phil from a dead sleep. "There was always the fear that a Jap in the dark might be sneaking up on you."[41]

Thousands of veterans share Bern Engel's nightly sleeplessness, the reprise of his agonies over the war years, his close calls, the friends lost. Having witnessed men during his war experiences in such excruciating states of physical and mental suffering induced Bern Engel to work as a Hospice volunteer in later life in an attempt to help minimize the trauma of the terminally ill.[42]

Having earned only 30 points when it took 35 to be sent home, Lee Conley soon found himself on occupation duty in Beijing, China. It was there that the extreme poverty experienced by the Chinese during the Japanese occupation proved an immense culture shock for Lee Conley and his fellow Marines. People in rags, children begging piteously on the streets for food, trucks that came through the streets at night to pick up the bodies of the dead, civilians who were marched through the streets on their way to be executed sans trials or hearings, people brutalized by an enemy on the rampage—all brought revulsion and nightmares for Lee that lasted a lifetime. The memory of a child swinging her only playtoy, a dead rat, became a memory impossible ever to forget.[43]

An airman who was uneasy about each mission, and always thrust his fingers into the gas tank to be sure they had sufficient fuel for the flight, vowed never to get on an airplane again as long as he lived—and kept his word. The Normandy Invasion cured Ken Almay of any desire to travel anywhere by ship. "I've 'swallowed the anchor' as they say, and haven't been on a boat since the war."[44]

Many veterans testified to being unable to watch violence, in movies or on TV. Some admitted walking out in movies that suddenly took a violent turn. The war impacted Frank Bourke tremendously and left a gnawing fear of ever again being away from one's loved ones.[45]

Alcoholism was a huge problem of returning veterans who had suffered through the terror and bloodshed of war. One soldier said that it took a fifth and a half of alcohol to enable him to kill people in war, but after that he never touched a drop of liquor.

Having been involved in six amphibious landings (in North Africa, Sicily, Salerno, Elba, Pinosa, and in southern France), Dave Anderson, of Lorain, Ohio, had been severely traumatized by his war experiences and admitted that he had not drawn a sober breath during his first five years out of service. He was an indifferent scholar after the war, suspended or dropping out of five different colleges in as many years. He was dismissed by three of the colleges under a cloud of alcoholism and rebelliousness. Fortunately, there was a happy postscript to Dave's story when later his life was turned around, thanks to the help of a caring professor and his devoted wife, Pat. (Dave later went on to complete a PhD in English, after which he became a college professor and author of more than 37 scholarly books.)[46]

Several shipmates were shocked after the war to discover that one of their favorite commanders was unable to readjust to civilian life after the war. The officer who had earned the immense admiration of his men for his ability and integrity was months later discovered in Detroit, a sot among drunken bums squatting in a dirty, darkened street. Not a few families testified that a father or brother "was brought down by alcohol" following the war.

Finding himself caught up with a group of veterans who found their chief occupation making the rounds of bars each night, Bud Rogne decided there was more to life than bar hopping and stayed in for the Korean War.[47]

Not all servicemen waited until the end of the war to do battle with alcohol. After the war in Europe was over, Van Hatcher recalled one fighter pilot that had "chickened out." Either scared or sickened by the bloodshed or plagued by the guilt of survival, the pilot refused to fly more missions and just sat in the Officers' Club and drowned himself in alcohol until late in the night when a fellow officer would help him into bed.[48]

As did many POWs, Lamar Rodgers found it very difficult to talk about his war experiences, and he, too, at first had had a drinking problem. The period of adjustment was extremely difficult as the men, particularly POWs, attempted to take up a normal life once again. The memories of what their lives had been like during the fighting and their imprisonment kept flooding back, often overpowering reason and endeavor.[49]

Although most veterans were impatient to come home to loved ones and to resume a normal life once again, there were those "that really didn't want to go home. They didn't know whether they were going to be able to take it or not. They didn't know what was waiting for them." For example, a good many changes had transpired in Lamar Rodgers' family while he was gone. His fiancée had married someone else, his grandmother had died, his father had disappeared, and he found it difficult "to come home and face that." As they were waiting to be discharged in San Antonio, Lamar remembered several of his POW buddies who spent their nights getting drunk at the local bars. They were given special treatment as POWs and therefore spent much of the day sleeping off their previous night's imbibing until they could once again jump in a car and go out for another night of carousing. For the moment alcohol could—and did—provide the camaraderie of "a band of brothers" and the transient courage to face the unknown. His 22 months as a German prisoner of war had rendered Lamar Rodgers an emotional wreck. Years later Lamar Rodgers admitted, "At times I can't even get along with myself. My nerves, you know, and what have you. I've been mean at times." Lamar was embarrassed that even "My kids have suffered from it." He continued: "This thing does warp you. It warps your personality to the point that you don't ever recover. It took me years and years to realize this." Even Lamar's mother had complained that "she sent a boy to war and she didn't know what she got back, because of the reactions here. There are times that I have such a short fuse that I explode over nothing that is of no consequence at all. And I recognize this and this is—they call it a concentration camp syndrome."

Coping with his prisoner of war experiences after the war was a challenge Lamar Rogers believed he never really mastered. "There's many things I still can't cope with. I don't like—I'm not going to be anywhere where there's a closed up room too long. I don't like people. Really, I don't like people. That's a tragedy in itself. I go to church, but once I'm out of there, I don't want to go back to where there's a lot of people. I don't want any of this. . . . Given a choice in the matter, I wouldn't be anywhere close to a group of people."[50]

It was not easy being married to a former POW Robbie Belle Bishop Rodgers admitted. For a time, her husband's war experiences of constantly taking orders and having most decisions made for him conditioned him to shun responsibility, on a job, in dealing with money, or in life situations in general. "Just those few months took years out of our lives. It did something to us that we didn't realize fully back then. We've had to live with it and our wives as well have put up with how that internment affected us. Some ex-POWs are hard to live with. Getting slugged in the back of your head with a rifle butt leaves emotional scars along with lumps."[51]

As can be observed, most POWs suffered devastating emotional scars from their war experiences. Nightmares about the German Shepherd guard dogs were a frightening occurrence for soldiers who had witnessed their viciousness in the German POW camps. Fred Douglas Williams, a former prisoner of war in Stalag VII-A, told of waking "up at night, you know, and be dreaming about those German Shepherds just eating you up and be scared to death. I guess it was two years I had those dreams." Williams confessed that he still despises German Shepherd dogs. "I have a cold chill every time I see one. They will eat you up and they won't ask

questions."[52] Lamar Rodgers shared the same abhorrence for the guard
dogs the Germans turned out on the POWs.

THE PHYSICAL SCARS

While tens of thousands of men carried psychological scars following
their service in World War II, thousands of other veterans carried crippling physical scars that would plague them for the rest of their lives.
Wendell "Wendy" Stanford Peterson, for example, spent 51 years in and
out of hospitals, seeking relief from a bullet wound to his right leg that
had nearly cost him his life.

At first the early assault waves in New Guinea seemed to have cleared
the path for the American forces that were later to secure the island. As
Wendy and his buddies hacked their way inland, however, Japanese who
were holed up in caves and crevices opened fire with a vengeance. Shrapnel took out a buddy standing next to Wendy, and minutes later as Wendy
was attending another fallen comrade, a Japanese gunner took aim and
succeeded in blowing away much of Wendy's right leg. The medics were
unable to reach him right away, and for 24 hours Wendy lay on the battlefield as bullets and shrapnel shore off tree limbs and peppered the ground
around him.

There followed four months of hospitalization at the base hospital,
a return to the States, and devastating assessments as to his condition.
Observations such as, "You'll never walk on that leg again" sent Wendy's
morale to "rock bottom." One day Wendy took new hope when he saw
"a patient with horrible foot wounds, but he was walking. So I said to
myself that if he could do it, so could I." For the next half century, Wendy
underwent countless operations, scores of skin grafts, innumerable torturous casts, and untold hours of physical therapy. Finally the ultimate
operation—the amputation of his leg. Always the optimist or at least
almost always, Wendy surmised: "It's been tough, but I think I've been
fortunate."[53]

Veterans' hospitals still resound with the thumps of crutches, the rum-
bling of wheelchairs, and the mumblings of the speech impaired—all
physical testimony to the horrors of the battle zones and the aerial warfare
of the forties. Malnutrition, dysentery, and "jungle rot" postponed the discharge for months of thousands of servicemen, such as Yeoman 2nd class
Jack Siebold who served with the Seabees in the South Pacific.[54] Countless
others still suffer from bouts of malaria.

DISCRIMINATION

African Americans often suffered considerable discrimination during the
war. Many northern blacks were angered by the second class treatment
accorded those in the South. Once George Taylor reached Washington,

D.C., as he was en route to Montford Point, the segregated Marine camp for African Americans near Camp Lejeune, he and his fellow African American comrades, the first to be inducted in the Marine Corps in 1943, were immediately transferred from train coaches for whites to straw-seated, unheated coaches for blacks. Objecting to his treatment, George explained that they were with the Government and not independent African Americans. "That don't mean a thing down here" was the reply as they were herded back to the unsavory coaches. They were surprised, although they should not have been, that they were not welcomed in white restaurants and assigned balcony seats in theaters and back seats on buses.

Taylor was repeatedly in trouble—fined and sent to the guardhouse for having the picture of a white woman inside his locker door, for refusing to obey orders that he thought were discriminatory, for punching a sergeant who kicked him without provocation. True, he admitted, he "raised a fuss" from time to time, but only when he saw himself as being picked on because of his color. His youth spent on Chicago's city streets made him forcibly stand up to what he considered demeaning, discriminatory treatment. For all of his tangles with officials, he was proud of his Marine Service and would be quick to join the Marines again if he had it to do over.[55]

Blatant discrimination resulted in an ugly confrontation at Fort Knox. Simply because of the color of their skin, Clinton Canady, a First Lieutenant and a dentist, along with several hundred of his African American comrades, also officers, who were serving with the Tuskegee Airmen at Fort Knox, had been refused entrance to the white-only Officers' Club at the base. The officers were incensed. Had they not gone through the same Officers' training? Had they not been duly commissioned, and were they not conscientiously giving their all to serving the same country as the white officers? Clearly this demeaning treatment did not go over well with the black officers. In protest, some 100 of them, led by Coleman Young (later to become mayor of Detroit), organized a march on the club. The men marched, were summarily repulsed, ordered back to their quarters, *and arrested!*

Rounded up by MPs, the protesters were quickly sent to Indiana and incarcerated in an Indiana prison area. However, once the outrage hit the African American newspapers, the event gained considerable media attention. As a result of the caustic criticism, in time the men were sent back to Fort Knox *but* with black officers replacing the white officers who had previously been in charge. Some months later, after the men were returned to Fort Knox, the protest eventually paid off, and the men were provided with their own attractive clubhouse and first-run movies. Away from the base, however, they were denied admittance to nearby Louisville theaters, restaurants, and hotels and gawked at by Louisville residents who were shocked to see black *officers.*

Lieutenant Clinton Canady and a group of his fellow African American officers still remember the indignity they suffered as they were being deployed to a new base in Texas. At a stop at a Ft. Worth railroad station, they were humiliated when they were prohibited from eating in the station's restaurant—simply because they were black. The real irony occurred when a group of German POWs, who were stationed in a POW camp nearby and who were assigned to work in the station's ground department, were graciously served in the station restaurant, while Clint's group of blacks was ordered to sit in a remote back room to be served. To pile insult upon injury, the POWs, the enemy, waved and laughed heartily at the humiliation of Clint and his fellow officers.[56]

The tables were turned for Wayne Lesher while stationed in St. Louis. Wayne's favorite spot on any bus was the back seat, that is until a St. Louis city bus driver came back and in no uncertain terms ordered him to move up "to the *front* of the bus."[57]

CHANGES IN RACIAL PERSPECTIVES

Before going overseas, Wilson Evans II, an African American from Gulfport, Mississippi, found that his stay in the North, in Worcester, Massachusetts, considerably changed his views on the racial question. Accustomed to the strict segregation of whites and blacks in the South, Wilson was pleasantly surprised at his acceptance in Worcester. Wilson explained that by living with kindly white people, he himself became more tolerant and considerate. "I treated them kinda like I would treat people at home, my grandmother and mother, after a while. I had an attitude when I first went there."

It was a complete change of relationships in the service during the Battle of the Bulge when for the first time in his over two years in service Wilson found himself "an American soldier. For those, what six, maybe eight, ten days, there were no black or white soldiers. We were all soldiers and for about six hours we were trapped behind the line, and whites were [as] afraid of dying as blacks. And blacks were afraid. And there was no color, no nothing. Nobody, you know. And during the breakthrough there were no separate water bounds; if coffee [was] made and someone couldn't find their canteen or couldn't find their cup, they'd borrow somebody else's, and they didn't think about it. I did see that Americans could become American for about eight or nine days."[58]

John Peoples, an African American from Starkville, Mississippi, who served in the black U.S. Marine Corps, credited his Marine Corps experience with maturing him and his technical electronics training with putting him far ahead of his Jackson State classmates when he opted to use the GI Bill to go to college after the war. As an African American during the war John, felt he was held back and discriminated against because of his color. At Camp Pendleton, California, John Peoples and his men were promised by their colonel that there would be "no discrimination." Minutes later, John and his fellow African Americans were ordered to sit at a separate table in the corner of the mess hall. A stalwart young New Jersey man insisted "We're not going to sit here, fellows. Let's just go back to the colonel." There was a sense of justice among the men when the colonel told them to sit anywhere. "So that was the first time I had seen someone in the Marine Corps defy desegregation because it was understood that in the Marine Corps that we had a separate Marine Corps for blacks."

When John was consistently given lower scores than his white colleagues for his correct answers in electronics school, he questioned his instructor who replied, "Peoples, there's no way that you could be smarter than these other guys. Now, you went to this all-black camp over in North Carolina. You went to school in Mississippi. There's no way. And I don't care what, you know, there's no way. You're just not that smart" An appeal higher up to a captain was returned with a, "You're going to get your promotion. What are you bitching for? Just relax and just go on and go to school. Just quit bitching." With that, John gave up. From this and other similar experiences John "gained confidence because for the first time I got a chance to compete with blacks and whites from the North and came out at the top."[59]

Vernon J. Baker of Cheyene, Wyoming bore first-hand testimony to the racism in World War II. Even before Pearl Harbor, Vernon, an African American, volunteered but was turned away by a recruiter who told him, "We don't have quotas for you people yet." Later, he enlisted through a different recruiter and en route to his base in Texas he was humiliated by being forced to ride in the back of the bus. Even as a graduate of Officers' Candidate School, he suffered racial abuse from his superiors who openly referred to blacks as "cowards." Much later, as he recuperated from being wounded in 1944, he was assigned a bed in a segregated ward in the hospital.

Routinely Vernon was given a royal putdown when he, as an officer, cautiously offered suggestions about combat tactics to less experienced white officers. Justice finally won out, however, when after several daring feats of bravery in Europe involving seizing possession of enemy bunkers, taking out enemy machine gun nests, and leading his men to safety when their situation seemed doomed, Vernon was awarded the Distinguished Service Cross for his courageous acts in April 1945. In 1997, his DSC was upgraded, and he was presented with the prestigious Medal of Honor.[60]

The story of the Tuskegee Airmen paints a dramatic picture of discrimination in the military services. "We had two enemies in the war," Joseph Phillip Gomer, a Tuskegee Airman declared, "the Germans and discrimination." Early on, Joe, an Iowa Falls, Iowa native, discovered the ubiquitous segregation attitudes that muddled the thinking of military officials and often demeaned black men who risked their lives for a country that was often oblivious to their abilities and commitment. During 1940–41, plans began to take shape to get blacks into the Army Air Force and to establish the Tuskegee Airmen, a prestigious group of black flyers who would receive training at Tuskegee Institute in Alabama. Joe noted, "There was an attitude that blacks would be unable to learn how to fly, or that they would turn coward if they got close to combat conditions . . . Even airfields were segregated. We could not land our trainers at a regular military airfield, so one was built just for us Tuskegee Airmen."

Despite the fact that all 13 of the first class in 1941 had college degrees, only 5 of them were graduated. "To get our wings, we had to be good and we had to be lucky," Joe Gomer acknowledged. "In fact, we learned by the grapevine that some of our Tuskegee cadets who washed out were better than white pilots who passed."

After 68 missions flying a P-47 and a P-51 as escort for the Allied bombing raids over Germany and Italy, Joe Gomer was finally replaced by another black pilot and was waiting in line to board a troop transport that would take him back to the States. (White fighter pilots could be returned to the States after 50 missions.) It was at that point that Joe experienced his most irritating experience with discrimination. At the checkpoint table, the officer in charge was busily checking over papers, and as Joe approached, he looked up, took a second look at Joe's color and waved him back to the end of the line "several hundred bodies back." Joe was infuriated. He had several narrow escapes flying P-47 and P-51 fighters, his plane had been riddled with gunfire from the enemy, but this was his most traumatic moment of the war. "I never felt such hostility toward anyone during the war, even towards the Germans, as I did to that man. That was as close as I ever came to wanting to kill anyone. After a year of serving my country, getting shot at, and losing fellow pilots in action, it was as though I had become a second-class citizen again. Without question, that was my most traumatic moment of the war. And strangely enough, it came at the end of my war in Europe."

At a fiftieth reunion of the 459th Bomber Squadron in St. Paul, Joe was asked to represent the Tuskegee Airmen, pilots to whom the bomber crews felt they owed their lives during the war. One former airman said: "I've waited 51 years to thank you fellows."[61]

The accomplishments of the Tuskegee Airmen and the 367,000 African Americans who served in World War II, without question led to President Truman's Executive order 9981 of 1948. "It is hereby declared to be the policy of the President that there shall be equality of treatment and opportunity for all persons in the armed services without regard to race, color, religion or national origin." The Civil Rights movement of the 1950s followed, thanks in part to the African Americans' contributions during the war.[62]

His children reminded Roy Herbert that it is not very Christianlike to
retain one's hatred of the Japanese. But his observations of some Japanese
atrocities, cutting off the ears of some POWs, for example, left him still
bitter and resentful. Forgiving and forgetting are two different things, he
insisted. After Pearl Harbor and his experiences in India and the Pacific,
Ted Bauer also harbored a grudge against the Japanese that for many years
continued to fester.[63]

Having seen so many of his buddies die, it was too much for Bill Keezer
to just forgive and forget. Keezer was awarded the Silver Star for bravery
for standing by his machine gun placement when everyone else ran. To
this day, he refuses to watch war movies or TV shows. They bring back too
many terrible memories.[64]

WASP Dorothy Dodd Eppstein was so turned off by the war that she
became a peace advocate and later was fired from her job as a school coun-
selor for being a peace marcher.[65]

THE RELIGIOUS PERSPECTIVE

It is surprising that anyone could come away from the bloody combat of
the South Pacific battlefields with wounds that would take a lifetime to
heal and not harbor a deep hatred for the Japanese. The recipient of not just
one but two Purple Hearts, Robert Rieder Boardman, a native of Salem,
Oregon, credits his military experience with turning his life around. On
Peleliu, Bob survived a minor wound that killed two Marines who were
standing with him. In the Battle for Okinawa, Bob's tank was hit and set
afire, and as he and four of his crew attempted to escape the inferno, three
of his comrades were shot down by the enemy. Bob narrowly missed their
fate, but suffered a devastating wound to his throat and the loss of half a
finger. His experiences led him to take up the ministry as his life's work,
and beginning in 1951, he served as a missionary in Japan. At one time
he conducted a Bible class in a high school in Okinawa that was "a few
hundred yards" from the scene of his life-threatening wound during the
battle for Okinawa.[66]

Pearl Harbor had a marked effect on Allan Rice and his family. Allan's
father, a Methodist minister, felt compelled to leave his Kokomo, Indiana
congregation to sign up as a navy chaplain. Early on Allan had divided
feelings about the war. In his father's church in Kokomo, he was part of a
youth group and was greatly influenced by taking part in a pacifist play.
When the war came, however, enlistment became so universal that Allan
felt it important to volunteer his services to the Army. As the ASTP (Army
Specialist Training Program) closed down (Allan was enrolled at Iowa
State College), he and the other ASTP men were assigned to the infantry.
For Allan there was amphibious training in California, then a temporary
assignment as an assistant to his father who was a chaplain aboard a troop

ship, and later on an assignment to Patton's Third army as the General made his way across Europe.

Later Allan was engaged in ferocious fighting for 30 days as the Americans made their perilous way across the Rhine. Fortunately he was a survivor despite the fact that there were 20 casualties in his battalion alone. Thirty days after the armistice was signed, Allan was sent to Yokohama.

After being a part of so much death and destruction in Europe and after seeing the devastation in Europe and Japan where whole areas had been leveled from the bombings, Allan became committed to "going back home and working for people and freedom." His future was settled. Almost his first words upon his return home were, "Well, I think I am going to become a minister." Allan had come from a long line of ministers, and the war had given him the impetus for his peacetime pursuits.[67]

In one of those famous foxhole promises, Ken Springer bargained with the Lord. "Lord, if I ever get out of this war alive, I'll do your work. . . I somehow felt that perhaps I was being saved for something better than just existing for myself." Ken Springer kept that promise and used his GI Bill to go to college, to teach, to work his way up to principal, and finally to Superintendent of Schools. He never forgot his bargain and has devoted countless hours to working for his church and volunteering for needy causes.[68]

As navigator on a B-17 mission to take out the oil refinery at Ploesti, Rumania, Robert "Bob" John Clemens, of White Bear Lake, Minnesota, was sweating out the German fighters and anti-aircraft flack that kept bombarding his plane. One engine was gone, the windshield was smashed, a piece of shrapnel had dented his helmet, and a plane to his left had been blown up. Bob and his crew were coming in on a prayer. Softly he muttered under his breath, "Oh God, if you get me out of this, I'll help you out somehow." The pilot managed to limp back to their base in Foggia, Italy, and the promise was momentarily forgotten. It was difficult enough to cope with the loss of 20 friends who died as members of the two bomber crews who were shot down that day.

Bob Clemens summed up the losses. "When I returned to the USA in early October 1944, only 150 crew members were left from the original 400 who arrived in Italy that year. In the month of June alone, we lost 318 bombers on air raids."

Following his discharge, Bob spent several years first in the heating and later in the insurance business. For almost 30 years, his top priorities were his work and his home. Yet, somewhere in the deep recesses of his mind lurked that promise to God made in the heat of battle so many years before. In honoring that pledge, Bob became involved in Prison Fellowship (the organization begun by President Nixon's advisor, Chuck Colson), which focuses on providing hope to prisoners and assistance following their release. That experience and zealous participation in his local church activities groomed him for his later extensive work as an associate in the Navigator lay ministry. His pledge, when a navigator on a B-17 bomber that had dispersed such widespread death and carnage during WWII, had led him to undertake another special mission later in life, this time as a Navigator of men for peace and justice in the postwar world.[69]

Leo Chick prayed each day just hoping to make it through the hell of war. "I have a lot of work to do yet," he kept reminding God. To this day he doesn't know why he came through alive and so many of his friends perished.[70] In a letter to his parents (August 14, 1945), Claude Fike, of Ahoskie, North Carolina, marveled over his "having been spared without even a scratch; it certainly bolsters my faith in Christianity."[71]

Asked "if a religious or spiritual dimension to their lives made any difference to one's peace of mind . . . and soul . . . in the stress of dangerous living?" Dick Elasky stated that he had had a long-standing relationship with God. It was not merely prayers during the war in time of crisis, but a commitment made when he was 14 and continued after his military service in church activities and with the lay ministry The Navigators.[72]

Richard Jones believed his time in the Air Force had been memorable— times that he would never forget. Although he thought that he had not changed appreciably, he felt the bomb damage in London was extremely depressing. As he helped load napalm on the planes he knew the devastation it would cause. His experiences caused him to give serious thoughts to war and its inhumanity. If anything, Dick believes it strengthened his religious convictions.[73]

Did the war change Phil Brain? Although before the war he had already been vaguely contemplating a career with the YMCA, the first year of his captivity in the Philippines and later time in Japan convinced him that *if* he managed to survive the war, he would devote the rest of his life to working with youth through the YMCA—and that was a promise he succeeded in keeping.[74]

On one of his early missions, the flack was so thick and his brush with death so close that B-17 navigator Bill Love canceled out the fear factor, calmed down, and "turned it over to God." For the rest of his life, Bill Love, as a result of his war experience, tended to take things in stride. Nothing much seemed to rile him, and he believed he could handle almost any situation.[75]

Asked if the war had strengthened his religious beliefs, Paul Niland answered in the affirmative. "Since I didn't think I would survive, I wanted to be ready."[76]

"With the war over, we returned to the U.S. on June 30, 1945," Woodrow Respects Nothing recalled. Their arrival in Norfolk on July 7, 1945, was heralded with crowds of welcomers. "They treated us like heroes. We marched single file between the mobs of people assembled to see us and greet us with kisses, yells, and handshakes." Some four months later, Woodrow returned to his home on the Pine Ridge Indian Reservation in southeastern South Dakota. "Shortly after I got home, my aunt Mildred wanted me to attend a ceremonial Prayer Service. I wasn't much for Indian ceremonies but she said I had to because it was in my honor. She had hired a medicine man to send Indian spirits to watch over me while I was in the war. I didn't know anything about it, but someone watched over me. My religious background was Episcopalian more than spirit worship. But still, it's part of our culture."[77]

CHAPTER 18

The Later Years

THE GI BILL

Thousands of servicemen had left as teenagers and had returned home as men. Homecoming, joyous though it was, brought about momentous choices. Maybe stay in the service and serve in the peacetime occupation of Europe and Japan? Go back to the comforts of home and family and to albeit a lackluster job waiting for one's return? Take advantage of the GI Bill and start or finish college? Would the old job be satisfactory, or had one's war experiences imbued one with a newfound courage and determination to seek greater heights and more demanding challenges?

For thousands upon thousands of returning servicemen the GI Bill (the Servicemen's Readjustment Act of 1944) provided funds for a college education that otherwise would have been financially impossible for most veterans. (By 1947, over one million servicemen were enrolled in colleges and universities.) For many of those who had been half-hearted students before the war, the advantages of an education had become abundantly clear during their wartime service, and following their discharge they took up their books with an unwavering commitment. Every opportunity was a chance to learn, to get ahead in life. Not a few veterans took up college life with an enthusiastic determination to get the most out of their studies as well as campus life. It was great to be alive, and no aspect of college life should be missed. Tom Dutch went out for the glee club, the drama group, cheer leading, wrote for the student newspaper, worked as headwaiter in the dining hall, served as student council president, and graduated with honors.[1]

After the war and his discharge, Bill Emerson could stand only one week of regular high school. His classmates were too juvenile and immature. Transferring to veterans' classes, Bill had his high school diploma in a matter of three months.[2]

Did his war experiences change Bruce Helmer? You bet they did! Following his discharge Bruce returned to his studies at Michigan State College with quite a change in attitude. Before the war, Bruce admitted to being an incredibly poor student. Only his father's intervention with the dean allowed him to remain in school on a probationary status. For the rest of his college career after the war, Bruce made grades that astonished his parents. The war had changed him from a zilch student to top of the line. From an irascible, flamboyant individual, Bruce now knew where he was going and what direction his life was taking. Twenty-eight years in the reserves, the last eight in intelligence service, concluded with Bruce's retiring in 1975 as a Lieutenant Colonel. To date, Bruce has returned nine times to England to meet with his former buddies and check out the old hang-outs.[3]

June Milks remembered her youngest brother as a carefree, fun loving young bachelor before the war. His wartime service, June remembered, had changed him immensely. He returned home a serious, confident "adult," who was determined to go to college and make something of his life. The GI Bill offered the perfect opportunity.[4]

"The GI Bill was the greatest thing to happen to this country," Jack Cawood believed. One could stay in the service, leave and seek civilian employment, or take the 17 credits awarded for one's war experience and use the GI Bill to further one's education. For Richard Crum, the GI Bill was a godsend. Studies were all important and freshman pranks, beanies, and fraternities seemed juvenile.[5]

The son of African American tenant farmers in Mississippi, Jimmy Carter Fairley had moved around so often that his schooling before he joined the Army Air Force in 1942 had concluded with the fourth grade. At the end of the war, following his military service as a truck driver, work that often involved the hazardous job of transporting bombs and ammunition through the country roads of England, Jimmy returned to school. Despite protests from envious members of the community, he finished his grade school and high school education. The GI Bill enabled him to go on to complete two years of college at Prentis Normal and Industrial Institute in Prentis, Mississippi. His military service gave impetus to his later work in the Civil Rights Movement, in the NAACP, in local Voters Leagues, and in Head Start Programs.[6]

At the time of his discharge, Bill Noonan realized that there would be little demand after the war for gunners' mates able to fix 40-millimeter guns, or three-inch 50s, or five-inch 38s; within three weeks following his return home he was enrolled at Michigan State College (later University) using the GI Bill to finish his education. Harry George credited the GI bill with paying for his medical degree. He had worked at a local hospital to help earn his tuition for his undergraduate studies, and thanks to the GI Bill he could continue on for his MD degree.[7]

Mel Buschman kept hoping he'd make it home alive, but after being wounded twice, he wondered if it were not about time for his number to come up. A third time wounded, Mel conceded he would eventually be going home, that is if the stretcher bearers would stop stumbling and dropping him as they struggled through a deep ravine in northern Italy en route to an ambulance, headed for the nearest hospital. A stay at the hospital, a hospital ship to the States, and then 18 months in a hospital in Annapolis, and he was finally sent home with three purple hearts and a disability discharge. Mel used the GI Bill to complete a Master's Degree, as noted earlier, but was disappointed that he had not designated his wish to go on for a PhD Degree, an oversight that forced him to pay out of his own pocket for his doctorate.[8]

After the war, Al Boettcher was offered his former job in Detroit, but decided instead to use the GI Bill and go back to college. First, however, he was required to sign a waiver that he had been offered his former position and had turned it down. He received $65 a month for room and board and books and tuition and headed for the University of Michigan and a degree in engineering. Ah! But when he married a year later, he received the munificent sum of $105 a month![9]

With Wayne Adgate's service time winding down and just prior to his discharge, Wayne's good friend, a flight surgeon, queried him on his plans for the future. As Wayne shrugged his shoulders in "don't know" uncertainty, the flight surgeon decided it was time for some fatherly advice. Partially in seriousness and partially in jest, the surgeon laughingly advised him, "Whatever you do, be sure to become a professional man! Actually, you have no gift of gab so you can't be a lawyer. You can't stand the sight of blood, so you can't be a physician, so you had better go into dentistry." Wayne spent the next few months mulling over his friend's advice, and following his return to civilian life enrolled in Albion College, completed dental school at Northwestern, and set up a most successful dental practice. Bob Wilson held such great respect for the dentist in his unit that that there was no question about his future career.[10]

The onrush of veterans utilizing the GI Bill after the war sent college administrators scurrying to provide professors, classrooms, and living quarters for the tens of thousands of veterans. Quonset huts were moved in and turned in to classrooms—and also for living quarters for veterans with families. Even college gymnasiums were turned into "dormitories." By 1946, for example, at Michigan State College (later University) some

2,000 veterans had enrolled. The shortage of housing meant that some 380 men had little choice but to be squeezed into temporary quarters in Jenison Hall Gymnasium. New dormitories were built as fast as construction companies could build them.

There were trailer camps on thousands of campuses. Married veterans and their wives found life somewhat difficult in improvised trailer camps where there was no running water closer than a general quarters a couple of blocks away. Toilets were the same—a block down the street. Imagine getting dinner and washing dishes and bathing a baby without immediate running water. But rent was cheap, and there was a tremendous feeling of camaraderie among the veterans.

A PILGRIMAGE TO THE SCENE OF BATTLE

There were those who made it home safely after all the bloodshed and destruction, and yet, in the years to come they were drawn as if by an unrelenting magnet back to the scenes of horror. There were thousands whose sleep was murdered nightly by successive seizures of terror and unrelieved panic. There were men so traumatized by their experiences that they were utterly unable to bring themselves to a catharsis of emotions by confiding to family or friends the anguish of those dark days. There were also those who in their later years, following the realignment of their lives, were compelled to travel back—sometimes alone; sometimes with a wife, a son, or a grandson; or with a tour of fellow pilgrims—to visit the places where death and annihilation had reigned supreme. For Walter Adams, his return to the beaches of Normandy was certainly no vacation. "If anything, it was a pilgrimage. To remember. To reflect. To contemplate. To gain perspective on the most cataclysmic event in my life."[11]

Normandy's massive military cemeteries tug at even the most callous observer's emotions—perhaps most of all the hearts of those who but for inches, or minutes, or luck, or the grace of God might well have been interred in the somber white-crossed fields. "Remembering them is an obligation for those of us lucky enough to have survived," one visitor humbly acknowledged. "An obligation, as well, for all of us who, thanks to their supreme sacrifices, are enjoying the advantages and opportunities of freedom today!"[12]

"There were moments too emotional to be put into mere words," Walt Adams said of his return visit to Normandy. "These random, unplanned encounters were emotional—and revealing." There were unembarrassed tears when the owner of a house next to the Pegasus Bridge, one of the first to be liberated in France, now a souvenir shop, refused to take his money for a handful of postcards. Observing his old fatigue uniform, the middle-aged proprietor intuitively surmised that Walter surely must have been a member of the undaunted liberation forces that had stormed her town so many years ago. As he nodded assent to her query, she waved aside his French francs "in grateful appreciation of what you and your comrades did for us."

In 1944, at Sainte-Marie-du-Mont, near the Utah beach, intrepid citizens of the town had courageously directed the 101st paratroopers to the sites of the German machine gun nests poised to repel the liberating forces. There, in 1993, an elderly Frenchman appreciatively filled a wine bottle with Utah beach sand, yet another addition to Walt's already unwieldy collection of sand from Omaha, Utah, Gold, Juno, and Sword beaches.[13]

At St. Lo, veterans remembered Major Thomas D. Howie who had so fervently vowed to be "the first American to set foot in the liberated St. Lo." It appeared Major Howie's wish would go unfilled when the Major was killed just hours before the town was taken. In a gesture of honor and respect, "His men of the 2nd Battalion, 116th Regiment, 29th Infantry Division, loaded his body on the first jeep to enter St. Lo and thus made his wish a sentimental (however macabre) reality."

Veteran John H. Winant in an article for *Alligator Alley* wrote:

Those of us who fought in, lived through and survived the battle of Okinawa as frontline U.S. Marines know that battle is an ugly and vicious machine that crushes all manner of beings that lie in its pathway. Playing guessing games about American losses, were there to have been an invasion of Japan, totally ignores the horrors that also would have been visited on British troops, on the many thousands of American and British prisoners of war held in inhumane conditions, on the Chinese, Koreans and others dominated by the Japanese, and finally on the civilian population of Japan, at home and elsewhere in Asia, and on the Japanese armed forces. Is there a way to compare the physical and emotional impact on all of these to that sustained at Hiroshima and Nagasaki?

A handful of us will return to Okinawa in this month (July 1995) not to celebrate a 50th anniversary, but to make a pilgrimage to extremely important places and things, seen and unseen. There, at the very spots where we witnessed or committed acts of bravery, fear, foolhardiness, leadership and cruelty, we will be searching for things that have long been hidden, half asleep inside ourselves.

Perhaps we'll be fortunate and will find something of ourselves that we left behind 50 years ago, and will come away feeling a sense of wholeness that has been elusive all these years. Whether that happens or not, we will remember comrades, shed tears for those many who were killed, feel the great surge of honest pride that comes with being a combat Marine, and lament that the great battle brought death to so many innocent bystander Okinawans, also to so many brave young Japanese.[14]

At a recent reunion Howard "Gov" Miller reminisced: "We'll remember hundreds of our colleagues. Many of them we never knew or had never met but none will return or live to celebrate V-J Day in 1945. By rows of white crosses, or beneath the sea, or as ashes on some remote place they have gone to eternity and will remain forever young. For us, now beyond four score after 18 reunions, we'll once again recall and re-live a significant chapter in our lives."[15]

A man whose father had been killed on his final mission from Tinian to Japan faithfully attends 505th Bomb Group reunions. He was but six months old when his father was killed; however, contact with his dad's comrades, he feels, gives him insights into the father he never knew.

For some men for whom later life had been unkind, a trip back to Europe to visit the gravesites of comrades who had died in battle gave them pause to wonder whether their comrades had found greater peace in their eternal rest than had they lived to experience some of the trauma of postwar living.

Veterans attending the 30th reunion in 1974 of the D-Day participants often received an exuberant welcome from the citizens of towns in France that they had helped liberate. Ev Hohn reported that the whole town of Chateau Sur Moselle put on a gala reception for his old 772nd Tank Destroyer Battalion. There was wild celebration in the streets despite the fact that "we couldn't convince them that we were not the ones who liberated their town. But it didn't seem to matter. We were American veterans of WWII and that was enough for them." With a sly smile he added, "They gave us more champagne than we could handle."[16]

After the war, there were seamen who made provisions in their wills that their bodies be carried to Hawaii and be buried at sea with their comrades who lost their lives during the December 7th attack. Others, who on business or for pleasure traveled to Hawaii after the war, were unable to bring themselves to visit the memorial, feeling the emotional strain would be overwhelming. Tom Dutch had been in Hawaii twice, both times unable to go to the Memorial. On his third visit, he told himself, "I've just got to do it." His emotions ran high, but tears led to both a painful remembering of his dead comrades and at the same time a certain resignation to anguish that would never truly be assuaged.[17]

It did not take a trip to the battlegrounds of Europe and the South Pacific to trigger painful memories and waves of survivor's guilt. Some years after the war, Alan Suits returned to his small hometown Kirkwood, Missouri and counted on the town's memorial 27 names of friends who had lost their lives in World War II and in the Korean war.[18]

A RETURN VISIT

Years later, Mel Buschman was invited back to northern Italy as a representative of the Armed Forces to take part in an anniversary in remembrance of the liberation of several small villages from German occupation. "Never have I seen a more grateful people," Mel marveled. As the honored guest in many of the tiny villages, Mel was asked to speak at the banquets being held in celebration. At one gathering, following the dinner, Mel was unable to leave the table. Everyone wanted his signature. For an hour and a half Mel signed papers, napkins, books, helmets—anything that could sustain a signature.

Nothing could be more memorable for Mel than a young Italian lad who approached him hesitantly, explaining that he had recently lost his father and his grief was growing more and more unbearable. In a tremulous voice he begged Mel, "Would you be my father?" The answer was an enthusiastic affirmative and for years afterward Mel continued a fatherly correspondence with the young man.

How times had changed, Mel mused, where in one village during the war years a young 14-year-old boy had begged left-over food from the company's kitchen, and now many years later he owned the restaurant, the scene of the celebration banquet.[19]

Fifty years after his service in Europe, Jim Church and his wife retraced some of Jim's steps during the war. It turned out that the older residents in the Vrenen/Tongeren area had certainly not forgotten what had transpired almost half a century earlier. In grateful appreciation of the courage and sacrifices of Jim and the brave Americans who helped free their village, the townspeople joined together to stage a gala celebration replete with a parade, gifts, and a banquet. Memories of the ghastly carnage of those days and the euphoria of success kept flooding back, unwilled and irrepressible, with the words of the town's mayor. "You're being celebrated here today not only because of yourselves, but also because you represent all America and that because of you, we can live in freedom and democracy today."[20]

A MEMORABLE EVENING

The riverboat cruise ship had stopped after dinner one evening on the River Marne and a group of jovial tourists set out to look over the town. In the distance there was the sound of music that grew louder as through the narrow streets appeared a band of young boys playing horns and drums followed by a parade of not so agile, elderly men. The scene was jubilant and the fascinated tourists strolled along behind.

Suddenly the streets were empty, completely devoid of marchers and din. With difficulty the little group of Americans espied the revelers disappearing into what surely must be the town hall. Hospitality reigned, and the curious onlookers were beckoned inside and urged to join in the celebration of what turned out to be a festive commemoration of the World War II liberation of the town. It was a merry evening with both hosts and guests trying eagerly through sign language and fractured French and broken English to converse with each other. The evening simply evaporated until finally it was time to return to the ship. It had been an evening to remember for a lifetime. There were vigorous handshakes and warm hugs as the grateful Americans endeavored to express their appreciation for the evening's gracious hospitality. It was their French hosts, however, who bowed and in tearful remembrance of that glorious day so long ago solemnly insisted, "Oh, no, indeed, it is *we* who thank *you*."[21]

ON THE POSITIVE SIDE

Fritz Bennetts believed his philosophy was relatively unchanged by the war. Since he had been a child he had held to his grandmother's advice to get up each morning asking God "to please help me to help someone today." Before the war, during the war, and for the rest of his life Fritz sought to put that prayer into action on a daily basis. He was also grateful for the training he received in the U.S. Navy, crediting it with preparing him for almost any work he wished to do after the war. He thought his training had taught him obedience, how to follow rules, how to treat people, and how to help them. In addition he learned some important lessons about "never giving up."[22]

Lessons learned? "It took four good years out of my life," Chuck Lindberg reflected. Nevertheless, he added: "The war taught me to be ready to accept anything and to never let things bother me. Also, I've always wanted to be ready to help others, because in combat, we survived by helping one another as best we could."[23]

Never, Fred Wickert explained, would he ever have had the experience and responsibility of working with and directing as many men as his wartime experience provided. After the war as the Air Force began demobilizing, part of his duties involved working with returnees with combat fatigue and evaluating the men for special help in the convalescent hospitals.[24]

Betty Louise Isom (Leiby), who served with the American Red Cross as Program Director of the Red Cross headquarters at Handley Stoke-on-Trent, believed she had not changed much as a result of her war experiences. However, she was proud of what the Red Cross was doing in the war, and she emerged with a greater appreciation of what America was doing to help Europe rebuild after the war. Her experiences conditioned her to do volunteer work where even today, as an octogenarian, she continues to volunteer considerable time to the Radio Talking Book, the Red Cross, and helping new patients at the ophthalmology clinic.[25]

Had Irene Kenneck (Johnson) changed as a result of her service as a dietitian with the U.S. Army during the war? Not appreciably, she admitted. However, it gave her an indelible picture of the strength and courage of the English people. It is often difficult to realize what the British went through: their sacrifices, the terrible devastation of the bombings, their

tremendous losses of men and property. On the positive side, the war gal-
vanized a sense of cooperation and patriotism in America that is not seen
everyday.[26]

A native Mississippian, George Rogers remarked that although "people
talk about the sacrifices that people did for their country, [but] it was no
sacrifice for me at all. It was a tremendous experience for me and a wonderful education." By enrolling in the Army Specialist Training Program,
George Rogers was sent to college first at Vanderbilt, then to North Carolina State, then to the University of Minnesota, and then to Yale. Having
studied and become proficient in the Japanese language, he was sent to
Fort Holabird, Maryland, where he underwent counterintelligence training and was sent to Japan for a year. Following the war he returned to
Yale, graduated, and was awarded a Rhodes scholarship to Oxford. After
he finished his two years at Oxford, he returned to Mississippi, and in
1952, he was elected to the Mississippi House of Representatives. Later he
received his law degree from Old Miss. All in all, his time in the military
provided a wealth of educational and travel experience—his good fortune
perhaps underlying the old saying, "It's an ill wind that blows nobody
good."[27]

In retrospect, Larry Hartman wondered if he had made the right decision in not continuing after the war in the Coast Guard service. The travel
and adventure had proved much more exciting than a job that might prove
routine and boring.[28]

Early on Jim Church was convinced that he would need a good background in math for later life, and whatever free time he had in the service
was spent pouring over the math book that he constantly carried with
him. His commitment paid off in later life when he took advantage of
the GI Bill, finished his education in electrical engineering, and eventually
did important work in helping develop equipment that made possible the
Apollo's flight to the moon.[29]

The "52–20" plan, whereby the government would pay veterans $20 a
week for 52 weeks to help with their readjustment to civilian life, at first
sounded good to Clair Nash. Why not just loaf around for a year and
then go to work? After all the trauma during his time overseas with the
U.S. Infantry, Clair was restless after three weeks of loafing, and when his
friend offered him a job with the local power company, Clair jumped at
the opportunity and happily stayed on to retirement.[30]

Jack Gunther, serving in the Twelfth Anti-aircraft Battalion attached to
the First Marine Division, credited his war experiences with helping him
to appreciate all the good things life had to offer that he had so taken for
granted before the war. The dependence on others gave Jack Gunther a
greater realization of cooperation and the vital need to work together on a
mission—and in later life.[31]

When asked about being members of "the Greatest Generation," Alice Diggins responded, "I guess every generation in its way is a great generation, if we survive and improve life for people."[32]

William Horton believed he really became aware of what closeness meant during his service, and that bonding carried over to his relationship with his family. To this day his family has been a close-knit family, with a family love bond spanning the miles. Asked how he and his family managed to stay so close, he always answered, "Well, they're my family."[33]

Joe Spinosa agreed that life for him and most servicemen was never to be the same after the war. In contrast to William Horton, however, Joe thought the struggle for survival at almost any cost made men selfish and primarily concerned with their own self interests, a perspective that continued to motivate one's future actions.[34]

Allan Rice found his relationships with the Japanese remarkably cordial during his time in Japan with the troops of occupation. When the Japanese found that the Americans were not the demons they were thought to be, they became friendly. Other units, he remembered, however, had great difficulties being nice to the Japanese.[35]

Bill Noonan recalled going home on leave and sitting in a restaurant enjoying a lively conversation with a civilian tablemate. His companion finished his dinner and left, and when Bill signaled for the check, the waiter smiled and replied that it had "already been paid for." His tablemate had picked up his check. It was a kindness not easily forgotten. "I figured I owed that dinner to someone else, somewhere, sometime." Several years later, Bill was able to repay that debt when he picked up the dinner tab for two Korean servicemen.[36]

During the war, Emily Hobbs (Wolf) explained, in small towns such as in her hometown of Amity, Arkansas, people moved out to take jobs in defense plants, to enlist in the services, to follow a husband in the military. After the war, many families sought more gainful employment and more challenge in larger cities. Many never returned. "First honeysuckle and then trees covered the farms where these families had lived before the war. Now crepe myrtle bushes, wisteria vines and pear trees show where they had been."[37]

Joseph Clemens, a corporal with the 254th Engineer Combat Battalion of the U.S. Army, had done patrol duty on the docks in Seattle, Washington before being sent overseas. On a return trip years later after the war, Joe saw the same wharf he had patrolled now being used to unload Japanese automobiles. "Now that's a paradox," he observed.[38]

CHAPTER 19

A Collage of Memories

ANXIOUS MOMENTS

Bailouts from planes were always terrifying ordeals. Would the chute open? Would one be killed by enemy gunfire on the descent? Would the landing be in trees, in bushes, or in plain sight of enemy patrols? Would the landing be in Allied or enemy territory? In November of 1944, while flying a P-38 in a mission over Belgium, Richard Gasser Nelson, found himself too far out over the target to turn back when the mission was aborted because of foul weather. A climb to 9,000 feet failed to keep the wings from icing, and the plane made a nose dive straight for the ground. At 1,000 feet John bailed out and into a blinding snowstorm. Although John landed safely, there were some anxious minutes. Suddenly there was the sound of voices laughing as a truck rolled by. John drew a huge sigh of relief—they were American voices! Within hours he was back at his home base in France.[1]

Colbert Graham, of Hattiesburg, Mississippi, was already counting the minutes until he would have completed his final bombing mission (his 25th) over Germany and be ready for a transfer to the States. His dream was shattered in seconds when the engine of his B-17 caught fire, and he was forced to parachute into German territory where he was immediately taken prisoner. Scared! You better believe it. "Anybody tells you that getting shot at is not scary is either stupid or a liar, one or the other," Graham admitted.[2]

As a Japanese American serving with the 100/422nd regimental combat unit, Tom Takeshi Oye had serious doubts about ever getting out of the Italian campaign alive. Enemy shells burst overhead in the trees and hailstorms of shrapnel showered down on the troops. "That was where I got my baptism by fire. When I dared look up, I could see tree leaves and limbs getting clipped and fall to the ground. We were not in simulated battle anymore. This was the real thing. The trauma of this, which still sticks with me, was to see buddies getting wounded or killed by bullets and shrapnel. Our steel helmets were not totally effective to deflect the enemy gunfire that was coming with such velocity. My weapon at the time was the M-l rifle, and at times I wished I could have doubled its output." In Italy and in action all during the war, "Some of our guys went beyond their own expectations in battle to prove that they were as loyal as any American . . . It was as though *we had to* in order to prove that we meant it. We took a lot of casualties on account of this mind set."[3]

Jim Pyle still gets misty-eyed remembering his time on the battlefields of Italy and the loss of 28 of the 101 men in his group in three assaults of a hill near Rome. The ground water was hip high and shells were bouncing around like popcorn. The ominous instructions had been: "You are all going up, but not all of you will be coming back, so get that bastard before he gets you." It was scary enough waiting to be called up to replace the dead and injured on the front line, but the fear and despair became overwhelming as retreating forces informed Jim that his best buddy had already been killed in the fighting. Through the murky darkness, huge trucks kept tracking down the hill with bodies stacked high and blood oozing over the sides of the trucks. Jim was prepared for what he was sure would be his last moments on earth. Although he had prayed to get "just a little sick," to keep him out of the fighting, the frigid temperatures and icy waters produced not even a noticeable sniffle. Eventually the hill was won, and Jim survived and moved on with his unit to challenge the next German stronghold.[4]

Bob DeVinney and his unit had just arrived in England where they were readying for further training as paratroopers. Suddenly on a training jump there was the thunder of planes overhead, and as they looked up, the skies were filled with gossamer white silk parachutes floating down to earth. Just as suddenly there was the gut-wrenching sight of two men plummeting to earth whose parachutes failed to open. It took only seconds for two of the new trainees to quit on the spot. "There's no way we are going to get involved in this," they announced emphatically.[5]

One can scarcely imagine a worse first mission than that of Howard "Gov" Miller's 15-hour bomb run to Japan on Ground Hog day 1945. All seemed well until about five hours out when Japanese zeros circled in, and suddenly an enemy bullet smashed into a hydraulic line in the plane, spelling near disaster for the crew. "Terror? You bet!" Gov remembered. With fuel gauges dropping, the crew readied parachutes, standing by to jump or "ditch" at sea with the plane, whose float time was about two minutes.

Hours later, however, with luck and skillful maneuvering, they made it safely back to their Tinian base. Not so for eight crews (40%) of their group. One plane had crashed on takeoff—all 11 on board were killed. "Two of our planes had been shot down, two collided over the target—all four crews lost! Three others had mechanical trouble or were hit and reported ditched at sea. Their crews were later rescued. Odds didn't look too great to make thirty-five missions." This was the first of 32 missions for Gov over Japan! Fortunately, the entire crew returned unscathed for 31 more!

"The next morning," he recalled, "there were funerals for the crew lost on the runway crash. It was one of my young life's most somber moments. From my squadron—crew members left who were not killed, missing, or pall bearers—there were few left as mourners—I was ONE! . . . It was a sickening feeling when the crew next to you was shot down and when you had seen them only that morning. It was almost worse when the staff gathered up their belongings to send home to their families."[6]

Kamikaze attacks during the latter part of the war marked a last ditch effort by the Japanese to attempt to turn the tide of war in their favor. The attacks were savage in their devastation of the pilot and the ships and the men they zeroed in on. Dr. Jack Bates, a navy dentist aboard the USS *Callaway*, an attack transport with secondary duties to serve as a hospital ship, drew a gruesome picture of a kamikaze attack on their ship on January 8, 1945, as they were heading toward an invasion of Lingayen Bay. "Have you ever awakened in the morning and wondered what was ahead for the day? Well, aboard our ship were 19 officers and crew who never would have believed they would be dead by lunch time. Another thirty did not know they would never again see their families or enjoy another Christmas. Our ship's family would never be the same," Jack wrote.

It was a weekend, and as Jack was standing at the ship's railing with five other medical officers visiting and enjoying the view from the port side, out of the blue "there was a soft whoosh and the whole sky and ship lit up like the light from a monstrous bonfire."

Jack scrambled to safer quarters and moments later returned to a sight that absolutely sickened him. "It is impossible to describe what I saw, but there, above where we had been standing, was a crumpled-up Jap fighter plane wadded up like a piece of paper resting against our stack and over one of the gun mounts. The pilot was standing upright, rigid and burned to a crisp, in what had been his cockpit a few minutes earlier." Fortunately, the kamikaze's bomb had missed the ship and thus hundreds of lives had been saved.[7] (Generations later were to observe some of the same suicidal fanaticism in the attacks of 9–11 and in Iraq that obsessed the kamikaze pilots during World War II.)

Although generally optimistic about life, Tom Dutch (Group 16, Sixth Fleet) began to have serious doubts about his safe return home when the kamikazes kept raiding their ships in the South Pacific. "You could even see their resolute expression on their faces," Tom remembered and re-enacts the scene in nightmares to this day. The smaller ships circled the larger ships, and in the morning and at dusk ignited diesel fuel geared to create a smoke screen and thus hide the larger vessels. Battleships were a primary target, but any ship, destroyer, carrier, or cruiser was a fit target. The demonic kamikaze pilots swept down out of the skies creating infernos and spreading fear and devastation on hapless ships and their crews. With every strike, Tom Dutch was sure his time was up.[8]

"Just as on land where there are no atheists in foxholes, I didn't find any on board ship when the shells were falling in on us or a Kamikaze was headed our way." Kenneth William Larson's keen observations were founded on his groups' narrow escapes from kamikazes while they were serving on board an attack transport ship in the Pacific during the last 18 months of the war. Particularly in the invasion of Okinawa where 1,500 Allied ships were prime targets for the Japanese suicide planes, Ken and his buddies experienced first hand the stark terror engendered by the dive bombers.[9]

While standing on the bow of an LST during the invasion of Okinawa, Bill Pace and a tough, seasoned buddy narrowly escaped a direct hit by a suicide plane. "Radar didn't detect them at that point and the first thing you'd know, you'd look up and here comes a crazy man in an airplane at you." The near miss nearly brought on heart attacks. The final line to "when the going gets tough, the tough get going" was changed that day to "the tough can get really scared." Bill Pace observed: "But I can tell you one thing, tough guys don't always stay tough during a time like that. I discovered that in life right then. It was about midnight before that fellow, that tough guy, was able to talk, it scared him so damn bad."[10]

On January 9, 1945, Ensign Bill Summers was part of the amphibious forces accompanying MacArthur's landing on Luzon at Lingayen Gulf. As an Ensign helping to unload thousands of gallons of high airplane fuel on the beaches, Bill and his shipmates were plagued by the kamikazes who came "screaming in over the tree tops" in an effort to disrupt the naval delivery service. The work was perilous at best and the "one way" pilots simply added to the precariousness of the venture.[11]

During his service with the Sixth Fleet in the South Pacific, Tom Dutch's nerves were on edge as he and a group of 16 ships—LCI (G) gunboats—

were sent into Leyte Gulf on a scouting mission three days before the actual invasion. No one knew how well or how poorly prepared the Japanese were for an attack and how much enemy gunfire could be expected. Tom (QM 2/c) and his men breathed easier after their ships had "neutralized" the beaches and headed out to join the armada of ships in the distance. As they made their way to the larger ships, their elation over an assignment safely completed was tempered by the sobering sight of the countless boatloads of men at the ready and crowded onto the landing craft going in for the perilous invasion now getting underway in earnest.[12]

It was a close call for Norm Pierce when their landing craft sank as they were beginning their assault on Bougainville. He and several of his buddies dumped their rifles and backpacks and swam ashore only to find themselves in Japanese territory. Having disposed of their guns, it was a treacherous three days of tiptoeing around the shoreline to get back to headquarters. Even a sneeze would have given them away. Just as they were reaching the Allies, the Japs spotted them and began shooting, but fortunately they made it to safety. Needless to say, they relished the furlough they were awarded after Bougainville.[13]

Sent to Nuremberg, Germany, as part of a ground party to check out and maintain the B-29 planes, Charles Wallace Grosse was assigned to fly couriers while awaiting the delivery of the B-29s. The assignment seemed simple enough, until Grosse discovered he was flying with two drunks. On at least one occasion, he had to fly the plane while the other two men drank themselves into oblivion. When it came time to land, Grosse put the plane on automatic pilot while he went back to the rear of the plane and dragged the pilot out to the cockpit. The administering of oxygen sobered the man up enough for him to land, but after that traumatic experience, Grosse had had enough and insisted on being reassigned.[14]

If he didn't have a cat's nine lives, Don Ely was sure he had been given at least five lives. From the moment he reached northern Luxemburg as a combat infantryman replacement, Don lived day to day, thinking everyday would be his last. His first day with his new unit in Luxembourg proved a chilling experience as he looked up to see two trucks maneuvering down the roadway loaded with frozen dead American bodies. Secretly he wondered if this was not an ominous "preview of coming events." Near misses included passing a doorway while fighting on the outskirts of Saarlautern, where one step back would have meant disaster. Friendly fire almost took him out another time as did a barrage of 88-millimeter German artillery on yet another occasion. Fortunately, an 88 was a dud as it crashed through the roof, ceiling, out the front wall, and stopped on the front lawn of the outpost where six of them were stationed. Riding on top of a tank over a pontoon bridge as his unit crossed the Rhine left him a perfect target for German aircraft fire. Small wonder nightmares and war dreams still plague him to this day, but they are less intense as the years pass by.[15]

One didn't have to be fighting in Europe or in the Pacific, there were lots of scary times right here in America. Don Langworthy remembered that during his flight training, "When we had flown 4 1/2 hours of dual (instructional time), he [the flight instructor] taxied to a take off spot where he got out of the airplane and said to me: 'Okay, Langworthy, take the plane around the field, land and touch and go around again and land and taxi back to here. I'll be waiting for you.' So, I did as I was told. Scared to death!" Later during further training, Don admitted: "It was pretty scary when we were to fly the night hops. I'm certain that GOD heard my prayers on those occasions as I was not at all comfortable with that activity, especially night in-the-dark takeoffs and landings and the formation flying that was too close for comfort."[16]

Running out of gas on a flight could result in a disastrous crash or merely a heart stopping moment. One day in 1945 Don Langworthy and three buddies were ordered to fly from their base at Cherry Point, North Carolina to Memphis, where their planes were to be "cocooned" for later use. "There was no 100 octane gas there so we took off without filling our tanks. It was Mississippi River flood time and the area around Newport was all fouled up so we went to an auxiliary field at Walnut Ridge, Arkansas, about fifty miles NE of Newport. All three of us got our planes on the runway there but the engines quit either on the runway or on the taxi strip. Bone dry of gas. Hard to believe then, and harder still to believe it today!"[17]

To say that he was scared was putting it mildly as Dick Guernsey, radioman and gunner on a B-24 bomber, headed out on his third mission over Germany. Would he make it back alive? The casualty lists were getting longer by the day. Was today the day anti-aircraft gunfire would bring down his plane? The adrenaline was surging when from behind his seat Dick felt a tap on his shoulder. "Don't worry, you're coming through ok," a voice sounded in his ear. As he turned around, Dick was astonished to find the space behind him empty. It was one of those "out of body" experiences, but from then on, come what might, Dick knew he would eventually be going home unscathed.

There were a number of near misses for Dick, who flew 51 missions over southern France, Germany, Vienna, and the Ploesti Oil Fields. When enemy gunfire crippled both engines on a bombing mission over Vienna and a crash appeared inevitable, the crew hurriedly tossed out guns, ammunition, everything disposable in order to lighten the load. Desperate for a place to land, the pilot suddenly spotted a British Fighter Airstrip, and despite the British efforts trying to radio them to convince them that the strip was too short for their bomber, they nosed in for a safe, but terrifying emergency landing.

Although Dick Guernsey usually flew lead plane, it was a miracle that during their 51 missions there were no casualties save when one crew member took a minor hit to his ankle. Sometimes, Dick shuddered, the flack was so thick one could almost walk on it. Once after landing safely the crew counted 244 holes in their plane. Among the heart stoppers of their tour of duty was the day when another plane during takeoff crossed in front of them, and it appeared that they would never be able to gain sufficient altitude to miss it. Somehow their pilot succeeded in gaining altitude, but it would be iffy if the plane could miss the power lines. As the plane lifted off, miraculously missing the power lines, hearts resumed beating again, and they headed out on their mission.[18]

News of the death of President Franklin Roosevelt stunned the Allies. He was their mainstay, their chief, their unflagging supporter. Where possible there were minuscule services, brief memorials, small groups of bowed heads. Few servicemen escaped a tug at the heartstrings, a lump in the throat. Dorothy Schroeder, a nurse with the Army Nurse Corp, was one of the few to be able to attended the "invitation only" mass at the Cathedral of Notre Dame in Paris with her chief of nurses. Servicemen were resplendent in uniforms from countries all over the world, flags from all of the nations flew in a kaleidoscope of colors. Thousands of mourners crowded the grounds as the world bowed in sorrow.[19]

As a special agent in military intelligence and later as a team commander in the Counter-Intelligence Corps in the European Theater of Operations, Jon Young had been working very closely with the French resistance, and it was impossible to refuse their demand that he witness the execution of a Nazi collaborator. "But this is Thanksgiving Day in the United States," Jon begged to be relieved of the grisly job. "But this is execution day in France," they insisted. To make matters worse, the young man's father knelt and tried to kiss Jon's shoes as he pleaded for his son's life. The next day a firing squad dispatched the collaborator. "It was indeed the saddest day of my life," and Jon shuddered to think of it.[20]

There were some scary minutes for Leo Stone when his flight instructor fell asleep during an early practice run. Later Leo and his crew were sure they had had it when they lost an engine and failed to gain altitude, but the men held their breath and continued on to the target, dropped their bombs and luckily stopped at Iwo Jima before running out of fuel. Many veterans never worried about going to hell. "We've been there," they agreed. Laurence Gavento braved danger through the war years with the conviction that "If God wants me—I'm ready."[21]

While stationed in London, WAC Dorothy Schieve found herself fortunate to have frequent meetings with her brother, George, a B-17 pilot who made runs across the Channel to Germany from Bedford, England. It was with great anticipation that Dorothy made a trip to Bedford to meet with her brother on March 26, 1944. They were to meet at the Red Cross headquarters in Bedford. It was a long wait, and Dorothy became ever more anxious as the hours passed with no word from George. At long last there was a call, but surely the last one she wanted to receive. George's plane had gone down. Two apprehensive weeks passed before Dorothy learned that her brother had been killed. By this time when a plane was shot down the Germans often took the enlisted men prisoners but often killed the officers. George's plane has gone down in Alsace Lorraine, and his flight group confirmed that George had been hanged by the Germans. Dorothy's parents had enough grief to bear knowing that their son had died when his plane was shot down. The true story of his death tormented Dorothy for the rest of her life, but she never told her parents, knowing that would merely add to their grief.[22]

"Scared??" Jim Pyle responded: "You better believe it. Atheists, infidels, theists, everyone prayed."[23]

STRANGER THAN FICTION

A flip of a coin—albeit a nickel—turned out to be the difference between life and death for Aviation Mech 3rd Edward Krenkel. Ed had joined the Navy in February of 1940 and following early training, Ed had been assigned to the aviation unit of the USS *Arizona* as an Aviation Mechanist Third Class. Less than a year before the Japanese attack, Ed was awaiting reassignment at Pearl Harbor. Both Ed and a buddy wanted to remain with the *Arizona,* but only one Aviation Mechanist Third Class was needed, the other to be assigned duty at the Naval Air Station at Pearl. How to solve the dilemma? Why a flip of a coin, of course. Ed remembered very clearly.

"It was the flip of a nickel. There were two of us, Aviation Mechanist Third Class, and I lost the flip. The guy that won is still aboard the *Arizona.* He's one of the eleven hundred and fifty some sailors who are still aboard."[24]

After extensive training for the crucial raid on the Ploesti oil complex in Rumania, Tom McGrain and his 376th bomb group left their Benghazi base in Libya on August 1, 1943, and headed out on their mission. (The Astra Romana oil refinery was thought to provide almost half of the Axis supply.) Although navigator Tom McGrain and his men were not on the lead plane, they were in the lead group and were, after all their training, appalled to see the navigator of the lead plane make a critical wrong turn.

Everyone knew it was a huge mistake, but radio silence prevented any notation of the error. Then followed a circuitous circling down to Bucharest and back up again in time to make the bombing run to help ignite the infamous inferno. (A total of five bomb groups—178 B-24 bombers—participated in the raids, some from Libya, some from England and other bases. Fortunately Tom and his planes were not among the 41 planes downed or the 13 lost in the raids.) To think a simple navigational error had almost botched the plan—an error that clearly caused the commandant considerable embarrassment![25]

As the war was ending, Fritz Bennetts and the men on his ship stood by in amazement when their captain and the captain of a nearby ship got into an argument that resulted in fisticuffs. Right before their eyes their staid, respected captain was dukeing it out with another commander. Instantly bystanders leaped up to try to pull them apart; however, wiser minds prevailed urging them to leave the two alone to settle their differences. "Hands off!" they counseled. "Let them get it out of their systems." Clearly the two captains had been through hell in recent weeks and needed to give vent to their anger and frustrations. Soon, tempers had cooled and two somewhat embarrassed, although still defiant officers, resumed command of their ships.[26]

At the airbase near Clovis, New Mexico, Romayne Hicks told of a series of mysterious B-24 crashes supposedly involving mechanical problems. Further investigation indicated that there was a saboteur on the base who was sabotaging the planes by putting sugar in the gas tanks. In short order a clever commandant closed down the base and later issued a false report that the problem had been remedied and the flights would resume. That night two sniper squads were placed in strategic positions and sure enough in the dark of night out came the saboteur toting a bag of sugar ready for his deviltry. In an instant the floodlights illuminated the field, and the culprit was dispatched on the spot. True to military tradition, the details of the incident were kept under wraps. Rumor ran rampant, however. Was he a spy? An enemy agent? A disgruntled airman who was being washed out? A deranged GI who had somehow fallen through the cracks? With all the precautions about "Loose lips," the censorship of mail, and the elaborate cryptography, it was unnerving for the flight crews to think of a demented saboteur in their midst.[27]

Alan Suits, an electronic technician, was stunned to learn of a group of thugs aboard his ship, the *Vogelgesong,* as it plied the Atlantic Coast and the Caribbean who often took off when the ship was in port to assault and rob innocent civilians. Afterward they had the audacity to brag about it to their crewmates! And were they not fighting to promote world peace? What a black eye for Americans![28]

World War II saw tremendous advances in manufacturing, health care, and food preservation to mention a few. Even horticulture came in for some innovative research. It was apparently the belief of the Army Air Force Command that the Pacific Theater of Occupation would require conquering each enemy stronghold one by one, which meant a lengthy process of years instead of months. The U.S. Army Air Force was hard put to provide fresh vegetables for servicemen in the South Pacific where traditional farming was impossible on the rocky, volcanic islands and atolls. The need for fresh produce was critical for nutrition, and adding at least a "little greenery" to the dehydrated "meals" rendered them considerably more healthful and appealing. Hydroponics, the growing of plants in chemically treated water without soil, provided the solution, and in early 1945, the U.S. Air Force was the first to employ hydroponics.

It was not easy for the Air Force to find just the right niche for Milton Baron, already in possession of a Master's Degree in Landscape Architecture from Harvard. However, an observing officer scrutinizing Milton's qualifications noted his diploma in Horticulture from Massachussetts Agricultural College, and Milt was assigned to acquire current information from experiments being conducted at a foremost center of hydroponics research, the University of California. (Scientists had been seeking application of this type of agriculture for years, but the war's needs gave the work considerable impetus.) For Milton it was stimulating and satisfying to be made part of a team specially trained to be capable of producing diet supplements for combat flying soldiers of the Air Force that probably would hasten the war's end. (The later commercial success of hydroponics is well known in every supermarket in the country. During the occupation of Japan, hydroponic culture was particularly important as the Japanese habitually fertilized their produce with "night soil," a process that eventuated in extensive health problems for the American troops of occupation.)[29]

Treatment of POWs has come in for some careful examination these days. Bill Worgul's marriage to a German girl and the ramifications of his extended German family led to a friendship with Hans Siegner, a German who had been sent to a POW camp in Wyoming in 1943. In contrast with the experiences of many Americans incarcerated in German POW Camps, Hans insisted that his time in the Wyoming POW camp "had been some of the happiest days of his life." He recalled one experience when a captain had come through his barracks on a routine inspection tour, and Hans had mentioned his fondness for apple pie. Several days later Hans returned to his bunk to find a suspicious lump under his pillow. As he peeled back the covers, there was a delectable apple pie that the captain's wife had made for him. It was an extremely emotional moment for a young serviceman thousands of miles away from home and family. So touched by the woman's kindness, Hans was unable to hold back the tears and simply put his head down in his arms and wept uncontrollably.[30]

For Paul and Dorrie Souder, natives of Indiana, the year at Harvard (where Paul as an Ensign had been sent for additional study in the Harvard Business School) had been a pleasant one. Dorrie had secured a job at the Widener Library, while Paul pored over Keynesian theory and Dow Jones charts. Graduation, in the summer of 1943, was a scene of revelry and jubilation. The men were resplendent in their white uniforms, marching about on a parade ground awash in bright sunshine, and in the stands proud wives and sisters, all done out in their best wartime finery, sat smiling and chatting. Amidst all the cheering and levity, Dorrie's attention was riveted on one disconsolate woman who stood sobbing and in heartrending gasps of weeping kept murmuring, "I'll never see him again. I know I'll never see him again." Although friends immediately rushed to comfort her, no amount of consolation could assuage the woman's grief. The painful memory of the poor woman's anguish that day would continue to haunt her friends for a lifetime. Actually, at the time, friends were convinced it was the emotion of the day that evoked such gloomy premonitions, and for the moment they put aside her morose foretelling. Many months later, however, in a chance encounter in Washington, the Souders were hailed on the street by a fellow classmate. During their exchange of the news of their Harvard comrades, the Souders were heartsick to discover that the woman had indeed been prescient. During his tour of duty in the Pacific in the midst of a typhoon, the Harvard classmate had watched in anguish as the ship to which the woman's husband had been assigned floated by— bottom up—all hands lost.[31]

Tom Culpepper, a native Mississippian, noted that during his early days in the Navy, the men in his unit observed that there were always two buddies with one questionably literate recruit. Whenever the guy in question had to sign papers, his two friends invariably accompanied him. There was always a signature, but no one knew "how in heck they brought it off."[32]

On leave one time in England, Al Jones and his friend found time for a game of golf at the nearby Eaton Country Club. It came as a surprise that the course consisted of only 14 holes so that the additional land could be devoted to raising crops for the undernourished English people. The Red Cross had provided some golf clubs for their use, and somehow Al had managed to keep with him five new golf balls from home. When they finished their round, Al was afraid for a moment that the golf pro at the club was going to kiss him when Al gave gifted him with the precious white treasures. The pro had not seen a new golf ball in five years![33]

When Al Wolf and his unit were transferred from the Houghton School of Mining and sent to Chicago, they decided on their first free Sunday to check out "The Loop," Chicago's downtown. "We were told it was an easy walk down a particular street to the station. [Probably the "elevated"— Chicago's rapid transit system.] After several blocks we became uncertain that we were going in the right direction. There was no traffic on the street except for one man walking toward us. We asked him if we were headed in the right direction. He assured us that we only had a few more blocks to go. He was right. It was only after the war that we discovered that the man was no one less than Enrico Fermi. It was also a surprise to learn that the atom bomb was being developed in the stadium opposite our office on the University campus."[34]

At Keesler Field in 1943, Captain Fred Wickert encountered one young GI who was determined not to be sent overseas. Hoping that an entire mouthful of extremely bad teeth would prevent him from being sent out of the States, he continually and adamantly refused to keep appointments to go to the camp dentist. Finally, rather than see their friend court-martialed, four buddies grabbed him up and plunked him in the dentist's chair at which time the dentist filled 30 teeth at one sitting! After a brief recuperation, the dentist's masterpiece was sent overseas.[35]

Young men brought up on farms often differed in their perspectives about military life. "I joined the army because I didn't want to pick cotton for the rest of my life," Johnie Courtney admitted. "Everyday in the army was like Sunday on the farm," he laughed. Po Weatherford and other southerners thought the army was a breeze compared to chopping and picking cotton.[36]

Believe it or not, two farm boys from West Virginia complained bitterly and incessantly that the army was letting them sleep too long. On the farm they were accustomed to rise with the chickens and were out in the fields long before roll call at the base. In time, the army finally lost patience and conceded that apparently they would serve more effectively on the West Virginia farms than on a battlefield, and they were released from duty and sent home![37]

Now and then, as Skipper Vince Schumacher and his USS *Tigrone* submarine crew roamed the Pacific, they were rewarded not only in keeping the Japanese at bay and in dodging bullets and torpedoes, but also by being able to come to the aid of at least 30 downed aviators. On one occasion, Vince intercepted a radio call from a pilot who was in trouble and was bailing out. As Vince steered his sub under the white silk of the parachute, he expertly timed it so a burly crew member could grab the pilot and pull him to safety aboard ship. The happy pilot exclaimed that not even his shirt got wet![38]

Some of the most terrifying experiences for any bomber crew were when a bomb got hung up in the bomb bay. Bombardier Al Jones remembered

tip-toeing across the catwalk of his plane for five minutes without a parachute, the plane 20,000 miles above the ground and the temperature 60
degrees below zero, to pry loose a bomb that was caught in the bomb
bay.[39]

The normal dangers of flying over the Himalayas [flying the Hump] were
compounded by what John Kast, a radioman trained in navigation and
special radar equipment on a C-109, called the "worst weather in the
world." A veteran of 90 missions hauling gasoline from Jorhat, India to
Kumming, China, John recalled losing more men to volatile weather conditions than to the Japanese. As the war was ending, John declined the
offer of his pilot to head out to Bombay for a leisurely visit of partying
and sightseeing. For some reason, rational or otherwise, John decided that
he would go another time. It had been the wisest decision of his life, for
he soon learned that the ill-fated plane had met with disaster. Although
piloted by an experienced airman, the plane had hit a mountain, and all
aboard were killed. Blind luck? An inner voice? God's hand?[40]

One of Clair Nash's most sobering memories of the war was the day when
two of his buddies were tossing grenades in a river in anticipation of a
bounty of fresh fish. The grenades were German and different from U.S.
grenades, and to everyone's horror both grenades exploded prematurely
killing one friend and severely wounding the other comrade. The ultimate tragedy was the fact that this was the last day of the war—a day
that should have been one of the happiest days, not one of the most tragic
days.[41]

GIs in the Pacific theater marveled at Tokyo Rose's fund of knowledge
about their activities. On Christmas eve of 1944, John Kast and his C-109
crew were called upon for a top secret mission to northern China. A Navy
commander was assigned to their plane, and they carefully loaded on a
long cylindrical object. They flew the Hump in the dead of night, landed,
and unloaded their secret cargo as guards immediately rushed them back
into their plane and they headed home. To their surprise in short order
Tokyo Rose announced the names and rank of each of the crewmen on
the mission. Where could she have obtained the information so quickly?
As it was, John and his men never knew what mysterious object they had
delivered in such secrecy, and for a change apparently it was one item that
escaped Tokyo Rose's information source.[42]

Immediately following the war, Dudley Rishell, a Wichita, Kansas native,
was part of a group of 21st Infantry 24th Division men assigned to take in
supplies and set up barracks for the next units to come in to occupy Japan.
He was in a state of disbelief by the devastation at Nagasaki. "Twelve inch
vertical I beams looked like match sticks," he remembered. "All that was

left of the city looked like toothpicks stuck in the ground that someone had struck a match to."[43]

After the war, it came as a shock to Don VanGorder to be assigned to ferry planes to a graveyard for no longer needed planes in Walnut Ridge in Arkansas. There, thousands of planes that had once been so vital to the war sat awaiting their demise. One B-32, sister to the B-29s, Don noted, had been flown for 36 hours and now was relegated to the junkyard. The same astonishment overcame Russ Hilding when in November of 1945 he flew a B-17 to Kingman, Arizona, where his plane joined acres of other planes to be stripped of engines, instruments, radios, propellers, and anything of value, and then lined up to be scrapped and sold for salvage. He, as did Don, noted that some of the planes were brand new. The planes were still filled with gasoline, and Russ remembered that at least one enterprising man bought up planes simply to get the fuel.[44]

Eugene Patterson was profoundly affected by an accidental meeting with two German officers in Gera Bronn that resulted in the death of one of the officers from a bullet from Eugene's M-1 rifle. It was a matter of "kill or be killed" when the German officers somersaulted from their motorcycle in front of Gene's column of light armored vehicles and refused to raise their hands when ordered to surrender. Gene had no choice but to shoot. (The one German officer escaped around the corner of a building, but the other man took a direct hit.) "I felt sick. In one accidental instant that neither of us had wanted, my .30-caliber bullet had torn life from that still being. I was the squeamish Georgia farm kid who'd never like to shoot quail or rabbits and who'd insisted my older brother be the one to wring the chicken's neck for Sunday dinner. Now here, much nearer than the cannon's reach, lay a man dead at my feet. I wished I had missed him."

In 1989, Gene returned to the exact location of the unfortunate shooting in Gera Bronn. How he wished his shot had missed!

Luck left long avenues of life ahead for me. I have walked them with the memories of those two men present in my heart, and with two certainties about war lodged firmly in my mind.

First, there is my certainty that war is the ultimate obscenity. I came away from the terror convinced that it is the antithesis of civilization for human beings to organize the killing of one another when, unlike animals, they aren't even hungry. Civilized ways simply must be found to settle man's post-jungle conflicts.

Second, I am certain that pending the discovery of these civilized ways to deter violence, decency requires peaceful people to stand up and stop human predators from savaging the helpless when conscience is called to meet brute force with just strength. Shrinking from that duty has ill-served peace, I think.

I see a sadness in this paradox, but not a contradiction; just a logical duty to act as conscience compels until intelligence can elevate the animalism that coarsened the history of my century.[45]

Chuck Larrowe, a survivor of the Battle of Okinawa, summed up the war well in saying, "I don't see how anybody who was involved with World War II, even building tanks or being on the home front could go through anything that would even begin to compare with World War II in importance!"[46]

Epilogue

Attempting to summarize memories of people who lived through the fateful years of World War II would constitute an exercise in futility. A few men echoed General Sherman's oft-repeated, "War is Hell," and a good number confessed, "I wouldn't take a million dollars for the experience, but neither would I be willing to go through it again for a million dollars."

World War II memories, for some, make up vital, vibrant remembrances of a tremendously important segment of their lives. For others the memories are repressed, never ever to be unlocked or examined. Hundreds of veterans still continue to battle memories that torture their minds by day and murder their sleep at night. Some are still fighting the guilt of survival, post traumatic syndrome, or the battle with alcohol. Millions remember being dipped in "instant age."

The preceding pages of battlefield and home front remembrances surely clue the reader to the fact that each person's experiences were unique— moments that would leave an indelible stamp on each individual for as long as life itself.

For the reader, some experiences may stir up old memories; some incidents may trigger a camaraderie of long ago; some may unveil new insights or new perceptions about the war itself. For everyone, however, the experiences reveal the world at its worst—the world at war.

Abbreviations

ECAS: The Eisenhower Center for American Studies at the University of New Orleans.

HMM: Historic Middletown Museum, Middletown, Kentucky.

MCL: The Special Collections and Archives at the McCain Library & Archives of the University of Southern Mississippi.

MWHC: Michigan Women's Historical Center, Lansing, Michigan.

PML: The Nelson Poynter Memorial Library at the University of South Florida, St. Petersburg, in the Special Collections Department.

S AND R: "Survival and Re-entry" by Allan Taylor. *WW II Experiences of Vets Who Survived Combat Conditions and Returned to Civilian Careers.* Bloomington, MN: Brewster Publishing House, n.d.

WHPNM: Women's History Project of Northern Michigan.

WOSL: The Women' Overseas Service League papers at Michigan State University Library, East Lansing Michigan, and at Louisville, Kentucky.

Notes

CHAPTER 1

1. A lady from Lake Wales, Florida related this experience, but asked that her name not be revealed.

2. Mary Sharp, letter, December 8, 1942; interview, Lansing, MI, September 29, 1997.

3. Mahlon (Mike) Sharp, MD, interview and diary, Lansing, MI, September 29, 1997.

4. Ivan Wright.

5. Ivan Wright.

6. Charles Glasco, letter, November 8, 2000.

7. Paul Gillesse, interview, April 2, 2006.

8. Edward Krenkel, telephone interview, April 25, 2006.

9. Donald Hines and Marshall Hines, interview, November 29, 2005.

10. Jon Young, telephone interview, April 21, 2004.

11. Emily Hobbs Wolf, letter, January 16. 2002.

12. Pat Rittenhour Anderson, interview, January 16, 2002.

13. Rachel Brunner McComb; interview, January 30, 2006.

14. Kathleen Allen, telephone interview, December 8, 2005.

15. John Irvin Nichols, interviews, Sanibel, FL, February 19, 1998.

16. David D. Anderson, frequent interviews, 2000–2007.

17. Robert Flores, telephone interviews.

18. William M. Pace, MCL.

19. Kenneth MacDonald, telephone interview, December 8, 2005.

20. Don Kona, telephone interview, January 9, 2006.

21. Bern Engel, interview, July 1, 1998.

22. Charles Grosse, HMM.

23. Donald Langworthy, telephone interviews and letters, August 22, 2007.

24. Frank Forsyth, MCL.

25. Conrad Taschner, telephone interview, January 9, 2006.

26. David Ruff, interview, August 29, 1997.

27. Hall Tennis, personal memories, DVD.

28. Thomas A. Dutch, telephone interview, April 28, 2004.

29. Don MacKenzie, telephone interview, December 9, 2005.

30. Levin Culpepper, interviews, Meridian, MS, August 14, 1997.

31. Jon Young, telephone interview, April 21, 2004.

32. Legrand, K. Johnson, ECAS.

33. Lloyd G. Wilson, interviews, July 11, 2005, and September 12, 2006.

34. Bob Hutchins, telephone interview, December 8, 2004.

35. Rollin Dart, telephone interview, Spring 2004.

36. Frederic R. Wickert, telephone interviews, August 26, 2005 and October 7, 2005.

37. Kenneth Springer, telephone interviews, April 20, 2004.

38. Melvin Bushman, telephone interview, April 20, 2004; Bill Worgul, telephone interview, June 10, 2004.

39. Daniel Suits, telephone interview, March 29, 2006. The CPS program had some 12,000 men working at 151 camps throughout the country. For more information about Conscientious Objectors in Civilian Public Service, see Heather T. Frazer and John O'Sullivan, *We Have Just Begun To Not Fight: An Oral History of Conscientious Objectors in Civilian Public Service During World War II* (New York: Twayne Publishers, 1996).

40. Dorrie Souder, interviews, February 13, 1998.

41. Iwao Ishino, interview and letters, September 12, 2005.

42. Hall Tennis, personal memories, DVD.

43. Tom Oye, S AND R, 241.

44. Yoshio "Bill" Abe, S AND R, 1–6.

45. Excellent information on the heroic activities of Japanese Americans can be found in Lyn Crost, *Honor By Fire: Japanese Americans at War in Europe and the Pacific* (Novato, CA: Presidio Press, 1944.)

46. Yoshio "Bill" Abe, S AND R, 6.

CHAPTER 2

1. Spencer C. Tucker, ed., *The Encyclopedia of World War II: A Political, Social, and Military History* (Santa Barbara, CA: ACC CLIO, 2005).

2. Eleanor Robinson, MWHC.

3. Marian Cyberski, MWHC.

4. Alice Haber, MWHC.

5. Eleanor Smith, MWHC and interviews.

6. Harriet Wever, MWHC.

7. Adelaide Gould, MWHC.

8. Betty Drake, telephone interview, Hattiesburg, MS, May 31, 2004.

9. Dorothy Schieve, telephone interview, May 10, 2004.

10. Christine VanderZalm Kittleson, telephone interview, November 21, 2005.

11. Betty Drake, telephone interview, Hattiesburg, MS, May 31, 2004.

12. Alice Haber, MWHC.

13. Essie Woods, MWHC.

14. Hazel Percival, WOSL (MSU) and *Time*, xlv, No. 15 (April 9, 1945): 26.

15. Kathryn Guthrie Wetherby, HMM.

16. Gloria Bouterese, telephone interview, April 2, 2007.

17. Marilyn Overman, interview, January 30, 1989.

18. Edna Penny Rice, WOSL (MSU).

19. Ruth Riordan, MWHC and interview, April 28, 2002.

20. Eleanor Robinson, MWHC.

21. Alma Mattison, telephone interview, August 26, 2005.

22. Alice Haber, MWHC.

23. Harriet Wever, MWHC.

24. Lenore Woychik Moe, telephone interview, December 12, 2005, and WOSL (MSU).

25. Frances Steen Suddeth Josephson.

26. Stella Staley, MWHC.

27. Betty Drake, telephone interview, Hattiesburg, MS, May 31, 2004.

28. Alice Haber, MWHC.

29. Elizabeth Anesi, MWHC.

30. Eleanor Smith, MWHC and interviews.

31. Dorothy Schieve, telephone interview, May 10, 2004.

32. Elizabeth McIntee, WOSL, Louisville, KY.

33. Barbara Brown, MWHC.

34. Prudence Burrell, MWHC.

35. Ruth Riordan, MWHC interview and letter.

36. Ruth Johnson, S AND R.

37. Irene Kenneck Johnson, telephone interview, August 11, 2004.

38. Wanda Kearns, telephone interview, June 9, 2005.

39. Marion Schoor Brown, telephone interview, July 23, 2005.

40. Shirley Martin Schaible, telephone interview, and letters, August 27, 2005, and March 9, 2006.

41. Sally Swiss, interview, January 16, 2002.

42. Mary Hoagland Gruen, letters and diaries, February 4, 2002.

43. Margaret Oaks, WOSL (MSU).

44. Dorothy Wilkie, MWHC.

45. Marian Mosher, WOSL (MSU).

46. Catherine Cross, S AND R, 71–80.

47. Catherine Cross, S AND R, 71–80.

48. Helene Gram Forster, WOSL (MSU).

49. Dorothy Drolett Doyle, MWHC.

50. Kathryn Wetherby Guthrie, HMM.

51. Marjorie Varner, WOSL (MSU).

52. Winifred Gansel, WOSL (MSU).

53. Dorothy Wilkie, MWHC.

54. Winifred Gansel, WOSL (MSU).

55. Martha Marshall Baker, WOSL (MSU).

56. Martha Marshall Baker, WOSL (MSU).

57. Catherine Cross, S AND R, 71–80.

58. Betty Drake, telephone interview, Hattiesburg, MS, May 31, 2004.

59. Shirley Schaible, telephone interview and letters, August 27, 2005, and March 9, 2006.

60. Elizabeth Anesi, MWHC.

61. Ruth Riordan, MWHC, interview, April 28, 2002.

62. Barbara Brown, MWHC.

63. Essie Woods, MWHC.

64. Helen Minor, MWHC.

65. Elizabeth Brown, WOSL (MSU).

66. Lillian Kivela, WOSL (MSU).

67. Virginia Rogers.

68. Dorothy Doyle, MWHC and interview.

69. Helen Minor, MWHC.

70. Helen Minor, MWHC.

71. Eleanor Robinson, MWHC.

72. Elizabeth Anesi, MWHC.

73. Helene Gram Forster, WOSL (MSU).

74. Gertrude Gay (Neff) Louisville Kentucky, WOSL (Louisville, KY).

75. Anita Dean, interview, April 22, 2004.

76. Dorothy Doyle, MWHC.

CHAPTER 3

1. Bruce Helmer, telephone interview, June 7, 2004.

2. Al Alvarez, ECAS.

3. William Burke, ECAS.

4. John MacPhee, ECAS.

5. Roland Johnson, ECAS.

6. Harold Cunningham, interview, February 10, 2002.

7. Eugene E. Eckstam, MD, ECAS.

8. Eugene E. Eckstam, MD, ECAS.

9. Eugene E. Eckstam, MD, ECAS.

10. Kenneth Almy, ECAS.

11. Andrew Hertz, ECAS.

12. Po Weatherford, interview, Niceville, FL, February 10, 1998.

13. Edward Boccafogli, ECAS.

14. Paul Bouchereau, ECAS.

15. Edward Boccafogli, ECAS.

16. Anthony Drexel Duke, ECAS.

17. Paul Bouchereau, ECAS.

18. Edward Boccafogli, ECAS.

19. Legrand K. Johnson, ECAS.

20. Bill Lodge, ECAS.

21. George Loomis, interview, November 17, 2004.

22. Richard Crum, telephone interview, January 3, 2006, and letter.

23. Victor Fast, ECAS.

24. Louie Ryder, telephone interview, April 9, 2007.

25. John Kirkley, PML.

26. John Robert Lewis, Jr., ECAS.

27. Harley Reynolds, PML.

28. Ray Aeibischer, ECAS.

29. Wallace Gibbs, Jr., ECAS.

30. Felix P. Branham, ECAS.

31. Dick Conley, ECAS.

32. Andrew Hertz, ECAS.

33. William Burke, ECAS.

34. Bill Pace, MCL.

35. Frank Feeley, interview, October 14, 2004.

36. Harold Cunningham, interview, February 10, 2002.

37. Kenneth T. Delaney, ECAS.

38. Anthony Drexel Duke, ECAS.

39. Carl Evans, ECAS.

40. John MacPhee, ECAS.

41. Robert Hall, PML.

42. Paul L. Curry, HMM.

43. B. Ralph Eastridge, ECAS.

44. B. Ralph Eastridge, ECAS.

45. B. Ralph Eastridge, ECAS.

46. Edward Boccafogli, ECAS.

47. Paul Bouchereau, ECAS.

48. Harold Cunningham, interview, February 10, 1992.

49. Harold Cunningham, interview, February 10, 1992.

50. Ted Thomas, tape, interviews, and DVD, "East Lansing WWII: Stories From the Front," created by the East Lansing Historical Society by Cheeney Media Concepts2. Produced/Directed by Ed Cheeney and Kevin Epling, 2006.

51. Reid Gilland, telephone interview, February 23, 2005.

52. Houston "Rip" Bounds, MCL.

53. B. Ralph Eastridge, ECAS.

54. Felix Branham, ECAS.
55. Felix Branham, ECAS.
56. Dick Conley, ECAS.

CHAPTER 4

1. Dick Elasky, S AND R, 99–104.
2. Don Strand, S AND R, 329–334.
3. C. Andrew Ryan, HMM.
4. Don Strand, S AND R, 332.
5. Don Strand, S AND R, 333.
6. Frederic R. Wickert, telephone interviews, August 26, 2005 and October 7, 2005.
7. Paul Niland, interview, March 28, 1999.
8. Joe Spinosa, HMM.
9. John R. Walker, "Memories of World War II," passim.
10. John R. Walker, "Memories of World War II," passim.
11. Wayne Lesher, interview, June 21, 2007, and personal memories, DVD.
12. Jon Young, telephone interview, April 21, 2004.
13. Lloyd Wilson, telephone interviews and correspondence, July 11, 2005 and September 12, 2006.
14. Ray Young, interview, May 5, 2004.
15. James Cecil Church, S AND R, 45.
16. Lloyd Wilson, telephone interview and correspondence, July 11, 2005 and September 12, 2006.
17. Louie Ryder, telephone interview, April 9, 2007.
18. Everett William Hohn, S AND R, 139.
19. Walt Szpara, interview, July 4, 2005.
20. Ray Young, interview, May 5, 2004.
21. Joe Spinosa, HMM.
22. Leroy Schroeder, telephone interview, August 8, 2006.
23. Gertrude Neff Gay, WOSL (Louisville, KY).
24. Richard Crum, telephone interview, January 3, 2006.
25. Woodrow Respects Nothing, S AND R, passim.
26. Albert Fine, personal memories, tape.
27. Leonard Zimmerman, telephone interview, November 22, 2005.
28. Bill Worgul, telephone interview, June 10, 2004.
29. Everett William Hohn, S AND R, 140.
30. William Wallace Henniger, S AND R, 149.
31. Kossie Atkins, telephone interview, August 6, 2005, and correspondence.
32. Lloyd Wilson, interview and correspondence, July 11, 2005 and September 12, 2006.
33. Delbert Kuehl, S AND R, 169.

34. Delbert Kuehl, S AND R, 163–74.
35. Jim Church, S AND R, 45.
36. Woodrow Respects Nothing, S AND R, 277.

CHAPTER 5

1. Helen and Larry Deason, letter, May 28, 1944, and diary.
2. Robert Hutchins, telephone interview, December 8, 2004.
3. Richard Sorenson, S AND R, 321–28.
4. Stanley Nelson, S AND R, 232.
5. Richard Newcomb, *Iwo Jima* (New York: Holt, Rinehart, and Winston, 1965), 296; and Richard B. Stoley, ed., *Life World War 2: History's Greatest Conflict in Pictures* (Boston: Bulfinch Press, 2001), 312. Some of the *Iwo Jima* material is corroborated in Karl Ann Marling and John Wetenhall, *Iwo Jima: Monuments, Memories, and the American Hero* (Cambridge: Harvard University Press, 1991); Richard Newcomb, *Iwo Jima* (New York: Holt Rinehart and Winston, 1965); and Jeter A. Isley and Philip A. Crowl, *The Marines and Amphibious War: Its Theory and Its Practice in the Pacific* (Princeton, NJ: Princeton University Press, 1951).
6. Charles Willard Lindberg, S AND R, 189–96.
7. Charles Willard Lindberg, S AND R, 189–96.
8. Hall Tennis, personal memories, DVD.
9. Conrad Taschner, interview, January, 6, 2006.
10. Rollie Dart, interview and speech, Spring 2000.
11. Charles Willard Lindberg, S AND R, 189–96.
12. George Dike, interview, September 26, 2006.
13. Hall Tennis, personal memories, DVD.
14. Ray William "Buck" Wells, MCL.
15. Donald R. Rudolph, Sr., S AND R, 285–90.
16. Clarence Joseph Stubbs, S AND R, 337.
17. Richard Newton, Scott, S AND R, 291–98.
18. Richard Newton Scott, S AND R, passim.
19. George Feifer, *Tennozan: The Battle off Okinawa and the Atom Bomb* (New York: Ticknor & Fields, 1992).
20. For more detailed information see Feifer, *Tennozan*, xvii. Also see Reader's Digest Association, *Reader's Digest Illustrated Story of World War II* (Pleasantville, NY: Reader's Digest Association, Inc., 1969), 488–95; Stoley, ed., *Life World War 2*, 319; and John S. D. Eisenhower, "The Invasion That Never Was," in *Life World War 2*, ed. Stoley, 306.
21. Chuck Larrowe, interviews and letter.
22. Robert Flores, telephone interviews, Spring 2000.
23. Robert Flores, telephone interviews, Spring 2000.
24. David Ruff, interview, August 29, 1997.
25. Walter P. Maner, interview, February 3, 2002.

CHAPTER 6

1. Jerry Mitchell, interview, August 15, 2002.

2. Richard Thelen, speeches. Excellent sources for more information on the *Indianapolis* disaster include Jerry Mitchell; Richard Thelen; and Doug Stanton, *In Harm's Way: The Sinking of the USS Indianapolis and the Extraordinary Story of Its Survivors* (New York: Henry Holt and Company, 2001); L. Peter Wren, *We Were There: The USS Indianapolis Tragedy* (Richmond, VA: Wren Enterprizes, 2002); L. Peter Wren, *Those in Peril On The Sea: USS Bassett Rescues 152 Survivors of the USS Indianapolis* (Richmond, VA: Wren Enterprises, 1999); Raymond B. Lech, *All the Drowned Sailors* (New York: Stein and Day, 1982); USS Indianapolis Survivors, *Only 317 Survived!* (Indianapolis, IN: Printing Partners, 2002); and Lyle "Duke" Pasket, in *Survival and Re-entry*, ed. Allan Taylor (Bloomington, MN: The Brewster/Alden Publishing House, n.d.).

3. Bob Gause in *Only 317 Survived!*, 165.

4. Bob Gause in *Only 317 Survived!*, 165.

5. L. Peter Wren, telephone interview, March 2, 2005.

6. Wren, *Those in Peril On The Sea*, 87. The story is corroborated by several seamen who heard it all.

7. Richard Thelen, speeches.

8. L. Peter Wren, telephone interview, March 3, 2005.

9. Jerry Mitchell, interview, August 15, 2002.

10. Wren, *Those in Peril On The Sea*, 87.

11. Jerry Mitchell, interview, August 15, 2002.

12. Lyle "Duke" Pasket in Taylor, S AND R, 250.

13. Stan Wisniewski in *Only 317 Survived!*, 490.

14. L. Peter Wren, telephone interview, March 3, 2005.

15. Robert Rubert, Frankenmuth (Michigan)Veterans Oral History Project, 244.

16. L. Peter Wren, *We Were There*, Epilogue.

17. Wren, *Those In Peril On The Sea*, 91.

18. Jerry Mitchell, interview, August 15, 2002.

19. Thomas G. Goff in *Only 317 Survived!*, 180.

20. Richard Thelen, speeches.

21. Cozell Smith in *Only 317 Survived!*, 452.

22. Bonnie Campbell in *Only 317 Survived!*, 83.

23. Herbert J. Miner in *Only 317 Survived!*, 328.

24. Richard Thelen, speeches.

25. Dan van der Vat, *The Pacific Campaign* (New York: Touchstone, 1991), 392.

26. Gus Kay in *Only 317 Survived!*, 242.

27. Harry George, telephone interview, March 14, 2005.

28. Hall Tennis, personal memories, DVD.

29. Robert Rubert, Frankenmuth (Michigan)Veterans Oral History Project, 244.

30. C. Raymond Calhoun, *Typhoon: The Other Enemy: The Third Fleet and the Pacific Storm of December 1944* (Annapolis, MD: Naval Institute Press, 1981), 119.

31. Calhoun, *Typhoon*, 90.

32. Joseph C. McCrane in Calhoun, *Typhoon*, 77–78.

33. A. S. Krauchunas in Calhoun, *Typhoon*, 79–80.

34. For a more detailed description of the sinkings, see Calhoun, *Typhoon*, Ch. 8.

35. Calhoun, *Typhoon*, 109–18. For more detail of the rescues see Chapter 11; an extensive analysis can be found in Hans Christian Adamson and George Francis Kosco, *Halsey's Typhoons* (New York: Crown Publishers Inc., 1967).

36. Bill Emerson, interview, August 20, 1999, and clippings.

37. Ralph Moulton, telephone interview, March 15, 2006.

38. Bill Noonan, interview, September 14, 2004.

39. Bill Noonan, interview, September 14, 2004.

40. Paul Gillesse, telephone interview, April 2, 2006.

41. Doris Kearns Goodwin, *No Ordinary Time: Franklin and Eleanor Roosevelt: The Home Front in World War II* (New York: Simon and Schuster, 1994), 317.

42. Bill Noonan, interview, September 14, 2004.

CHAPTER 7

1. Paul Van Oordt, frequent interviews, 2002–2007.

2. James Edward Clark, MCL, 35.

3. James Moye, MCL.

4. Patrick E. Carr, MCL, 10–13.

5. Robert E. Lee Eaton, MCL.

6. Carl Moss, telephone interview, January 6, 2006.

7. Morris Williams, MCL, 27.

8. Charles Boyd Woehrle, S AND R, 371–84.

9. Willis Emmanuel Eckholm, S AND R, 81–92.

10. Jim Tyler, MCL, 16–31.

11. Lamar Rodgers, MCL, 58.

12. Jim Clark, MCL, 43.

13. Jim Tyler, MCL.

14. Carl Moss, telephone interview, January 6, 2006.

15. Jim Tyler, MCL.

16. Gilbert Blackwell, MCL. Details of buildings and camp activities are spelled out in numerous accounts of POW camps such as: Lewis H. Carlson, *We Were Each Other's Prisoners: An Oral History of World War II*

American and German Prisoners of War (New York: Basic Books, 1997); Angelo M. Spinelli and Lewis H. Carlson, *Life Behind Barbed Wire* (New York: Fordham University Press, 2004); and Thomas H. Taylor, *The Simple Sounds of Freedom* (New York: Random House, 2002).

17. Jim Tyler, MCL.

18. Lamar Rodgers, MCL, 65–66.

19. Jim Tyler, MCL, 30.

20. Jim Tyler, MCL, 25–28.

21. Jim Tyler, MCL, 25–28.

22. Jim Tyler, MCL, 25–28.

23. Pat Carr, MCL, 16–17.

24. Carl Moss, telephone interview, January 6, 2006.

25. Colbert Graham, interview, May 31, 2004.

26. Lamar Rodgers, MCL.

27. Paul Van Oordt, frequent interviews, 2002–2007.

28. Lamar Rodgers, MCL, 59–60.

29. Willis Emmanuel Eckhol, MS AND R, 81–92.

30. Lamar Rodgers, MCL.

31. See Arthur A. Durand, *Stalag Luft III: The Secret Story* (Baton Rouge: Louisiana State University Press, 1988), passim.

32. Lamar Rodgers, MCL, 59.

33. Lamar Rodgers, MCL, 64.

34. Frederick Douglas Williams, Sr., MCL, 28.

35. Jim Moye, MCL, passim.

36. For details of the planning and execution of "The Great Escape" see Durand, *Stalag Luft III.* See the movie version of *The Great Escape* still available at many video stores.

37. Chuck Woehrle, S AND R, 371–84.

CHAPTER 8

1. Arthur A. Durand, *Stalag Luft III: The Secret Story* (Baton Rouge: Louisiana State University Press, 1988), 339.

2. Chuck Woehrle, S AND R, 377. For further information on the evacuation and liberation of POW camps, particularly Stalag Luft III, see Durand, *Stalag Luft III,* 326–56.

3. Chuck Woehrle, S AND R, 378.

4. Paul Van Oordt, frequent interviews, 2002–2007.

5. Chuck Woehrle, S AND R, 378.

6. Church Woehrle, S AND R, 378.

7. Morris C. Williams, MCL, 74–75.

8. Chuck Woehrle, S AND R, 381.

9. Paul Van Oordt, frequent interviews, 2002–2007.

10. Lamar Rodgers, MCL, passim.

11. Lamar Rodgers, MCL, passim.

12. Pat Carr, MCL, 18.

13. Leland McLendon, MCL, 26.

14. Carl Moss, telephone interview, January 6, 2006; and David Dennis, diary.

15. David Dennis, diary.

16. David Dennis, diary.

17. Willis Lott, MCL, passim.

18. Russ Hilding, interview, June 8, 2006, and tape.

19. Henry Wolcott, telephone interview, June 16, 2006.

20. Raymond Young, interview, May 5, 2004.

21. Brewster Chamberlin and Marcia Feldman, eds. *The Liberation of the Nazi Concentration Camps 1945* (Washington, D.C.: United States Holocaust Memorial Council, 1987), 80.

22. See Ray Young, "Never To Be Forgotten: The Liberation of a Nazi Death Camp," *Michigan History Magazine* (March–April 1995): 46–47; and Brewster Chamberlin and Marcia Feldman, eds., *The Liberation of the Nazi Concentration Camps 1945: Eyewitness Accounts of the Liberators* (Washington, D.C.: United States Holocaust Memorial Council, 1987). For an informative account of Buchenwald, see Edward R. Murrow, "Nazi Death Factory at Buchenwald," *Reader's Digest Illustrated Story of World War II* (Pleasantville, NY: The Reader's Digest Association, Inc., 1969): 428–31.

23. Ted Thomas, tape, interviews, and DVD, "East Lansing WWII: Stories From the Front," created by the East Lansing Historical Society by Cheeney Media Concepts2. Produced/Directed by Ed Cheeney and Kevin Epling, 2006.

24. Raymond Young, interview, May 5, 2004 and Walter Adams, speech and "Return to Normandy," *Lansing State Journal* (October 24, 1993): 1F; Henry Kane, interview with sister Martha Niland.

25. John R. Walker, *Memories of World War II*, self-published, n.d., passim.

26. Sam Dann, *Dachau 29 April 1945: The Rainbow Liberation-Memoirs* (Lubbock: Texas Tech University Press, 1998), 48, 62. In his book Dann presents a riveting collection of official documents and eye-witness accounts of the liberation of Dachau. Wendell Rimer told of serving on a war crimes investigating team in Leipzig, Germany, that was investigating a German hospital that took in concentration camp workers, Poles, Frenchmen, Russians, and Bulgarians, who were so feeble from lack of food and disease that they could no longer work. The hospital and its staff were being investigated on charges that despite the innumerable admissions no one was ever dismissed from the hospital. It was suspected that the Germans simply allowed the workers to starve to death or gave "them an injection and they'd die." The recovery of dozens of bodies that had been buried on a hill in back of the hospital tended to corroborate the team's suspicions. Wendell Dean Rimer, MCL, 30.

27. Lloyd Wilson, telephone interviews, July 11, 2005, and September 12, 2006.

28. Andrew Candler Leech, MCL.

29. Kossie Atkins, telephone interview, August 6, 2005.

30. Donald R. Brown, telephone interview, Professor Emeritus, The University of Michigan.

31. Bernard Engel, interview, July 21, 1998.

32. June Covert Bohn, telephone interviews, April 18 and 26, 2006.

33. Charles Grosse, HMM; Betty Leiby, interview, March 22, 2004; Po Weatherford, interview, February 10, 1998.

CHAPTER 9

1. Phil Brain in Allan Taylor, S AND R, 27–34.

2. John Lewis Hinkle, Jr., MCL, passim.

3. Frank Forsyth, MCL, 69.

4. Ruth Benedict, *The Chrysanthemum and the Sword: Patterns of Japanese Culture* (Cambridge, MA: The Riverside Press, 1946), 38. Ruth Benedict explained: "Honor was bound up with fighting to the death. In a hopeless situation a Japanese soldier should kill himself with his last hand grenade or charge weaponless against the enemy in a mass suicide attack. But he should not surrender. Even if he were taken prisoner when he was wounded and unconscious, he 'could not hold up his head in Japan' again; he was disgraced; he was 'dead' to his former life." This deeply ingrained philosophy of the Japanese warriors and civilians no doubt colored Truman's decision to drop the atomic bomb.

5. Sam Abbott, MCL, 36.

6. John Hinkle, MCL, 14.

7. Sam Abbott, MCL, 36.

8. Frank Forsyth, MCL, 28.

9. Frank Forsyth, MCL.

10. Sam Abbott, MCL, 4.

11. Frank Forsyth, MCL, 18.

12. Joe Kish, telephone interview, November 20, 2005.

13. George B. Thornton, MCL, 20, 22.

14. Frank Forsyth, MCL.

15. Sam Abbott, MCL, 36.

16. Frank Forsyth, MCL, 12–19.

17. John Hinkle, MCL, 19.

18. Frank Forsyth, MCL, 12.

19. Sam Abbott, MCL; and Frank Forsyth, MCL.

20. Sam Abbott, MCL.

21. Frank Forsyth, MCL, 28.

22. J. Cecil Chambliss, MCL, 72.

23. Frank Forsyth, MCL, 28.

24. John Hinkle, MCL, 21.

25. Philip Brain, S AND R, 30.

26. Gregory F. Michno, *Death on the Hellships: Prisoners at Sea in the Pacific War* (Annapolis, MD: Naval Institute Press, 2001), Preface. Michno states, "About 93 percent of POW deaths at sea were caused by friendly fire," p. 292. See also Manny Lawton, *Some Survived* (Chapel Hill, NC: Algonquin Books of Chapel Hill, 1984); and Gavan Daws, *Prisoners of the Japanese: POWS of World War II in the Pacific* (New York: William Morrow and Company, Inc., 1944).

27. Michno, *Death on the Hellships,* 306.

28. Philip Brain, S AND R, 30.

29. Philip Brain, S AND R, 30.

30. Roger H. White, personal memories, tape. For some 10 years afterward, Roger White was jumpy, easily upset. Night after night his nightmares of three and a half years as a POW continued.

31. James E. Romero Jr., *Skyblue 79, Over and Out Lacey* (Lacey, WA: James E. Romero, Jr., 2005), 77.

32. Roger H. White, personal memories, tape.

33. J. Cecil Chambliss, MCL.

34. J. Cecil Chambliss' oral history account of his experiences on the *U.S. Houston* and in Burma is documented in more detail in H. Robert Charles' book *Last Man Out* (Austin, TX: Eakin Press, 1988) and in James D. Hornfischer's *Ship of Ghosts* (New York: Dell Publisher, 2006). Although *The Bridge Over the River Kwai* turned out to be an extremely popular movie, most historians note that it omits much of the reality and horror that took place during the building of the "Death Railroad." In many sources the Dutch doctor Henri Hekking is acclaimed as one of the real heroes of the Burmese camps. Thanks to his use of herbal medicines and his courage and stamina in standing up to the Japanese and their heartless brutality, Dr. Hekking was credited with having saved hundreds of lives. His story is an integral part of *Last Man Out,* whose author, H. Robert Charles, tells of Dr. Hekking's expertise in saving his life. According to Robert Charles, 21 percent of the Americans, Australians, English, and Dutch who worked on the railroad died. Of the 270,000 Asians, the death rate reached 90,000. "Next to the holocaust in Europe, the inhumanity displayed at Burma ranks with the worst in recorded history" (Charles, *Last Man Out,* 167). See also, Stanley Sandler, ed., *World War II in the Pacific: An Encyclopedia* (New York: Garland Publishing Inc., 2001).

35. Frank Forsyth, MCL. Stories paralleling Frank's manufacture of "sulfa pills" are corroborated in other accounts of POWs.

36. J. Cecil Chambliss, MCL.

37. Frank Forsyth, MCL.

38. Sam Greene, interview, Westlake Village, CA, December 24, 2005, and letter.

39. J. Cecil Chambliss, MCL. For further information see McCormack Gavan and Hank Nelson, *The Burma-Thailand Railway: Memory and History* (St. Leonards, NSW: Allen & Unwin, 1993).

CHAPTER 10

1. John R. Walker, *Memories of World War II,* self-published, 38, n.d.

2. Ted Thomas, tape, interviews, and DVD, "East Lansing WWII: Stories From the Front," created by the East Lansing Historical Society by Cheeney Media Concepts2. Produced/Directed by Ed Cheeney and Kevin Epling, 2006.

3. Donald Hines, interview, November 29, 2005.

4. Ted Thomas, tape, interviews, and DVD, "East Lansing WWII: Stories From the Front," created by the East Lansing Historical Society by Cheeney Media Concepts2. Produced/Directed by Ed Cheeney and Kevin Epling, 2006.

5. Joseph Brochin, S AND R, 19–26.

6. Ted Thomas, tape, interviews, and DVD, "East Lansing WWII: Stories From the Front," created by the East Lansing Historical Society by Cheeney Media Concepts2. Produced/Directed by Ed Cheeney and Kevin Epling, 2006.

7. Billy Benton, interview, Madison, MS, made by Levin Culpepper, March 18, 1998.

8. Andy Andrews, interview, August 18, 1997.

9. Karl Legant, letter, April 18, 1997.

10. Eugene Pigg.

11. Roy Herbert, interview, March 16, 2004.

12. Humphrey Sears Taylor, S AND R.

13. John Goodell, interview, January 14, 2002.

14. James C. Veen, Jr., telephone interview, January 31, 2007.

15. Dick Robinson, interview, Summer 2000.

16. Larry Hartman, telephone interview, April 13, 2006.

17. Gerald (Bud) Rogne, HMM.

18. Joe Spinosa, HMM.

19. Ray Young, telephone interview, May 5, 2004.

20. Dudley Rishell, telephone interview, March 19, 2006.

21. Wayne Adgate, interview, January 29, 2002.

22. Paul Niland, interview, March 28, 1999.

23. John Joseph Murphy, S AND R, 211–16.

24. John Gail McKane, S AND R, 197–210; Jay Sterner Hammond, S AND R, 128.

25. Jack Shingleton, telephone interview, September 20, 2005.

26. Claude Fike, MCL.

27. Richard Jones, interview, August 29, 2005; Bill Noonan, interview, September 14, 2004; Robert Stern, interview, Gulfport, FL, February 25, 2006.

28. Dudley Rishell, telephone interview, March 19, 2006.

29. Joe Kish, telephone interview, November 20, 2005.

30. Romayne Hicks, telephone interview, January 13, 2006.

31. Robert L. LaBouy, "Where Did We Get Such Men?" *Delta Chi Quarterly* (Spring/Summer, 1999): 12–13.

32. Johnie Courtney, telephone interview, September 2, 2005.

33. John Kennedy, interview, Westlake Village, CA, December 24, 2005.

34. Karl Leitz, telephone interview, August 23, 2005.

35. Gradus Shoemaker, HMM.

36. Phil Montgomery, interview and letter, December 15, 2005.

37. Dan Kona, telephone interview, January 8, 2006.

38. John Hoagland, interviews, summer 2006. For detailed first-hand information about the sinking of the USS *Spence,* see C. Raymond Calhoun, *Typhoon: The Other Enemy: The Third Fleet and the Pacific Storm of December 1944* (Annapolis, MD: Naval Institute Press, 1981), especially pages 78–80.

39. Claude Fike, MCL.

40. Austin Hines, interview, March 14, 1998.

CHAPTER 11

1. Janet Hicks Ronk, interview, November 17, 2005, and clippings.

2. John Haus, interview, August 25, 1997.

3. David D. Anderson, frequent interviews, 2002–2007.

4. John R. Walker, *Memories of World War II,* self-published, n.d.

5. Owen Marmon, telephone interview, September 23, 2004.

6. Jim Pyle, interviews, Hattiesburg, MS, Summer 1990.

7. Po Weatherford, interview, Niceville, MS, February 10, 1998.

8. Austin Hines, March 14, 1998.

9. Carl Tychsen in Allan Taylor, S AND R, 357–66.

10. Vince Schumacher, telephone interview, April 15, 2006.

11. Robert Drake, telephone interview, April 28, 2004.

12. Wayne Adgate, interview, January 29, 2002.

13. Richard Pearse, interviews, September 13, 2006.

14. Robert Stern, interview, Gulfport, FL, February 25, 2006.

15. Helen and Larry Deason, letters and diary, July 24, 1944.

16. Paul and Dorrie Souder, interviews, February 13 and 14, 1998.

17. Donald Langworthy, telephone interview, August 22, 2007.

18. Gradus Shoemaker, HMM.

19. Ginny Bennetts, interview, April 13, 2005.

20. Rachel Jones, telephone interviews, August 29, 2005.

21. June McIntosh Milks, interview, January 16, 2002.

22. Carl Arthur Tychsen, Jr., in Taylor, S AND R.

23. Alice Diggins, HMM.

24. Robert Overholt, telephone interview, September 6, 2005.

25. Kossie Akins, telephone interview, August 6, 2005.

26. Henry LaBrosse, telephone interview, September 22, 2004.

27. Catherine Cross, S AND R, 71–80.

28. Donald Bancroft, interview, Hattiesburg, MS, Summer 1999.

29. John Hoagland, interviews, Summer 2006.

30. Hilma Wilcox, telephone interview, September 13, 2005.

31. Albert Smith in Taylor, S AND R, 313–18.

CHAPTER 12

1. John Goodell, interviews, January 14, 2002.

2. John Goodell, interviews, January 14, 2002.

3. Donald VanGorder, telephone interview, August 2, 2006.

4. Paul Niland, interview, March 28, 1999.

5. Walter Maner, interview, February 3, 2002.

6. Claude Fike, MCL.

7. Joe Foster, telephone interview, December 1, 2005.

8. Douglas Dunham, interview, September 15, 2006.

9. Paul Bouchereau, ECAS.

10. Douglas Dunham, interview, September 15, 2006.

11. Helen Brush Hiscoe, interview, October 2, 2006.

12. Douglas Dunham, interview, September 15, 2006.

13. Karl Legant, letter, April 30, 2002, and Eugene Cornelius, telephone interview, August 1, 2006.

14. Henry Nelson, telephone interviews, April 27, 2004.

15. Joseph Victor Brochin in Allan Taylor, S AND R, 22.

16. Legrand Johnson, ECAS.

17. Ken Springer, interviews, April 20, 2004.

18. Frank Bourke, interviews, June 24, 2004, and correspondence, October 27, 2004, March 4, 2005, and December 19, 2005.

19. Frank Young, interview, Niceville, FL, January 12, 2004.

20. Robert Stern, interviews, St. Petersburg, FL, February 25, 2006.

21. Bill Noonan, interview, September 14, 2004.

22. Frank Feeley, interviews, October 14, 2004.

23. Lee Conley, telephone interview, March 17, 2004.

24. Richard Bacon, telephone interview, June 12, 2006.

25. Bob Wilcox, telephone interview, June 13, 2006, and correspondence.

26. Milton Ames, Frankenmuth, MI, "Veterans Oral History Project," 2004.

27. June McIntosh Milks, interview, January 16, 2002.

28. Vince Schumacher, telephone interview, April 15, 2006.

29. Lenore Moe, interview, December 12, 2005.

30. Norm Pierce, HMM.

31. Bill Noonan, interview, September 14, 2004.

32. John Rodgers, telephone interview, December 7, 2004.

33. Paul Souder, interviews, February 14, 1998.

CHAPTER 13

1. Ginny Rath Bennetts, telephone interview, April 13, 2005.
2. Maxine Hari George, telephone interview, April 14, 2005.
3. Beverly Doane Marshall, letter, memories, World War II.
4. Janie Boyd (Tabler), telephone interview, July 4, 2007.
5. Dorrie Souder, interview, February 13, 1998.
6. Ruby Martin Bancroft, interview, August 19, 1997.
7. Ginny Bennetts, interview, April 13, 2005.
8. Janet Goodell Iddings (Haley), interview, January 14, 2002.
9. Dell Boettcher, interview, September 26, 2004.
10. Richard Bates, diary, "Medical school in the war years 1941–1945."
11. Richard Bates, diary, "Medical school in the war years 1941–1945."
12. Theodore R. Kennedy, interview, August 25, 2007.
13. Monna Heath, interview, April 17, 2006.
14. Jane Leipprandt (Scandary), interview, June 21, 2005.
15. Janet Sullivan (O'Leary), interview, Summer 2006.
16. Sue Coleman (Johnson), telephone interview, Spring 2004.
17. Bunny Brunner (McComb), interview, January 30, 2006.
18. Shirley Dean (Guider), interview, Summer 2006. In small towns where a paucity of teachers remained after the draft and the flurry of enlistments, often the town's ministers would fill in to teach the classes.
19. Sue Sims Schulze, interview, July 24, 2000.
20. Bernice "Bunny" Roe (Smith), telephone interview, Fall 2006.
21. Rex Shugart, WHPNM.
22. Dorrie Elliott Souder, interview, February 13, 1998.
23. O. H. Barnett, MCL.
24. Mary Sharp, interview, September 29, 1997.
25. Helen and Larry Deason, letter, May 28, 1944, and diary.
26. Carolyn Talbot Hoagland, letter and interview, Sanibel, FL, February 18, 1998.
27. Christy Clark (Nichols), interview, Sanibel, FL, February 18, 1998.

CHAPTER 14

1. Ilah Meyers, interview, February 4, 2002.
2. Maxine Grissett, interview, January 14, 2004.
3. Marjorie Pearson, interview and memories letter, September 3, 2004.
4. Alice Haber, MWHC.
5. Muriel Rokeach, telephone interview, November 30, 2005
6. Doris Warden, telephone interview, Fall 2006.
7. Janet Sullivan (O'Leary), interview, Summer 2006.
8. Annie deVries (Robinson), interview, Summer 2000.
9. Harold Cunningham, interview, February 10, 2002.

10. Iona Shugart, WHPNM.

11. Dan McHugh and Donald Hines, interview, November 29, 2005.

12. Jane Hootman (Drake), telephone interview, April 28, 2004.

13. Sue Coleman (Johnson), telephone interview, May 5, 2004.

14. Agnes Parsons (Pulling), telephone interview, January 11, 2006.

15. Lillian Lockwood, telephone interview and letter, June 28, 1998.

16. Signe Hegge Bates, interview, Sanibel, FL, February 18, 1998.

17. Mary Saltzman (Baron), interview, October 4, 2006.

18. Mary Jane Schmierer, S AND R, 117–23.

19. Don Swope, telephone interview, April 3, 2006.

20. Sonia Dudek, telephone interview, December 5, 2005.

CHAPTER 15

1. Romayne Hicks, telephone interview, January 13, 2006.

2. Howard "Gov" Miller, interview, June 4, 2006; Greg Deliyanne, interview, October 12, 2004. See Kumiko Kakehashi, *So Sad to Fall in Battle* (New York: Ballantine Books, 2007), 175–77; Peter Young, ed. *The World Almanac Book of World War II* (Englewood Cliffs, NJ: World Almanac Publications, 1981); and Robert Goralski, *World War II Almanac: 1931–1945* (New York: G.P. Putnam's Sons, 1981).

3. Claude Fike, MCL.

4. Robert Wilcox, telephone interview and correspondence, June 13, 2006.

5. David Ruff, interview, August 29, 1997.

6. Louis D'Valentine, telephone interview, September 6, 2005; Miller Perry, interview, March 16, 2004. The Allies were also ready for the invasion of Japan. Hall Tennis, stationed in Maui, told of the extensive and elaborate practice sessions preparatory to an invasion. "We are in Maui, where we live in a big tent camp, training to invade Japan and have the pleasure of walking through shooting 'ranges' built like city streets, village streets, where targets shaped like people pop out of doors and windows and we shoot our carbines quickly, from the hip or however to hit the targets." There was training in "night infiltration where the password was the sound of scratches on the butt of the rifle with your fingernail. They were standard courses we went through to keep us busy and remind us how to shoot." personal memories, DVD.

7. David D. Anderson, frequent interviews, 2002–2007; Robert Drake, telephone interview, April 28, 2004.

8. Gus Ganakas, telephone interview, September 11, 2006, and speech.

9. Eugene Cornelius, telephone interview, August 1, 2006.

10. Mary Moir Groves, interview, Harbor Springs, MI, Summer 2006.

11. Henry LaBrosse, telephone interview, September 22, 2004.

12. William Ewing, letter, April 13, 2000.

13. Roy Herbert, interview, March 16, 2004.

14. Wayne Adgate, interview, January 29, 2002.

15. Louis D'Valentine, telephone interview, September 6, 2006, and correspondence.

16. Lee Conley, telephone interview, March 27, 2004; Bill Pace, MCL; James Pyle, interviews.

17. Downey Milliken Gray, Jr., HMM.

18. David D. Anderson, frequent interviews, 2002–2007.

19. Dorothy Schieve, interview, May 10, 2005.

20. Fritz Bennetts, telephone interview, April 13, 2005

21. David Ruff, interview, August 29, 1997.

22. Clarence Kallback, shipboard fellow traveler interview.

23. Barbara Brown, MWHC.

24. Elizabeth McIntee, WOSL (Louisville, KY), telephone interview, September 8, 2006, and correspondence.

25. Mel Buschman, telephone interview, April 20, 2004.

26. Andrew Leech, MCL.

27. Vince Schumaker, telephone interview, April 15, 2006

28. Howard "Gov" Miller, interview, June 4, 2006.

29. Bill Emerson, interview, August 20, 1999.

30. Harry Hedges, telephone interview, September 26, 2006.

31. Paul Nielsen, clippings, correspondence, and article from *Today's Seniors*, August 1985.

CHAPTER 16

1. Lois Ella Gill, interview, April 26, 1998.

2. Ilah Meyers, interview, February 4, 2002.

3. Po Weatherford, interview, Niceville, FL, February 10, 1998.

4. James Pyle, interview, Hattiesburg, MS, February 3, 1998.

5. Frank Bourke, interview, June 24, 2004, and correspondence, October 27, 2004; March 4, 2005; March 10, 2005.

6. James Clark, MCL, 99.

7. Elizabeth McIntee, telephone interview, WOSL (Louisville, KY), September 8, 2006.

8. Ralph Moulton, telephone interview, March 15, 2006, and letter.

9. Lamar Rodgers, MCL.

10. Ted Thomas, tape, interviews, and DVD, "East Lansing WWII: Stories From the Front," created by the East Lansing Historical Society by Cheeney Media Concepts2. Produced/Directed by Ed Cheeney and Kevin Epling, 2006.

11. John R. Walker, *Memories of World War II,* Self-published, n.d., 60.

12. William Horton, HMM.

13. Genevieve Luckey, MWHC.

14. Barbara Brauker (Kaye), interview, April 2002.

15. Donald Bancroft, interview, Hattiesburg, MS, February 14, 1998.

16. Paul Souder, interview, February 14, 1998.

17. Carolyn Hoagland, interview, Sanibel, FL, February 18, 1998.

18. Fritz Bennetts, telephone interview, April 13, 2005.

19. Walter Maner, interview, February 3, 2002.

20. Ray Young, telephone interview, May 5, 2004, Don Bancroft, interview Hattiesburg, MS, Summer 1997; Joe Spinosa, HMM.

21. Bill Keezer, interview, March 16, 2004.

22. Joe Foster, telephone interview, December 1, 2005.

23. Don Strand, S AND R.

24. Jim Perkins, "A Tale That is Told: The Life and Times of James W. Perkins."

25. Al Jones, war letters and tapes, 1944–1945.

26. Paul Souder, interview, February 14, 1998.

27. Willis Libolt, "Things I Can Remember."

28. John Irvin Nichols, interview, Sanibel, FL, February 18, 1998.

29. Wayne Adgate, interview, January 29, 2002.

30. Bill Noonan, interview, September 14, 2004.

31. Claude Fike, MCL, 34–38.

32. Alexander Jefferson with Lewis H. Carlson, *Red Tail Captured, Red Tail Free* (New York: Fordham University Press, 2005); John Kennedy, interview, Westlake Village, CA, December 24, 2005. Alexander Jefferson, in *Red Tail Captured, Red Tail Free,* wrote about his degrading homecoming. He had been held as a POW of the Germans for nine months, and in all respects he was a hero. Yet, at the New York dock he was greeted by "A short, smug, white buck private [who] shouted, 'Whites to the right, niggers to the left' " (107).

33. Bill Noonan, interview, September 14, 2004.

34. Robert Flores, telephone interview, Summer 2000.

35. Albert Fine, tape, n.d..

CHAPTER 17

1. Claude Fike, MCL.

2. Hall Tennis, personal memories, DVD.

3. Johnie Courtney, telephone interview, September 2, 2005; Paul Van Oordt, frequent interviews, 2002–2007; Dudley Rishell, telephone interview, March 19, 2006.

4. William Summers, telephone interview, September 25, 2005; Lawrence Von Tersch, telephone interview, August 1, 2006.

5. Walter Woodhouse, interview, September 12, 2004.

6. Ted Bauer, telephone interview, January 25, 2006.

7. Walter Adams, "Return to Normandy," *Lansing State Journal* (October 24, 1993).

8. Paul Niland, interview, March 28, 1999.

9. John Irvin Nichols, interview, Sanibel, FL, February 18, 1998.

10. Lee Conley, telephone interview, March 17, 2004.

11. Mel Buschman, telephone interview, April 20, 2004.

12. Paul Niland, interview, March 28, 1999.

13. Anita Johnson Dean, interview, April 22, 2004.

14. Mahlon Sharp, interview, September 29, 1997.

15. Paul L. Curry, HMM.

16. Al Boettcher, interview, September 26, 2004.

17. Philip Sidney Brain Jr., S AND R.

18. Robert Stern, interviews, Gulfport, FL, February 25, 2006.

19. Robert Drake, telephone interview, April 28, 2004.

20. Alan Suits, telephone interview, July 31, 2006.

21. Leroy Schroeder, telephone interview, August 8, 2006.

22. Henry LaBrosse, telephone interview, September 22, 2004.

23. Elizabeth McIntee, WOSL (Louisville, KY), telephone interview, September 8, 2006.

24. John Key, interview, July 10, 2000; Jane Weatherford, interview, Niceville, FL, February 10, 1998.

25. Don Swope, telephone interview, April 3, 2006.

26. Wayne Lesher, interview and personal memories, DVD.

27. Dorothy Dodd Eppstein, MWHC.

28. Robert Fisher, telephone interview, May 5, 2002.

29. Inez Flanders and Louise Cullefer, interviews, Hattiesburg, MS, August 18, 1997.

30. Frank Feeley, telephone interview, October 14, 2004; Alice Diggins, WHPNM.

31. Charles Larrowe, telephone interview, September 11, 2005.

32. Hall Tennis, personal memories, DVD.

33. Joe Kish, telephone interview, November 20, 2005.

34. Hall Tennis, personal memories, DVD.

35. Phil Montgomery, interviews, December 15, 2005.

36. David Ruff, interview, August 29, 1997.

37. Joe Spinosa, HMM.

38. Robert McCollough, HMM.

39. Leo Chick, telephone interview, Fall 2004.

40. Lloyd Hamlin, telephone interview, December 9, 2005.

41. Phil Montgomery, interviews, December 15, 2005.

42. Bernard Engel, interviews, July 21, 1998.

43. Lee Conley, telephone interview, March 17, 2004.

44. Kenneth Almay, ECAS.

45. Frank Bourke, interview, June 14, 2004, and correspondence, October 27, 2004, March 4, 2005, March 10, 2005.

46. David D. Anderson, frequent interviews, 2002–2007.

47. Gerald "Bud" Rogne, HMM.

48. Van Hatcher, MCL.

49. Lamar Rodgers, MCL, 89–90.

50. Robbie Belle Bishop Rodgers, MCL.

51. Willis Emmanuel Eckholm, S AND R, 85.

52. Fred Douglas Williams, Sr., MCL, 48.

53. Wendell Stanford Peterson, S AND R.

54. Jack Siebold, telephone interview, August 28, 2006.

55. George Taylor, telephone interview, April 28, 2006 and personal memories DVD.

56. Clinton Canady, telephone interviews, March 26, 2007.

57. Wayne Lesher, interview and personal memories DVD.

58. Wilson Evans, II, MCL.

59. John Peoples, MCL, 114–16.

60. Vernon J. Baker, S AND R, 7–12.

61. Joseph Philip Gomer, S AND R, 105–13.

62. For more information see Alexander Jefferson with Lewis H. Carlson, *Red Tail Captured, Red Tail Free* (New York: Fordham University Press, 2005).

63. Roy Herbert, interview, March 16, 2004.

64. Bill Keezer, interview, March 16, 2004.

65. Dorothy Dodd Eppstein, MWHC.

66. Robert Rieder Boardman, S AND R, 16.

67. Allan Rice, telephone interview, August 27, 2004.

68. Kenneth Springer, telephone interview, April 20, 2004.

69. Robert John Clemens, S AND R, 51–60.

70. Leo Chick, telephone interview; Claude Fike, MCL.

71. Claude Fike, MCL.

72. Richard Elasky, S AND R.

73. Richard Jones, interview, August 22, 2004.

74. Philip Sidney Brain, Jr., S AND R.

75. Bill Love, interview, March 18, 2004, and letter, October 1, 2004.

76. Paul Niland, interview, March 28, 1999.

77. Woodrow Respects Nothing, S AND R, 278.

CHAPTER 18

1. Thomas Dutch, telephone interview, July 13, 2006.

2. Bill Emerson, interviews, May 6, 2006.

3. Bruce Helmer, telephone interview, June 7, 2004.

4. June McIntosh Milks, interview, January 16, 2002.

5. Jack Cawood, telephone interview, August 30, 2005; Richard Crum, interview, January 13, 2006, and "Memories of WWII."

6. Jimmy Carter Fairley, MCL.

7. Bill Noonan, interview, Lansing, MI, September 14, 2004; Harry George, telephone interview, March 14, 2005.

8. Mel Buschman, telephone interview, April 20, 2004.

9. Al Boettcher, interview, September 26, 2004.

10. Wayne Adgate, interview, January 29, 2002.

11. Walter Adams, "Return to Normandy," *Lansing State Journal* (October, 24, 1993), 1F.

12. Walter Adams, "Return to Normandy," *Lansing State Journal* (October 24, 1993): 1F.

13. Walter Adams, "Return to Normandy," *Lansing State Journal* (October 24, 1993): 1F.

14. John H. Winant, interview and article in *Alligator Alley,* no. 22: 5, and personal memories, DVD.

15. Howard "Gov" Miller, interview, June 4, 2006.

16. Everett William Hohn, S AND R, 143.

17. Thomas Dutch, telephone interview, July 31, 2006.

18. Alan Suits, telephone interview, July 31, 2006.

19. Mel Buschman, telephone interview, April 20, 2004.

20. James Cecil Church, S AND R, 47.

21. Christy Clark Nichols, interview, Sanibel, FL, February 18, 1998.

22. Fritz Bennetts, telephone interview, April 13, 2005.

23. Charles Willard Lindberg, S AND R, 22.

24. Frederic Wickert, telephone interviews, August 26, 2005 and October 7, 2005.

25. Betty Louise Isom (Leiby), telephone interview, March 23, 2004.

26. Irene Kenneck (Johnson), telephone interview, August 11, 2004.

27. George Rogers, MCL.

28. Larry Hartman, telephone interview, April 13, 2006.

29. James Cecil Church, S AND R.

30. Clair A. Nash, interview, October 31, 2006.

31. Jack Gunther, interview, June 27, 2000.

32. Alice Diggins, WHPNM.

33. William Horton, HMM.

34. Joe Spinosa, HMM.

35. Allan Rice, interview, August 27, 2004.

36. Bill Noonan, interview, September 24, 2004.

37. Emily Hobbs (Wolf), letter, December 29, 2005.

38. Joseph Clemens, S AND R.

CHAPTER 19

1. Richard Gasser Nelson, S AND R, 221.

2. Colbert Graham, interview, May 31, 2000.

3. Tom Takeshi Oye, S AND R, 239. After the war the citizens of the French town of Biffontaine erected a monument in gratitude for the 442nd's fighting to liberate their city.

4. James Pyle, interview, Hattiesburg, MS, February 2, 1998.

5. Robert DeVinney, interview, November 25, 2005.

6. Howard "Gov" Miller, interview, June 4, 2006.

7. Jack Bates, Memoirs.

8. Thomas A. Dutch, telephone interview, July 13, 2006.

9. Kenneth William Larson, S AND R.

10. William Pace, MCL.

11. William Summers, telephone interview, September 25, 2005.

12. Thomas Dutch, telephone interview, July 13, 2006.

13. Norm Pierce, HMM.

14. Charles Wallace Grosse, HMM.

15. Don Ely, telephone interview, November 4, 2005.

16. Donald Langworthy, telephone interviews and correspondence, August 22, 2007.

17. Donald Langworthy, telephone interviews and correspondence, August 22, 2007.

18. Richard Guernsey, telephone interview, August 4, 2005.

19. Dorothy Schroeder, telephone interview, WOSL (Louisville, KY), August 8, 2006.

20. Jon Young, interview, April 21, 2004.

21. Leo Stone, personal memories, DVD. Laurence Gavento, interview, August 26, 1997.

22. Dorothy Schieve, interview, May 10, 2004.

23. James Pyle, interviews, Hattiesburg, MS, Summer 1990.

24. Edward Krenkel, telephone interview, April 25, 2006.

25. Thomas McGrain, telephone interviews, September 7, 2006.

26. Fritz Bennetts, telephone interview, April 13, 2005.

27. Romayne Hicks, telephone interview, January 13, 2006. WASP Dorothy Dodd Eppstein told of disgruntled mechanics who resented women pilots were found guilty of putting sugar in the fuel tanks and causing serious accidents. MWHC.

28. Alan Suits, telephone interview, July 31, 2006.

29. Milton Baron, interview, October 4, 2006. As early as the 1930s hydroponics was employed on rocky Wake Island to grow vegetables for travelers served by Pan American Airlines.

30. William Worgul, telephone interview, June 10, 2004.

31. Dorrie and Paul Souder, interviews, February 13 and 14, 1998.

32. Thomas W. Culpepper, interview.

33. Al Jones, tapes, letter, and diary, 1944–1945.

34. Al Wolf, letter, n.d.

35. Frederic Wickert, telephone interviews, October 7, 2005.

36. Po Weatherford, interview, Niceville, FL, February 10, 1998.

37. Frederic Wickert, telephone interview, October 7, 2005.

38. Vince Schumacher, telephone interview, April 15, 2006.

39. Al Jones, tapes, letter, and diary, 1944–1945.

40. John Kast, telephone interview, March 27, 2006.

41. Clair A. Nash, interview, October 31, 2006.

42. John Kast, telephone interview, March 27, 2006.

43. Dudley Rishell, telephone interview, March 19, 2006.

44. Donald VanGorder, telephone interview, August 2, 2006; Russ Hilding, tape interview.

45. For more detail, see *St. Petersburg Times,* Sunday June 5, 1994, PML.

46. Charles Larrowe, telephone interview, September 11, 2005.

Selected Bibliography

Adamson, Hans Christian, and George Francis Kosco. *Halsey's Typhoons: A First-hand Account Of How Two Typhoons, More Powerful Than the Japanese, Dealt Death and Destruction to Admiral Halsey's Third Fleet.* New York: Crown Publishers, Inc., 1967.

Ambrose, Stephen E. *Band of Brothers: E Company, 506th Regiment, 101st Airborne from Normandy to Hitler's Eagle's Nest.* New York: Simon & Schuster, 1992.

———. *Citizen Soldiers: The U.S. Army from the Normandy Beaches to the Bulge to the Surrender of Germany June 7, 1944–May 7, 1945.* New York: Simon Schuster, 1997.

Asahina, Robert. *Just Americans: How Japanese Americans Won a War at Home and Abroad.* New York: Gotham Books, 2006.

Benedict, Ruth. *The Chrysanthemum and the Sword: Patterns of Japanese Culture.* Cambridge, MA: The Riverside Press, 1946.

Bennett, Scott H., ed. *Army GI, Pacifist Co: The World War II Letters of Frank and Albert Dietrich.* New York: Fordham University Press, 2005.

Bilyeu, Dick. *Lost in Action: A World War II Soldier's Account of Capture on Bataan and Imprisonment by the Japanese.* Jefferson, NC: McFarland & Company, Inc., 1991.

Blair, Clay, Jr. *Silent Victory: The U.S. Submarine War Against Japan.* Philadelphia: J. B. Lippincott Company, 1975.

Blunt, Roscoe C., Jr. *Inside the Battle of the Bulge: A Private Comes of Age.* Westport, CT: Praeger, 1994.

Bradley, James. *Flyboys.* New York: Little, Brown and Company, 2003.

Bradley, James, with Ron Powers. *Flags of Our Fathers.* New York: Bantam Books, 2000.

Breuer, William B. *The Great Raid on Cabanatuan: Rescuing the Doomed Ghosts of Bataan and Corregidor.* New York: John Wiley & Sons, Inc., 1994.

Brokow, Tom. *The Greatest Generation.* New York: Random House, 1998.

Callahan, Raymond. *Burma: 1942–1945.* Newark: University of Delaware Press, 1978.

Callhoun, C. Raymond. *Typhoon: The Other Enemy: The Third Fleet and the Pacific Storm of December 1944.* Annapolis, MD: Naval Institute Press, 1981.

Carlson, Lewis H. *We Were Eeach Other's Prisoners; An Oral History of World War II American and German Prisoners of War.* New York: Basic Books, 1997.

Chamberlin, Brewster, and Marcia Feldman, eds. *The Liberation of the Nazi Concentration Camps 1945: Eyewitness Accounts of the Liberators.* Washington, D.C.: U.S. Holocaust Memorial Council, 1987.

Charles, H. Robert. *Last Man Out.* Austin, TX: Eakin Press, 1988.

Coleman, John S., Jr. *Bataan and Beyond: Memories of an American POW.* College Station: Texas A & M University Press, 1978.

Crost, Lyn. *Honor By Fire: Japanese Americans at War in Europe and the Pacific.* Novato, CA: Presidio Press, 1994.

d'Albert-Lake, Virginia. *An American Heroine in the French Resistance: The Diary and Memoir of Virginia d'Albert-Lake.* New York: Fordham University Press, 2006.

Dann, Sam. *Dachau 29 April 1945: The Rainbow Liberation-Memoirs.* Lubbock: Texas Tech University Press, 1998.

Daws. Gavan. *Prisoners of the Japanese: POWS of World War II in the Pacific.* New York: William Morrow and Company, Inc., 1994.

Duboscq, Genevieve. *My Longest Night.* New York: Arcade Publishing, 1978.

Dunnigan, James F., and Albert A. Nofi. *Victory at Sea: World War II in the Pacific.* New York: William Morrow and Company, Inc., 1995.

Durand, Arthur A. *Stalag Luft III: The Secret Story.* Baton Rouge: Louisiana State University Press, 1988.

Falk, Stanley L. *Bataan: The March of Death.* New York: W.W. Norton and Company, Inc., 1962.

Fauntleroy, Barbara Gavin. *The General and His Daughter: The Wartime Letters of General James M. Gavin to His Daughter Barbara.* New York: Fordham University Press, 2007.

Feifer, George. *Tennozan: The Battle of Okinawa and the Atomic Bomb.* New York: Ticknor & Fields, 1992.

Fessler, Diane Burke. *No Time For Fear: Voices of American Military Nurses in World War II.* East Lansing: Michigan State University Press, 1996.

Frazer, Heather T., and John O'Sullivan. *"We Have Just Begun To Not Fight": An Oral History of Conscientious Objectors in Civilian Public Service During World War II.* New York: Twayne Publishers, 1996.

Freeman, Roger A. *Zemke's Wolf Pack: The Story of Hub Zemke and the 56th Fighter Group in the Skies over Europe.* New York: Orion Books, 1988.

Fuchida, Mitsuo, and Masatake Okumiya. *Midway: The Battle That Doomed Japan.* New York: Ballantine Books, 1955.

Gansberg, Judith M. *Stalag: USA. The Remarkable Story of German POWs in America.* New York: Thomas Y. Crowell Company, 1977.

Good, Michael. *The Search for Major Plagge: The Nazi Who Saved Jews.* New York: Fordham University Press, 2005.

Goodwin, Doris Kearns. *No Ordinary Time: Franklin and Eleanor Roosevelt: The Home Front in World War II.* New York: Simon & Schuster, 1994.

Gordon, Richard M. *Horyo: Memoirs of an American POW*. St. Paul, MN: Paragon House, 1999.

Hallas, James H. *Killing Ground on Okinawa: The Battle for Sugar Loaf Hill*. Westport, CT: Praeger, 1996.

Hart, B. H. Liddell. *History of the Second World War*. New York: G.P. Putnam's Sons, 1970.

Hearn, Chester G. *The Illustrated Directory of the United States Navy*. London: Salamander, 2003.

Hornfischer, James D. *The Last Stand of the Tin Can Sailors*. New York: Bantam Books, 2004.

———. *Ship of Ghosts: The Story of the USS Houston, FDR's Legendary Lost Cruiser, and the Epic Saga of her Survivors*. New York: Dell Publisher, 2006.

Hoyt, Edwin P. *The GI's War: The Story of American Soldiers in Europe in World War II*. New York: McGraw-Hill Book Company, 1988.

———. *The Invasion Before Normandy: The Secret Battle of Slapton Sands*. New York: Stein and Day, 1985.

Isley, Jeter A., and Philip A. Crowl. *The U.S. Marines and Amphibious War: Its Theory, and Its Practice in the Pacific*. Princeton, NJ: Princeton University Press, 1951.

Jefferson, Alexander, with Lewis H. Carlson. *Red Tail Captured, Red Tail Free*. New York: Fordham University Press, 2005.

Kakehashi, Kumiko. *So Sad to Fall in Battle: An Account of War Based on General Tadamichi Kuribayashi's Letters from Iwo Jima*. New York: Presidio Press, 2007.

Kaminski, Theresa. *Prisoners in Paradise: American Women in the Wartime South Pacific*. Lawrence: The University Press of Kansas, 2000.

Keith, Billy. *Days of Anguish, Days of Hope*. Garden City, NY: Doubleday & Company, Inc., 1972.

Kenny, Catherine. *Captives: Australian Army Nurses in Japanese Prison Camps*. St. Lucia: The University of Queensland Press, 1986.

Kerr, E. Bartlett. *Surrender and Survival: The Experience of American POWs in the Pacific 1941–1945*. New York: William Morrow and Company, Inc., 1985.

Kitagawa, Daisuke. *Issei and Nisei: The Internment Years*. New York: Seabury Press, 1967.

Knaefler, Tomi Kaizawa. *Our House Divided: Seven Japanese American Families in World War II*. Honolulu: University of Hawaii Press, 1991.

Knox, Donald. *Death March: The Survivors of Bataan*. New York: Harcourt Brace Jovanovich, 1981.

Kurzman, Dan. *Fatal Voyage: The Sinking of the USS Indianapolis*. New York: Broadway Books, 2001.

LaBouy, Robert L. "Where Did We Get Such Men?" *Delta Chi Quarterly* (Spring/Summer 1999): 12–13.

Lawton, Manny. *Some Survived*. Chapel Hill, NC: Algonquin Books of Chapel Hill, 1984.

Lech, Raymond B. *All the Drowned Sailors*. New York: Stein and Day, 1982.

Leighton, Alexander H. *The Governing of Men: General Principles and Recommendations Based on Experience at a Japanese Relocation Camp*. Princeton, NJ: Princeton University Press, 1945.

Levine, Alan J. *Captivity, Flight, and Survival in World War II*. Westport, CT: Praeger, 2000.

Lord, Walter. *Day of Infamy.* New York: Henry Holt and Company, 1957.

MacArthur, Douglas. *Reminiscences.* New York: Fawcett World Library, 1965.

Marling, Karal Ann, and John Wetenhall. *Iwo Jima: Monuments, Memories, and the American Hero.* Cambridge: Harvard University Press, 1991.

McCormack, Gavan, and Hank Nelson. *The Burma-Thailand Railway: Memory and History.* St. Leonards, NSW: Allen & Unwin, 1993.

McGuire, Melvin W., and Robert Hadley. *Bloody Skies A 15th AAF B-17 Combat Crew: How They Lived and How They Died.* Las Cruces, NM: Yucca Free Press, 1993.

Merriam, Robert E. *The Battle of the Ardennes.* London: Souvenir Press, 1958.

Michno, Gregory F. *Death on the Hellships: Prisoners at Sea in the Pacific War.* Annapolis, MD: Naval Institute Press, 2001.

Miller, Lee. *The Story of Ernie Pyle.* New York: The Viking Press, 1950.

Morison, Samuel Eliot. *The Battle of the Atlantic September 1939–May 1943,* Vol. 1. Boston: Little, Brown and Company, 1947.

Moskin, J. Robert. *The U.S. Marine Corps Story.* Boston: Little, Brown and Company, 1992.

Mullener Elizabeth. "Flying For His Life," *The Times Picayune,* East Jefferson Edition, no. 203: 1, 14.

Murrow, Edward R. "Nazi Death Factory at Buchenwald." *Reader's Digest Illustrated Story of World War II.* Pleasantville, NY: The Reader's Digest Association, Inc., 1969: 428–31.

Newcomb, Richard F. *Iwo Jima.* New York: Holt, Rinehart and Winston, 1965.

Nichols, Charles S., Jr., and Shaw, Henry I., Jr. *Okinawa: Victory in the Pacific.* Rutland, VT: Charles E. Tuttle, 1966.

Parker, Pauline E., ed. *Women of the Homefront: World War II Recollections of 55 Americans.* Jefferson, NC: McFarland & Company, Inc., 2002.

Patton, George S., Jr. *War As I Knew It.* Boston: Houghton Mifflin Company, 1995.

Perkins, James W. "As a Tale That is Told." Jim's typed memoirs of his World War II experiences.

Petty, Bruce M. *Saipan: Oral Histories of the Pacific War.* Jefferson, NC: McFarland & Company Inc., 2002.

Prefer, Nathan N. *Patton's Ghost Corps: Cracking the Siegfried Line.* Novato, CA: Presidio, 1998.

Pyle, Ernie. *Brave Men.* New York: Grosset & Dunlap, 1944.

Reader's Digest Association. *Reader's Digest Illustrated Story of World War II.* Pleasantville, NY: Reader's Digest Association, 1969.

Ross, Bill D. *Iwo Jima: Legacy of Valor.* New York: The Vanguard Press, 1985.

Sanders, Charles J. *The Boys of Winter: Life and Death in the U.S. Ski Troops During the Second World War.* Boulder: The University Press of Colorado, 2005.

Sandler, Stanley, ed. *World War II in the Pacific: An Encyclopedia.* New York: Garland Publishing, Inc., 2001.

Saylor, Thomas. *Remembering The Good War: Minnesota's Greatest Generation.* St. Paul: Minnesota Historical Society Press, 2005.

Saywell, Shelley. *Women in War.* New York: Viking Penguin, Inc., 1985.

Sides, Hampton. *Ghost Soldiers: The Forgotten Epic Story of World War II's Most Dramatic Mission.* New York: Doubleday, 2001.

Sledge, E. B. *With The Old Breed at Peleliu and Okinawa.* Novato, CA: Presidio Press, 1981.

Sloan, Bill. *Given Up For Dead. America's Heroic Stand at Wake Island.* New York: Bantam Dell, 2004.

Spiller, Harry, ed. *Prisoners of the Nazis: Accounts of American POWs in World War II.* Jefferson, NC: McFarland & Company, Inc., 1998.

Spinelli, Angelo M., and Lewis H. Carlson. *Life Behind Barbed Wire: The Secret World War II Photographs of Prisoner of War Angelo M. Spinelli.* New York: Fordham University Press, 2004.

Stanton, Doug. *In Harm's Way: The Sinking of the USS Indianapolis and the Extraordinary Story of Its Survivors.* New York: Henry Holt and Company, 2001.

Stevens, E. Michael, ed. *Women Remember the War 1941–1945.* Madison: State Historical Society of Wisconsin, 1993.

Stolley, Richard B., ed. *Life World War 2: History's Greatest Conflict in Pictures.* Boston: Bulfinch Press, 2001.

Summerfield, Penny. *Women Workers in the Second World War: Production and Patriarchy in Conflict.* London: Croom Helm, 1984.

Taylor, Allan. *Survival and Re-entry: WW II Experiences of Vets Who Survived Combat Conditions and Returned to Civilian Careers,* Vol. 1. Bloomington, MN: The Brewster/Alden Publishing House, n.d.

Taylor, Thomas H. *The Simple Sounds of Freedom: The True Story of the Only Soldier to Fight for Both America and the Soviet Union in World War II.* New York: Random House, 2002.

"The War In the Pacific." *Time,* xlv, no. 15 (April 9, 1945): 26.

USS Indianapolis Survivors. *Only 317 Survived!* Indianapolis, IN: Printing Partners, 2002.

van der Vat, Dan. *The Pacific Campaign: The U.S. Japanese Naval War 1941–1945.* New York: Simon & Schuster, 1991.

Walker, John R. *Memories of World War II.* Self-Published, n.d.

Wheeler, Richard. *IWO.* New York: Kensington Publishing Corp, 1980.

Whitehead, Don. *"Beachhead Don": Reporting the War From the European Theater 1942–1945.* New York: Fordham University Press, 2004.

Williams, Eric. *The Tunnel Escape.* New York: Berkley Highland Books, 1952.

Willis, Donald J. *The Incredible Year.* Ames: Iowa State University Press, 1988.

Wood, Winifred. *We Were WASPS.* M. Winifred Wood and Dorothy Swain Lewis, 1978.

Wren, L. Peter. *Those in Peril On The Sea: USS Bassett Rescues 152 Survivors of the USS Indianapolis.* Richmond, VA: Wren Enterprizes. 1999.

———. *We Were There: The USS Indianapolis Tragedy.* Richmond, VA: Wren Enterprizes, 2002.

———. *World War II Revisited.* Carmel, IN: Cork Hill Press, 2005.

Yellin, Emily. *Our Mothers' War: American Women at Home and at the Front During World War II.* New York: Free Press, 2004.

Young, Donald J. *The Battle of Bataan: A History of the 90 Day Siege and Eventual Surrender of 75,000 Filipino and United States Troops to the Japanese in World War II.* Jefferson, NC: McFarland & Company, Inc., 1992.

Young, Ray. "Never To Be Forgotten: The Liberation of a Nazi Death Camp." *Michigan History Magazine* (March/April 1995): 46–47.

Index

About the Author

MARILYN MAYER CULPEPPER is the author of *Trials and Triumphs: The Women of the American Civil War* and *All Things Altered: Women in the Wake of the Civil War.* She received her PhD from the University of Michigan and is Professor Emerita at Michigan State University.

1018

PLEASE SHARE YOUR THOUGHTS
ON THIS BOOK

comments:	comments:
comments:	comments:
comments:	comments:
comments:	comments:
comments:	comments:
comments:	comments: